TRAVAUX
D'HUMANISME ET RENAISSANCE

XXXV

BY THE SAME AUTHOR

L'inspiration personnelle et l'esprit du temps chez les poètes métaphysiques anglais. — Paris : Corti, 1960. 3 volumes.

A Midnight's Trance. By William Drummond. Edited from the Edition of 1619. — Oxford: Blackwell, 1951.

ROBERT ELLRODT
Maître de conférences
à la Faculté des Lettres de Toulouse

NEOPLATONISM
IN THE
POETRY OF SPENSER

Ouvrage publié avec le concours
du Centre National de la Recherche Scientifique

THE FOLCROFT PRESS, INC.
FOLCROFT, PA.

First Published 1960

Reprinted 1969

ROBERT ELLRODT
Maître de conférences
à la Faculté des Lettres de Toulouse

NEOPLATONISM
IN THE
POETRY OF SPENSER

Ouvrage publié avec le concours
du Centre National de la Recherche Scientifique

LIBRAIRIE E. DROZ
8, rue Verdaine
GENÈVE
1960

"... é possibile di convertir quasivogla fola, romanzo, sogno et profetico enigma, et transferirle in virtu di metaphora et pretesto d'allegoria a significar tutto quello che piace a chi piu comodamente é atto a stiracchiar gli sentimenti, et far cossi tutto di tutto, come tutto essere in tutto disse il profondo Anaxagora."

GIORDANO BRUNO,
De gl' Heroici Furori (1585).

"... & me semble qu'il n'est séant d'imaginer telz songes, & rechercher de si hault les Allegories."

LOYS LE ROY,
Le Sympose de Platon (1558).

FOREWORD

This book was written as a "complementary thesis", in partial fulfilment for the requirements of the French "Doctorat d'Etat". It was completed as early as 1949 in a slightly different form, but could not be published before I had maintained my major thesis: "L'inspiration personnelle et l'esprit du temps chez les poètes métaphysiques anglais".

The present study was recast and thoroughly revised in 1958. Yet it has not been substantially altered. Spenserian criticism in the last decade has been little concerned with the poet's Platonism. Some important contributions in other fields had to be taken into account and some new material was incorporated, but the lapse of ten years has not led me to modify any of my conclusions. I only wish I could have toned down the controversial eargerness, but the rewriting would have been too extensive. Should any Spenserian scholar be hurt by my onslaughts, let him blame the spirit of youth and believe me a soberer, if not a wiser man.

This work was undertaken at a time when I enjoyed the opportunities offered for research by the Fondation Thiers and the Centre National de la Recherche Scientifique. I have great pleasure in recording my obligation. Professor Michel Poirier has many claims on my gratitude: after perusing the first version and giving wise advice, he did not shrink from resuming this "paineful pilgrimage" when the book was revised. Lastly, I must extend my thanks to M. René Helsmoortel whose observations on language and style have enabled me to remove a number of blemishes from these pages. The many imperfections that remain are the tribute a scholar must often pay for venturing to write in a foreign language.

The following sonnet is but a further tribute to the English language from a lover of English poetry. Since a recantation was expected from a Renaissance poet, the author of a scholarly work on Spenser may be allowed to heave a sigh of relief, even though the regret for "wasted pains" be no more genuine than the recantation of a Petrarchist usually was.

TO EDMUND SPENSER

In thy delightful land of Faëry,
Listening the murmur of thy gentle stream
By sylvan haunt, how sweet it were to dream
And drink from thy pure well of melody!
To living springs I fain had followed thee,
Rather than fields where briars only teem.
Why search for "sources" in dry dust? Sad theme,
And only fit for mournfull Memory.

Yet only to remove whatever stain
Or shadow, on the troubled water cast,
From wiser eyes long hid thy meaning plain
Have I the wild of Learning travelled past.
So may my labour seem not harsh and vain,
Long poring o'er thy smooth unhurrying strain.

R. E.

INTRODUCTION

Spenser's direct acquaintance with the *Dialogues* of Plato and the dominantly Platonic character of his thought were unchallenged at the beginning of the present century. L. Winstanley's edition of the *Fowre Hymnes* (1907), with its sketch of Platonic influence throughout Spenser's works, was a fair representative of the reigning opinion. Harrison, J.B. Fletcher and Winstanley herself also called attention to the Italian Neoplatonists.[1] But they did not question the poet's familiarity with Plato, and the influence they claimed for Ficino, Bruno and Benivieni rather brought further grist to the Platonic mill.

Then a double reaction set in. Other sources were detected, other influences were given prominence. On the one hand, Spenser's allegiance to Calvinism was emphasized.[2] On the other hand, "naturalistic" notions were discovered in his cosmogony. Beside the Platonist, a Lucretian adept and a dabbler in "old religious cults" appeared on the stage of criticism.[3] They were soon joined by a disciple of Empedocles[4]. Outlandishness was fortunately tempered in W.L. Renwick's wise comment and, with C.S. Lewis, honest Spenser, divested of foreign apparel and antique garb, trod the stage in Elizabethan dress[5]. Meanwhile the poet's familiarity with the dialogues of Plato was called in question[6], and it was at last recognized by editors and scholars that many of his notions could have been obtained at second-hand. As to Renaissance Neoplatonism, his indebtedness to Hoby's translation of Castiglione was stressed[7]. Yet, no critic went so far as to deny altogether his acquaintance with the Italian Neoplatonists[8]. And, of late, a new and spirited champion took up arms against the miscreants who doubted Spenser's scholarship. The banner of Neoplatonism has been planted again, not only on all *Fowre Hymnes*, but also on *Colin Clout*, the Garden of Adonis and the Mutabilitie Cantos[9]. The pendulum,

---

[1] See Harrison's *Platonism in English Poetry* and Fletcher's articles listed in the *Bibliography*, D.2.

[2] See Padelford's articles in Bibliography, D. 2.

[3] See Greenlaw's articles in Bibliography, D. 2.

[4] See Albright's article in *PMLA* 44 (1929), 715-59.

[5] See Renwick's *Spenser* (1925) and various editions; Lewis's *Allegory of Love* (1936). Cf. Stirling's position in *PMLA* 49 (1934), 501-38.

[6] See Taylor's article in *MLR* 29 (1924), 208-10.

[7] See R. W. Lee's article in *PQ* 7 (1928), 65-77.

[8] Direct knowledge of Plato has been more frequently impugned. Taylor (see note 6) doubted whether he was acquainted with any of the Platonic dialogues. Grierson assumed that he knew Plato through Cicero (*Cross-Currents*, p. 39).

[9] See J. W. Bennett's articles in Bibliography, D. 2.

which had been slowly approaching the resting-point, has swung again in the Platonic direction.[10]

In tracing the influence of Platonism over the thought and imagination of Spenser two lines of approach must be distinguished. One may rest satisfied with a broad definition of the poet's world as one in which "the values of Neoplatonism and of Christianity are familiarly blended":

> Through the growing pattern of the poem [the *Faerie Queene*] can be traced levels of being which extend from pure intelligences to inanimate nature, distinct but related by their common reference to the guiding and informing spirit which gives unity and order to a multiple world. It is not a dual world of pointless change contrasting with eternal changelessness; the changing world derives from and returns to unity, and each of its levels is good in its degree, being a reflection of the eternal. In ascending scale, created things are more beautiful because more pure — clear manifestations of the spirit which informs them:
>
> Still as everything doth upward tend,
> And further is from earth, so still more cleare
> And faire it growes, till to his perfect end
> Of purest beautie, it at last ascend (*H.H.B.*, 43-47).
>
> But though distance from the home of pure spirit, and involvement in matter, must lessen the purity and beauty of the creatures at certain levels, all have their beauty and in Spenser's symbolism their goodness. All
>
> are made with wondrous wise respect,
> And all with admirable beautie deckt, (*H.H.B.* 34-35)
>
> and in no part of Spenser's universe is the hand of God absent.[11]

The description is unimpeachable, but with a change in emphasis, this blend of Christianity and Neoplatonism could be discovered in the world of Dante. Neither St Augustine nor St Bonaventura, nor even St Thomas for all his Aristotelianism, would have challenged the statements on the scale of being, the levels and correspondences, the one informing spirit and the essential goodness of all created things[12]. We may readily acknowledge an infusion of Neoplatonism in Spenser's thought as in Christian thought at large. But more evidence is required to turn him into a thorough Platonist.

And yet the search for precise parallels is liable to make confusion worse confounded. Source ascription may be deceptive. Many and various are the channels through which Platonism can have reached Spenser and permeated his poetry. The works of Plato and of the Alexandrian Platonists were available

---

[10] In a recent appraisal, C. S. Lewis rejects most of the earlier claims concerning the Platonic "Ladder" in the *Four Hymns* but he persistently illustrates the poet's thought from the *Symposium*, the *Phaedrus* and the *Republic; English Literature in the Sixteenth Century*, pp. 366, 374-77, 385-86.

[11] Kathleen Williams in *That Soveraine Light*, pp. 39-40.

[12] See Dante, *Paradiso*, XIII, 52-78, XXVIII, XXIX, 13-36. Cf. Gilson, *L'esprit de la philosophie médiévale*, Ch. V, "Analogie", and Ch. VI, "L'optimisme chrétien"; *La philosophie de Saint Bonaventure* (Paris, Vrin, 1943), Ch. VII; *Le Thomisme* (Paris, Vrin, 1945), pp. 216, 248. Medieval cosmology, based on the *Timaeus*, had always acknowledged the hierarchy of being and the correspondences between the many levels. On the variety and grading of all created things according to their excellence, on the perfection of the world as a whole and the goodness of all *being*, including *ens in potentia*, see St Thomas, *Summa*, Ia, q. 47, art. 1, 2; q. 48, art. 1-4.

both in the original Greek and in Latin translations. But these works would be read — if the poet read them at all — in the light of Renaissance commentaries. The syncretic nature of Renaissance Platonism is well known and requires no further emphasis. Zoroaster, Pythagoras, "thrice-great Hermes", the Orphic hymns, the Cabbala and Arab philosophy entered into it, together with Plato and Plotinus. Far from being exiled from the new Platonic Republic of philosophers, Aristotle was reconciled with Plato by thinkers like Pico and Leone Ebreo. All known systems of philosophy were tortured into harmony by the minds of men more alive to likenesses than sensitive to discrepancies ; and the whole was loosely related to Christianity. That seething mass of confused thinking will be referred to as *Neoplatonism.* But a distinction should be drawn between the more esoteric aspects of the Neoplatonic philosophy, developed by cabbalistic scholars like Pico, and the broader, simpler notions vulgarized by the poets and the writers of "trattatti d'amore". A courtly and literary Platonism, mainly concerned with the metaphysics of love and the theory of poetry first sprang up in Italy, whence it spread to France and England. Again for the sake of convenience, I will call the new literary convention *aesthetic Platonism.* But aesthetic Platonism, too, had various aspects, for the tradition of courtly love was not discarded by the poets, but merely suffused with the glow of Platonic idealism. Besides, from the earliest times, scholars like Ficino had brought into Platonic exposition both the metaphysics and the psychophysiology of love evolved by the Italian poets of the "dolce stil nuovo" [13].

Renaissance Neoplatonism, then, was a mixed body of thought, and not an entire break-away from the past. Yet, undoubtedly, the atmosphere of the age was Platonic, although Plato may have been more praised than understood. In a way, the existence of a diffuse Platonism in literary criticism, poetry and conversation, makes it often unnecessary to ascribe any Platonic notion we meet in a poem to a direct acquaintance with the dialogues of Plato or with the more scholarly commentaries. In our own days, among those, including *literati,* who talk and write about Freudianism and existentialism, how many have ever read *Die Traumdeutung* or *L'Etre et le Néant*?

The Platonic philosophy of love reigned in courtly circles. Platonic ethics, long known through Cicero, inspired Renaissance moralists. But, besides the contemporary atmosphere, tradition should be taken into consideration, especially when one deals with a poet whose links with the past are obvious. His cosmology and his mystical divinity may have had a more remote ancestry than Ficinian theology. Nor did they imply any departure from the mediaeval tradition. The Plato of the *Symposium* was the new sun that rose on the horizon of the "renascent" world. But the Plato of the *Timaeus* had lighted the mediaeval world with constant rays. He was known through the Latin translation of Chalcidius and through the *De Consolatione* of Boethius. The Platonic account of Creation had been reconciled with *Genesis* by the theologians of the School of Chartres. It inspired many mediaeval allegorists, including Jean de Meung and Alanus, with whom Spenser was acquainted, either directly or through Chaucer. Platonic influence was all-pervading. To quote an eminent historian of mediaeval philosophy, "Plus on étudie le Moyen Age, plus on y remarque le polymorphisme de l'influence platonicienne. Platon lui-

---

[13] See Kristeller, *Ficino,* p. 287.

même n'est nulle part, mais le platonisme est partout." [14] Besides the philosophical tradition of the Middle-Ages, derived from Chalcidius and Boethius, Cicero and Seneca, Apuleius and Macrobius, a more mystical stream of Neoplatonic influence flowed from Dionysius and Augustine, the double fountainhead of Christian mysticism. When Renaissance scholars like Ficino attempted to write a *theologia platonica,* they naturally turned to Augustine and Dionysius for inspiration and support [15]. On the other hand, the Reformation exalted Augustinian theology, and much increased its popularity. A Christian poet, therefore, might conceivably come into his Platonic inheritance through Dionysius and Augustine as well as through Ficino or Pico with regard to the mystical aspects of Platonism.

Several scholars have traced the rise and progress of Renaissance Platonism in England [16]. The early English humanists, from Sir Thomas More and Sir Thomas Elyot to Roger Ascham, were chiefly attracted by the moral and political wisdom of Plato. More himself knew the dialogues, but later scholars were often satisfied with Cicero's interpretation. This "Socratic" Platonism, as Jayne describes it, was nevertheless a new and important development. But the very interest taken by John Colet in Platonic cosmology, although awakened in Italy, had been anticipated by mediaeval speculation. Both More and Colet were impressed by the "Hermetic" Neoplatonism of Pico as set forth in the *De Dignitate* and the *Heptaplus,* but uninfluenced by his Commentary on Benivieni's *Canzone*: they were concerned with the dignity of man and the mysteries of Creation, not with the philosophy of love and beauty whose chief exponent had been Ficino. [17] Nor is the love poetry written in the period suffused with Platonism. The *trattati* d'amore were as yet unknown to the "courtly makers", despite the well-known links between the Court of Navarre and both the English and the Scottish Court [18]. When Queen Elizabeth herself translated one of Marguerite's poems, she chose the highly mystical, but quite un-Platonic *Miroir de l'Ame Pécheresse* [19].

---

[14] E. Gilson, *La Philosophie au Moyen Age*, p. 268.

[15] See Robb, *Neoplatonism*, p. 59. — Petrarch's veneration for Plato rested on the testimony of Augustine and Cicero.

[16] See Schroeder's *Platonismus in der Englischen Renaissance,* Walter Schirmer's *Antike, Renaissance und Puritanismus* (pp. 133-54), Caspari's *Humanism and the Social Order* (pp. 10-2 and *passim*). R. Weiss covers an earlier period in *Humanism in England during the Fifteenth Century* (Oxford, 1941). Schoell only deals with Chapman's borrowing from Ficino in *Etudes sur l'humanisme continental en Angleterre à la fin de la Renaissance* (Ch. I). Cassirer is mainly concerned with the later Cambridge Platonists in *Die Platonische Renaissance in England*. Jean Jacquot has closely analysed the Platonism of Chapman and traced the Platonic element in Ralegh's *History of the World.* These works are listed in my Bibliography. C Jayne's article on "Ficino and the Platonism of the English Renaissance" (Bibl. C) is a good introduction to the subject, though questionable on minor points. Other studies are: John Burnet, "How Plato came to England" in *Essays and Addresses* (London, 1929); Friedrich Dannenberg, *Das Erbe Platons in England* (Berlin, 1932); Walter Schrinner, *Castiglione und die Englische Renaissance* (Berlin, 1939).

[17] Cf. Jayne, *op. cit.*, pp. 223-5.

[18] Anne Boleyn had been brought up in the court of Marguerite.

[19] The "nothingness" and utter indignity of man is emphasized, contrary to the humanistic tendencies of the Neoplatonists. Not the soul's longing for the Heavenly Beauty, the Good or the One, but God's love to sinful man, overcoming his blindness and resistance as in Francis Thomson's *Hound of Heaven,* is celebrated: "Hélas! mon Dieu, je ne vous cherchais pas,/ Et vous ça bas à moy estes venu" (*Les Marguerites*

According to Jayne, the "period of Platonic poetry opened about 1570". Then did "a new Plato burst upon the English scene — not Plato the cosmologist or Plato the politician, but the Plato of the *Symposium,* Plato the apostle of love and beauty, of refinement and gentility, of art and poetry, of every thing to which the "barbarous" English aspired to catch up with the civilized continent" [20]. The date suggested, however, may be thought too late or too early. Too late, if some awareness of courtly Platonism is to mark off the beginning of the period: the publication in 1561 of Sir Thomas Hoby's translation of Castiglione's *Cortegiano,* is, of course, a better landmark from this point of view. But, if the period is to start from the moment when the new ideals were expressed in poetry, the first gleam of Platonism will be discernible in *The Shepheardes Calender* (1579) and in the sonnets that Sidney probably composed in the early eighties. More years elapsed before the gleam strayed fitfully through the sonnet sequences of Daniel, Drayton and Shakespeare, shone more steadily in Greville's *Caelica* and Spenser's own *Amoretti,* and brought, at last, intellectual light to the graver poetry of Chapman and Sir John Davies. Spenser's first two *Hymns* undoubtedly are the fullest exposition of the Renaissance philosophy of Love and Beauty, more conventional but more straightforward and of wider scope than Chapman's individual and crabbed *Banquet of Sense* (1595). Whether they were written shortly before the publication of the *Fowre Hymnes* in 1596, that is in the hey-day of poetic Platonism, or were composed in an early blaze of enthusiasm at the very beginning of the new period, that is about 1580, is open to discussion and will be debated in the following pages. In any case, from his early defence of love in *The Shepheardes Calender,* a persistent strain of Platonic inspiration is said to run through Spenser's works.

But, by the time he wrote, Platonism or Neoplatonism flowed from different channels, in England as on the Continent. Mere source ascription is dangerous and unrewarding. Many Platonic notions had always been or had lately become commonplaces. They circulated freely. It may be that even the closest scrutiny will not reveal the original stamp on the well-worn coins. Yet the brand-new ones, stamped with the effigy of the Renaissance God of Love and Beauty, should attract our attention at once. The distinction already sketched between cosmological, mystical, ethical and aesthetic Platonism invites a labour of discrimination. To the historian, whether of literature or ideas, it would be of interest to make out whether Spenser was more deeply influenced by the new trends displayed in the works of the Italian Neoplatonists or by an older tradition inherited from the Middle Ages. Source-hunting has been so eagerly pursued and so little discrimination shown by some adepts at this scholarly game that the first task, invidious though unambitious, must be a careful sifting of evidence. Spurious parallels will be rejected ; new ones will occasionally be

---

de la Marguerite, vol. I, p. 19). Divine love is described throughout as a personal relationship between the Lover of souls and a soul whom heavenly grace turns into the "mother", "daughter" and "sister" of God as in traditional Christian mysticism (p. 16 ff.). Only the paradoxes on life and death ("En vous je vy, quand en moy je suis morte..."; p. 48) may recall Ficino's description of the paradoxes of love in the *Commentarium in Convivium* (II, 8), but the occasion and meaning are quite different and such conceits abound in mystical writings uninfluenced by Platonism. Jayne's description of Marguerite's *Miroir* as a "Platonic handbook" is therefore quite unwarranted (*op. cit.,* p. 233).

[20] *Comp. Lit.,* 4 (1952), p. 225.

offered to support new interpretations. For a clear understanding of the poet's meaning, not an accumulation of parallels, is the end devoutly to be wished. And, in many cases, the poet's characteristic handling of notions borrowed from Platonic philosophy will turn out to be more important than the immediate "source" : for the source may be some Renaissance treatise but the spirit may be thoroughly mediaeval. This line of approach should enable us to gain a clearer insight into Spenser's own mind and discover its individual bent and bias.

Though subservient to the task of interpretation, a close examination of sources, ruling out the more improbable, may have a further interest. The problem of Spenser's indebtedness to Plato and the Neoplatonists has so far been approached as if from the very beginning the poet had freely drawn inspiration from all available works. An enquiry conducted on chronological lines may disclose a deepening of knowledge and interest, a ripening of thought. It may thus afford new and safer grounds for an ultimate synthesis.

CHAPTER I

CHRONOLOGICAL PROBLEMS

To trace the evolution of Spenser's interest in, and knowledge of Platonism, one has to know whether his more distinctly Platonic poems were early or late compositions. The following chapters will show that some of the sonnets in the *Amoretti* and the first two *Hymns* alone imply a precise acquaintance with Renaissance Neoplatonism. Both works were published at the end of Spenser's literary career, in 1595 and 1596. But the poet claimed that the profane Hymns were written in the "greener times" of his youth and the dating of the sonnets is still open to debate.

The chronological problem concerning the sonnet sequence need not detain us long. It was meant to tell a story and, according to "the simplest reading", "may cover the period from late in 1592 to spring of 1594, or, allowing for a longer separation, 1591-1594" [1]. The truth of the story, of course, has been questioned. But P.W. Long's theory must be rejected. [2] The identification of the lady of the *Amoretti* with Lady Carey makes nonsense of Sonnets LVI, LXVIII, LXXI, etc., obviously addressed to an intended bride, and the suggested date, 1590-91, can hardly be reconciled with Sonnet LXXX, written after Spenser had completed the first six books of the *Faerie Queene* [3]. Yet Renwick and other scholars wisely admit that earlier sonnets, written at various times, may have been embedded in the sequence and the whole re-arranged for publication. But the natural presumption is that the earlier poems are the conventional Petrarchan sonnets lamenting the lady's cruelty in the tone and spirit of the poetry inspired by "Rosalind", whoever she was, or by the mere desire of writing in the fashionable strain. Now, these largely make up the first half of the sequence, up to Sonnet LII, while the influence of the Platonic philosophy of love is most distinctly felt in the latter half, from Sonnet XLV

---

[1] Renwick in *Daphnaida*, p. 193.

[2] See his articles in *MLR* 3, 257-67 and *MLR* 6, 390-7.

[3] It has even been claimed that Spenser's statement that Books IV-VI were complete was an "exaggeration": J. Bennett, *Evolution of the Faerie Queene*, p. 15, n. 2. This does not mean that Spenser could have so exaggerated as early as 1591. Besides, the poet only states that he has run through Faery land a long race, "which those six books compile". This means completion of the narrative as a bulk, but time may have been required for further adjustments in the pattern of interwoven stories and for the usual polishing before publication. Another indication concerning the date is afforded by Sonnet LX. The poet speaks of "those fourty [years] which my life outwent." The statement implies that he was *over* forty and this particular sonnet, at least, must have been written later than the poet's fortieth birthday in 1592.

onward. The arrangement of the poems in this part of the sequence may well be chronological since they clearly allude to personal circumstances. As Sonnet LXXX, implying the completion of the first six books of the *Faerie Queene,* is unlikely to have been written earlier than the spring of 1594[4], there is at least a strong probability that the Platonic sonnets, from Sonnet XLV to Sonnet LXXXVIII, were written in 1593-94.

The *Fowre Hymnes* call for closer examination. There are grounds for presuming that the first two Hymns, at least as they now stand, were not composed in the poet's youth. The absence of any previous reference to them in the Spenser-Harvey correspondence and the *Shepheardes Calender,* the maturity of the style and its freedom from archaisms, are strong motives to reject an early date of composition[5]. It is also agreed that Spenser's apology for "these former two Hymnes in the praise of Love and beautie" as written "in the greener times" of his youth, cannot be taken at its face-value[6]. It may have been a poetic — or a politic — statement. Dramatic convenience — or the taste of his patrons — may have required a recantation; fashion no less, if we judge from contemporary Petrarchan sonnet-sequences. J.W. Bennett has pointed out a similar apology in a letter prefixed to Benivieni's *Eclogues.* The parallel even extends to the scattering abroad of copies and the impossibility of recalling them, presented as an apology for a further publication[7]. This is by no means a single instance. Castiglione's excuse for publication was not unlike Spenser's and Benivieni's[8]. Besides, considerations on the abuse of love-poetry and the honey-poison contrast were hackneyed. Thomas Lodge, in his *Defence of Poetry, Music and Stage Plays* issued in 1579, had declared:

> ... those of judgment can from the same flower suck honey with the bee from whence the spyder (I mean the ignorant) take their poison[9].

This is exactly Spenser's argument and imagery:

> ... finding that the same too much pleased those of like age & disposition, which being too vehemently carried with that kind of affection, do rather sucke out poyson to their strong passion, then honey to their honest delight...

Further parallels could be quoted from Whetstone's *Dedication* of the *Historye of Promos and Cassandra* (1578) and Thomas Nashe's *Anatomie of Absurditie* published in 1589[10]. The same argument was taken up again by Sidney in his *Apologie for Poetrie* (1595) and the same metaphor used by Francis Meres in his *Palladis Tamia*[11].

Although recent critics agree on a late date of composition for the first two hymns, they partly disagree in their interpretation of the evidence, P.W. Long suggesting a date "shortly subsequent to the publication early in 1590 of

---

[4] Allowing time for the completion of the series and the writing of the *Epithalamion* published with the sonnets; the *Amoretti* were entered in the Stationers' Register on November 19, 1594.

[5] See *Variorum, MP* I, p. 657 ff., and Long, *Eng. Stud.* 47, p. 200 ff.

[6] See J. W. Bennett, *SP* 28, p. 50 ff.

[7] Bennett, *SP* 28, p. 50. Benivieni, *Opere,* ff. 73 r°-v°.

[8] *The Courtier,* Everyman, p. 9.

[9] Reproduced in *Elizabethan Critical Essays,* ed. Gregory Smith (O.U.P. 1904), vol. I, p. 79.

[10] *Ibid.,* I, 59; I, 322-3.

[11] *Ibid.,* I, 186; II, 304.

Books I-III of the *Faerie Queene*" [12], and J.W. Bennett holding that a thorough revision — if not actual composition — took place "sometime between the publication of the *Amoretti* in the spring of 1595 and september 1596" [13]. The different considerations that have been brought to bear on the date of composition are:

1° Alleged biographical evidence in the first two hymns.

2° The allusion to poems of love written "of late" in the Proem to the Fourth Book of the *Faerie Queene.*

3° Parallels in the *Amoretti* and *The Teares of the Muses.*

4° The long parallel in *Colin Clouts Come Home Againe.*

5° Prosodic criteria.

6° The structural unity of the *Fowre Hymnes.*

To these considerations should be added an exhaustive examination of parallels in the several books of the *Faerie Queene.*

P.W. Long believed that the "lengthy and so far unsucessful siege" of an obdurate lady described in the first two hymns had reference to Spenser's courtship of the lady of the *Amoretti.* He assumed that the lover's complaints had a biographical significance, and the "new flame" of the *Hymnes* was the "new love" mentioned in *Amoretti IV* [14]. But is it safe to fasten a biographical meaning on two formal hymns, obviously meant to give poetic expression to the Renaissance philosophy of love? Besides, even though the hymns indeed conveyed allusions to personal circumstances, we do not know how many "new flames", the poet entertained in his life. The parallel offered with *Amoretti IV* is unconvincing, for the Sonnet is a New-Year sonnet (therefore an April sonnet according to the Elizabethan calendar), and the poet, when he calls to his beloved "Prepare yourself new love to entertain" is only inviting her to be in harmony with Nature awaking from her wintry sleep — a charming but conventional idea.

More interesting, and even tantalizing, is the allusion in the Proem to Book IV of the *Faerie Queene* :

> The rugged forhead that with grave foresight
> Welds kingdomes causes and affaires of state,
> My looser rimes (I wote) doth sharply wite
> For praising love, as I have done of late,
> And magnifying lovers deare debate;
> By which fraile youth is oft to follie led,
> Through false allurement of that pleasing baite,
> That better were in vertues discipled,
> Then with vaine poemes weeds to have their fancies fed.

P. W. Long argued that, since there was no love-poetry in the *Complaints* and the *Amoretti* had only praised chaste love, while the *Faerie Queene* exalted chastity and condemned lechery, the reference could only be to the earlier hymns, both susceptible of a sensuous interpretation, both pagan and blas-

---

[12] Long, *Eng. Stud.*, 47, p. 200.
[13] Bennett, *SP* 28, p. 56.
[14] Long, *Eng. Stud.*, 47, pp. 199-200.

phemous in the closing stanzas [15]. His conclusion was "Here, I think is the blameful blot (*F.Q.*, VI.xii.41) which brought Spenser's writings into a mighty peeres displeasure." The inference is unwarranted. Some sonnets in the *Amoretti* were no less "blasphemous" and others far more "sensuous" than any stanza of the hymns. P. W. Long did not mention *Colin Clout,* in which the celebration of love is equally sacrilegious — if it is a sacrilege to say that Love is God [16]. Lastly, even in the *Faerie Queene,* a Puritan moralist might have objected to the sensuous pictures of passion and the frivolous love-stories.

Indeed, out of all possible references, an allusion to the yet unpublished hymns is the least likely. Spenser declared in September 1596 that the earlier hymns had been composed in his youth. The statement may be suspected, but would the poet have committed himself to a false assertion if, in a work issued a few months earlier, he had openly alluded to the same poems as written "of late"? He may not have cared to be truthful, but he should have minded the contradiction. Besides, it is doubtful whether Burghley would have stooped to take notice of stray pieces of love poetry. A better case might be made for connecting his expression of disapproval with the first three books of the *Faerie Queene,* for a national epic that claimed the highest patronage would attract his attention and call for comment. He may have resented allusions to Leicester's and Raleigh's courtship of Queen Elizabeth, much more likely to provoke his "displeasure" than any harmless love poetry. At the close of the second instalment of the *Faerie Queene* Spenser complained that his "former Writs" had been slandered ("bacbite") by wicked tongues who brought them into Burleigh's displeasure (*FQ.* VI.xii.41). He obviously alluded to the same "writs" in the proem to the Book with which the new instalment opened. Now, there was little to misconstrue in the *Hymnes* — or in the *Amoretti,* at that — but an allegorical Poem lay open to slander. And, had not the strictures been aimed at his *Faerie Queene,* would the Poet have thought it necessary to answer them repeatedly in the self-same poem? In the *Letter* to Raleigh, Spenser had already tried to forestall criticism of a like nature:

> To some I know this Methode will seem displeasaunt, which had rather have good discipline delivered plainly in way of precepts, or sermoned at large as they use, then thus clowdily enwrapped in Allegoricall devises.

Part, at least, of his motive in writing the Proem to Book IV was to rebutt the charge that youth "better were in vertues *discipled,* then with vaine poemes weeds to have their fancies fed". The statement that the "looser rimes" had been written "of late" agrees with this interpretation, whether the Proem to Book IV was written shortly after the appearance of Books I-III, or, as seems more likely [17], composed just before the 1596 publication. Since the Proem

---

[15] Long, *Eng. Stud.,* 47, p. 201.

[16] Cf. *Amoretti* XXII, where the poet builds an altar to his "sweet Saynt"; *Amoretti* LXXII, where he chooses earthly beauty instead of heavenly beauty. In *Colin Clout* 771-834. the "religion" of Love is expounded. See ll. 773, 795-99, 809-10, 828-34.

[17] I agree with Craik's observation: "These introductions to the several Books of the *Fairy Queen...* have all the appearance of having been written after the poem itself, and inserted, like the Dedicatory Sonnets, by the author when he was preparing it for the press". (Quoted by Bennett, *The Evolution of the Faerie Queene,* p. 48). This is still more probable when applied to the Proem heading the first of the three new books published in 1596. Besides, it should be contemporary with the concluding stanza of Book VI, which refers again to Burleigh's displeasure.

introduced a "continuation", the phrase "of late" may have been used to denote "sequence" as well as "time", and it may refer to the earlier episodes of the story.

The phrase "looser rimes" has so far been taken to indicate such parts of the *Faerie Queene* as could have been misconstrued by a stern moralist. But it may be contended that Spenser meant to contrast the seriousness of epic poetry with the lighter pieces of love-poetry he had been indulging in. Nevertheless, there is no reason to assume that he was alluding to the *Hymnes*. J. W. Bennett takes it for granted that the Proem refers to the *Amoretti* and the sonnet to Lodowick (*Amoretti* XXXIII) in a way supports her thesis. Yet *Colin Clout* should not be left out of consideration since it contains a formal praise of love. The evidence we have, therefore, does not justify any rash conclusion. The very ease with which we frame different hypotheses bids us beware not to lay undue stress on any of them.

Any assumption that the Proem alludes to the Hymns must then appear entirely gratuitous. It were strange, indeed, that Spenser should have called attention to unpublished poems of his, however widely circulated, as if all the readers of the *Faerie Queene* were expected to know them well. This alone would tempt me to reject Long's assumption outright. Yet there is a tiny bit of evidence that might have been adduced in support of his thesis, but was apparently overlooked. In the fifth stanza of the Proem, the poet calls to Cupid to sprinkle the heart of Elizabeth:

> .... with drops of melting love,
> Deawd with ambrosiall kisses, by thee gotten
> From thy sweete-smyling Mother from above.

The lines clearly recall the *Hymne in Honour of Love* (22-25):

> Come then, ô come, thou mightie God of love,
> Out of thy silver bowres and secret blisse,
> Where thou doest sit in *Venus* lap above,
> Bathing thy wings in her ambrosiall kisse.

The question is: are we entitled to infer from echoes of that kind that the poems in which they occur were fairly contemporary? An exhaustive study of such parallels will reveal that they range over wide periods and are of doubtful significance as to the date of composition. Spenser, a copious poet, often indulges in a kind of stereotyped diction. Whenever he handles the same themes, the same phrases are apt to recur.

Accordingly, we cannot rely on the parallels Long pointed out in the *Teares of the Muses* [18]. On the one hand, the *Teares* cannot be dated with any certainty [19]. On the other hand, if Erato's complaint affords parallels to the first two hymns, Urania's offers as many parallels to the *Hymne of Heavenly*

---

[18] *Eng. Stud.* 47 (1913), p. 204 ff.

[19] See the various arguments collected in the *Variorum MP* II, 533-40. My own inclination is to join Renwick in dating *The Tears* 1578-80. Renwick bases his opinion on certain characters of the style and the fact that the Muses' complaints are not in harmony with both literary and national circumstances in 1590. (*Complaints*, pp. 181-2). Furthermore they closely agree with Cuddie's complaints in the *Shepheardes Calendar* (*October*, ll. 58-83).

Beautie. The fifth stanza is a fair summary of the progress through "the heavens great hierarchie" described in *HHB* 41-98 [20]. In the next stanza (ll. 511-14), the attributes of God are listed as in *HHB* 106-12. And Urania's "contemplation of things heavenly wrought" (*TM* 524-28) shows verbal resemblance to *HHB* 1-4. Since the *Hymne of Heavenly Beautie* was admittedly written years later it follows that parallels in the first two hymns do not necessarily imply that the poems were written in the same period.

Of greater weight are the parallels noted by Long in the *Amoretti* [21]. Not that any trust should be placed in casual echoes, but a general likeness in tone and tenor is, to my mind, a better — though by no means decisive — testimony. But the sonnets were probably composed somewhat later than Long assumed. Besides, since the biographical meaning of the hymns is highly doubtful, there is no reason to suppose that they were written just before the sonnet in which the lady is pictured as yielding. Since the hymns were conceived as invocations to Love and Beauty (or Venus), the poet was bound to represent himself as begging for grace, and not as a contented lover, if he wished to express the full power of love and beauty. In weaving the web of biographical interpretation, critics sometimes forget, not only Renaissance conventions, but the bare necessities of subject-matter. Lastly, no one will deny that the glow of personal feeling whose radiance lights many of the sonnets — a more intimate form of expression — is entirely wanting in the formal hymns, dedicated to the impersonal power of love.

Even granting the similarity of style the hymns therefore cannot be dated with any great precision by reference to the *Amoretti.* At best, it may be surmised that they were composed not long before or not long after — or at any time during the two years' period of composition. Yet they are not likely to have been written at a time when Spenser was still engaged in expressing a present and personal passion. Men in love — unless they have Donne's intellect, and Spenser had not — seldom indulge in speculations on the abstract nature of the passion. When he was in love, Spenser wrote of Rosalind or Elizabeth Boyle, whether in the *Shepheardes Calender* or in the *Amoretti.* When he talks of the universal nature of love, as in *Colin Clout* and the *Hymnes,* it looks, at best, like "passion recollected".

The probable date of composition of the first two hymns being somewhat earlier than 1592 or later than 1594, we might turn to the *Faerie Queene* in the hope of finding further evidence that would enable us to choose between the earlier or later period. What I believe to be an exhaustive list of parallels will be found in the first *Appendix*. Results only need be discussed here.

The parallels listed fall into three categories: mere verbal echoes, general parallels in idea and a few precise parallels both in diction and idea. Stray verbal echoes, as already suspected, are devoid of significance. They occur whenever the subject-matter or the occasion is the same, especially in all invocations, either to Elizabeth, the Muses, Love or Venus; in the descriptions of poetic fury, of love's conquering power, of Cupid, of the Graces, or of angels "in their trinall triplicities on high." The last hymn as well as the first offers echoes of Book I.

---

[20] Cf. *H.H.B.* 50-60 and *T.M.* 505-8; *H.H.B.* 78-84 and *T.M.* 509; *H.H.B.* 96-8 and *T.M.* 510.

[21] Long's parallels are: *H.L.* 8: *Am.* IV; *H.L.* 149-52: *Am.* X; *H.L.* 294-300: *Am* XXV; *H.B.* 248-9: *Am.* XXXVI; *H.B.* 274-80: *Am.* XII. See *Eng. Stud.* 47, pp. 202-4.

Parallels in idea, when they remain vague, are equally unreliable. They are mostly called for by the subject matter of each hymn and each book of the *Faerie Queene.* Thus, the hymns on earthly love and beauty afford the largest number of parallels to Books III and IV in which the same topics are dominant. The divine hymns will offer parallels both to the episode of the Mount of Contemplation in Book I, and to the cosmological speculations in Books IV and V. Lastly various invocations inevitably show some family likeness.

Important parallels both in words and ideas occur only in the first and last hymn, and surprisingly enough it is the same stanza of Book IV that calls for comparison with passages in both hymns. This alone, if any weight is to be attached to parallels, might suggest that all four hymns were written together. J. W. Bennett, who had earlier defended this thesis [22], apparently abandons it in her latest Book on *The Evolution of the Faerie Queene* (p. 173), since she suggests a contemporary date of composition for the Temple of Venus in Book IV, the praise of love in *Colin Clout* and the first two of the *Fowre Hymnes.* Her opinion is based on the assumption that "it seems fairly clear that when he began to write again after his trip to court with Raleigh, Spenser was much interested in theories about the metaphysical nature of love, and he had been freshly impressed with the beauty of the Lucretian Hymn to Venus". To this I object:

1° The largest number of parallels to the first two hymns — and the clearest ones — occur in Books II and III of the *Faerie Queene* published before 1590. The hymns offer a great many more echoes of the description of Belphoebe, the Mask of Cupid and the Venus-Adonis canto than of the Temple of Venus.

2° On the one hand, there is no Platonism in the Lucretian hymn to Venus in Book IV and "naturalism" is still dominant in Colin's praise of love (as shown in Chapter IV below). On the other hand, there is not the slightest hint of Lucretian influence in the hymns. To assume that poems are contemporary merely because they evince an interest in the metaphysical nature of love may strain our "willing suspension of disbelief" when their metaphysics are so wide apart.

I naturally agree that the subject-matter of *Colin Clout* was taken up again (or conversely) when Spenser wrote the first two hymns. The parallel is the best we have, and since it has been extensively studied, I need not produce the evidence once more [23]. The difficulty lies in the interpretation. The hymns may have been written either before or after Colin's praise of love. And, since several critics maintain that the first two hymns, as they now stand, have been "reformed" and "amended" before publication as the Dedication suggests [24], a further alternative is to be taken into consideration: the hymns may have been written first in a more sensuous — or in a solely Petrarchan — vein, and later idealized in the light of the Platonic philosophy of love. Out of this double alternative four possibilities arise.

---

[22] In *SP* 32, pp. 152-57.

[23] See J.W. Bennett, *S P* 28, pp. 52-3.

[24] On the controversy as to Spenser's meaning in the Dedication, see Bennett, *S P* 28, pp. 51-52, and Padelford *SP* 29, p. 216. The controversy is not relevant to our purpose. Since Spenser's words are doubtful and the whole Dedication suspect, we had better abstain from grounding any assumption on it. Spenser had condemned "loose rimes" in his early poems (*S.C.*, "October" 73-78; *Mother Hubberds Tale,* 810 ff.).

Now, these may be reduced and we may work our way to the truth by elimination. If the hymns were written after *Colin Clout,* that is after 1591 — or even after 1595, since Spenser revised the poem before publication — they must have been written from the first in their final form. And if they were composed before *Colin Clout,* it is highly unlikely that they existed in their present shape. This assumption might be based on the absence of the more "technical" notions of the Neoplatonic philosophy of love in Spenser's poetry up to the *Amoretti* (as Chapter II will show). But this consideration must be left out for the present since my theory concerning the late composition of Spenser's distinctly Platonic poems must first be grounded on arguments irrespective of any inferences, however natural, from a gradual growth of interest in, or knowledge of, Platonism. Fortunately my assumption is also supported by the prosodic uniformity and symmetrical structure of all four hymns, a uniformity that could hardly have been attained if the hymns had not been composed together or, at least, wholly rewritten before publication [25]. We are left therefore with a simple alternative. The first two hymns were either composed before *Colin Clout,* and later re-written ; or they were written as they now stand some time after the composition of Colin's definition of Love. There is no imperative reason nor any necessity to choose between the two hypotheses. For, if the hymns existed in an earlier shape, it must be admitted that they were entirely re-written at a later period, since prosodic and stylistic uniformity would not have been attained otherwise.

The results of the enjambment test applied to the *Fowre Hymnes* and a comparison with other poems will be found in Appendix II. Of chief interest in the present discussion is the uniformity of the enjambment ratio within each of the first two hymns. If there was any incorporation of older material as J. W. Bennett maintains [26], that material must have been thoroughly rehandled, for, whenever Spenser embedded in a later poem an earlier piece of work, the insertion is clearly betrayed by a marked difference in the enjambment ratio. I have given instances from *Colin Clout* and the *Faerie Queene* in the Appendix. It is therefore interesting to notice that the third hymn alone affords a sharp prosodic contrast between the devotional stanzas on the life of Christ and the remainder of the poem (see Appendix II). Furthermore, immaturity is betrayed by the style, by the number of exclamations (11.155, 169; 170 etc.) and the use of rhetorical and alliterative antitheses, especially rife in the *Shepheardes Calender* and the First Book of the *Faerie Queene* [27]. I therefore suggest that lines 155-252 mark the insertion of an older devotional poem. Among Spenser's lost works, the *Hours of the Lord* mentioned by Ponsonby, and the *Dying Pelican,* alluded to in Spenser's correspondence with Harvey, may have been the original poem. The sacrifice of Christ was commonly compared to the sacrifice of the Pelican.

As regards the first two Hymns, in return, no compelling reason is found to dismiss as "older material" the Petrarchan stanzas that will not fit J. W. Bennett's Neoplatonic interpretation of Spenser's design [28]. In the mind of a

[25] See Appendix II, and Bennett, *S P* 32, pp. 155-6.
[26] *SP* 28, pp. 54-6.
[27] Examples need hardly be given for the *Shepheardes Calendar.* In the *Faerie Queene* some instances are: I.i.2.7.; I.i.25.9; I.ii.19.7; I.iii.44.9; I.iv.30.8; etc.
[28] *S P* 28, pp. 54-6.

Renaissance poet, there does not seem to have been as clear a distinction between Petrarchan and Platonic love as now exists in the mind of a modern scholar. Both influences were commonly blended in poetry. As late as 1594 Spenser had been writing purely Petrarchan sonnets, together with a few more or less Platonic ones. On composing hymns of love and beauty he was unlikely to abandon the Petrarchan style altogether. One must needs father upon the poet the absurdity of tagging on a meaningless close to the second hymn if one reads into the poem the Neoplatonic *scala*. But I will show in Chapter VII that the "Petrarchan" stanzas imply no falling-off from a higher pitch of Platonic idealism.

The odds are, then, that the hymns in their present shape were written after the composition of *Colin Clout*. Whether the poet drew for subject-matter on unpublished hymns, or simply on his earlier published love-poems, is of little consequence. Now, on the one hand, the different metaphysics of love in *Colin Clout* and in the *Hymnes* suggest an interval : the difference will be emphasized in the fourth chapter. On the other hand, prosodic uniformity with the last two hymns implies that they were written at the same time. But parallels to *Colin Clout* in the *Hymnes* are so close as to suggest that Spenser had recently re-read the earlier poem, and decided to improve upon it. We know that *Colin Clout* was revised and augmented some time before its publication in 1595. It therefore seems reasonable to assume that the *Fowre Hymnes* were composed after that revision. This would explain the presence of parallels to *Colin Clout* in the fourth Hymn as well as in the first two. It has not been noticed that Elizabeth in *Colin Clout* and Sapience in the *Hymne of Heavenly Beautie* are addressed in an identical language. Speaking of his vision of the Queen (II. 40-6), Colin said:

> And since I saw that Angels blessed eie,
> Her worlds bright sun, her heavens fairest light,
> My mind full of my thoughts satietie,
> Doth feed on sweet contentment of that sight:
> Since that same day in nought I take delight,
> Ne feeling have in any earthly pleasure
> But in remembrance of that glorious bright,

This is the feeling conveyed and the language used at the close of the fourth *Hymne*:

> So full their eyes are of that glorious sight,
> And senses fraught with such satietie,
> That in naught else on earth they can delight,[29]

In *Colin* (ll. 344-7), Queen Elizabeth is endowed with divine attributes:

> But vaine it is to think by paragone
> Of earthly things, to judge of things divine:
> Her power, her mercy, and her wisedom, none
> Can deeme, but who the Godhead can define.

Power, mercy and wisdom, together with beauty, are the characters most emphasized in Sapience, I do not mean that Sapience was intended to stand

---

[29] *H.H.B.* 11.281-3. Cf. 11.256-7 ("sweete contentment") and 11.267-8.

for Queen Elizabeth, but knowing the allegorical habit of the Renaissance mind, its easy conjunction of the divine and the profane, there is no unlikelihood in assuming that Spenser purposely depicted Sapience in a language that might have befitted the Queen, a language he had applied to her in an earlier poem.

These parallels suggest that Spenser when he composed the *Hymnes* may have intended to "platonize" his earlier praise of love, to "christianize" his earlier praise of queenly majesty. Now, *Colin Clout* may have been the poems — or one of the poems — alluded to in the *Proem* to the Fourth Booke. If we take the phrase "for praising love" literally, it even applies more correctly to the close of *Colin Clout* than it would to the *Amoretti,* written in praise of the poet's beloved rather than in praise of the universal passion. Besides, Burghley was less likely to take offence at a sonnet-sequence than at a poem designed as a move in favour of Raleigh. It is therefore tempting to frame the following conjecture.

Hearing of Burghley's criticisms, Spenser, late in 1595, wrote or re-wrote the *Proem* to the Fourth Booke introducing a keen retort. That first retort, in the flush of indignation, was defiant. Spenser did not apologize for his love-poetry; indeed, he could not, since out of the three new books he was publishing two, the fourth and sixth, were mainly devoted to "earthly love". But he himself was at the time interested in a more purely Platonic and intellectual conception of love with which he had played in the *Amoretti.* He may have been reading or re-reading Ficino, and may have found the very seed of the *Fowre Hymnes* in a French translation of his *Commentary on the Banquet,* as a later chapter will show. La Boderie's dedicatory epistle to the Queen of Navarre would not only suggest a rejection of earthly love, but a contrast between Platonic and Christian love. The idea of a subtler retort to the critics of his love-poetry occurred to him. Since the palinode was in vogue, he would apparently disown his "looser rimes" as belonging to "greener times". He would write on earlier themes, or re-write from earlier poems, two profane *Hymnes* as a foil to the divine *Hymnes.* But he would take care to make the *Hymnes* he affected to disclaim unobjectionable by refining away the sexual element, still present in *Colin Clout.* In the earlier poem the mating of men was distinguished from the mating of beasts by the presence of "the sparke of reason's might" and the attraction of beauty, but its object remained the enlargement of the "kind" through sexual generation. In the *Hymne in Honour of Love,* the idea is refined and obscured so as to leave us in doubt whether the Platonic "marriage of true minds" is to be accompanied by sexual relationship [80]. Accordingly, the poet could claim, as in the Proem to Book IV, that his love-poetry had been misunderstood, and yet disown even a love so pure — as he did in the Dedication — in so far as it led the mind away from the Christian love of God.

I have offered a conjecture, and no more than a conjecture, for we cannot be sure that *Colin Clout* was the poem criticised by Burghley [81]. But whatever

---

[80] *H.L.* 11.99-105. Explained in Ch. VII, p. 128.

[81] I have given above my reasons for dismissing the *Hymnes* out of consideration. I have made out a plausible case for the *Faerie Queene,* but acknowledged the claims of the *Amoretti* and *Colin Clout.* It cannot be proved that any of these poems is the one alluded to. I only wish to show there may have been strong grounds for Burghley's special displeasure with *Colin Clout.* Its publication was meant to promote Raleigh's return into favour. It recalled Leicester's time (1.736) and glanced at

the occasion for their composition may have been, it is highly probable that all four hymns, in their present shape, were written some time after the publication of *Colin Clout* in 1595, and, in all likelihood, after the *Faerie Queene* I-VI had been entered in the Stationer's Register in January 1596. For the contrast between the "recantation" in the Dedication and the "vindication" in the Proem suggests a change of mind or policy, whether my conjecture be retained or not. And, obviously, the "recantation" must have followed the attempt at "vindication".

Accordingly, though absolute certainty is not attainable, it may be assumed that Spenser's most distinctly Platonic poems belong to the later years of his life. Should a survey of all the poems printed before the publication of the *Fowre Hymnes* disclose no evidence of any thorough acquaintance with the niceties of the Neoplatonic philosophy of love, but for a few sonnets probably written in 1593-94, this would be no mean confirmation of our chronological assumption. For this is not arguing in a circle, but buttressing one argument with another. Should I be proved wrong as to the date of composition by the discovery of new evidence — which is unlikely — the consequence would be an inversion of the chronological development rather than a subversion of my main thesis. Had the Platonic sonnets in the *Amoretti* and the first two hymns been written in Spenser's youth, or, as Long assumed, in 1590-1, this would merely mean that their author was earlier initiated and interested in "technical" Platonism, as I shall call it, than he need have been according to my present theory. If so, he must have rapidly outgrown this interest, as one might expect. From my own view of the poet's character and frame of mind, I should even welcome this new prospect. It would be more satisfactory to find young Spenser dabbling in quintessential metaphysics of love, but soon discarding the more cumbrous or fanciful notions to retain the larger outlines only, the glowing spirit and whatever could enter into his own sober and Christian view of virtuous love, as set forth in the *Faerie Queene.* But there are no grounds for the alternate theory, not even greater psychological likelihood since the *Fowre Hymnes,* on closer examination, will turn out to be in essential agreement with the poet's other pronouncements on love.

From this narrow discussion of chronological problems, one turns with relief to a more spacious consideration of Spenser's Platonism. The unusual precision and density of Platonic notions in the *Fowre Hymnes,* allowing a

---

present "enormities" (1.665). It was published later than the *Amoretti:* "of late" therefore better applies to it. Besides, in the same issue *Astrophel* was included; the pastoral travesty of Sidney's heroic death, and the emphasis on his love for Stella may have further irritated Burghley. Spenser complains his "Writs" have been slandered. The slander may not have been unconnected with the dedication to Sidney's wife of a poem praising the mutual love of the hero and Stella. Since the Stella of the Sonnets was Penelope Devereux, Lady Rich, it has to be assumed that "Spenser tacitly puts Lady Sidney into the place of Stella". Renwick's other assumption that "Sidney's love for Lady Rich was a purely literary *amour courtois* in which there was neither sin nor embarrassment for any one" (*Daphnaida,* p. 191) cannot be retained in view of the passionate and sensuous character of some of the sonnets. I suggest that Spenser, living in Ireland and writing several years after the event, had never known the connection of the sonnets with Lady Rich and believed they were addressed to the poet's wife (as his own were). He therefore innocently dedicated *Astrophel* to her. His enemies may have seized upon the occasion to father on him a malicious design (wite", *F.Q.* VI.xii.41.4), and this *faux pas* may have brimmed the cup of Burleigh's *displeasure.*

clearer discrimination among sources, invited separate attention: hence the division of the present study. Emphasis on the hymns was further required by the results of my own investigation. In my survey of the poems he had previously published, I shall be mainly concerned with pruning off an overgrowth of Platonic interpretation in order to bring out the poet's own line of thought. Since my contention is that most of the alleged parallels with Plato or with the Renaissance expositions of Plato are simply forced upon the text, influences as yet unnoticed will only be mentioned to show the conservative and traditional trend of Spenser's Platonism. With the *Fowre Hymnes* the case is different. Direct influence of the Renaissance Neoplatonists is unquestionable and newly-discovered parallels will conduce to the full elucidation of the meaning.

CHAPTER II

AESTHETIC PLATONISM AND THE THEORY OF LOVE PRIOR TO THE PUBLICATION OF THE "FOWRE HYMNES"

In the Platonic philosophy of love and beauty elaborated by Ficino, Pico and others, the main points relevant to the present study are the new emphasis on the divine origin and nature of beauty, the distinction between the earthly and the heavenly Venus and the progress along a "ladder" leading up from sensual to spiritual love and from the perception of earthly beauty to the contemplation of, and union with, the Heavenly Beauty.

Under the influence of Platonism the Fathers of the Church had already described God as Beauty's self and the fount of beauty [1]. In Dionysian theology the One was at the same time the Good and the Beautiful, raying forth beauty upon all things as light flows from heaven [2]. The Augustinian and Dionysian tradition kept the notion alive throughout the Middle Ages. Yet the schoolmen were not highly concerned with beauty as a "name" or attribute of God; St Thomas only discussed the identification of the Son with Beauty within the Trinity [3]. The Renaissance Neoplatonists rushed into fields the schoolmen had not entered or had trodden warily. But, in the wider view of the Christian tradition, they did not innovate when they defined beauty as "the splendour of the face of God", "the radiance of divine Goodness", "an influence of the heavenly bountifulness." [4]. They could rely on the authority of the Areopagite: Ficino, indeed, interpreted the *Symposium* in the light of his mystical divinity [5]. Yet their insistence on beauty, the attention they lavished on the subject proved distinctive, even in comparison with the early Church Fathers. Their influence, direct or indirect, may therefore be surmised whenever beauty is described in Renaissance literature as an effulgence and effluence of the Divine.

---

[1] St Augustine's well-known invocation to God as "pulchritudo tam antiqua et tam nova" is but the most familiar instance: *Confess.* X. xxvii. On God as the fount of beauty see *Confess.* IV. x; *De Vera Religione,* xvii; *De Civitate Dei,* XI, iv; *Enarratio in Psalm.* XLIV (ed. 1586, t. I, p. 41 d. 1, p. 306 a. 1; t. V, p. 124 a. 1; t. VIII, p. 162 c. 2).

[2] *De Divinis Nominibus,* IV, 7; ed. 1634, pp. 651-2. God is also called "fons & principium pulchrorum omnium" (p. 652).

[3] *Summa,* Ia, q. 39, art. 8, ad primum.

[4] Ficino, *In Convivium,* V.iv, "Pulchritudo est splendor divini vultus"; II.iii, "Pulchritudo est splendor divinae bonitatis"; Castiglione, *Courtier,* Everyman, p. 304.

[5] Cf. *In Convivium,* II. ii, III. i; VII. xv. Ficino's quotations chiefly refer to the Dionysian circle of love: *Amor circulus est bonus a bono in bonum perpetue revolutus* (II.ii: cf. *De Div. Nom.* VI.xiv, 712 C). But he was also at one with the Areopagite in stressing the part played by beauty as principle and final cause: "Hocce pulchrum

The very definition of love they borrowed from Plato implied a change in outlook, a shift of emphasis. Whether sensual or spiritual, love was defined as "a desire for beauty"[6]. To the Pseudo-Dionysius the one object of love had been the "Good-and-Beautiful: no distinction could be introduced between the two[7]. St Thomas agreed that the good could be praised as beautiful, but he referred the good to the final cause and the beautiful to the formal cause[8]. From his careful distinctions the impression emerges that the good was more comprehensive in his eyes and, since it involved the beautiful, could be said to be the only cause of love[9]. Ficino and his followers reverted to the position of Dionysius with a difference. The beautiful was one with the good, not only *in subjecto,* as St Thomas had pointed out, but in its very nature. The good was praised as beautiful, according to the very words of Dionysius. But the tendency was to *picture* the Beautiful as an emanation from the Good[10]. Not the "Good-and-Beautiful" in undivided unity, but the Beautiful alone could therefore be described as the cause of all love, though the Good, as the very essence of God and the fount of being[11], was still its ultimate source and end. Since love was first awakened by beauty alone, the new point of view, in fact, invited more *attention* to Heavenly Beauty than to Divine Goodness and therefore proved more attractive to the poetic imagination.

Meanwhile the spiritual nature of beauty was emphasized. St Thomas and the schoolmen had been quite unmystical about it. Beauty required *integritas,* that is wholeness, *proportio sive consonantia,* and *claritas,* which meant brightness, and even bright colours[12]. As a later chapter will show, the Renaissance Neoplatonists, following Plotinus[13], emphatically rejected those sensible and rational criteria. Beauty became an unaccountable gleam or spark of the divine or even a "hidden odour" of God[14]. Yet, to account for imperfection in the creatures, philosophers had to elaborate a theory on the informing of matter by the divine ideas, deformities arising from "unaptnesse in the substance

---

est omnium principium ut causa efficiens; & ut causa finalis ad quem tendit omne studium & appetitus" (*De Div. Nom.*, IV.7; p. 652). Therefore may the Circle be called Beauty as well as Love, "prout in deo incipit et allicit" (*In Conv.* II.ii).

[6] *In Convivium* I.iv: "Cum amorem dicimus, pulchritudinis desiderium intelligite." The definition applies to divine love since «divina pulchritudo amorem parit" (II.ii). To Castiglione "love is nothing else but a certaine coveting to enjoy beautie" (*Courtier*, p. 303).

[7] *De Div. Nom.*, IV.vii: The latin rendering had to be "bonum sic & pulchrum", or even "pulchrum vel bonum" (ed. 1634, p. 653).

[8] *Summa*, Ia, q. 5, art. 4, ad primum.

[9] *Summa*, Ia-IIae, q. 27, art. 1, "Utrum bona sint sola causa amoris". The approach is realistic. The perception of the beautiful implies cognition and is therefore reserved to the eye and ear; odours are not called beautiful. The beautiful may not differ from the good, but the good is more inclusive.

[10] The Good was the centre and Beauty the circumference: Ficino, *In Convivium*, II.iii.

[11] *In Convivium*, II.v: "bonum quidem ipsa supereminens dei existentia dicitur. Pulchritudo actus quidam sive radius inde per omnia penetrans." *Existentia* was rendered by *essenza* in the Italian version.

[12] Thomas, *Summa*. Ia, q. 39, art. 8, ad primum; cf. Ia, q. 5, art. 4, ad prim.

[13] See his treatise on the beautiful in *Enneads*, I. vi. Jayne unaccountably ascribes to Plotinus *the very opinion he combats*, that "beauty is a certain symmetry of parts and a charm of color" (Jayne, p. 130, n. 36: see *Enneads*, I. vi. 1).

[14] Cf. Ficino, *In Convivium*, II. vi: "superni numinis splendorem per corpora refulgentem", "deum... cujus sapor occultus odorem quemdam sui dulcissimum operibus suis inseruit" (Marcel, p. 152).

fownd" (*H.B.* 144). Through this elaboration, the requirements of proportion, colour, etc., were more or less openly re-introduced [15]. The hall-mark of the new philosophy was, of course, the assumption that "comelines is imprinted more and lesse (as it were) for a marke of the soule, whereby she is outwardly knowne" and "therefore is the outwarde beautie a true signe of the inward goodnesse" [16]. Poets and lovers naturally seized upon so sweet an assurance.

The beauty that awoke love was always a reflection of the Heavenly Beauty. Yet observation showed that that love did not always tend upward, nor would it always "contemplate" but, in Donnean phrase, would sometimes "do". How did it happen? An explanation was sought in a distinction between the heavenly and the earthly Venus founded on the Plotinian emanation theory and hierarchy of principles: the One (or the Platonic Good), the First Intellect or Angelic Mind, and the World-Soul.

> "To sum it all up" in Ficino's own words, "Venus is twofold: one is clearly that intelligence which we said was in the Angelic Mind; the other is the power of generation with which the World-Soul is endowed. Each has as a consort a similar Love. The first, by innate love is stimulated to know the beauty of God; the second by a love of its own kind to procreate the same beauty in bodies. The former Venus first embraces the Glory of God in herself, and then translates it to the second Venus. This latter Venus translates sparks of that divine glory into earthly matter. It is because of the presence of sparks of this kind that an individual body seems beautiful to us, in proportion to its capacity. The human soul perceives the beauty of these bodies through the eyes. The soul also has two powers, since it has the power of intellection and the power of generation. These two powers in us are the two Venuses which are accompanied by their twin loves. When the beauty of a human body first meets our eyes, the mind which is the first Venus in us, worships and loves the human beauty as an image of the divine beauty, and through the first, is frequently aroused to the second. But the power of generation in us, which is the second Venus, then desires to create another form like this. Therefore, there is a love in each case: in the former, it is the desire of contemplating Beauty; and in the latter, the desire of generating it" [17].

The Renaissance Neoplatonists were not agreed in their views on sexual love. Ficino had been tolerant. His position, indeed, has sometimes been judged inconsistent and shifting [18], and its very complexity may have bred some confusion among later writers on love and beauty. But contradictions, I believe, are only apparent. In the first Oration love had been defined as a desire of enjoying beauty, and thereby limited to the pleasures of the mind, the eyes and the ears, since beauty is not apprehended by the other senses of smell, taste and touch. The desire for physical union, therefore, is not love, but lust or madness, inasmuch as it arouses sensations "which are so impetuous and irrational that they jar the mind from its stability" and, "being so intemperate, are the opposites of beauty", for beauty consists in harmony, and "harmony is a kind of temperance" [19]. Yet, after drawing a distinction between the desire of con-

---

[15] Ficino, *In Convivium,* V. iii-vi: see Chapter VII.
[16] Castiglione, *Courtier,* p. 309; see Chapter VII.
[17] *In Convivium,* II. vii; Jayne's translation, pp. 142-3, slightly modified: cf. Marcel, pp. 154-5.
[18] Robb, *Neoplatonism,* p. 80, Festugières, *Ficin,* pp. 59-60.
[19] *In Convivium,* I. iv; Jayne, p. 41; Marcel, p. 142.

templation and the desire of generation in his commentary on the Second Oration, Ficino declared both loves "honourable and praiseworthy, for both loves seek the divine image" [20]. Physical union between the lovers is free from all blame when inspired by a recognition of beauty in the beloved and the wish to propagate it. Such a conjunction no longer proceeds from the desire of tasting the baser pleasures afforded by the senses of smell, taste and touch. Sex is no longer branded with infamy when ruled by the higher faculties [21]. Yet it did not enter into "Platonic" love as Ficino conceived it: "intellectual love between friends, love which unites the members of the Academy into a community, which is based on the individual's love for God" [22]. Socratic love meant Agape rather than Eros.

Although he admitted the marriage of bodies as well as the marriage of true minds between man and woman, Ficino had divested "vulgar" love for woman of its special glamour, since he transferred the nobler feelings and pleasures to the plane of divine love; Platonic love and divine love were interchangeable terms in his correspondence [23]. Sexual love, though approved, was reduced to an "office" or "function" to be performed "within the bounds prescribed by natural law and civil laws drawn up by men of wisdom" [24]. This implied marriage. Thus Ficino's views on sexual love appear predominantly rational and prudential, in close agreement with the mediaeval Catholic conception. They did not invite a romantic idealization of love between man and woman, whether married or unmarried.

Platonic asceticism was carried further by Pico and Benivieni, both destined to come under the spell of Savonarola [25]. In his *Commento* on the *Canzone dell'Amore Divino*, Pico distinguished between heavenly, human and brutish love [26]. "The appetite of carnal conjunction" he immediately dismissed, "Human love" he defined as a rational apprehension of sensible beauty, already severed from the body; heavenly or "angelic" love, as a desire for intellectual beauty [27]. Emphasis is laid throughout on the distinction between sensible and intelligible beauty; the delights of the eyes and ears are evoked by the former, and, until they are "intellectualized", belong with vulgar love [28].

The development of the Neoplatonic conception of love at the hands of later writers need not be traced as yet. This outline of the theory as set forth by its earlier and major exponents was meant to show that the new philosophy of love in its inception and original spirit ran contrary to both the earlier romantic

---

20 *In Convivium*, II. vii; Jayne, p. 49; Marcel, p. 155.

21 *Ibid.*, "Of what, therefore, does Pausanias disapprove in love? I shall tell you. If a man is too eager for procreation and gives up contemplation, or is immoderately desirous of copulation with women, or consorts unnaturally with men, or prefers the beauty of the body to that of the soul, insofar he abuses the dignity of love... Therefore, a man who properly respects love praises, of course, the beauty of the body; but through it he contemplates the more excellent beauty of the soul, the mind, and God, and admires and loves this more fervently than the other" (Jayne, p. 143).

22 Kristeller, *Ficino*, p. 286.

23 *Ibid.*, pp. 285-6.

24 *In Convivium*, II. vii; Jayne's translation, p. 143.

25 Robb, *Neoplatonism*, pp. 60 and 112.

26 *Commento*, II. xxiv.

27 In the language of Pico, intellect is to reason what reason is to understanding in the language of Coleridge. In Hoby's Castiglione, "understanding" is used to translate "intelletto".

28 *Commento*, II. xxiii.

devotion to one's lady in courtly love and the later romantic ideal of married love. With Petrarch and Dante, no doubt, courtly love had already moved beyond chivalric devotion and away from adulterous desire. It could inspire the lover not only with virtuous thoughts, but with the love of God. In the soft haze of idealism and mysticism the earlier exaltation of love and the Neoplatonic philosophy of love could melt into each other, as the poetry of the age often shows. Besides, even the more scholarly Renaissance Platonists relied on mediaeval notions when they sought a psychological explanation for the birth of human love. Platonic metaphysics called for aid on a materialistic physiology. The Renaissance philosophy of love included various and often jarring elements and invited compromises which will be more closely reviewed in later chapters as occasion may require. For the present, one only needs to be reminded of the inherent conflict, whether conscious or unperceived. From a clear realization of it greater strictness in the evaluation of Platonic influence should result. Not because it includes elements also found in the Neoplatonic treatises of the age should a poem be styled Platonic, when those very elements happen to be alien to Platonism or Neoplatonism in spirit or ancestry. To warrant such a labelling, the notions involved should be integral with the Neoplatonic philosophy of love in its original spirit, and some, at least, of its distinctive tenets, explanations, ways of thinking and key-words or images should be reflected in the poetry.

The distinction between base lust and spiritual love will obviously prove far too general for Platonic identification unless it be clearly connected with the Neoplatonic mythology and metaphysics concerning the two Venuses, as outlined above, or with the philosophical explanation for the birth of individual love which Ficino derived from the Neoplatonic account of the soul's descent into the body, or again with the soul's ascent along a ladder reaching up to the Heavenly Beauty and the First Mind whence it came. The new metaphysical elaboration of the time-honoured *innamoraménto* need not be discussed before we consider the *Fowre Hymnes*. But the lover's progress along the Platonic ladder, or stair, must be traced since the "steps" or "grades" have been read into the *Amoretti*. There are minor discrepancies but no major disagreement between the various descriptions of the *scala*[29]. As Hoby's translation of Castiglione's *Cortegiano* must have been widely read in England and was certainly known to Spenser, the following account will be based on the speech ascribed to Bembo in the Fourth Part of *The Courtier*. I find it suitable to distinguish seven stages in the whole *process*, but the *ascent* only begins with the second stage which is the first rung of the ladder in Pico's commentary on Benivieni's *Canzone*.

1. The eyes of the lover snatch the image of a beautiful woman and carry it to the heart; sensual desire is stirred (*Courtier*, 312-13).

2. (Grade I) The lover must consider that "beautie is bodilesse, and an heavenly shining beame", therefore abstain from all the pleasures of sense but sight and hearing, for "these have little bodily substance in them, and be ministers of reason" (*Courtier*, 313).

---

[29] Fletcher's and Casady's descriptions of the *scala*, as recorded in the *Variorum* (*M.P. I*, p. 677 and *M.P.* II, p. 642) are not wholly reliable. The apparent transposition of stages 3 and 4 when Castiglione's account is compared with Benivieni's (*M.P.* II, p. 642, editor's note) is only due to a wrong interpretation or inaccurate phrasing.

3. (Grade II) The lover "that considereth onely the beautie in the bodie, loseth this treasure and happinesse, as soon as the woman beloved with her departure leaveth the eies without their brightnesse...". "To avoide therefore the torment of his absence, and to enjoy without passion", the lover must call back the coveting of the bodie to beautie alone and turn his whole attention to the image of the beautiful woman he retains "in his imagination sundred from all matter." This image he will enjoy "without mistrust ever to lose it" and, "through the vertue of imagination, hee shall fashion with himselfe that beautie much more faire than it is in deed" (*Courtier,* 316-17).

4. (Grade III) The lover, "meddling all beautie together... shall make an universall conceite". "And thus shall he behold no more the particular beautie of one woman, but an universall, that decketh out all bodies". That universal beauty is still apprehended by imagination, and therefore not clearly discerned "by reason of the agreement that the fancies have with the bodies" (*Courtier,* 316-18).

5. (Grade IV) Generalization must be followed by introversion. The lover must "come into his wit", look into his own mind, "to beholde the beautie that is seene with the eyes of the minde, which then begin to be sharpe and throughly seeing, when the eyes of the bodie lose the floure of their sightliness". In other words, the senses and the imagination must be laid asleep, as in mystical contemplation, before "the soule ridde of vices, purged with the studies of true Philosophie", may turn to "the beholding of her owne substance" and see "in her selfe a shining beame of that light, which is the true image of the Angelike beautie" (*Courtier,* 318-19).

6. (Grade V) "Ravished with the shining of that light", the soul in a manner "waxeth dronken and beside herselfe (as in mystical rapture) for coveting to couple her self with it" (the mystical longing for union), and therefore "ariseth to the noblest part of her which is the understanding", as Hoby phrases it, that is the intuitive intellect as distinguished from the rational or discursive [80]. This "noblest part" of the soul, brought into play for the contemplation of heavenly things while the other faculties are in abeyance, calls to mind the part played in contemplation by the "summit" or "apex" of the soul in Christian mysticism (*Courtier,* 319).

7 (Grade VI) Yet the soul is not satisfied with beholding the heavenly beauty "onely in her particular understanding". Whereupon love "guideth her to the universall understanding", Pico's *prima mente.* Thus the soul "seeth the main sea of the heavenly beautie, and receives it into her, and enjoyeth the soveraigne happiness", that is the beatific vision (*Courtier,* 319).

There is no going beyond this point, as Pico observed: the seventh grade is but "the sabbath of divine love", the soul's "repose by the side of the First Father, the fount of all beauty" [31]. The merging of the individual intellect with the universal intellect and the coupling of the soul with the heavenly beauty characterize the "union" achieved on the highest rung of the Platonic ladder;

---

[80] Although we are not told that the soul "hath no more need of the discourse of reason" until the last stage is reached (*Courtier,* p. 319), discursive reasoning obviously plays no part once the soul has "waxed blinde about earthly matters" and opened "the eyes that all men have, and few occupie" (pp. 318, 319).

[31] *Commento,* III. x: "Et ad quella pervenudo lanima grado in ordine sesto termina el suo camino, neglie licito nel septimo, quasi sabbato del celeste amore, moversi piu oltre, ma ivi debbe come in suo fine a lato al primo padre fonte dogni bellezza felicemente riposarsi" (f. 65r° in Benivieni's *Opere*). This does not justify Fletcher's description of the seventh grade as "the merging of the soul with God" (*Variorum, M.P. I,* p. 677).

no further merging of the soul with God is expected although the soul may be described as coupled with God himself in a Christian context [32].

This outline of the Neoplatonic philosophy of love and beauty shows that the image of the beautiful woman is displaced by a "universal conceite" as early as Grade III. Mystical introversion is required from Grade IV onward, when all the natural faculties are laid to sleep. Whenever Renaissance love poetry takes on a Platonic colouring, the poet may therefore be expected not to proceed beyond the second or third grade. Random allusions to the "heavenly beauty" must be referred to the general assumption that God is the fount of beauty: they need not imply that the poet himself claims he has reached the stage of contemplation. Attempts to read the ladder into profane love poetry will mostly prove unfruitful and misleading whenever the poet is assumed to proceed beyond the second grade; the rest is metaphor or hyperbole.

Besides the philosophy of love and beauty, aesthetic Platonism, as loosely defined in the Introduction, may include the doctrine of poetic inspiration. They were closely related since the soul could be rapt and "elevated" by four different kinds of "divine fury", *furor divinus*: the first poetic, the second mystical, the third prophetic, the fourth amorous [33]. It was a favourite subject with Ficino, whose commentary *In Platonis Ionem, vel de furore poetico* was widely read and probably more influential than the original dialogue.

With the publication of *The Shepheardes Calendar,* aesthetic Platonism appeared in Spenser's poetry before ethical and cosmological Platonism. In the October eclogue the heavenly origin of both "pierlesse Poesye" and "lofty love" was proclaimed. But, although the ideas expressed are unmistakably of Platonic descent, there is no serious evidence that they were directly borrowed from Plato or even from the more philosophical Renaissance treatises. By 1579 Spenser was likely to have read Castiglione's *Courtier,* but, whatever his knowledge of Renaissance Neoplatonism may have been at the time, he only availed himself of the more general notions; his handling of the Platonic commonplaces is loose and poetical.

As regards the theory of poetic inspiration, Fletcher has pointed out that Spenser, like Sidney, could have derived it from Minturno's *De Poeta,* which makes any first-hand acquaintance with the *Ion* or the *Phaedrus* or even with Ficino's commentary *In Platonis Ionem* unnecessary [34]. Renwick further notes that the phrasing of the *Argument* suggests reminiscence of the *Pro Archia,* and the Greek word *Enthousiasmos* used by E. K. also occurs in a letter of Cicero [35]. Cuddie's Emblem is taken from the *Fasti,* and from both the Emblem

---

[32] *Courtier,* p. 322: "The fathers of olde time, whose soules... thou didst hale from the bodie, and coupledst them with God". Bembo had just asked that the soul might be "coupled with an everlasting and most sweet bond to the heavenly beautie" (*Ibid.*). No difference seems to have been intended between the two expressions. "Coupling" with God was Christian language and does not seem to imply a higher form of union. Casady's alternative (*Variorum, M.P.*, II, p. 642) is unwarranted.

[33] *In Convivium,* VII. xiv.

[34] "Spenser, the Cosmopolitan Poet", in *English Graduate Record,* Columbia University (1905), pp. 69-71. The Platonic theory had also been expounded by Landino in his *Disputationes,* ff. XXXVIIr° - XXXVIIIr°. Strangely enough Ficino's *Commentary* is not mentioned in the *Variorum* Spenser among the alleged sources of the October eclogue. French sources could also be suggested. See R.V. Merrill, *Platonism in French Renaissance Poetry,* ch. VI.

[35] See *Variorum, MP* I, p. 376.

and Fletcher's parallel with the *Ars Amatoria* it appears that Spenser's theory of heavenly inspiration was mainly grounded on Ovidian authority [36]. These remarks are not meant to belittle the momentous change in the very conception of poetry and the poet's office for which Renaissance Platonism was ultimately responsible in England as on the Continent [37]. Spenser as a "professional" poet, fired with a genuine literary ambition, would naturally welcome a theory proclaiming the "vertuous intent" of poetry and the "worthines" of poets and, together with this ideal, take it for granted that "poetry is a divine instinct and unnatural rage" [38]. But he may have imbibed these notions from the French Pléiade [39] and from the very air about him. While Mantuan's Fifth Eclogue is clearly echoed, there is no *proof* that Spenser was indebted to Plato or the Italian Neoplatonists, even if he were responsible for E. K's scholarly gloss.

On the power of poetry "to restraine the lust of lawlesse youth", E. K. observes that "this place seemeth to conspyre with Plato, who in his first booke de Legibus sayth that the first invention of Poetry was of very vertuous intent". Unfortunately he attributes to Plato a statement about the "Panegyrica" and a distinction between the terms "vates" and "poet" which is not in the *Laws* [40]. His later statement about the "working of Musick" according to Plato and Pythagoras is so muddled that Renwick's source ascription to the *Republic* (3.398-9) is less "evident" than he claims [41]. It seems safer to assume, as Renwick himself did for the earlier reference to Plato, that it was borrowed from some commentator, or "a confused memory of Cambridge lessons". It might have been added that Cicero once more was at hand. Plato's discussion of music in the *Republic* was twice echoed in the Ciceronian *Laws* [42].

As to Piers's rhapsodic defence of love, its Platonic character is obvious, but its vagueness and generality do not allow any rash inference as to its sources. C. J. Osgood finds in the second statement "the first mention of the Platonic Mirror, which is here described in language close to that of the *Phaedrus*" [43]. But in the *Phaedrus* the image was used to explain how the lover comes to be loved in return by his beloved, who sees himself in the lover as in a mirror. The birth of love in the lover's soul was ascribed to reminiscence. Spenser here simply says that the lover admires a reflection of heavenly beauty in the beloved as in a mirror. This was the commonest of Neoplatonic notions, not foreign either to the Christian idea that God is seen in his creatures as in a glass. Both the idea and the image constantly recur in Renaissance poetry and in the *trattati d'amore*: they are no proof of Platonic or Ficinian influence.

---

[36] See *Variorum, MP*, I, pp. 391, 389; *Ars am.* III, 549-50.

[37] See our thesis, *Les Poètes Métaphysiques Anglais* (Paris: Corti, 1960), Part II, Ch. III, Sect. 1.

[38] Gloss on ll. 21, 65, and on the Embleme. Though Spenser time and again declares himself "rapt" with a "heavenly fury" (*Colin*, l. 623, *Amoretti*, LXXXV, l. 11; *H.H.B.*, l. 1), it should be noticed that he is describing a rapture evoked by moral or heavenly beauty. He is not concerned with exalting a "divine instinct" above the art and industry he never spurned.

[39] Cf. Janet Scott, *Les Sonnets Elisabéthains*, p. 174.

[40] *S.C.* Oct, Gloss, 21; *Variorum M.P.* 100. See notes by Mustard and Renwick in *Variorum*, p. 391, and *Calendar*, p. 219.

[41] *Ibid.*, Gloss 27; *Calendar*, p. 219.

[42] Cicero, *De legibus*, II. 15; III. 14.

[43] *Variorum, M.P.* I. 372; *S.C. Oct.*, 93; *Phaedrus*, 255 D.

Nor are we entitled to assume from the first statement

> Ah fon, for love doth teach him climbe so hie,
> And lyftes him up out of the loathsome myre:

that Spenser was already acquainted with Diotima's teaching how to "climbe' the Platonic ladder to Beauty" [44]. The ennobling power of love is here stressed in connection with poetic inspiration. The lines breathe the very spirit of Renaissance Platonism, but the imprecision of the statement, the absence of the more "technical" points of the Neoplatonic philosophy of love (such as the theory of "abstraction" or "ideas") forbid any rash conclusion as to the extent of the poet's knowledge either of Plato himself, or even of his commentators, at the time when he wrote the *Shepheardes Calendar.*

Since a Platonic significance has been ascribed time and again to Spenser's imagery — be it the "mirror" or "wings" — and its origin traced back to the *Phaedrus* [45], a more general observation may be in point here. According to that kind of source ascription, we are apparently to believe that Spenser's Muse would have "walked to heaven with a staff" like Herbert's philosopher, but would have borrowed "wings" on no occasion if the poet had never read Plato. But the Platonic metaphor is the only metaphor Spenser could have used. Only if allusion were made to the winged team of horses (*Phaedrus* 246 a) or to the itching growth of feathers in the soul (*Ibid.* 251 c) could we trace the influence of the *Phaedrus.*

The mirror image might be of greater significance. It recurs throughout the *Faerie Queene,* but mostly for complimentary uses. Elizabeth is called "Mirrour of grace and Majestie divine" (I *Pro.* 5.2). Under the name of Belphoebe, she is described again as a "glorious mirrhour of celestiall grace" and this vaguely Platonic imagery is associated with the Petrarchan imagery of "Graces" and "belgardes" (II.iii.25). As to the magic mirror in which Britomart beheld her future lover *before* she had ever set eyes on him (III.ii.18-21), it is difficult to see how "the Platonic meaning of the mirror is intended" [46]. Plato here would be made responsible not for reminiscence, but foreknowledge. One had better leave the task to Merlin, as the poet himself wisely did. Only in the Proem to

---

[44] *Variorum, M.P.* I. 371.

[45] *Variorum, M.P.* I. 372. *Winstanley,* notes on *H.B.* 181-2, *H.H.L.* 1-5, Winstanley (p. XXI) also discovers "the imagery of the Phaedrus" in the lines that show us Britomart seeking to restrain her passion:

> Whereby the passion grew more fierce and faire
> Like to a stubborne steede whomo strong hand would restraine
> (*F.Q.* IV. vi. 33. 8-9)

It is hard to believe that the comparison would not have occurred to Spenser unless he had been reading Plato. Do we think of the two horses of the *Phaedrus* each time we speak of "briddling" our passions? — Yet, should an exacting scholar still require a "source", why not Castiglione? See *Courtier,* p. 272.

The cave of the *Republic* has also been mentioned each time Spenser spoke of a "den" or "myne" (See *Variorum M.P.,* I. p. 525, note on *H.B.* 46). But there is not the least suggestion of the metaphysical significance of the Platonic cave when Spenser compares men deprived of wisdom to "brute beasts [that] lie in loathsome den." (*T.M.* 531), or when he speaks of the influence of beauty refining "the grosse matter of this earthly myne" (*H.B.* 46). In the first instance, "den" is called for by the comparison with beasts; in the second instance "myne" is used, as Winstanley observed, because the earth provides material for heavenly influence to work upon: cf. *F.Q.* III. vi. 9. 3-4.

[46] Lotspeich, in *Variorum, F.Q.* III, p. 217.

Book VI is the mirror image used with a precision of thought and language that may imply awareness of its Neoplatonic significance [47]. That the one probable instance of a "technical" use of Platonic imagery should have occurred so late is a noteworthy circumstance that should be borne in mind.

If from imagery we turn to Spenser's conception of love and beauty as expressed in the *Faerie Queene,* we must acknowledge again a general Platonic character. But the absence of any definite parallel makes source ascription to Plato or the Italian Neoplatonists equally unreliable. Only the more common Platonic notions are developed, and often further simplified or blended with notions that alter or destroy their more metaphysical implications. Obviously Spenser was more interested in the moral and psychological aspects of the Renaissance philosophy of love. A fair instance of the poet's habit of bringing Platonism down to earth, and interpreting it in terms of ethics, is afforded by the invocation to Love in the third book of the *Faerie Queene.* It opens with the orthodox distinction between two kinds of love:

> Most sacred fyre, that burnest mightily
> In living brests, ykindled first above,
> Emongst th'eternall spheres and lamping sky,
> And thence pourd into men, which men call Love;
> Not that same, which doth base affections move
> In brutish minds, and filthy lust inflame,
> But that sweet fit, that doth true beautie love,
> And choseth Vertue for his dearest Dame,
> Whence spring all noble deeds and never dying fame.
>
> (*F.Q.* III. iii. 1).

The opening lines raise an expectation of the Neo-Platonic contrast between love as a desire of contemplation kindled by intellectual beauty, and love as a desire of generation excited by earthly beauty [48]. But from the closing lines it appears that the higher love is conceived as a spur to virtuous action on earth rather than an invitation to fly back to heaven. Moreover, in the next stanza, it will be noticed that the poet — if he needs must be following Plato — deliberately sides with Agathon against Socrates when he chooses to make Love a deity: "Well did Antiquity a God thee deeme". [49] Any poet would have done so,

---

[47] *F.Q.* VI, Proem 6.:

> But where shall I in all Antiquity
> So faire a patterne finde, where may be seene
> The goodly praise of Princely curtesie,
> As in your selfe, O soveraine Lady Queene,
> In whose pure minde, as in a mirrour sheene,
> It showes, and with her brightnesse doth inflame
> The eyes of all, which thereon fixed beene;
> But meriteth indeede an higher name:

See editor's note in *Variorum, F.Q.*, VI, p. 186.

[48] Ficino, *Commentarium,* VI. vii; Pico, *Commento,* II. x; II. xxiii; Conti, *Mythologiae,* III. xii, p. 380.

[49] It will be noted that Natalis Comes only quotes from the *Symposium* texts in which Cupid is spoken of as a God (*Mythologia,* IIII. xiiii, p. 399). Renaissance commentators usually were at the pains of reconciling Socrates' definition with Agathon's for both classical and mediaeval tradition made it impossible for them to "ungod" Cupid. See Ficino, *In Convivium* VI. ii: "Amor est medius inter pulchritudinem et turpitudinem atque inter deum et hominem". Cf. VI. iv: "Quoniam [Amor] a Deo descendit, Deus, quoniam a daemonibus confirmatur, daemon est apellandus".

and the departure was usual, but it shows that the classical god of Love, not the Socratic "daemon", was uppermost in Spenser's mind. The effects of Love he next describes belong with both the classical and the Neoplatonic tradition:

> The fatall purpose of divine foresight,
> Thou doest effect in destined *descents*,
> Through deepe impression of thy secret might,
> And stirredst up th'Heroes high intents.

The love that sent Britomart on her quest for a husband, the love that "afterwardes did rayse most famous fruites of matrimoniall bowre" is obviously not a "desire of intellectual beauty". Yet that same love has been described as "ykindled first above", and contrasted with brutish love. The distinction therefore was not drawn on the metaphysical level, between the earthly and the heavenly Venus, but on the ethical — and Christian — level, between virtuous love and "filthy lust". I grant that the poet's distinction was countenanced by the more Christian Neoplatonic commentators, and I will further show that it may have been inspired by Louis le Roy. But it is characteristic of Spenser that his conception of love, whenever he echoes the Platonists, should remain either purely ethical when human love is considered, or purely natural when "cosmic" love is discussed. To both human and cosmic love, he ascribes a heavenly origin, but in the *Faerie Queene* he has no place for "heavenly love" as conceived by the Platonists, love "ad divinam pulchritudinem cogitandam" (*In Conv.* VI.vii). For, when he ascends the mount of Contemplation, he no longer speaks the language of Plato, nor even of a Christian Platonist: he speaks the language of Christian devotion unalloyed and holds forth the vision, not of the Intelligible World, but of the Heavenly Jerusalem (*F.Q.* X.46-7).

Spenser does not appear to have seriously entertained the Renaissance ideal of Platonic love between men and women. Both his ethical bent and his frank acceptance of physical love within the bonds of honesty ran contrary to it. C. S. Lewis has shown that true love in the *Faerie Queene* is always accompanied by fruition [50]. The pairs of lovers who, in the Temple of Venus could enjoy

> Their spotlesse pleasures and sweet love content

have been spoken of as Platonic, because pairs of lover-friends are next introduced into the Temple. But the names of those lover-friends were not borrowed from Plato, but from Elizabethan literature [51]. Their love-relationship is described as solely grounded on "vertue", without any mention of *beauty* of body and *beauty* of mind, the ground of friendship according to Plato and Ficino [52]. Lastly, the lover-friends are sharply distinguished from the lovers:

> But farre away form these, *another sort*
> *Of lovers* lincked in true harts consent;
> *Which loved not as these, for like intent,*
> But on chast vertue grounded their desire,
> (IV. x. 26. 3-6: my italics)

---

[50] *The Allegory of Love*, pp. 330-1. See also Chapter VIII.
[51] See Commentary on *F.Q.* IV. xxvi-xxvii, in *Variorum* IV.
[52] Cf. *Symposium*, 180 d.-184 c and *In Convivium*, II, ix. Beauty of mind, I agree, is virtue, but Spenser's language at any rate, is more Ciceronian than Platonic: cf. De *Amicitia*, viii.

What the poet means by ascribing a different "intent" to lovers of different sexes is obvious enough. Their love sports are "spotless", not because they are Platonic, but because they are "lovers trew". For further instances, we might turn to the Arcadian love-scenes of Book VI, to Aladine and Priscilla "Joying together in *umblam'd* delight" or to the "jolly knight" who "In covert shade himselfe did safely rest, — To solace with his Lady in delighte"[53].

Even when the authority of Socrates is claimed — probably at second hand[54] — love is still described as a "*kindly* flame" or "*natural* affection", and praised as the promoter of "brave exploits"[55]. The association of love and heroism was countenanced, indeed, by Plato and the Renaissance Platonists, but it had been a commonplace of courtly love throughout the Middle-Ages. That Spenser should have chosen to emphasize the most traditional and least metaphysical aspect of the Platonic philosophy of love shows how near in spirit to the mediaeval and chivalric ideal he remained. Yet his very address to Elizabeth has been given a Platonic significance:

> **To her I sing of love, that loveth best,**
> **And best is lov'd of all alive I weene:**[56]

But this is a far-fetched interpretation[57]: the poet was speaking to the Queen the language of love she expected, even in her old age. Apart from the complimentary design, his object may have been to emphasize the love relationship between Elizabeth and her subjects, a relationship established on the day when the Virgin Queen decided to "wed" the English people. Whether uniting lover with lover, friend with friend, or subjects with their ruler, love in men's hearts remains a "human" feeling, addressed to "human" objects throughout the *Faerie Queene.*

Apparently more metaphysical — and therefore Platonic — is the conception voiced by Erato in the *Teares of the Muses* (387-90):

> Sweete Love devoyd of villanie or ill,
> But pure and spotles, as at first he sprong
> Out of th'Almighties bosome, where he nests;
> From thence infused into mortall brests.

Even here, however, Platonism is qualified. Not only the language ("th'Almightie"), but the thought is Christian, since no Platonic mediators between God and man are needed. The Venus next invoked is the mythological "Cytheree", a literary figure, not the Heavenly Venus. Furthermore, the same confusion arises as in the *Faerie Queene.* The love nesting in "th'Almighties bosome" cannot be anything but heavenly love; yet "infused into mortall brests", he will "blazon foorth an *earthlie* beauties praise" (1.369). The inconsistency can only be explained away if the poet's *feeling* is recognized as Petrarchan rather than Platonic. To Petrarch the beloved object was divine; passion therefore was purifying, love for Laura led "al ciel", "al sommo ben". But the

---

[53] *F.Q. VI.* ii. 43 and *VI.* iii. 20.
[54] See Chapter V, p. 96 below.
[55] *F.Q.* IV. Proem 2. 2, 4 and 3. 4.
[56] *F.Q. IV.* Proem 4. 6-7.
[57] See I. E. Rathborne, *Spenser's Fairyland,* pp. 220-21.

feeling remained "incarnate", focused on a human being[58]. Between Platonic love and Petrarchan love lies, as it were, the same difference as between love for God *through* Christ and love for God *in* Christ. Now, when he speaks of love, Spenser with the Platonists starts from heaven, whence all love proceeds. But instead of returning love to heaven, to intellectual Beauty, he dwells on Beauty incarnate. What he loves is Beauty *in* the beloved rather than Beauty's self.

So far for the *feeling.* I do not mean to deny the Platonic character of Spenser's *notion* of beauty. But, as expected, the notion, suffused with a feeling inappropriate to it, will lose in precision and consistency. Furthermore, in his rhapsodizing on beauty, Spenser in the *Faerie Queene* never goes beyond the more widespread Renaissance commonplaces. Beauty proceeds from God. It is "The great Creatours owne resemblance bright," (*F.Q.* IV.viii.32.2). For eyes are "lamps" "Kindled above at th'heavenly makers light," (*F.Q.* II. iii.23,2). This is Platonism, no doubt, but poetic and Christian Platonism. On the one hand, the thought is vague and general, the language no less. Beauty is declared to be divine, but the more distinctive Platonic notions, such as participation and the beauty of ideas, or the Neoplatonic conception of the soul as transcendent form, never once appear[59]. On the other hand, the Christian poet has no room for the Neoplatonic "intermediaries": the beauty of the creation is the immediate reflection of the beauty of God who created it. Neither the Angelic Mind nor the World-Soul are wanted.

To write thus, the poet need not have been deeply read in Platonic philosophy. No more knowledge was required than could have been gathered from a chapter of that popular compendium, *The French Academie* by Pierre de la Primaudaye. Indeed, the following passage in its very generality and avoidance of metaphysical subtlety is in the right key of both Platonic enthusiasm and philosophical unsophistication when compared with the poetry of Spenser. I quote from the French original, available as early as 1580:

> Puis donc que Dieu l'a créé & formé par amour, il n'y a point de doute qu'amour ne soit respandüe par tout le monde, & qu'elle ne soit tousiours attiree par beauté: à fin qu'elle soit conforme & semblable à la fontaine dont elle est sortie. D'autre part, toute beauté est comme un ray de celle beauté infinie & divine qui est en Dieu. Parquoy comme la forme divine attire les vrayes amours, ainsi l'image d'icelle attire les images d'amour. Et l'amour qui induit Dieu tout puissant à la création de toutes choses, est procedee de la bonté d'iceluy. Et pourautant que beauté est un ray de bonté qui est répandu par tout, comme le Soleil respand sa lumiere par ses rays, tant plus une chose

---

[58] Sonetto XII (ed. Mestica, p. 16). Laura is time and again described as "Uno spirto celeste, un vivo sole" (Sonetto LXIX, Mestica, p. 135) — which shows that epithets like "celestial," or "heavenly," and sun-imagery are no Platonic hallmark. The ennobling power of love is stressed in terms of *ethical* significance: cf. Canzone IX (XIX), Mestica, p. 110. See Petrarch's apology for youthful passion in the *De Contemptu Mundi:* "Illa juvenilem animum ab omni turpitudine revocavit ...atque alta compulit spectare" (*Opera,* I. 335): cf. *F.Q.* III. v. 1-2.

[59] Spenser describes the soul as ruling the body and directing its actions rather than as "informing" it when he argues in the Fourth Book that "love of soule doth love of bodye passe". This, I admit, is in agreement with Plato's own point of view in the *Timaeus.* But it is hardly consonant with the metaphysical views and the language or the Renaissance Neo-platonists who combined Aristotle's definition of the soul as form with the Platonic conception of transcendent form, as in *H.B.*: "For soule is forme..." (133 ff.).

est belle, & tant plus elle est aimable. Car la mere d'amour est bonté: & bonté, la mere de beauté: de sorte qu'elles sont toutes deux engendrees comme d'une mesme mere. Et selon la diversité des natures creës de Dieu, il y a aussi diverses especes de beauté, qui sont toutes comme rays & flammes & splendeurs de celle beauté divine & infinie, qui est la fontaine de toutes les autres [60].

Instead of keeping apart the earthly and the heavenly Venus, Spenser, according to Lotspeich, telescopes their attributes and functions in the Venus of the *Faerie Queene*, "Queene of beautie" and Mother of all things [61]. If the Platonic Venus was, indeed, "primarily" intended, the confusion would amount to no less than a confusion of matter and form, unthinkable for any true Platonist. The poet, I agree, was not above making the confusion. But, in fact, it seems much more likely that the "Queene of Beautie" was in his mind the classical Goddess of Beauty, beautiful herself and beauty-bestowing. Her associations in all the examples cited by Lotspeich are poetic or literary [62].

The unmetaphysical nature of Spenser's conception of beauty is best illustrated by his occasional description of it as a gift of Nature. Paeana is spoken of as "she whom Nature did so faire create" (*F.Q.* IV.ix.16.5). Britomart is praised as:

> That peerelesse paterne of Dame natures pride
> And heavenly image of perfection, (*F.Q.* IV. vi. 24. 5-6)

The latter quotation is interesting, for the second line is loosely Platonic in language and might be given a Platonic meaning. But the "Dame Nature" of the first line is obviously the Nature of the mediaeval allegorists. This shows that Spenser drew on all available notions indiscriminately — a Renaissance characteristic. But it further suggests that he was not fully alive to the intellectual nature of beauty and the Platonic doctrine of participation. Paeana and Britomart owe their beauty to Nature — not to a reflection of the Heavenly Venus. And when Britomart is described as:

> ... so goodly workmanship of nature
> The maker selfe resembling in her feature? (*F.Q.* IV. vi. 17. 4-5)

the words echo the Christian conception of the creation of man in the likeness of God, hardly reconcilable either with the Platonic pattern or the Neoplatonic emanation theory. Beauty is conceived as direct resemblance of the creature to the Creator, not as conformity to an ideal model, nor as the raying down of heavenly beauty through the hierarchy of being.

---

[60] *Suite de l'Academie Françoise*, Ch. 49, f. 110 r° (Paris, 1580). The first part of the Academy was translated into English in 1586; the second part in 1594. The passage quoted is followed by a distinction between spiritual and sensible love and beauty phrased in general terms again and yet with more philosophical precision and truly Platonic austerity than anything found in Spenser so far.

[61] *Mythology in Spenser*, p. 116.

[62] In *S.C.* Aug. 138, Venus is associated with "the shepheard Ida"; in *F.Q.* *Ded. Son.* 17, with "the Chian Peincter"; in *F.Q.* IV. iv. 3-4 (misquoted by Lotspeich IV. iv. I) with her girdle and her husband Vulcan; in *F.Q.* VI. x. 17, with the Graces; in *T.M.* 398 (misquoted by Lotspeich *T.M.* 138) she is the mythological Venus, without any Platonic "overtone"; in *F.Q.* IV. v. 26 she presides over a mediaeval Court of love tournament. As to the Venuses of the Garden of Adonis and the Temple, they will be discussed in Chapter IV; the latter is Lucretian, the former has a mixed philosophical allegiance.

Spenser's distinction between beauty of body and beauty of mind, and his "habit of contemplating the beauty of the beloved in reverent fear" have been urged as proofs of Platonic influence [63]. Again, the parallel is so general that it can be used at best to point out an affinity, not to support any source ascription. Even the affinity is relative, for to Plato and to orthodox Platonists, the beauty of mind which surpasses the beauty of body is apprehended by the intellect; but Spenser's conception does not appear to be intellectual [64].

As to the feeling of awe and adoration experienced by the lover in presence of the beautiful object — "T'adore thing so divine as beauty were but right" — it betrays a high sensitiveness to beauty, but whether due to the reading of the Platonists, or to the traditions of courtly and Petrarchan love which also required awe and reverence [65], or perhaps to both (the likeliest assumption), we have no means of ascertaining.

From this rapid survey of Spenser's statements on love and beauty in the *Faerie Queene* and the minor poems — still excepting the *Amoretti* and the *Hymnes* — a twofold conclusion may be drawn:

1° The poet who wrote of love and beauty in the *Shepheardes Calender*, the *Teares of the Muses* and the *Faerie Queene* [66] was "in tune" with Platonic enthusiasm, but he did not conceive of Beauty as abstract or intellectual and emphasized the human rather than the metaphysical nature of Love.

2° Since the notions of "participation", "ideas", "abstraction", and all the niceties of the Neo-Platonic ladder discernible in the first two hymns never once appear, it looks as if Spenser either was not yet acquainted with them, or was hardly interested in them at the time. I am assuming that the hymns were written after the first six books of the *Faerie Queene*. But if my conclusions in Chapter I are not fully granted, they will be found to be further supported by the vagueness of the poet's Platonism in the works published up to 1595. For increasing richness and precision in the handling of Platonic notions is a more likely evolution than increasing looseness of thought and language. Besides it has been noticed that the first really "technical" use of the Platonic mirror occurs in the Proem to Book VI, which may have been written shortly before publication, as late as December 1595. Lastly, knowing Spenser's habit of repeating himself, it is hard

---

[63] Williamson, *Platonism*, pp. 31-40.

[64] Williamson quotes ll. 167-203 of the *Epithalamion* as a piece of Platonism. Two qualifications should be added:

1) "The inward beauty" of the bride is the beauty of Christian virtues — not intellectual beauty.

2) Petrarch and the Petrarchans had praised the excellencies of their ladies' minds above the beauty of their bodies. To do so, Spenser need not have read Plato and the Neoplatonists. See Petrarch, *Sonnetto CXIV:* "O d'ardente vertute armata..."

[65] The Petrarchan lover is awe-struck by the beloved. For Petrarch's own explanation, see *De Contemptu Mundi:* "Dicunt enim stuporem amoris esse principium..." (*Opera,* I. 359).

[66] Colin Clout's definition of love will be discussed in Chapter IV since it emphasizes the cosmological nature of love.

to believe that none of the distinctly Neo-Platonic notions expressed in the still unpublished hymns should have cropped up in later-written poems.

A study of the *Amoretti* further strengthens the probability of late acquaintance with — or late interest in — the niceties of Platonism. The sonnet-sequence leads us half way from the soft haze of Platonism in the *Faerie Queene* to the hard glare of the Neo-Platonic theory of love in the hymns. More remarkable still is the late appearance of the more "technical" notions in the sequence. Far too many sonnets as usual have been loosely labelled Platonic. When Spenser, praising his lady's beauty, declares "fairest" "her mind adornd with vertues manifold" (Sonnet XV) or when he rings the changes on the ennobling power of love (Sonnets III, VIII, etc.), he is still writing in the tradition of courtly love, as handed over and refined by Dante and Petrarch [67]. The emphasis on the divine nature of beauty, I admit, seems to be his own in Sonnets III and VIII as compared with their Italian models. In Sonnet III the beloved is the "soverayne beauty":

> the light whereof hath kindled heavenly fyre
> in my fraile spirit by her from basenesse raysed.
> That being now with her huge brightnesse dazed,
> base thing I can no more endure to view: [68]

Sonnet VIII calls her:

> More than most faire, full of the living fire,
> Kindled above unto the maker neere: [69]

But this "soverayne beauty" is Petrarch's "somma beltà" (Sonnet CXXI), not the Platonists' Heavenly Beauty. The light and fire imagery was also used by Laura's lover. When he invests the lady with a heavenly radiance, the English poet seems to be chiefly concerned with outdoing the hyperboles of his predecessors. That he did so by stressing the metaphysical background and liked to evoke the raying down of beauty from its fount after the manner of the Neoplatonists need not be denied if the generality and vagueness of the Platonic reference is acknowledged.

Yet M. Bhattacherje and Edwin Casady claim that rungs of the Platonic ladder are conspicuous in individual sonnets from the very beginning of the sequence, especially in Sonnet XXII. The former, indeed, notes the same religious imagery in a sonnet by Desportes, but assumes that "both poets", when mentioning the "image" of the lady, allude to that early stage in the Platonic ladder when the lover, to avoid the torment of absence, frames in his mind an image of the beloved "sundred from all matter" and so may "make it

---

[67] See Sonnet CXXI, 11. 9-14 in Petrarch's *Canzoniere*. Cf. Guinicelli's *Al Cor Gentil* and Dante's poem quoted below, p. 122.

[68] There is nothing comparable to these lines in Petrarch's sonnets "Vergognando talor ch'ancor si taccia" and "Perch'io t'abbia guardato di menzogna", cited as parallels by Renwick, nor even in Tasso's sonnet "Veggio, quando tal vista Amor impetra" despite its fire imagery ("le gran fiamme ond'arsi": "Rime", I. 23, p. 7 in *Opere*, ed. 1736, vol. VI: cf. *Variorum, M.P.*, II, p. 421.

[69] Petrarch's Sonnet CXVIII "NON d'atra e tempestosa onda marine", mentioned by Renwick, only offers a parallel between the power of light and the power of his lady's eyes. See also Sonnet CXXI, "Le stelle, il cielo...".

friendly and loving to his soule, and there enjoy it, without mistrust ever to lose it" [70]. Now, this happens to be a downright misconstruction of the French sonnet, for Desportes, building an altar to his "proud Goddess" in a "solitary wood" merely extends a metaphor into a myth [71]. It might, then, be claimed that Spenser intended to "platonize" this fanciful myth and invest it with philosophical truth:

> Her temple fayre is built within my mind,
> in which her glorious ymage placed is,
> on which my thoughts doo day and night attend
> lyke sacred priests that never thinke amisse.

But Tasso, too, had erected a temple "dentro la mente" in a sonnet uninfluenced by Platonism [72]. The process of abstraction is neither mentioned nor suggested in Spenser's own poem. The reason given for beholding the beauty of the beloved within the mind is alien to the motives advanced by the Neoplatonists and does not pave the way to a further ascent. The poet only means to find "some service fit" for his "sweet Saynt" in a "holy season fit to fast and pray". This religious adoration which verges on sacrilege is not the produce of Platonism, but a bold poetic inversion of Christian feeling ultimately traceable to the mediaeval "trouvères". By Spenser's time it was little more than innocuous poetic diction, fashionable among sonnetteering lovers [73]. Sonnet XXXV was written in the same spirit. The lover's eyes are so filled with the beauty of the beloved that he can endure no other sight:

> All this worlds glory seemeth vayne to me,
> and all their showes but shadowes saving she.

This is no "step" in the Platonic ladder, as Casady will have it. It *might* describe the feelings experienced when the soul turns inward and "waxed blinde about earthly matters, is made most quicke of sight about heavenly" [74]. But the "beauty" celebrated in the sonnet is not the Heavenly Beauty "that is seene with the eyes of the minde" [75]. The "shadowiness" of all things is mere poetic hyperbole and the idea of the world's vanity is deliberately phrased so

---

[70] *Platonic Ideas in Spenser*, pp. 187-8; Castiglione, *Courtier*, p. 317.

[71] *Diane*, I. 83 (*Œuvres*, p. 31):

> Solitaire et pensif dans un bois escarté
> Bien loin du populaire et de la tourbe espesse,
> Je veux bastir un temple à ma fiere deesse,
> ....
> Mon œil sera la lampe ardant continuelle,
> Devant l'image saint d'une dame si belle,
> Mon corps sera l'autel, et mes soupirs les vœux.

[72] Cf. his poem "Io per me vo'..." cited by Viglione in *La Poesia Lirica di Edmondo Spenser*, p. 289, and quoted in *Variorum, M.P.* II, p. 427.

[73] Cf. instances from Scève, Ronsard, Desportes, listed by Renwick, *Daphnaida*, p. 199.

[74] Castiglione, *Courtier*, p. 319.

[75] *Courtier*, p. 318.

as to recall once more, not the Platonic tradition, but the language of Christian devotion [76].

In *Sonnet* XLV, midway between the first Easter and the second New Year, the Platonic notion of the image of the beloved, abstracted by the lover and treasured by him, first appears. The term "Idea" is also used for the first time. But both the thought and the language show that Spenser either did not care for philosophical accuracy or had not yet fully grasped the theory of abstraction and idealization. The sonnet is not susceptible of a truly Platonic interpretation, for, unless Idea meant image, the conceit would be absurd:

> Within my hart, though hardly it can shew
> thing so divine to view of earthly eye:
> the fayre Idea of your celestiall hew,
> and every part remaines immortally: [77]

Casady's attempt to trace the lover's ascent along the Platonic ladder in Sonnets LX to LXXVI is thoroughly unconvincing. It rests on the assumption that in Sonnet LXVII "the poet compares his experience to that of the weary huntsman in order to reiterate that 'rational love is happier than sensual'", and "develops the comparison to assert that not until he had spent the violence of his sensual love in long, unsuccessful pursuit of the *gentle deare* could he get close to the object of his desire. But once he had put on the 'mylder looke' of rational love, the *gentle deare* immediately permitted him to approach *'and with her owne goodwill hir fyrmely tyde'* " [78]. On an unprejudiced reading of the poem, no grounds are discovered for this far-fetched interpretation [79]. And an examination of the neighbouring sonnets will simply rule it out. The traditional interpretation holds good: the "happy shore" descried is not Platonic love but married love and its "spotless pleasure", which need not be solely spiritual to be chaste in the poet's eyes, as his highly sensuous delight in his lady's lips and "goodly bosome" reveals. What Platonism he has infused into this part of the sequence will only be discovered in individual sonnets and stray allusions or images. The second New Year sonnet (LXI) rhapsodizes on "The glorious image of the makers beautie", and proclaims that "Such heavenly formes ought rather worshipt be, then dare be lov'd by men of meane degree". The enthusiasm and even the language betray the influence of Platonism [80]. But the notions involved are vague as compared with *An Hymne in Honour of Beautie* and the imagery of the Sonnet is dominantly Christian [81]. The very perception of "heavens glory" in the light of his lady's beauty will not further the poet's flight to the purest sky, but on the contrary defeat it, for "Hart need not wish

---

[76] As another instance of semi-sacrilegious hyperbole see the closing couplet of Sonnet IX, describing the lady's eyes:

> Then to the Maker selfe they likest be
> Whose light doth lighten all that here we see.

[77] The Idea is identical with "the goodly ymage of your visnomy" dimmed and deformed by sorrow in the next lines.

[78] Casady, *Studies in Honor of Hardin Craig*, p. 100.

[79] Even the assumption that "with mylder looks" almost certainly modifies *me* in 1. 9. seems to be unwarranted.

[80] Yet only the stress on beauty is Platonic in the first line since it reproduces the Christian idea that man was made in the image of God.

[81] See 11. 2, 5-8 and the preceding note.

none other happinesse, but here on earth to have such hevens blisse." (Sonnet LXXII). As in Tasso's similar sonnet[82], the winged spirit, yearning for heavenly beauty, finds it incarnate in the "soverayne beauty" that feeds his *fancy* (not his intellect) "with full delight". As the sonnetteers sacrilegiously availed themselves of religious imagery for complimentary purposes, so did they subvert the Platonic hierarchy and invert the "ladder" to give higher praise to an earthly beauty.

Sonnet LXXIX is the first piece of really consistent and "argued" Platonism. But the argument is concerned with "the trew fayre", not with Platonic love, which would be irrelevant in the sequence. The praise of the lady's "gentle wit, and vertuous mind "in the first quatrain might have come from the pen of Guinicelli or Petrarch and the reminding her of universal mortality in the second was a religious commonplace. Only in the sestet is the Platonic note distinctly sounded, though in Christian language still[83], and in full harmony with the Augustinian and Dionysian tradition:

> Men call you fayre, and you doe credit it,
> For that your selfe ye dayly such doe see:
> But the trew fayre, that is the gentle wit,
> and vertuous mind, is much more praysd of me.
> For all the rest, how ever fayre it be,
> shall turne to nought and loose that glorious hew:
> but onely that is permanent and free
> from frayle corruption, that doth flesh ensew.
> That is true beautie: that doth argue you
> to be divine and borne of heavenly seed:
> deriv'd from that fayre Spirit, from whom al true
> and perfect beauty did at fist proceed.
> He onely fayre, and what he fayre hath made,
> all other fayre lyke flowres untymely fade.[84]

---

[82] Tasso's sonnet (quoted by Janet Scot in *Les Sonnets Elisabéthains*) is a fair instance of his so-called Platonism, which Spenser is said to have emulated. A comparison of the two poems will show that Spenser's language and "atmosphere" are slightly more Platonic and "ideal" than Tasso's although the poets are at one in abjuring the higher ambition. I translate the Italian sonnet:

"The soul, yearning for light and beauty, spreads her amorous wings to soar to Heaven, but her human nature makes these so heavy that she slips down to what she prizes on earth. And to the soul accustomed to the sweet bait of pleasure which Love displays on an unclouded face, among white pearls and the roses of morn, it seems as if there were no greater sweetness. And she does as the bird that soars aloft, yet swoops down to the place where it finds food and is held captive as of its own will. Among so many gifts gratefully received from Heaven, the delight that my soul finds in you seems so great that she feeds on you alone and dwells in you" (*Rime*, I. 47 ; *Opere*, VI. 11).

[83] "Spirit" is Christian and "made" suggests creation though "derived" might seem to imply emanation.

[84] Tasso's sonnet "Vergine Illustre" cited as a source by Janet Scoot (*MLR* 22, p. 195), offered the same contrast between the decay of bodily beauty and the immortal worth of the "gentle soul" but the bare mention of *immortal bellezza* hardly gave Tasso's tercets the Platonic colouring of Spenser's:

"Not from this [bodily beauty] but from the immortal beauty do you expect it [high worth], and, with a proudly humble view, seclude yourself and dwell on the heights dear to you. And if the inner worth of the gentle [i.e. noble] soul through gracefulness is still far more prized, how fortunate the spouse for whom you thus adorn yourself!" (*Rime*, I. 330, *Opere*, VI. 58).

The last sonnets in the sequence describe a separation and 'the torment of absence", which the lover could conquer, according to the Platonists, by framing and enjoying in his own mind an image "simple and pure" of the beauty that delighted him in a beautiful woman [85]. Sonnet LXXXVIII is obviously reminiscent of this process of abstraction first confusedly suggested in Sonnet XLV:

> Since I have lackt the comfort of that light,
> the which was wont to lead my thoughts astray:
> I wander as in darknesse of the night,
> affrayd of every dangers least dismay.
> Ne ought I see, though in the clearest day,
> when others gaze upon theyr shadowes vayne:
> but th'onely image of that heavenly ray,
> whereof some glance doth in mine eie remayne.
> Of which beholding the Idaea playne,
> through contemplation of my purest part:
> with light thereof I doe my selfe sustayne,
> and thereon feed my love—affamisht hart.
> But with such brightnesse whylest I fill my mind,
> I starve my body and mine eyes doe blynde.

When the lover claims he now beholds the Idea of the beloved "through contemplation of (his) purest part", Idea may not be loosely substituted for image as in the earlier sonnet. We may read into these lines a condensation of the process described in the *Hymne in Honour of Beauty,* when the lover, abstracting the *image* of the beloved, compares it with a like image formed in the inner part of his soul from its very generation. This is not an image formed in the fancy, but an actual *form,* described by Ficino as the *idea* informing the individual soul [86]. Since love arises from a perfect identity between the "forms" of the lovers' souls, through the contemplation of the "purest" or innermost part of his soul the lover does indeed contemplate both his own Idea and the identical Idea of the beloved. Should a simpler but, to my mind, awkward interpretation be retained [87], the sonnet would none the less give evidence of closer interest in the intricacies of the Neoplatonic philosophy of love than the earlier poems had evinced. Yet, the lover's persistent gloom, his complaint about starving his body, disclose that intellectual contemplation cannot really feed his "love affamisht hart" as the last lamenting sonnet clearly confesses (LXXXIX). This was not in keeping with Bembo's requirements for "the good and happie lover" in the *Courtier,* but found precedent in Ficino's admission that, although the soul might be satisfied with the Idea of the beloved, the eyes and the spirits "demand the presence of the body and the soul being very compliant with them, is led to desire the same thing" [88].

---

[85] Castiglione, *Courtier,* p. 317.

[86] *In Convivium,* VI. vi; quoted below, p. 133.

[87] According to Fletcher's and Renwick's interpretations, quoted in *Variorum, MP* II. 454, the *Idaea* is the image of the lady as a "concrete lovable person" contemplated by the lover's "purest part" "i.e. the spiritual or intellectual" (Fletcher, *MLN,* 18, pp. 112-3.) Spenser, I agree, often used *idea* for *image,* but "Idaea" here is reinforced with "playne". Besides, I take "through contemplation of my purest part" to mean "through contemplating my purest part" rather than "through contemplating by means of my purest part", which sounds awkward.

[88] *In Convivium* VI. vi; Jayne's translation, p. 189. Note that this admission occurs in the very chapter that may have suggested the beholding of "the Idaea playne".

Sonnet LXXIX precedes the sonnet that announces the completion of six books of the *Faerie Queene,* and is therefore likely to have been written as late as the Spring of 1594 [89]. The sonnets on separation close the sequence, and though the chronological arrangement cannot be blindly trusted, the odds are that they were, indeed, written last [90]. A survey of the *Amoretti,* as arranged by the poet himself, therefore reveals increasing ease, consistency and "technicality" in his handling of Platonic notions. His interest in the Neo-Platonic metaphysics of love seems to have sharpened markedly during the period of composition. This was only natural since the French and Italian sonnetteers he imitated had been influenced by Platonism. Vagueness of thought or impropriety of language in several sonnets may imply that he had first taken his philosophy at second hand from the poets rather than from the more scholarly expositors. But an interest in the Platonism of the sonnets of Tasso [91] may have sent him to Ficino and other Neoplatonists, and may have ripened into the *Fowre Hymnes* [92].

---

[89] See Chapter I, p. 13.

[90] The poet tells a consistent story, whether true or not, and Sonnet LXXXVI implies that the separation of the lovers did follow, or was intended to follow, a period of sweet peace and intimacy: the last sonnets, therefore, must have been written after the sonnets that showed the lady relenting for the first time.

[91] According to Janet Scott, this poet was one of the sources of the Platonism of Spenser's sonnets: see *MLR* 22, p. 19. and *Sonnets Elisabéthains,* 162-7. The parallels I have quoted show that Spenser usually out-Platonizes Tasso, though they agree in rejecting genuine Platonic love.

[92] Spenser may have felt, too, that love sonnets, addressed to a lady did not call for the same display of philosophical knowledge as the formal Hymns.

CHAPTER III

PLATONIC ALLEGORY AND ETHICS IN THE FAERIE QUEENE

In my survey of Platonism in the *Faerie Queene,* I have thought it wise to restrict myself to an examination of Spenser's direct *statements* on love and beauty. I am aware that several characters and episodes have been construed into Platonic significance and will be urged against my belittling of Platonic influence. The best that can be said of these interpretations is that wonderful ingenuity has been lavished on them. I cannot attempt to refute them all at length, but, to show how insecure they are, I will review the least improbable ones: they concern the two Florimells, Belphoebe and Gloriana.

According to C. G. Smith, the true Florimell represents true beauty, "beauty which has its source in a beautiful soul". "The make-believe Florimel [sic] is false beauty — beauty which does not have its source in a beautiful soul". He quotes in support from the *Hymne in Honour of Beautie* the lines teaching us that "Beauty is not, as fond men misdeeme, An outward shew of things, that onely seeme." He believes he has thus demonstrated strikingly the degree to which certain Neoplatonic concepts permeate Spenser's poetry, and concludes: "The allegory of the two Florimels as here interpreted furnishes a touchstone for Spenser's attitude toward true and false beauty in the entire *Faerie Queene*" [1]. Of all Neoplatonic constructions of Spenserian allegories, this is probably the most plausible, for the true Florimell undoubtedly stands for beauty, drawing all hearts after her [2]. Platonic emphasis on the compelling power of beauty is responsible for the conception in a general way. But the contrast between true and false beauty which runs through the *Faerie Queene* is not the Platonic opposition of ideal and phenomenal beauty: it is the contrast between Nature and false Art [3]. The false Florimell is a delusion and Spenser never says that sensuous beauty is a mere appearance. I have quoted the lines in which Britomart is described as the "peerlesse paterne of Dame Natures

---

[1] *SP* 31, pp. 140-51.

[2] As Woodhouse recently observed, "everyone whose path she crosses is drawn after her, impelled by love in some one of its forms, impure or pure, base or exalted, according to his own nature: the witch's son, the boatman, old Proteus, Sir Guyon, even Prince Arthur who believes or hopes that she is (or at least is like) the Gloriana of his dreams, and at last the resistance of Marinell himself is broken down" (*ELH,* Sept. 1949, pp. 217-8).

[3] C.S. Lewis has pointed out the contrast between Nature and Art: see his *Allegory of Love,* pp. 328-29. But Art may collaborate with Nature, as in the Temple of Venus where "all that Nature did omit, Art, playing second Natures part supplyed it" (*F.Q.* IV, x. 21. 8-9). Art is praised or condemned according as it is used to bring natural things to perfection or to create a mere delusion.

pride" [4]. The false Florimell, made up by the witch with artificial materials, is contrasted with the work of Nature, who "grudg'd to see the counterfet should shame. The thing it selfe" [5]. The allegory of the two Florimells furnishes, indeed, a touchstone for Spenser's attitude toward true and false beauty: but the touchstone is truth to Nature, in all her concreteness, rather than truth to an "ideal" model, the abstract truth of the Platonists. Artificial beauty is but make-believe, bound to vanish away like the snowy Florimell, once it has been exposed. But the natural beauty of the body, even when unaccompanied by beauty of mind, remains real, though defaced, and can be fully restored, as in the fair Paeana [6].

In connection with the allegorical interpretations of Virgil by Renaissance critics, it has been argued that Spenser embodied the Heavenly Venus of the Neoplatonists in Belphoebe [7]. C. W. Lemmi extends the allegory. He regards Britomart as the embodiment of Ficino's Earthly Venus, "the power of generation attributed to the Soul of the World", whereas Belphoebe is identified with the Angelic Mind, whose love is purely contemplative. Spenser tells the Queen that she may see herself both in Belphoebe and in Gloriana (*F.Q.* VII Proem 5). "She may indeed do so if we suppose that both are embodiments of Heavenly Venus; the one in her aspect of spiritual detachment, or chastity; the other in her completeness as the Universal Soul [sic] or Angelic Mind. To this last, power or rule may well be attributed, and thus we may see in Elizabeth the anointed viceregent of God. As heavenly Venus, Gloriana is ultimate Platonic truth, comprehending and embodying all Ideas" [8].

The brilliancy of the argument should not blind us to its speciousness. If Spenser really intended a Neoplatonic allegory, he must have been either a very inconsistent allegorist or a very unorthodox Platonist. Obviously, Belphoebe is to be compared — or contrasted — with her twin Amoret rather than with Britomart. The significance of their twin-birth otherwise escapes us. And if Amoret is "just a maiden", as C. W. Lemmi believes, I fail to see how her twin can be the Heavenly Venus. It might be argued that Amoret is human Love; then her twin should be Heavenly Love, not Heavenly Beauty [9]. And what is the Neoplatonic significance of Chrysogone? No explanation has been offered. The only analogue I find for her miraculous conception is the myth of Porus and Penia in the *Symposium* [10]. But if the Sun here is Porus and Chrysogone Penia, Belphoebe again is Love, born of Plenty and Penury. This hardly agrees with her rôle and description in the *Faerie Queene*. In any case, she cannot be the Heavenly Venus, for the celestial Beauty of the Platonists was born without a mother [11]. And if, having exhausted the resources of imagination

---

4 See Chapter II, p. 38 above.

5 *F.Q.* III. viii. 5-7.

6 *F.Q.* IV. ix. 16; cf. IV. viii. 49. 4-9.

7 M.Y. Hughes, *PMLA* 44, 696-705.

8 "Britomart; The Embodiment of True Love", condensed in *Variorum, F.Q.* IV, pp. 317-21.

9 The interpretation of Amoret as human love is C.S. Lewis's in *The Allegory of Love*, p. 345.

10 Even if Spenser had the myth in mind, which I very much doubt, it would not necessarily imply that he was acquainted with Plato or Ficino, since the myth had been related by Natalis Comes (*Mythologia*, p. 400).

11 All Platonists agree on this point. See Plato, *Symposium* 180 d, Ficino, *In Convivium* VI. vii. Even Natalis Comes had warned Spenser that Heavenly Venus "*sine matre* coeli filia existit" (*Mythologia*, p. 380).

and Neo-Platonic lore, we humbly turn to the poet's own statements, we may wonder why critics ever attempted to pitch the interpretation in so high a key. In her first apparition, Belphoebe is described as the "*mirrhour* or celestiall grace" [12]. The reflection is not the thing itself. In the third Book, she is offered as an "ensample" to all fair ladies, but she is spoken of as the "highest" among them, not as the one true Beauty and Beauty-bestowing power. Her praise is set in a much lower key than the praise of Venus in Book IV:

> To youre faire selves a faire ensample frame,
> Of this faire virgin, this *Belphoebe* faire,
> To whom in perfect love, and spotlesse fame
> Of chastitie, none living may compaire:
> No poysnous Envy justly can empaire
> The prayse of her fresh flowring Maidenhead;
> *For thy she standeth on the highest staire*
> *Of th'honorable stage of womanhead,*
> That Ladies all may follow her ensample dead. [13]

In the next stanza the poet describes her as "curteous and kind", speaks of her "goodly modesty" increasing "the prayse of woman kind". Not a word here but applies to Elizabeth; not a word but is a strange understatement when applied to the Heavenly Venus.

As to Gloriana, she is indeed the "anointed viceregent of God", but this does not mean that she is "ultimate Platonic truth". All Renaissance courtiers and poets saw in the Prince the image of God. Castiglione was voicing the conviction of an age when he wrote:

> Therefore even as in the firmament the sunne and the moone and the other starres, shew to the worlde (as it were) in a glasse, a certaine likenesse of God: So upon the earth a much more liker image of God are those good Princes that love and worship him, and shew unto the people the cleare light of his justice, accompanied with a shadow of the heavenly reason und understanding.
>
> And such as these be doth God make partners of his true dealing, righteousnesse, justice and goodnesse, and of those other happie benefits which I can not name, that disclose unto the worlde a much more evident proofe of the Godhead, than doth the light of the sunne, or the continuall turning of the firmament with the sundrie course of the starres [14].

No Neo-Platonic hierarchy of God, Mind and World-Soul was needed either by Castiglione or Spenser. Platonism in both is subdued to Christianity, and the Platonic mirror is combined with the "glass" of St. Paul:

> But in the triall of true curtesie,
> Its now so farre from that, which then it was,
> That it indeed is nought but forgerie,
> Fashion'd to please the eies of them, that pas,
> *Which see not perfect things but in a glas:*
> Yet is that glasse so gay, that it can blynd
> The wisest sight, to thinke gold that is bras,

[12] *F.Q.*, II. iii. 25. 6.
[13] *F.Q.*, III. v. 54; my italics.
[14] Castiglione, *Courtier*, pp. 276-7.

But vertues seat is deepe within the mynd,
And not in outward shows, but inward thoughts defynd.

But where shall I in all Antiquity
So faire a patterne finde, where may be seene
The goodly praise of Princely curtesie.
As in your selfe, O soveraine Lady Queene,
In whose pure minde, as in a mirror sheene
It showes, and with her brightnesse doth inflame
The eyes of all, which thereon fixed beene; [15]

The "Dread Soverayne Goddesse, that doest highest sit — In seate of judgement, in th'Almighties stead" [16] remains a terrestrial ruler, unlike the Sapience of the *Hymne of Heavenly Beautie* that rules "both heaven and earth" [17]. If she needs must be identified with a Neoplatonic emanation, it could only be the World-Soul. But there is not a shred of evidence that Spenser ever intended the identification: the World-Soul plays no part in his cosmogony. That both Belphoebe and Gloriana should be described as "hevenly borne" [18] is of slender metaphysical significance when we know the kind of complimentary language Spenser and other poets used when they addressed the Queen. But of unmistakable significance is the contrast between "earthly" Cleopolis and heavenly "Hierusalem" seen from the Mount of Contemplation (*F.Q.* I.x.58). Gloriana dwells in Cleopolis, and unless we fly in the face of evidence, we cannot identify her with the Heavenly Venus. And we may further notice that the contrast of the two "cities" is a Christian — and Augustinian — idea, without the slightest infusion of Renaissance Platonism.

The episode of the Mount of Contemplation, indeed, affords the key to a right understanding of the symbolism of the *Faerie Queene*. It shows that the scene of the action is on earth, and the action itself, even though guided by a spiritual purpose, must find its accomplishment on earth. The contemplative bliss of the Heavenly Jerusalem is to be postponed until St. George has acquitted himself of his active task: Christian warfare on earth. He is to fight for Una: "Till from her cursed foe [he hath] her freely quit" (*F.Q.* I.x.63.9) — that is, until the *one* true Church be established in England. We may freely wonder at the perverse ingenuity that has interpreted his quest as the Platonic quest for Truth or Wisdom [19].

---

[15] *F.Q.*, VI. Proem. 5-6: my italics.

[16] *F.Q.*, V. Proem 11. 1-2.

[17] *H.H.B.* 197.

[18] *F.Q.*, II. iii. 21. 9; I. x. 59. 9.

[19] See Harrison, *Platonism*, pp. 1-12. The theory has since been entertained by many commentators. It is untenable for:

1° It does not rest on serious evidence. Harrison argues that Una is presented both as truth, or wisdom, and true beauty. But obviously the true church was to be the teacher of truth and wisdom, and the very quotations chosen by Harrison utterly defeat his purpose. Those who kept Una's company"... learnd her *discipline of faith* and veritie" (I. viii. I). As to her beauty, it is described in the language Solomon and St. John used when speaking of the church (see Upton's note in *Variorum*. *F.Q.*, I, 308).

2° A Platonic interpretation is not only superfluous; it jars with the atmosphere of Book I, for the "colouring" is mediaeval, the theology calvinistic and the main purport both religious and political in the Elizabethan way.

3° Lastly, if Una is ultimate Platonic truth, it makes the episode of the Mount of Contemplation contradictory and meaningless. For the knight, to embrace the

To read into the dream-vision of Arthur, enamoured of Gloriana, an allegory of "the human soul enamoured of the heavenly Sapience" [20] also requires more imagination than need be expended. It does violence, not only to Spenser's own declaration in the Letter to Raleigh, but to Arthur's relation (*F.Q.* I.ix.9):

> It was in freshest flowre of youthly yeares,
> When first the coale of kindly heat appeares
> To kindle love in every living brest;

Would heavenly love be described as "*kindly* [natural] heat" by a Platonist? But Arthur, some will say, scorned "that idle name of love", and when he was, at last, bound "in beauties chaine", his conqueror was heavenly love. Yet if we read further (*F.Q.* I.ix.12), we hear him confess:

> .... that proud avenging boy
> Did soone pluck downe, and curbd my libertie.

Obviously the "proud avenging boy" is Cupid, not love of "the heavenly Sapience". The whole account of Arthur's resistance and final submission to love is thoroughly Petrarchan. As to the dream-vision, not "Neoplatonism" but "Romance" is writ large on it. Its origin in Sir Thopas and fairy lore is well known [21].

An interpretation of Arthur as "Grace", though more in tune with the Christian meaning of the poem, also implies an over-statement. Arthur bears the shield of heavenly grace, but he is only the shieldbearer. If he was divine himself, he would not have to fight a doubtful battle in several occasions, until the blazing light of the shield is disclosed [22]. And once, at least, the veil of the shield is loosed "by chaunce", not by Arthur's will, "chaunce" being, in fact, the providence of God (*F.Q.* I.vii.19). Arthur is not Grace, still less a Neoplatonic intermediary [23]. He is the hero whom the grace of God never forsakes, as it forsook even the Red-Cross Knight when he fell captive to Orgoglio. He is what Spenser told us he was, not what critics may wish him to be:

> .... the prowest man alyve,
> And noblest borne of all in *Britayne* land (II. xi. 30. 6-7)

---

contemplative life, would have to "Forgoe that royal Maides bequeathed care". But, if Una were Heavenly Wisdom and Beauty, how could the highest contemplation be divorced from her?

[20] Fletcher *P.M.L.A.* 26, pp. 474-5.

[21] See *Variorum F.Q.*, I, p. 267.

[22] See *F.Q.*, I. viii 19; V. viii 37. Cf. "long doubtful fights" in II. viii. 30 ff and VI. xi. 4 ff. Woodhouse notes that Arthur would have been defeated by Maleger (*F.Q.*, II. xi. 30) but for a providential intervention (*ELH*, 1949, pp. 221-2). He assumes that Arthur figures forth the grace of God working upon the will in the first Book, which moves on the religious level: in the following books, moving on the natural level only, Arthur would represent both Aristotelian magnanimity and "the power and providence of God as they intervene to protect his creatures from outward evils". But *F.Q.*, I. viii. 19, as shown below, implies that Arthur is the instrument of divine Grace rather than Grace itself in Book I as well. Making allowance for this qualification, Woodhouse's reading of the *Faerie Queene* is not inconsistent with mine: it is based on a distinction between the order of grace and the order of nature long rooted in Christian tradition and irrelevant to Neoplatonism.

[23] The idea was put forth by M.Y. Hughes in *P.M.L.A.* 44, p. 702.

The next lines make it clear that he is but the recipient — and occasional instrument — of Grace:

> Yet thee fierce Fortune did so nearely drive,
> That, *had not grace thee blest,* thou shouldest not survive.

In so far as he is a symbol, he symbolizes the virtue which "conteineth in it them all" (Letter to Raleigh). The moralist, seeking for Aristotelian precedent, called it Magnificence, probably meant for Magnanimity [24]. But a Christian, imbued with Calvinistic teaching, could not conceive of the "perfection" of all vertues otherwise than as the full possession of heavenly grace [25].

It hardly appears necessary to discuss Janet Spens's "interpretation" of the *Faerie Queene*, since the writer fails to bring any evidence in support of her ingenious speculations. We are told that "Spenser discovers with the great Neo-Platonist Plotinus a natural affinity"; yet "it is possible that Spenser never read any complete work of Plotinus" [26]. As the *Variorum* editor observes, "Miss Spens seems to have consulted not Plotinus, but merely Dean Inge on Plotinus" [27]: in any case, no parallel is offered. Miss Spens's interpretation of the Mutability Cantos will be briefly discussed in Chapter IV, since it pertains to cosmology. As to the allegorical meaning of Arthur's quest for Gloriana, a sweeping statement on the "comparative unimportance of the personal and political allegory" is followed by a definite perversion of "the Authors" meaning in his Letter to Raleigh: "The *Faerie Queene* is 'glory in my generall intention', the spiritual loveliness which is the object of Prince Arthur's quest, and indistinguishable from the Sapience of the *Hymne of Heavenly Beautie...*" [28]. But Spenser does not give the least hint in the Letter that the Glory sought by "Magnificence" — or Magnanimity — is anything else but Fame. And though overtones in the poem itself suggest that the object of Arthur's quest is more than the fame "that grows on mortal soil" (to echo *Lycidas*), there is no evidence for Neoplatonic implications going beyond the romantic narrative, the political allegory and the Christian meaning.

Having rejected the Neoplatonic interpretation of characters and episodes in the *Faerie Queene,* we must take into consideration claims for Platonic influence on its ethics. Again we meet either with unsubstantiated statements or with mere commonplaces.

Whether Spenser's Holinesse is Aristotle's Manliness "in the more inclusive Platonic sense of moral courage" [29], is a problem that had best be left to Milton's fallen angels "who reason'd high... and found no end". We, "in thoughts less elevate", may rest satisfied with regarding it as a cross-breed, whose parents were, not Aristotle and Plato, but mediaeval piety and Elizabethan protestantism [30]. And when we are told that the temptation of

---

[24] M.F. Moloney's late plea for the "Magnificence" of St. Thomas (*Summa,* II-II, q. 134, art. 2) is unconvincing: see *JEGP* 52 (1953), 58-62.

[25] All virtuous action is due to God's grace: "If any strength we have, it is to ill (*F.Q.,* I. x. 1. 8; cf. I. viii. 1. 3.).

[26] *Spenser's Faerie Queene,* pp. 40; 39.

[27] *Variorum, F.Q.,* VI-VII, p. 419.

[28] Spens, *op. cit.,* pp. 113-114.

[29] Jones, *A Spenser Handbook*, p. 133; cf. p. 161.

[30] Woodhouse observes that "the attempt of Winstanley to extract holiness from a blend of Aristotle and Plato breaks down, (*ELH,* 1949, pp. 201-2).

Despair comes from the *Phaedo,* and "the whole account of the contemplative life in the House of *Holiness* owes much to Plato" [31], we feel inclined to hand the matter over to Meredith's Comic Spirit.

In the Legend of Temperance, Spenser's debt to Aristotle is clear [32], and not unaccountable, since the Nicomachean ethics were a University text-book [33]. It has even been claimed that Book II is "a poetic version of the whole of the *Nichomachean Ethics,* omitting the Intellectual Virtues other than practical wisdom" [34]. Whether the claim be justified or not, the poets' Poet and the Philosopher are agreed on many points.

Especially interesting in relation to Spenser's ethics is Aristotle's admission that *natural* desires are seldom sinful (*Nicom. Ethics,* III.xii.3). He recognizes both the claims of the body, such as physical *love,* and the nobler pleasures, arising from a desire of *glory* (*Nicom. Ethics,* VII.iv.). This is Spenser's ethical attitude to both love and glory, illustrated by Britomart and by Arthur's quest of Gloriana. It has little affinity either with the Plato of the *Symposium* or the Plato of the *Republic,* for whom the desire of honour belongs to an inferior type of government (*Rep.* 545 a). Lastly, it should be noticed that Aristotle had criticised Socrates for denying there was any such thing as intemperance, since all evil was mere ignorance (*Nicom. Ethics*, VII.ii.2., *Ethica Magna,* II.viii.2). In the *Faerie Queene,* Spenser, as a Christian, obviously conceives of intemperance as wilful, siding with Aristotle, not with Plato.

Yet the division of Guyon's temptations according to the Platonic distinction of three principles within the soul — reason, spirit or anger, and concupiscence — has been traced back to the *Republic* [35]. Now Spenser *may* have

---

[31] Winstanley, p. XV. Cf. Jortin, in *Variorum, F.Q.,* I. 280. For the argument against suicide, Jortin adds a much likelier source, the *De Senectute.* By Spenser's time, the argument was a stock one, but the best parallel is afforded by the *Commentary* of Macrobius on the *Somnium Scipionis,* a mediaeval text-book still in favour in the XVIth century (*In Somnium Scipionis,* lib. I, cap. XIII, p. 51). As to the House of Holiness, it is pure mediaeval allegory.

[32] See Jones, *A Spenser Handbook,* pp. 172-92; De Moss, *The Influence of Aristotles' "Politics" and "Ethics"* on Spenser, *M P* 16 (1918), pp. 245-70.

On temperance as a "mean" (*F.Q.,* II. ii.), see *Nicom. Ethics* II. ii. 6-9; II. vi-vii; *Eudem. Ethics,* II. iii; *Ethica Magna,* I. ix.

On temperance as half-way between debauchery and insensibility (cf. Marinell in *F.Q.* III) see *Nicom. Ethics* II. vii. 3; *Eudem. Ethics,* III. ii; *Ethica Magna* I. xx.

[33] See Mullinger, *The University of Cambridge from the Royal Injunctions to the Accession of Charles I,* pp. 110-112. None of Plato's dialogues had been printed in England, whereas Aristotle's *Ethics, Physics* and *Problems* had been issued by English printers. An early translation of the *Ethics* was available: *The ethiques of Aristotle, that is to saye precepts of good behavioure.* (London, R. Grafton, 1547.) Spenser's attention may have been caught by a 1581 edition: *Aristotelis ethicorum ad Nicomachum libri decem per quaestiones expositi per S. Heilandum.* London, H. Bynneman, 1581.

[34] Ernest Sirluck *MP* 49 (1941-2), 73-100.

[35] Williamson, *Platonism,* pp. 13 ff. A more moderate claim is advanced by Sirluck who points out that Medina and her sisters "children of one syre by mothers three" figure forth the three divisions of the soul in the *Republic* — the rational, the irascible and the appetive — but acknowledges Spenser's faithfulness to Aristotle in his conclusion: "In thus combining Aristotle's doctrine that virtue resides in the mean with Plato's doctrine that it resides in the government of the irrational part of the soul by the rational, Spenser may have assumed that the two were compatible, since the mean state in Aristotle involves possessing and obeying the right rule discerned by practical wisdom" (*MP* 49, p. 82).

known the *Republic,* which he mentions in the Letter to Raleigh, though without giving proof of personal acquaintance with it [36]. Out of all Platonic dialogues, the *Civitas* had proved most attractive to the politically-minded moralists of the early English Renaissance [37]. But the poet need not have read Plato to make the stock distinction between the rational principle, the irascible impulse and the appetitive instinct [38], or to ascribe temperance to the sovereignty of reason, an ethical commonplace [39]. Besides, writing of "the twelve private morall vertues, as Aristotle hath devised" [40]; he may have turned to the apocryphal *De Virtutibus et Vitiis,* usually included in the *Ethica,* and much favoured in the Renaissance [41]. This short treatise would teach him — if need were — "the triple division of the soul according to Plato" [42].

Other echoes of Plato in Book II have been suggested. Braggadochio was said to embody "certain subtle observations of both Plato and Aristotle" [43]. It requires some subtlety, indeed, to read the Protagoras into Braggadochio, the Italian swashbuckler. As to "the Platonic House of Alma" [44], it has been fully

---

[36] *Variorum, F.Q.,* I. 168: "For this cause is Xenophon preferred before Plato, for that the one in the exquisite depth of his judgment, formed a commune wealth such as it should be, but the other in the person of Cyrus and the Persians fashioned a government such as might best be". From so general a statement, no inference can be drawn as to Spenser's acquaintance with the *Republic.* The contrast of Plato's ideal commonwealth with Cicero's description of actual institutions was a stock one, clearly stated by Macrobius:

"Inter Platonis et Ciceronis libros, quos *de Republica* utrumque constituisse constat ... hos interesse prima fronte perspeximus, quod ille rempublicam ordinavit, hic retulit; alter qualis esse deberet, alter qualis esset a majoribus instituta, disserint (In *Somnium Scipionis,* lib. I, cap. I), Spenser knew Xenophon's *Cyropaidia* through Giraldi's *Three Discourses of Civil Life* and he substituted Xenophon for Cicero. Through Cicero, he would know the characteristics of the *Republic* (see *De Officiis,* I. xxv; *De Legibus* I. v; II. xv; III. xiv).

[37] Taylor characterizes the *Republic* as the "onlie begetter" of More's *Utopia* (*Platonism,* pp. 90-1). Cf. Cassirer, *Die Platonische Renaissance in England,* p. 77. Schroeder shows that the *Republic* and the *Laws* influenced More, Ascham and Elyot more than any other dialogue (*Platonismus,* pp. 66; 71; 87-93, 128). There is a reference to *Plato's Republic* in Robert Crowley's *One and thirtye Epigrammes, wherein are briefly touched so many Abuses, that maye and ought to be put away,* a popular work published in 1550.

[38] Harrison, *Platonism,* p. 13. The distinction was current in the Middle Ages since it occurs in the *Timaeus* (70 a) and was stated by Macrobius in his Commentary *In somnium Scipionis* I. 6, p. 25. It recurs in all discussions on ethics in Renaissance treatises; see for instance Equicola's *Di Natura d'Amore,* p. 115.

[39] If a source is required, Cicero is the likeliest. See Jones, *A Spenser Handbook,* pp. 191-2. But the idea was expressed in all Neoplatonic treatises; cf. Landino, *Disputationes,* fol. liii r°.

[40] *Variorum, F.Q.,* I, p. 167.

[41] It was separately published in Paris (1538, 1548) and Basel (1539, 1552), a mark of popularity.

[42] "Quum autem anima secundum Platonem, in tres distribuatur partes, rationalis quidem virtus est, Prudentia: animosae autem Mansuetudo, & Fortitudo: cupidae vero, Temperantia & Continentia: totius autem animae, Justitia, Liberalitas, & Animi Magnitudo". (*Aristotelis De Virtulibus & vitiis libellum were aureolum* appended to *Georgii Gemisti Plethonis... Quatuor Virtutum explicatio... Adolpho Occone... interprete,* Basileae, per Joanem Oporinum (1552), p. 100, col. I).

[43] C.G. Osgood *M L N* 46 (1931), p. 506. Osgood observes that according to Plato, both the coward and the foolhardy person are ignorant (*Protag.* 360). The philosopher's purpose is to show that fear springs from ignorance and courage from knowledge: no such concern is traceable in Spenser (*F.Q.* II. iii. 4 ff.).

[44] Winstanley, p. XVII.

explained in the light of mediaeval and Elizabethan physiology [45]. As regards the curious stanza describing the proportions of the human body, any unprejudiced critic will agree that Dowden's quotation from Bartholomew Anglicus is the only satisfying analogue, together with the *Somnium Scipionis,* quoted by Upton [46]. We need not assume Spenser had dabbled deep in Pythagorean lore. The not impossible influence of the *Timaeus* is not sufficiently established and I need not remind the reader once more that it may have reached Spenser through mediaveal channels [47].

More interesting and more conclusive than vague or doubtful parallels is a further disagreement between Plato's conception of temperance and Spenser's presentation of the virtue in Book II. In the *Republic* temperance is described as "a kind of harmony", which, diffused in a city, connects the high and the low, the strong and the weak, "all in one symphony" (432 a), just as in the individual man it is a kind of symmetry and a government of pleasures and desires (442 d). Now, the wider political conception is not even hinted at by Spenser, while his treatment of temperance in the individual is dominated by the Aristotelian notion of the "mean". The effect is to break up the Platonic symphony into a series of symmetrical adjustments. It is interesting to notice that even a Platonist like Castiglione did not discard the Aristotelian conception of virtue as a mean:

> For as it is a hard matter in a circle to find out the pricke in the centre, which in the middle, so is it hard to find out the pricke of virtue placed in the middle between two extreme vices, the one for the overmuch, and the other for the over litle [48].

Spenser, as a prentice courtier, must have read Hoby's translation in his Cambridge days. Through Castiglione, some Platonism undoubtedly crept into his ethics, but he seems to have borrowed only such notions as were best attuned to the mind of a Christian and an Aristotelian.

Spenser's handling of chastity has puzzled some commentators because they failed to distinguish between *one* aspect of chastity, virginity, incarnate in Belphoebe, and the all-inclusive virtue, pertaining both to maiden and wife. It is therefore as improper to suggest that chastity only meant to Spenser love ending in marriage [49] as to deny that Britomart was held up as a model of chastity on the grounds that she is unfit to personify that vertue since, unlike the Virgin Queen, she does not remain a maiden [50]. In the person of Britomart, the poet who, though a Protestant, recommended celibacy for priests [51], was not exalting married love above virginity. Belphoebe, as a type of Elizabeth

---

[45] See Fowler, Greenlaw, Powell and Strathman in *Variorum, F.Q.* II, pp. 279, 436-38, 456-7, 469-70.

[46] E. Dowden, "Elizabethan Psychology," *Atlantic Monthly* 100 (1907), pp. 391-2; Upton, quoted in *Variorum, F.Q.,* II. 479.

[47] See Introduction. Alanus de Insulis, Jean de Meung and Bartholomaeus Anglicus drew upon the *Timaeus.* Besides, Morley's literal interpretation of the stanza (*Variorum, F.Q.,* II. 481-2) cannot be lightly dismissed, for such speculations on the dimensions of the human body were popular in the age of Vitruvius: cf. Equicola, *Di Natura d'Amore,* p. 149.

[48] *Courtier,* p. 292; cf. p. 171, top.

[49] C.S. Lewis, *The Allegory of Love,* pp. 338-9.

[50] Bennett, *The Evolution of the Faerie Queene,* p. 137.

[51] See *F.Q.* V. vii. 19; *M.H's.T.* 475 ff.

and virginity, sheds about her a more "heavenly" radiance than Britomart. But Britomart was meant for a more "comprehensive", though less "exalted" virtue. In so far as she is a maiden warrior, like Belphoebe, she embodies virginal purity; but, as she is a lover and a bride, she embodies womanly purity. Instead of showing the two aspects in succession — an awkward method — Spenser most felicitously combined them from the first, by sending the maiden warrior on a quest for an unknown lover. But, on the other hand, we are not entitled to assert that the chastity personified in Britomart is "the noble love of the Phaedrus" [52]. For love as described in the *Phaedrus*, "philosophical love" (256 a-b), has not generation for its end; Britomart's Christian love has [53]. Chastity, besides, cannot be "love" of any kind: it is not an affection, but a "mode" of the affections, and a mode of being. Chaste is Belphoebe, chaste is Britomart, and chaste the bride's "wombe informe(d) with timely seed" [54]. No difficulty arises so long as we abstain from dragging in Platonism — or a supposed aversion to virginity [55], and abide by the Christian notion of chastity, which includes both virginity and purity in married love. Spenser's position on this point, one may add, is neither original nor individual in Elizabethan England. In Nicholas Ling's popular handbook, *Politeuphia, Wits Common-Wealth*, chastity was said to consist "either in sincere virginitie, or in faithfull matrimonie" [56].

The remaining books of the *Faerie Queene* may be briefly discussed for the purpose of the present inquiry, since even Harrison and Winstanley disclaim any consistent Platonic theory for the last three books [57]. Spenser's treatment of Justice is clearly not Platonic: it is best described as Aristotelian, Elizabethan, popular and Calvinistic. Plato, in the *Republic*, conceived of justice, within the city as "the habitual practice of one's own proper and natural work" (433 a-b) and within each man as the governement of the concupiscible and irascible parts by the rational part of the soul (441 e). Neither of these ideas is illustrated by Spenser's Legend of Justice. In fact, justice to Plato is like temperance an all-inclusive virtue, whereas "according to the English poet", as Harrison admits, "justice is purely retributive, a dispensing of reward and punishment" [58] Harrison pretends that Spenser had already exhausted the Platonic notion of justice in his explanation of temperance (*Platonism*, p. 29). But, as I have shown, Spenser's treatment of temperance is mainly Aristotelian. Aristotelian, too, is the presentation of retributive and distributive justice in Book V [59]. This does not mean that Spenser modelled the conduct of Book V on the *Nicomachean Ethics*: by his time, most of the ideas he developed belonged to the wisdom of the nations. Aristocratic prejudice, disdain for the mob and

---

[52] *Winstanley*, p. XVII.

[53] *F.Q.* III. iii. 3; V. vii. 16, 23.

[54] *Epithalamion*, 1. 386.

[55] It has been assumed that Spenser condemns virginity in Marinell as a "deficiency" (Jones, *A Spenser Handbook*, pp. 217-8). What Spenser condemns is not virginity, nor "bachelorship" (Padelford "The Allegory of Chastity in the *Faerie Queene*", *S.P.* 21, pp. 367-81) as a "state" bad in itself, but insensibility to human affections for a wrong motive. Marinell does not dedicate himself to a religious life, but to the acquisition of riches. Christianity has never exalted virginity apart from a religious purpose (Cf. Isis' priests in Bk. V).

[56] *Politeuphia*, p. 202; London, I.R. for Nicholas Ling, 1597.

[57] Harrison, *Platonism*, pp. 26-7. *Winstanley*, p. XIX.

[58] *Platonism*, p. 27.

[59] Cf. *Eth. ad Nicom.*, lib. V; *Magna Moralia*, I. xxxi.

violent attacks on the "levelling" principle of equality are the hall-mark of Elizabethan politics [60]. Lastly the identification of justice with the will of God is a Calvinistic characteristic [61].

For his conception of Courtesy the poet owes nothing to Plato, and though he owes much to Italian courtesy books, it is significant that he borrows none of their Neoplatonic refinements on the theory of love. Lovers "in this delightfull land of Faery" are purely Arcadian, not in the least Platonic [62]. As to Spenser's ideas on friendship, in an admirably documented article, C. G. Smith has shown that they were widespread and proverbial in Renaissance literature [63]. Although he finds authority for them in the Platonic dialogues, it is apparent from the mass of evidence set forth that they belong to "a diffused humanism", to which Cicero contributed more than Plato [64]. That body of thought has been loosely styled Neoplatonic, but it is informed with the spirit of Latin, not of Greek literature. Besides it represents no abrupt break with the mediaeval tradition, as the similarity of the Amyas story to the romance of *Amis and Amiloun* clearly shows [65].

Not only were Spenser's ethics scarcely — or at best, indirectly — influenced by Plato, but the whole plan of the *Faerie Queene,* with the clear-cut distinction and separate treatment of "the twelve private morall vertues" was repugnant to the spirit of his philosophy. To the Platonist, there is but one Idea of the Good, and one science of it; and therefore there is, in a way, but one virtue, wisdom,

---

[60] *F.Q.* V. ii. 30 ff. Fritz Caspari claims that "Like Plato, Spenser sees in unbridled democracy and in the ensuing tyranny the opposites of the just state, and he accordingly portrays both as such in his treatment of justice" (*Humanism and the Social Order,* p. 197). One may assent and find the resemblance one more proof that the *Republic* was the dialogue with which Spenser was best acquainted, beside the *Timaeus.* But, as these ideas were commonplaces and as the claim is unsupported by obvious parallels, direct influence is not established.

[61] *F.Q.,* V. ii. 39-42.

[62] e.g. the love of Aladine for Priscilla (VI. ii. 43), Calepine for Serena (VI. iii. 20 and *passim*), Calidore for Pastorell (VI. ix). The fair Mirabella is a *Petrarchan* coquette punished for her cruelty.

[63] *E.L.H.* 2 (1935), pp. 165-91.

[64] C.G. Smith brings in illustrations from the *Lysis,* the *Phaedrus,* and Ficino's *Sopra l'Amore.* But these are no evidence that Spenser derived such ideas from Plato or Ficino, since all had been expressed by Elizabethan writers. Besides, Cicero's *De Amicitia* — a standard work he is likely to have consulted before writing a Legend of Friendship — could have furnished him with all the ideas listed by C.G. Smith:
1° "Friendship is based on virtue": cf. *De Amicitia* viii-ix; xxvii.
2° "Friendship is based on equality": cf. *De Amic.* xix.
3° Friendship is based on similarity: cf. *De Amic.* xiv.
4° "Friends have but one soul": cf. *De Amic.* xxv.
5° A friend is a second self": cf. *De Amic.* xxi, end.
6° False friendship cannot last: cf. *De Amic.* xxii.
7° Friends' goods are common goods (rejected by Spenser): cf. *De Amic.* xvii.
The assertion of the superiority of friendship over "affection unto kindred" (*F.Q.* IV. ix. 1-2) is more distinctly reminiscent of the *De Amicitia* v than of the *Nicomachean Ethics* mentioned by the editor (*F.Q.* IV. 213). Spenser also departs from Aristotle and agrees with Cicero when he introduces the physical theories of Empedocles into his Legend of Friendship (*F.Q.* IV. x. 32, 35, cf. *De Amicitia,* vii, cst. *Nicom. Ethics,* viii. i. 7).

[65] H.M. Ayres "The Faerie Queene and Amis and Amiloun", *M.L.N.* 23 (1908), pp. 177-80.

which cannot be parcelled out. To the Aristotelian on the contrary, there are several sciences of the good since the good is found in all the categories: the different virtues therefore must be treated distinctly[66]. Obviously, his allegorical frame forced upon Spenser the Aristotelian point of view. Yet, with due allowance for poetic requirements, the fact remains: the *conduct* of the ethical allegory is Aristotelian even when the *atmosphere* is pervaded with Platonism. It may not be either an overhasty generalization to say that Plato envisages ethics from a metaphysical vantage ground in the light of ultimate truth, whereas Aristotle discusses them from a pragmatical point of view. Spenser's own position is neither truly Platonic nor purely Aristotelian. His is the standpoint of the politically-, ethically-, religiously- minded Englishman of the early Renaissance. At times, he is the humanist, concerned with human standards only. But, as a rule, his ethics have wider implications, religious rather than metaphysical. Human values are related, not to the ideal values of Plato, but to Christian values. True virtuousness does not lie in the participation of the Platonic Heavenly Wisdom, but in conformity to the will of God, manifest as well in the Law of Nature as in Scripture, or again in the mysterious working of grace[67].

But although ethical action in the *Faerie Queene* is constantly referred to a higher scheme of values, its purpose and scope remain, in a sense, "worldly", for its beginning and end are on earth. The New Jerusalem and "the pillars of Eternity" loom afar, as "a wished end", but an end beyond the story's end: world's end. Action in the *Faerie Queene* is completed on earth, concerned with present achievements and present rewards: the betrothal of the Knight of Holiness to the true Church (I.xii.17-40), the destruction of the Bower of Bliss[68]; the release of Love from the enchantments of courtly gallantry[69], the winning of a bride in the temple of Concord-Venus (IV.x), the slaying of Grantorto by the Knight of Justice[70], the blinding of the Blatant Beast by the knight of Courtesy[71]. From internal evidence, there is no reason to suppose that the meeting of Arthur and Gloriana was to be invested with a metaphysical significance. Metaphysical overtones, I agree, are not wanting in the epic. But they are heard, not at the close of each story, but, as it were, at resting places within each book. A pause in the action allows leisure for reflection. Time and again the poet ascends "the mount of contemplation" whence he surveys both heaven and earth and relates human affairs to the divine or cosmic scheme. The Mount of Contemplation (I.x.) and the Garden of Adonis (III.vi.) are both pauses and metaphysical peaks. The Cantos of Mutabilitie, labelled VI-VIII, were probably composed with a like intent. They were not meant for a conclusion, but for the metaphysical core of a Legend of Constancy, the action of which would

---

[66] See Aristotle's criticism of the Idea of the Good in the *Nicomachean Ethics*, I. iii. 1-7.

[67] On Spenser's religious ideas, see chapter XII.

[68] *F.Q.* II. xii. Has it occurred to any Spenserian critic that the puritanically-minded poet may have had in mind the often entreated closure of the Elizabethan brothels when he described the destruction of the bower where "some goodly swayne(s) of honourable place" defaced their nobility? The Bower is Italianate no doubt, but the "morality" is plain English: "Let Gryll be Gryll"... (II. xii. 87, 8).

[69] *F.Q.* III. xii. C.S. Lewis's interpretation.

[70] *F.Q.* V. xii. Grantorto may be the Pope or Philip II. See A.B. Cough in *Variorum*, *F.Q.* V. 318.

[71] *F.Q.* VI. xii. The Blatant beast is Slander, and probably the extreme Puritans.

have remained on the ethical and human level. In Book IV the story for once runs to a close against a cosmic background (IV.x.), but it retains its purely human interest and significance [72]. In Book II, the House of Alma (II.ix) also marks a pause and a peak. In the Legend of Justice, the metaphysical overtones occur in the debate of Artegall with the Giant (V.ii.30-43). An early introduction of the metaphysical "justification" was necessary for Spenser's justice had been unpalatable, unless conceived from the first in relation to world-order and the divine will. But this sense of the wider significance of human action does not imply, as the Neoplatonic philosophy did, the existence of a hierarchy of worlds, in which each world is a copy of the next above it. It invites us to read the episodes of the epic in a metaphysical context, but it does not require that an allegory of metaphysical realities should be read into the action, and the characters turned into Neoplatonic entities. Refreshed by a glimpse of eternity, the poet and his heroes consciously "turne againe Backe to the world". Metaphysical realities are either expressed through direct statement or embedded into the story. But "the continued Allegorye or darke conceit" of the story itself is purely ethical, historical or political. A needless expense of ingenuity would have been spared, had not some critics thought they knew what Spenser meant better than he knew himself. For once, the safest method is to abide by the *Letter of the Authors expounding his whole intention in the course of this worke.* It does not disclose any metaphysical intention. And, far from claiming the patronage of Plato, the poet admits he "laboured" to satisfy the "commune sense" of those by whom "is Xenophon preferred before Plato". Since his statements agree with the obvious ethical and historical significance of the epic and do not support the supposed — and unsubstantiated — Neo-Platonic meaning, we may definitely reject the latter.

It might be objected that the *Letter* was an afterthought and that I refused to take Spenser's declaration at its face-value when I discussed the dedication of the *Fowre Hymnes.* But there is a wide difference between indulging in a false statement for the sake of literary artifice and deliberately trying to mislead the reader into a wrong interpretation, or to conceal from him the deeper significance of a poem. I incline to disbelieve Spenser when he says that the first two *Hymnes* were written in his youth. But I believe he is telling the truth when he invites us to contrast the earthly with the heavenly *Hymnes.* A chronological or biographical lie for literary or other reasons is not unexpected from a poet. But he had no reason to conceal the true meaning of a poem unless it were for political safety. Now, the *Letter of the Authors* precisely invites a historical and topical interpretation of the *Faerie Queene* — the only one that offered any danger. Spenser knew that it lay open to suspicion, since he chose a story "furthest from the daunger of envy and suspition of present time". Had the idea of a Neo-Platonic interpretation but occurred to him, even as an afterthought, he would eagerly have seized on it and paraded it in the *Letter* or in a Proem. For, against the strictures of such as might be displeased by the topical allusions, his best defence would have been to flaunt a deeper allegorical purpose and openly identify Belphoebe not with Elizabeth,

---

[72] The structure of Book IV is loose. Marinell's winning of Florimell (IV. xi. xii) is but a duplicate of Scudamour's winning of Amoret. Neither offers a conclusion to the Legend of Friendship. For once the conclusion and the metaphysical "peak" coincide: the legend of friendship culminates in — and ends with — the stanzas on Concord "Mother of blessed *Peace* and *Friendship trew*" (IV. x. 34. 2).

but with the Heavenly Venus. This he did not. A Neoplatonic interpretation of the *Faerie Queene* has not "the authors" consent. Furthermore, it cannot be fastened upon the poem without glaring inconsistencies. For the sake of making Spenser a Neoplatonist, some critics make a bungler out of him, fathering upon him a design he failed to carry out if he ever entertained it. But there is nothing to show that he *did* entertain it.

CHAPTER IV

PLATONIC MYTHOLOGY AND COSMOLOGY

In the "Faerie Queene" and "Colin Clout"

The conduct of the action in the *Faerie Queene* does not admit of a Neoplatonic interpretation. But the human action is developed against a mythological and cosmological background. Besides, whole cantos are taken up by myths of metaphysical significance, such as the myth of Adonis, or the Mutabilitie Cantos. Might not the myths and the cosmology at least be permeated with Neoplatonic influences? The Alexandrian Neoplatonists had built up an allegorical mythology, turning the former Greek theogony into a figurative expression of their own metaphysics and emanation theories. The Renaissance Platonists followed in their wake. The second of Leone Ebreo's *Dialoghi d'Amore* offers, I believe, the fullest exposition of the various meanings fastened by the Neoplatonists upon the mythology of the poets [1]. But Ficino and Pico had shown the way [2], and even vulgarizers of mythology and Platonism like Natalis Comes (i.e. Natale Conti) and Equicola not unfrequently mention the various correspondences between the poetical genealogy of the gods and the Neoplatonic hierarchy of emanations [3]. It is therefore unlikely that Spenser should have been entirely unaware of the Neoplatonic significance attached to the classical myths, since we know he borrowed his mythology from Natalis Comes [4]. But it is highly characteristic of his trend of mind and his interests that he should have had no use for the Neoplatonic metaphysics in his *Faerie Queene.* The waiving of the more metaphysical allegories may be due only to his personal taste; but it would be objectively explained as well, if, up to the *Fowre Hymnes,* Spenser had derived his Platonic notions from Natalis Comes and Louis Le Roy only. For, as the next chapter will show, both the Italian compiler and the French commentator on the Banquet, sharing Spenser's naturalistic and ethical bent, showed a distrust of the more far-fetched metaphysical allegories. But, for the time being, let us examine Spenser's own use of mythology with an unprejudiced eye.

Our task is made easy by H. G. Lotspeich's invaluable study of *Classical Mythology in the Poetry of Edmund Spenser.* It may be seen at a glance that Uranus (or Caelus) and Saturn, the first two members of the Neoplatonic tri-

---

[1] *Dialoghi,* II, ff. 66 v° sq.
[2] Ficino, *In Convivium* V. xii, VI. vii; Pico, *Commento,* II. xi; II. xvii-xviii.
[3] See Natalis Comes on Venus (p. 380) and Jove (p. 104). Cf. Equicola on Venus equated with the world-soul: *Di Natura d'Amore,* p. 120.
[4] See Lotspeich, *Mythology in Spenser,* pp. 14 ff.

nity[5], are never invested by Spenser with any metaphysical significance[6]. Saturn is the Golden Age ruler of classical tradition. He appears also in his astrological character. This aspect of him, Lotspeich notes, "is more characteristically mediaeval"[7]. Daemogorgon is taken from Boccaccio[8]. Spenser rests satisfied with the mythological associations and, though the figure had a fascination for him, he nowhere suggests the Neoplatonic interpretation of the myth urged by Leone Ebreo[9]. The story of Pan and Syrinx, when he tells it, is the charming classical myth of Ovid, unburdened by metaphysical allegory[10]. Nor does the poet ever invite us to read an allegory of the creation into the childbirth of Latona or the amours of Alcmena[11]. Spenser's Apollo is the classical Phœbus untouched by Neoplatonic speculation[12]. The same is true of Diana, Mars and Mercury[13]. The Hours are daughters of Jove and Night, not because they figure "the union of the Divine Principle with Matter" as Dr. Spens profoundly suggests[14], but because Jove is Day[15], and the poet "is manifestly working from their [the Hours'] connection with divisions of time"[16]. They are "porters of Heaven's gate", not because from that gate, "the ideas of the yonder" issue into the lower world[17], but because Homer and Ovid had ascribed that function to them[18]. Even the myth of Psyche, distinctly Platonic in Apuleius and Boccaccio[19], is to some extent un-platonized by Spenser, for the Psyche that educates Amoret "in all the lore of love and goodly womanhead" in prevision of an earthly marriage in the temple of a Lucretian Venus[20] hardly recalls the rational soul, attaining through purgations "to the consummation of divine joy and contemplation"[21]. Other instances of Spenser's conscious or unconscious avoidance of metaphysical implications might be adduced[22]. But the former sufficiently show that he usually treated mythology as a poet, not as a philosopher, much less as a Neoplatonist. Among the mythological figures of the *Faerie Queene,* only Jove, Cupid or Love, Venus and Adonis are occasionally invested with a philosophical significance.

Now, each book of the *Faerie Queene* contains, usually in its second half, a central allegory, which, though related to the general allegorical frame, stands out, as it were, in climatic isolation, self-complete and self-contained. In the Legend of Holiness and the Legend of Temperance, the allegorical "peaks" reached in the House of Holiness and the House of Alma are clearly mediaeval

---

[5] Ficino, *In Convivium* II. vii; Pico, *Commento* I. vii.
[6] Lotspeich, *Mythology,* pp. 114, 105.
[7] *Ibid.,* p. 105.
[8] *Ibid.,* pp. 51-2.
[9] *Dialoghi,* II, ff. 67 r° et seq.
[10] Lotspeich, *Mythology,* p. 109. Contrast Leone, *Dialoghi,* II, f. 71 r°.
[11] Lotspeich, *ibid.,* pp. 77, 35. Cst. *Dialoghi,* II, 77 v°- 79 v°.
[12] Lotspeich, *ibid.,* pp. 37-8.
[13] *Ibid.,* pp. 53-4; 79-80; 80-81.
[14] *Spenser's Faerie Queene,* p. 43.
[15] Cf. *F.Q.* I. v. 25; I. vii. 23. 1. Cf. the Hour's parentage in *Epithalamion,* 1. 98 (Day and Night).
[16] Lotspeich, *Mythology,* p. 70.
[17] Spens, *Faerie Queene,* p. 43.
[18] Lotspeich, *Mythology,* p. 70.
[19] *Ibid.,* p. 104.
[20] *F.Q* III. vi. 50-51; cf. IV. x.
[21] Boccaccio V. 22, quoted by Lotspeich, p. 70.
[22] Spenser, for instance, has no use for the Neoplatonic allegory of the myth of Orpheus: cf. Le Roy, *Sympose,* f. 15 r°-v°; cst Lotspeich, *Mythology,* p. 94.

in character, untouched by Neoplatonic speculation [23]. In the Legend of Justice, the philosophical mount of centemplation is early ascended and again proves Christian and mediaeval [24]. Should such pre-eminence be claimed for the Isis Church episode, it should be noted that Spenser borrowed from Plutarch's *De Iside* the mythological details and both the evhemeral and the physical allegory, but did not in the least suggest the more metaphysical interpretations of the myth [25]. The culmination of the Legend of Courtesy is Sir Calidore's vision of the Graces dancing on Mount Acidale, a pastoral and classical picture, from which all metaphysical shadows were felicitously banned [26]. We are therefore left with three pieces of cosmological allegory: the garden of Adonis, the Temple of Concord Venus and the *Mutabilitie* Cantos — to which Colin's definition of love in *Colin Clouts Come Home Againe* must be added. An estimate of Spenser's cosmic philosophy prior to the *Fowre Hymnes* must rest on those four pieces. And since Jove, Venus, Adonis and Cupid nowhere appear in their philosophical character but in the four allegories just mentioned, the mythology and cosmology of Spenser, in relation to Platonism, may be studied at a time.

Since Dr. Janet Spens claims that the *Mutabilitie* Cantos are the key to Spenser's philosophy, and are "only to be interpreted by the light of Neo-Platonic doctrines" [27], these will be considered first. The Neoplatonic interpretation offered may contribute to our aesthetic enjoyment of the *Faerie Queene,* especially if we find Dean Inge's Plotinism congenial. But even Dr. Spens seems to have had some qualms of conscience, since, after asserting:

> The Olympian Gods are the attributes of the Divine Principle issuing into this secular world. That is the meaning of Nature's final judgment.

she feels bound to add:

> The choice of the name "Nature" for the judge of the question is a little confusing to the modern mind, as is also the form of a legal trial [28]

No such misgivings disturbed Dr. J. W. Bennett, who brought a wealth of material to bear upon the *Mutabilitie* Cantos. Unfortunately, all of it is not relevant, and the Neoplatonic superstructure thus erected rests on insecure foundations. Dr. Bennett begins by reminding the reader that Jove is not the Supreme Deity, for in the Neoplatonic hierarchy he is equated with the *anima mundi* [29]. She next proceeds to identify Nature with the World-Soul "as it acts as a creative force" [30], and asserts that to such a deity, "the immediate creator of the visible universe", Mutability might well say:

> For, heaven and earth I both alike do deeme,
> Sith heaven and earth are both alike to thee;
> And gods no more than men thou doest esteeme:
> For even the gods to thee, as men to gods do seeme.
>
> (*F.Q.*, VII. vii. 15)

---

[23] See above, pp. 52-55.

[24] For its Boethian and Biblical character, see *Variorum, F.Q.* V, pp. 178-9.

[25] *F.Q.* V. vii. 1-24.

[26] *F.Q.* VI. x. 8-28.

[27] Spenser's *Faerie Queene*, p. 35.

[28] *Ibid.*, pp. 43-44.

[29] *S.P.* 30 (1933), 162-63.

[30] *Ibid.*, p. 163. Professor Bennett quotes Pico and Ficino. The ultimate source is Plotinus, *Enneads,* IV. iv. 6; IV. iv. 9-10.

Now, this is only true if we admit that Spenser's Nature is the Nature of the Latin and mediaeval Platonists, not the nature of Plotinus, Ficino and the Renaissance Neoplatonists, for whom nature was definitely one grade lower than the World-Soul in the scale of being, an unconscious involuntary agent [31] or a mere "seminary" [32]. Can the lovest of all the Neoplatonic intermediaries be the "great goddesse" of the *Mutabilitie* Cantos, above whom no one sits, but the God of Sabbaoth? If Spenser had in mind the Neoplatonic hierarchy, how shall we account for the unfilled gaps between the fourth and the first degree? And would a Neoplatonist have introduced Jove merely in his mythological and astrological character — as J. W. Bennett is constrained to admit lest her theory should prove self-contradictory — when we know that he was commonly identified with the World-Soul, not only by Plotinus, Ficino and Pico, but even by vulgarizers like Natalis Comes [33]? It may be agreed, that Spenser pictured the Jove of Classical mythology and had in mind the Jupiter of classical astrology. But there are overtones, hinting at a deeper significance, and these overtones are always Christian, never Neoplatonic. How various soever the component elements may be, the *Mutabilitie* Cantos are dominated by mediaeval astronomy, mediaeval cosmology, mediaeval Christianity.

The assertion may appear paradoxical since the very theme chosen might, at first sight, be related to the impact of "the new astronomy" upon the poet's mind. To support her claim to "Heav'ns Rule" [34]. Mutability urges the late disturbances in the courses of the planets which had already been mentioned in the Proem to Book V and argued into a proof of the decay of the world [35]. But the term "new astronomy" should be reserved to the Copernican hypothesis or the discovery of new stars, not to speak of the later discoveries of Galileo. There is nothing really "new" in Mutability's arguments. Spenser's astronomy is purely Ptolemaic. Irregularities in the courses of the planets [36], the precession of the Equinoxes [37], "mutability in the Sunnes greatest declination" [38], these facts had puzzled ancient and mediaeval astronomers [39]. Of course, the progress of Renaissance astronomy had sharpened man's conscious-

---

[31] Plotinus, *Enneads* III. viii. 4-5; IV. iv. 11-13.

[32] Ficino *In Timaeum*, cap. X (*Opera*, p. 1442). In the *Commentarium in Convivium*, the four circles concentric to God are Mind, Soul, Nature and Matter (II. iii). Nature, I agree, is described as "the generative power of the Soul". Spenser, therefore, might have telescoped Nature and Soul into one, which would account for the line: "Still mooving, yet unmoved from her sted" (*F.Q.* VII. vii. 13. 3), since Ficino describes the Soul as *anima in statu pariter atque motu* (VI.xvi).

Since both Spenser and Ficino write in the Neoplatonic tradition, their conceptions are reconcilable. But Spenser's, as shown below, offers all the characteristics of mediaeval Platonism, and none of the characteristics of Renaissance Neoplatonism, since he does not develop nor hint at the emanation theory, and reduces the series God-Mind-Soul-Nature to God and Nature.

[33] *Mythologia*, II. i. p. 104. "Alii mundi animam Jovem esse crediderunt": Orpheus is quoted in support.

[34] *F.Q.* VII. viii. 1. 4.

[35] *F.Q.* VII. vii. 50-55; cf. V. Pro. 5-8.

[36] *F.Q.* VII. vii. 51. 3-4; 52. 1-6; 55. 1-4; cf. V. Pro. 8. 8-9.

[37] *F.Q.* VII. vii. 55. 6-7; cf. V. Pro. 5-6.

[38] In *F.Q.* V. vii. 5-9 only.

[39] See F.R. Johnson, *Astronomical thought in Renaissance England*, pp. 22-5; 60-1. See also Bainbridge's short history of "mutability in the sunnes greatest declination" in Hakewill's *Apologie... of the Power and Providence of God* (2nd. ed. 1630, pp. 101-3).

ness of irregularity in the heavenly revolutions. But none of the variations observed "of late" which Spenser mentions [40] were of a revolutionary nature; but for the Copernican hypothesis and the nova of 1572, they would have been dealt with by means of eccentrics and epicycles. The poet may have borrowed his notions from competent, but classical textbooks of astronomy, like Peurbach's *Theoricae Novae* [41]. "His poetry", F. R. Johnson notes, "although reflecting many of the currents of thought that inspired the new scientific movement, seems never to have been directly influenced by any of the events in its progress". "For example, there is no allusion to the new star of 1572, and the shattering of the Aristotelian doctrine of the changeless heavens, although in the "Mutabilitie Cantos" Spenser's theme offered an appropriate occasion for such a reference" [42]. Mutability acknowledges the Earth to be "unmov'd" [43], and makes a point of the "motions of (the) Spheares", the solid spheres of Aristotle which Copernicus and the best Elizabethan astronomers had discarded or questioned [44]. The astronomical theme of the *Cantos of Mutabilitie,* and the treatment of it are therefore traditional, and dominantly mediaeval in spirit [45]: their cosmology and metaphysics no less.

Claims have been made for a Lucretian influence [46]. These fragments of a Legend of Constancy may well be reminiscent of the fifth book of the *De Natura Rerum*, but their general argument is not the "mortality" of all things, as Greenlaw argues [47]. W. P. Cumming has shown that Spenser's primary indebtedness for his philosophy of change is to Ovid [48], a mediaeval and Elizabethan

---

[40] *F.Q.* VII. vii. 51-4, and possibly 52. 1-6; cf. V. Pro. 5-8.

[41] *Theoricae Novae Planetarum Georgii Purbachii...* Basileae, per S. Henricpietri, 1596. Originally written in the XVth century, the "new theories" were based upon Ptolemy and Arabic astronomy (cf. Johnson, *Astronomical Thought*, p. 63).

See especially: *De Mutatione Declinationum Solis maximarum* (p. 136), *De inaequali progressu stellarum fixarum* (p. 139), *De Variatione punctorum aequinoctalium* (p. 146) *De inaequali motu stellarum fixarum* (p. 149). Peurbach admits there is no fixity in the Zodiac (pp. 151-2).

In the *Quaestiones Novae in Theoricas Novas Planetarum ... Georgii Purbachii ... authore Christiano Vurstisio* (Basileae 1568), the irregularities "in multiformi motu Mercurii" are emphasized (p. 107; cf. *F.Q.* VII. vii. 51. 4). Various irregularities are also discovered in the motion of the sphere of fixed stars (pp. 400-430). See especially p. 403: "Ea namque testata fecerunt, eundem motium *nunc tardiorem, nunc velociorem* esse, eoque maximas Solis declinationes, annique quantitatem mutari, quinetiam aequinoctia atque Solstitia ad *diversas* repere sedes...". Cf. p. 411: "Verus motus inerrantium syderum idcirco *irregularis* est...". But most of the irregularities had long been known; before Copernicus, Albategnus and Alphonsus "apparentias istas excusare voluerunt" (pp. 403, 419).

[42] *Astronomical Thought*, p. 195 and Note 81.

[43] *F.Q.* VII. vii. 17. 7. This is the more remarkable since Harvey was aware of the Copernican hypothesis: cf. F.R. Johnson, *op. cit.*, p. 181. Spenser must have heard of it. Did he refrain from using it because he regarded the opinion as absurd or impious?

[44] On Copernicus, see Mc Colley's article in *Popular Astronomy*, vol. XLIV, 525-33. Ater the *nova* of 1572 "the idea of solid orbs had to be wholly abandoned" (Johnson, *Astron. Thought*, p. 155).

[45] G. Williamson defends a contrary thesis: "To call his belief in the decay of the world 'mediaeval' is to neglect one aspect of the Renaissance in a religious mind" (*ELH* 1953, pp. 121-50). I agree that such a belief is "one aspect" of the Renaissance as a period including ancient and new trends of thought and feeling. What I claim is that the belief in decay was a legacy of the "mediaeval mind", the belief in progress a character of the "Renaissance mind".

[46] Greenlaw, *SP* 17, pp. 439-64.

[47] *Ibid.*, pp. 455-64.

classic; and Rosemond Tuve rightly describes the theme of mutability as "a Mediaeval Commonplace", pointing out analogues in Gower and Lydgate[49]. Even if we mistakenly read into *Mutabilitie* the theme of decay treated in the Proem of Book V — the probable origin of Greenlaw's misinterpretation — differences still outweigh resemblances. For instance, the assertion of mutability in celestial bodies may be reminiscent of Lucretius, but the Epicurean poet ridiculed the identification of planets with gods, which Spenser retains, not merely for the sake of poetry but for the sake of astrology[50]. Besides, while emphasizing the mortality of heavenly bodies, Lucretius stressed the regularity of heavenly motions, which Mutability denies[51], whereas any idea that the sun one day might be spent, though appropriate to the theme, is not even implied[52]. The description of the four elements in transmutation has verbal echoes of Golding's Ovid[53] and again emphasizes Protean change, not decay and disintegration[54].

The predominantly mediaeval character of Spenser's philosophy is nowhere more clear than in his conception and portrait of Nature. E. C. Knowlton and C. S. Lewis have traced its descent through "Claudian, Bernardus, Alanus and Jean de Meung"[55]. Spenser's possible indebtedness to Alanus had earlier been emphasized by Greenlaw[56]. But as regards Nature, Lotspeich, Fowler and Allbright rightly pointed out that "the two descriptions are quite different"[57]. Some of the details have been traced to Plutarch[58]. Others were commonplaces in "the school of Alanus", which included Chaucer and Lydgate[59]. But in his emphasis on beauty and the poet's impotence to describe Nature, Spenser comes nearest to Jean de Meung[60]. Instead of the laboured description of Alanus,

---

48 *SP* 28, pp. 241-56. Cf. Stirling's "Two Notes" in *MLN* 50, pp. 154-5.

49 *SP* 30, pp. 145-7.

50 *De Natura,* V. 111-47. *F.Q.*, VII. vii. 50-54.

51 *De Natura,* V. 11. 678; 1183-4.

52 Spenser comes nearest to it in *F.Q.* V. Pro. vii, but only fears that the sun "will us quite forsake. In VII.vii.24.1-2, he asserts the immortality of fire, which Lucretius denies (noted by Allbright, *P M L A* 44, p. 73).

53 Stirling, *MLN* 50, p. 154.

54 Contrast *F.Q.* VII.vii.25 and *De Natura,* V. ll. 236-47.

55 C.S. Lewis *The Allegory of Love,* p. 355. Cf. Knowlton, *JEGP* 34, pp. 366-76.

56 "Some Old Religious Cults in Spenser", *SP* 20, pp. 216-43.

57 Lotspeich *Mythology,* p. 87; Fowler, quoted in *Variorum, F.Q.*, VII, pp. 292-3; Allbright, *SP* 25, p. 757.

58 Lotspeich, *Mythology,* p. 87.

59 Cf. Helen A. Kahin, *ELH* 8 (1941), 257-72.

60 In *The Parlement of Foules* (11. 316-18) Chaucer merely states that Nature apeared "right as Aleyn, in the Pleynt of Kinde, /Devyseth Nature of aray and face". Spenser twists the reference into an admission that Chaucer "durst not with it mell,/ But it transferd to *Alane*" (*F.Q.* VII. vii. 9). Spenser may have remembered Lydgate's *Reson and Sensuallyte* as Kahin suggests (*ELH* 8, pp. 259-62). But Lydgate's lines lack the nerve and feeling of the passage by Jean de Meung quoted below:

Touching the beaute and fayrenesse
Of this honourabill godesse,
Ther was no man her alyve
That konnyng hadde to discryve
The excellence of his beaute
Nor comprehende in no degre
Hyr comelynesse, hyr Woman-hede,
For al beaute hyt dyd excede.

(*Reson and Sensuallyte,* ll. 321-28.)

which takes away the awfulness of Nature [61], both the English and the French poet are content with describing her mainly "by negatives":

> Bien la vousisse descrire,
> Mais mes sens n'i pourroit soufire;
> Mes sens! Qu'ai-je dit? c'est du meins
> Non feroit veir nus sens humains,
> Ne par voiz vive ne par notes (*Roman*, ll. 16165-9).

Jean de Meung proclaims that no poet, painter or philosopher could describe Nature fittingly (*Roman*, ll. 16166-210) and ends by declaring that the beauty of her face "ne peut estre d'ome compris" (ll. 16247-8). Spenser tells us "That eye of wight could not indure to view" the face of Nature, which "could be seene but like an image in a glass" (*F.Q.* VII.vii.6).

The last image, with its distinct New Testament ring, implies the Christian character of Nature, not only as the vice-regent of God [62], but as the manifestation of the Deity. This is more clearly pointed out in the next stanza, when Nature's garment is compared to the garments of the transfigured Christ. There is nothing odd in the comparison, for Nature in mediaeval Platonism is the fecundity of God himself, and especially of God the Son, the "Noys" of Bernardus, who called her "*tu, natura, uteri mei beata fecunditas*" [63]. The charge of pantheism has been brought against Spenser, as against Bernardus, and may be as decisively refuted [64]. Spenser's philosophy is the "Christian naturalism" of the Middle Ages" [65], not the pantheism of Renaissance thinkers like Bruno. The final award of Nature comes as a surprise or an act of faith only to the reader who has not been aware of the undercurrent of Christian meaning from the very first stanzas. Mutability, as C. S. Lewis emphasizes [66], is presented as Rebellion and Sin:

> By which, we all are subject to that curse,
> And death instead of life have sucked from our Nurse.
> (VII. vi. 6)

Her father, Titan, is obviously identified with Lucifer, the fallen Angel:

> Then ceasse thy idle claime thou foolish gerle,
> And seeke by grace and goodnesse to obtaine
> That place from which by folly *Titan* fell;
> (VII. vi 34)

Indeed, Jove's rebuke reads like a rebuke of the Pelagian heresy or the Renaissance exaltation of the dignity of man. It is an exact parallel to the Calvinistic theology of the *Hymne of Heavenly Beautie*:

---

[61] Such a description of Nature's lips for instance: "Labia modico tumore surgentia Veneris tyrones invitabant ad oscula" (Migne, ccx, col. 432 c).

[62] Cf. *Roman*, 11. 16785 ff., and *Parlement of Foules*, 1. 379: "Nature the vicaire of th' almighty lorde".

[63] *De mundi universitate*, p. 9; quoted by Gilson in "La Cosmogonie de Bernardus Sylvestris", p. 22.

[64] For Bernardus, see Gilson, *op. cit.*, p. 20; for Spenser, C.S. Lewis, *The Allegory of Love*, pp. 355-6.

[65] Cf. Gilson, *La Philosophie au Moyen Age*, p. 315.

[66] *The Allegory of Love*, p. 354.

> But wote thou this, thou hardy *Titanesse,*
> *That not the worth of any living wight*
> *May challenge ought in Heavens interesse;*
> Much lesse the Title of old *Titans* Right [67].
> For, we by Conquest of our soveraigne might,
> And by eternall doome of Fates decree,
> Have wonne the Empire of the Heavens bright;
> Which to our selves we hold, *and to whom wee*
> *Shall worthy deeme partakers of our blisse to bee.*
>
> (VII. vi. 33; italics mine)

Throughout the Cantos, Jove has a double function. For the sake of the myth and the cosmic allegory, he is the planetary god. But for the sake of the moral allegory, he has to speak at times like the Christian God. The contemporary reader was too well trained in the complexities of allegory to mistake the poet's meaning [68]. "High Jove" is a "symbol of the true Godhead" in all the Books of the *Faerie Queene* [69].

The metaphysics of the *Cantos of Mutabilitie* are, indeed, no less traditional than the cosmology. It has been claimed that "the dominant timbre of Christian Platonism" is heard in their "polyphonic music" [70]. The pronouncement may win assent with one qualification: this is *mediaeval* Christian Platonism. Even the concluding stanzas do not betray the influence of Ficino or other Renaissance Neoplatonists. They distinctly echo the earlier Platonism of Boethius. The author of the *De Consolatione Philosophiae* was still a favourite with the Elizabethans but, in the words of Morris quoted by Stirling, "no philosopher was so bone of the bone and flesh of the flesh of Middle Age writers as Boethius" [71]. Yet even the striking parallel between the ideas expressed at the close of *Mutabilitie* and in a "prose" passage of the *De Consolatione* does not imply that Spenser like Boethius found the concept of permanence in change and the ideal of immutability reconcilable "in perfect union", as Stirling maintains. In the heart of change the poet, like the philosopher, discovered a "fated temporal succession", distinct from God but closely dependent upon His steadfast Will or Providence:

> I well consider all that ye have sayd,
> And find that all things stedfastnes doe hate
> And changed be; yet being rightly wayd,
> They are not changed from their first estate;
> But by their change their being doe dilate;
> And, turning to themselves at length againe,
> Do worke their owne perfection so by fate:
> Then over them Change doth not rule and raigne;
> But they raigne over change, and doe their states maintaine.
>
> (*F.Q.*, VII. vii. 58)

---

[67] Why "much lesse" unless Titan symbolizes Lucifer, as I have suggested?

[68] See, for instance, Leone Ebreo's distinction of a fivefold allegory in the myth of Perseus (*Dialoghi*, f. 61 r°-v°) and Harington's translation of it in his "Apologie of Poetrie" (in *El. Cr. Es.* II, pp. 202-3).

[69] Lotspeich, *Mythology*, p. 76. Lotspeich omits to list many examples, where Jove is clearly identical with the Christian God; I.v.25-6; I.v.42.9; I.vii.23,1, etc.

[70] E.C. Knowlton, *JEGP* 34 (1935), p. 375.

[71] Stirling, *SP* 30, pp. 193-204.

Igitur uti est ad intellectum ratiocinatio, ad id quod est id quod gignitur, ad aeternitatem tempus, ad punctum medius medium circulus; ita est fati series mobilis ad providentiae stabilem simplicitatem. Ea series caelum ac sidera movet, elementa in se invicem temperat et alterna commutatione transformat: eadem nascentia occidentiaque omnia renovat... Ita enim res optime reguntur, si manens in divina mente simplicitas indeclinabilem causarum ordinem promat. hic vero ordo res mutabiles et alioquin temere fluituras propria incommutabilitate coherceat [72].

Yet, although Spenser's mention of "fate" suggests he had this passage in mind, he is not here really concerned, as a Platonist would be, with tracing the expression of the timeless and the stable through the temporal and the mutable, nor with bringing multiplicity to unity [73]. The idea that mutable things may "worke their owne perfection" through change is alien to Platonism and bound up with the Christian conception of time not as a degraded image of eternity but as a teleological progress designed by God to bring all created beings to their mature perfection, natural or spiritual. [74] With the fulfilment of this design, time itself will be brought to an *end*; and "none no more change shall see" (vii.59). This transition from the idea of temporal immutability in change to the immutability of God, as Stirling observed, is *not*" a leap from uncomfortable naturalism to a refuge in religion" [75]. Yet, even though the concepts are "constituents of a single philosophical (or rather religious) doctrine", a *leap* there is, to my mind rather than a mere transition, when the poet, not satisfied as a Neoplatonist might be with discovering permanence as the very hub of change, looks forward to the day when "all shall changed bee" (vii.59). Nothing could suggest this approach in the distinction drawn by Boethius between fate and providence. Nor is the approach mystical. For the mystic — whether a Platonist or a Christian — may leap from time to eternity in

---

[72] *De Cons. Phil.*, IV, prose vi: "In consequence, what ratiocination is to intellect, the creature to Being, time to eternity and the circle to the centre, the temporal succession of moveable fate is to the stable unity of Providence. This temporal order sets the sky and stars in motion, tempers the elements in their interactions and transforms them through alternate mutations; it also renews whatever is growing and dying ... Thus are all things governed for the best, if the simplicity abiding in the Divine Mind expresses itself in an undeviating succession of causes and if that order by its own immutability controls the mutable things that would else drift aimlessly".

[73] This was the purpose of Boethius in his distinction between fate and providence; I quote from Chaucer's translation: "right so god disponeth in his purviaunce, singulerly and stably, the thinges that ben to done, but he administreth in many maneres and in dyverse tymes, by destinee, thilke same thinges that he hath disponed... the purviaunce is an unmoevable and simple forme of thinges to done; and the moveable bond and the temporel ordinaunce of thinges, whiche that the divyne simplicitee of purviaunce hath ordeyned to done, that is destinee" (*Cons. Phil.* IV. Prose vi; Chaucer, *Works*, p. 186, 11. 96-117).

[74] Cf. Georges Poulet, *Etudes sur le temps humain* (Paris, Plon, 1950), p. V, on time as conceived by the mediaeval schoolmen: "Soutenue par la continuité permanente de la forme, se déroulait donc la continuité mouvante du temps; ... ce qui distinguait ce temps du temps héraclitéen ou même platonicien, — temps de la pure mobilité —, c'est qu'il était mouvement vers une fin. La finalité du mouvement donnait en retour à celui-ci quelque chose qui en transcendait la matérialité. Même dans son corps, le chrétien du moyen-âge sentait une orientation continue vers une perfection spirituelle. Le temps avait une direction. Le temps finalement emportait le chrétien vers Dieu."

[75] *SP* 30 (1933), p. 203.

contemplation or ecstasy. But Spenser here only leaps from the changeable to the changeless over the very end of time:

> Then gin I thinke on that which Nature sayd,
> Of that same time when no more *Change* shall be,
> But stedfast rest of all things firmely stayd
> Upon the pillours of Eternity,
> That is contrayr to *Mutabilitie:* (VII. viii. 2).

However closely linked the concepts may have been through ages of Christian thought, the assurance that all things fulfil themselves through time and change and the yearning for eternal rest "With Him that is the God of Sabaoth hight" (viii.2) do not evoke the same emotional response. The uncompleted *Faerie Queene* does not end on a philosophical synthesis, but on the frank acknowledgement of the Christian paradox: the acceptance of temporal succession and historical development as required for the working out of God's purpose and the soul's longing for a divine order that transcends the order of nature and will bring all time and history to a close [76].

The question of permanence within change in the natural order had already caught the poet's attention in the "Garden of Adonis", a philosophical myth which ranks next in importance to the "Cantos of Mutabilitie". Again we meet with Lucretian and Neoplatonic interpretations [77]. Fortunately, all mooted points need not be discussed at length since Professor Stirling, a scholar who seems to have set himself the task of bringing the light of common sense upon Spenserian criticism, has clearly refuted both Greenlaw's and J. W. Bennett's theories [78]. It may be agreed that Spenser was clothing in the language of myth and poetry the popular conception of substance and form, and Ovid's "philosophy of turned shapes", as he found them in Golding's *Epistle*. But, whereas Stirling laid emphasis on the popular character of Spenser's notions, I mean to stress their *mediaeval* character: a change in perspective rather than

---

[76] My interpretation is close enough to J.L. Stampfer's, based on Woodhouse's distinction between the order of nature and the order of grace in the *Faerie Queene:* "In Canto VII, writing as a natural man, he discovers that order is the law of the universe, and that the end of change is self-dilation and self-perfection. In canto VIII, writing with the deeper yearnings of a Christian, he rejects the natural order, which however perfectly it operates, is still permeated with change, mutability and corruption" (*Univ. of Toronto Quarterly* 21, p. 152). Yet I disagree with the assertion that Spenser writes "as a natural man" only in Canto vii: the distinction is too sharp or over-simplified. The distinction is blurred, on the contrary, by Milton Miller's description of the final change as a sort of spontaneous return of Nature to an original perfection: "Nature having gone from perfection to mutability is ceaselessly regenerated in its decay and keeps something of its original nature which will at last take it back to its original perfection and that 'stedfast rest of all things'" (*ELH* 18, pp. 199-200).

[77] Respectively by Greenlaw in *SP* 17, pp. 440-54, and J.W. Bennett in *PMLA* 47, pp. 46-78, and *JEGP* 41, pp. 54-78.

[78] In *PMLA* 49, pp. 501-38, and *JEGP* 41, pp. 482-89. The controversy is so intricate that the reader must be invited to read the articles. Professor Bennett is not ready to own herself defeated, as appears from her postcript to Stirling's "Reply". But scholars now mostly agree with Stirling that the Garden shows the operation of the principle of generation in the natural order: see Woodhouse *ELH*, 1949, pp. 211-16, Bradner, *Faerie Queene*, p. 179, Milton Miller, *ELH* 18, p. 194. Harrison's distinction between the naturalistic "philosophy of the Garden" and the Platonic "philosophy of the Mountain" within the Garden episode has found little echo: it is reviewed on page 86 below.

substance, since the mediaeval had become the popular in Spenser's age. And I further wish to point out the genuine *Christian* meaning of the whole myth, which seems to have escaped notice so far.

Stirling believes that Golding and Spenser confused the popular and philosophical concepts of form and first matter [79]. In fact, they used them as they were understood throughout the Middle-Ages. Four lines of Bernardus Silvestris give in a nut-shell the form-substance relationship as conceived by Spenser:

> Res eadem subjecta manet, sed forma vagatur,
> Atque rei nomen dat nova forma novum.
> Forma fluit, manet esse rei mortisque potestas
> Nil perimit, sed res dissociat socias [80].

Those lines, which Etienne Gilson has illustrated by quoting Ronsard — "La matière demeure et la forme se perd" [81] — may also illustrate a stanza from Spenser:

> The substance is not chaungd, nor altered,
> But th'only forme and outward fashion;
> For every substaunce is conditioned
> To change her hew, and sundry formes to don,
> Meet for her temper and complexion:
> For formes are variable, and decay,
> By course of kinde and by occasion;
> And that faire flowre of beautie fades away,
> As doth the lilly fresh before the sunny ray. (*F.Q.* III. vi. 38)

The transiency of forms was admitted by mediaeval Platonists, but they did not confuse immanent forms with their models, the ideas of the divine mind [82]. As to the concept of first matter, it is hardly more crude in Spenser than it became soon after Plato and Aristotle at the hands of Theophrastus and Strato [83]. Later, St. Augustine and mediaeval commentators identified "hyle" or "prima materia" with the "materia informi" of the Book of Wisdom [84]; Golding follows the Augustinian tradition in his *Epistle,* fusing *Genesis* and *Timaeus* [85]. Bartholomaeus Anglicus, whose popular encyclopaedia Spenser certainly knew, either in the Latin version or in the English translation [86],

---

[79] *PMLA* 49, p. 513 ff.

[80] *De Mundi Universitate,* II. viii; p. 52.

[81] *Elegie aux bucherons de la forêt de Gastine,* quoted in "La Cosmogonie de Bernardus Silvestris," p. 21.

[82] The ideas are in the mind of God; the "forms" impressed upon matter are only copies of the divine models: cf. *Platonis Timaeus interprete Chalcidio,* ed. J. Wrobel, p. 361, ll. 13-18.

[83] "Dans la botanique de Théophraste, le terme *hyle* reparait souvent. Mais ... toujours il désigne non point le devenir en général, mais la matière immédiate ou seconde des commentateurs, c'est-à-dire *le corps dans lequel apparaît la forme.*" (A. Rivaud, *Le Problème du Devenir et la Notion de la Matière dans la Philosophie Grecque,* p. 462).

[84] Cf. Gilson, "La Cosmogonie de Bernardus Silvestris", p. 11.

[85] So did the Renaissance Neoplatonists (Bennett, *P M L A* 47, p. 37), but neither Golding nor Spenser adopted any of their refinements on a hierarchy of graded worlds, the hall-mark of Renaissance Neoplatonism.

[86] Dowden seems to have established Spenser's indebtedness to Bartholomaeus for his Castle of Alma (see *Variorum F.Q.* II, pp. 480-1; cf. *M.P.* II, p. 437, note on *Am.* lii). Spenser would know the popular Elizabethan translation: *Batman uppon Bartholome.*

offered a paraphrase of the *Timaeus* which described an eternal, invisible first matter assuming transitory shapes and qualities. The *De proprietatibus rerum* is certainly a better illustration of Spenser's stanzas on "substance" than the *De Natura Rerum*:

> Materiale igitur principium mundi inferioris fuit illa materia invisa scilicet *prima materia communis quae omnium formarum & qualitatum fuit susceptibilis, quae eciam sub diversis speciebus & formis conservatur. permanet enim haec materia quo ad substantiam incorrupta quamvis continue quo ad qualitates transmutabiles alteretur...*: ex quo patet quod *prima materia ex qua mundus naturaliter constat ingenerabilis et incorruptibilis esse* [*sic*] *a qua omnia materialia incipiunt et in quem redeunt tanquam ad matricem* [87].

For in the wide wombe of the world there lyes,
In hatefull darknes and in deep horrore,
An huge eternall Chaos, which supplyes
The substances of Natures fruitfull progenyes.

All things from thence doe their first being fetch,
And borrow matter, whereof they are made,
Which, when as forme and feature it does ketch,
Becomes a body, and doth then invade
The state of life, out of the griesly shade.
That substaunce is eterne, and bideth so;
Ne when the life decayes and forme does fade,
Does it consume, and into nothing goe,
But chaunged is, and often altred to and froe. (*F.Q.* III. vi. 36-7)

What "Platonism" can be traced in this description is therefore at best mediaeval Platonism derived from the *Timaeus*. It was not inconsistent either with traditional Christianity or with the prevailing Aristotelianism. The eternity of matter was, of course, a tenet hardly reconcilable with the dogma of creation. As asserted in Bruno's *De la Causa, Principio et Uno,* it was distinctly heretic [88]. Yet, from the time of Augustine, the perpetuity or indestructibility of the created world as to its "substance" had been asserted and widely acknowledged [89]. Immortality, at least, was thus granted to created matter. Spenser obviously meant no more since his "everlasting store" remains "As it first

---

[87] *De Proprietatibus Rerum*, VIII. i. "Accordingly, the material principle of the lower world was that yet unseen matter, that is the first matter, common to all things, which was susceptible of all forms and qualities and was even preserved under all aspects and forms. For this matter, indeed, remains unaltered as to the substance, though changing continually as to the transmutable qualities... Whence it appears that the first matter out of which the world is composed according to nature is neither generated nor corruptible: all material things arise out of it and revert to it as to the womb."

[88] Cf. G. Bruno, *Cause, Principe et Unité*, trad. E. Namer, Paris, 1930. In the *Zodiacus Vitae*, Palingenius, according to a French translator, "affirme en Phylosophe, que la Matiere est eternelle, & en sa qualité de Théologien, il nie que cela puisse être" (tr. La Monnerie — La Haye, 1731-32, p. 445). The dichotomy, of course, may be traced to Pomponazzi.

[89] Cf. *Batman uppon Bartholome*: "This world (he [St Austen] saith) shal passe touching the possibilities and kinde and shape that it hath now, but it shall abide evermore touching the substance and kinde, as it is saide there" (119, r°, c. 2). This substance had been identified with the "Massa and lumpe Plato calleth *Yle* in *Thimeo*" (118 v°, c. 2). This is one more instance of the degradation of the concept of first matter: *Massa* could be Ovidian or (later) Paracelsian.

created was of yore" [90]. Eterne is a poetic licence which even Christian theologians would not have reproved since Dionysius had noted the same in Scripture [91]. A further proof of the poet's perfect orthodoxy, whether from a Catholic or Protestant point of view, is afforded by a similar description of the first matter in the *First Week* of the French Huguenot poet Du Bartas. With Golding's *Ovid,* mentioned by Bennett and Stirling, this is probably the best analogue, as yet unnoticed. The first instalment of Sylvester's translation appeared only in 1592, but in France *La Sepmaine* had been published in 1578. Spenser, we are told by Harvey, "conceived much pleasure" in the fourth day of the first Weeke" [92]. As he could read French, his attention may have been early caught by this passage:

> Car tout ce qui se fait de la matiere,
> *Qui dans l'antique rien fut faite la première.*
> Tout ce qui se resoud, en elle se resout.
> Depuis que l'Eternel fit de rien ce grand Tout,
> Rien de rien ne se fait: rien en rien ne s'escoule:
> Ains ce qui naist ou meurt ne change que de moule.
> ....
> Un corps naistre ne peut, qu'un autre corps ne meure
> *Mais la seule matiere immortelle demeure,*
> Tableau du Tout-Puissant, vray corps de l'univers,
> Receptacle commun des accidens divers,
> Toute pareille à soy, toute en soy contenüë,
> Sans que le vol du temps l'accroisse ou diminuë,
> Immuable d'essence, & muable de front,
> Plus que n'est un Protée ....
> Telle qu'une Lays, dont le volage amour
> Voudroit changer d'ami cent mille fois le jour,
> Et qui n'estant à peine encore deslacee
> Des bras d'un jouvenceau embrasse en sa pensee
> L'embrassement d'un autre, & son nouveau plaisir
> D'un plaisir plus nouveau luy cause le désir, [93]

Du Bartas and Spenser are agreed on the creation of the first matter and its subsequent "immortality" underlying the fleetingness of "form" as mere phenomenal shape [94]. Further, the erotic imagery used to describe the union of form and matter is in harmony with the Venus — Adonis myth and may have suggested it if one of the functions of the myth, as some critics assume, is to symbolize again the form-substance relationship [95]. But this very relationship, similarly described by Bartas and Spenser, happens to be illustrated from Aristotle's *Physica* in a contemporary French Commentary on *La Sepmaine* [96].

---

[90] III. vi. 36: This applies to the "stock" of creatures, but apparently involves "the substaunces of Natures fruitfull progenyes", hence the first matter itself.

[91] *De Div. Nom.* Cap. X. Dionysius quotes *Ps.* XXIII, 7-9.

[92] G. Harvey, *Marginalia,* ed. G.C.M. Smith (1913), p. 161.

[93] *Sepmaine,* ed. 1589, ff. 45 v°-47 v°. My italics.

[94] Du Bartas also expatiated on the physical principle: "Rien ne se réduit en rien" (f. 46 r°). This is touched upon by Spenser: the "substaunce" cannot "into nothing goe" (xxxvii. 8).

[95] The image, of course, may be traced back either to Plato's *Timaeus* (50 d) or to Aristotle (*Phys.* I. 9, 192a, 6-25): both described matter as female and form as male.

[96] The *Commentaires* listed in my Bibliography, sect. B (see Du Bartas).

And well it might, since the concept of first matter was essential to both Aristotelian logic and physics and the transient forms are obviously not Platonic. Thus every reason for connecting Spenser's stanzas with Platonism vanishes.

Although Renaissance Platonism is not responsible in any way for the description of the form-substance relationship, the Garden of Adonis, as distinguished from the womb of Chaos, might conceivably be, as Professor Bennett claims, both the abode of souls between incarnations and a realm of forms, an immaterial world providing a pattern for the material [97]. Unfortunately this assertion rests on unjustified parallels.

Whoever reads the texts with an unbiassed mind will fail to discover any similarity between the running around "from old to new" of the "thousand thousand babes" in the Garden and the transmigration of souls in Plato's Vision of Er, Cicero's *Somnium Scipionis* or Plutarch's *De Facie quae in Orbe Lunae apparet* [98]. There is no distinction between the good and the bad, no judgment, no recompense or punishment, a constant feature of myths in the Er tradition [99]. Besides, were Spenser's Paradise located in the Milky Way as in the *Somnium,* were it even a middle place between the earth and the moon like "Pluto's orchard" in the *De Facie,* how could the poet bring Venus to this "joyous Paradize", "Wher most she wonnes, when she *on earth* does dwell" [100]? The Garden of Adonis is also utterly unlike Ariosto's earthly paradise on a mountain-top [101] or his highly fanciful and satirical world on the moon [102]. As Spenser was familar with the *Orlando Furioso,* this is one more indication that his purpose was not to describe the fate of souls after death. But the inaccuracy of the parallels offered hardly calls for further comment since the very assumption that souls grow in the Garden is at least questionable as I will later show. And should the babes turn out not to be rational souls, how could their transmigration be derived from the Vision of Er or the *Somnium*

---

[97] *PMLA* 47, pp. 51 sq., 60-1; *JEGP* 41, p. 54. With the "pictorial features of various descriptions of paradise also traced in the Garden by Dr Bennett, the present study is not directly concerned.

[98] Analogues mentioned by Bennett, *JEGP* 41, pp. 54-58.

[99] See Plato, *Republic,* Book X; Cicero, *Somnium Scipionis,* VII; Plutarch, *De Facie* XXXII.

[100] *F.Q.* III. vi. 29. 2. "Whether in *Paphos* or *Cytheron* hill, / Or it in *Gnidus* bee, I wote not well", the poet adds (29. 4-5): these were real places, however legendary, and should not have been mentioned if the Garden was not to be located on earth.

[101] *Orlando Furioso,* c. XXXIV. Ariosto follows a mediaeval tradition which Albertus Magnus traced to Strabo and Beda: *Summa theologica,* part II, tract. 13, quaest. 79. Dante had availed himself of it with greater earnestness: *Purgatorio,* c. XXVIII. The tradition has no connection whatever with the Neoplatonic philosophy in Albertus, Dante and Ariosto. Since the Garden of Adonis was an earthly Paradise Spenser may have borrowed "pictorial details" from it. But he nowhere suggests that his Paradise is close to the sphere of the Moon, "altitudinis tantae ut ad lunarem globum ascendat" (Albertus, *ibid.*). Nor is the setting cosmic as in the *Sommium* an dthe *De Facie.*

[102] *Orlando Furioso,* c. XXXIV-XXXV, so described by Bennett, *JEGP* 41, pp. 60-1. I failed to discover how the satirical vale on the Moon, which inspired Milton's "Paradise of Fools" in Limbo (*Par. Lost* III. 496), could be a "pattern world" in the Platonic sense. As to the brief description of the country at large, it emphasizes the "otherness" of the fields, rivers, lakes, mountains, cities and houses found on the Moon: this is romance, not Platonism.

Scipionis? Plutarch's essay *De Facie,* I admit, might offer a way out of the difficulty since the "souls" whose ultimate fate and highest bliss is to be dissolved in the Moon are distinguished from the intellect bestowed on man by the Sun. Spenser's "babes" (vi. 32) then would stand for Plutarch's souls and Plutarch's intellect would be described as a "reasonable soul" (vi.35). But one immediately perceives how far-fetched this interpretation would be. There is not the least resemblance between the planting of the "babes" in the Garden and the "account of the rejuvenating process" in Plutarch's essay [103]. Besides, one fails to see how this process could be reconciled with Christianity, even by Renaissance Platonists, and a definitely un-Christian theory should not be read into the *Faerie Queene* unless it were based on safer grounds than Professor Bennett's hypothesis affords.

While acknowledging that "Spenser" echoes the language of Moses' description of creation" in stanza 34, the same critic argues that the poet is not describing "the creation of this mundane sphere" [104]. Allegorical interpretations of Genesis, no doubt, had often been offered, but the passage from Golding's Epistle quoted in support of this interpretation is inapplicable since it refers to the creation of a world of Ideas. The Garden of Adonis is only planted with "forms" or even "shapes", which are obviously not the Ideas of the Divine Mind, whatever Spenser may have intended. For the vegetative growth of forms in the Garden, Professor Bennett finds precedent in Pico's description of the Garden of Jove, "perche in quella sono piantate le Idee, non altrimenti che il arbori in uno orto" [105]. But the parallel, though interesting, is again unsatisfactory since the Garden of Jove is the Angelic Mind, therefore far different from the Garden of Adonis, "So faire a place as Nature can devize" (vi.29.3). To argue that Spenser transferred the image to the lower plane of individual forms is both groundless and needles. In a "garden" and in a "seminary", how could forms do otherwise than develop as plants grow? The main allegory commanded the lesser metaphors.

[103] Bennett, *JEGP* 41, pp. 56-7. The reader must judge for himself. As the passage is too long for quotation, I have to give a summary. Man, as a compound of body, soul and intellect, suffers two deaths. The first suddenly and violently unbinds the soul from the body. Only by the second death is the intellect gradually and slowly unbound from the soul. Every soul, with or without intellect, when divorced from the body, must, as ordained by fate, wander for a time in the middle region between the earth and the moon. There the sinful souls endure a purgatory while the virtuous dwell in the serener region of the atmosphere, called Pluto's orchard or meadow (a Latin version reads "prata Ditis", a French version "verger de Pluton"). This region is also the abode of daemons or genii. Hence the purified souls rise to the moon. There they are invigorated and shine. After a time each soul is separated from its intellect, which flies up to the sun. Without an intellect and freed from bodily passions the soul then dissolves and fades into the Moon, as the body returns unto dust. But the souls of the ambitious, the avaricious, the irascible and the sensual lovers, subject to their own passions, suffer a reincarnation. Out of these arise Titans and Typhoons, whose souls are irrational. Yet even these souls may be rejuvenated after death and again receive an intellect from the sun. *De Facie,* XXXII; *Opera,* t. II, pp. 925-45. I fail to see how *any part* of Plutarch's relation may apply to Spenser's myth in *F.Q.* vi. 29-50.

[104] Bennett, *PMLA* 47, p. 60. The claim that the Garden cannot represent the material world since the "babes" are sent out of it (33. 8; cf. 36. 1) and Adonis is "hid from the world" (46. 6) is hardly justified. The "babes" might be sent out of the wide wombe of the world" (36.6), as plants sprout — or as babies come into the world. And Adonis is hid from the world by "a grove of mirtle trees", which may be literal or symbolic as we choose (43-44).

[105] *Commento* II. xi, quoted by Bennett in *PMLA* 47, p. 58.

Our first concern, indeed, should not be to hunt for Neoplatonic parallels but to discover the meaning of the main allegory. Stirling's description of the Garden as "a place where continuous generation takes place" is not entirely satisfactory. It hardly accounts for the echoes of *Genesis* in stanza 34. It does not explain the preexistence of all future shapes in the Garden from the first act of Creation (st.36,1.5). And it does not reveal the full significance of the Garden in the story of Amoret.

The last is the most serious defect, for obviously the poet's intention throughout the Canto is not merely to describe the "form-substance relationship". The Garden was first conceived for Amoret there "yfostered to bee". An interpretation of it should not start only from the prelude on the Sun — "great father he of generation" (sts. 8-9) — but from the miraculous conception of Chrysogone. Now Amoret is Love[106], human love, both divine and earthly, as Spenser conceived it. She is begotten by heaven, like her sister Belphoebe, the type of virginity. Both are God's daughters since "th'author of light" is obviously "the Lord of life and Light", "highest God"[107]. The emphasis, accordingly, is on the purity, the "sinlessness" of her generation. Chrysogone:

> ... bore without paine, that she conceived
> Withouten pleasure .... (III. vi. 27. 2-3)

Sinlessness again is emphasized in the description of the growth-process in the Garden. Only when they leave the Garden, are the "naked babes" clothed "with sinfull mire" (vi.32-7). On their return, they "grow afresh, as they had never seene *Fleshly corruption*" (vi.33.4). Obviously the Garden is a place of innocence; yet love even physical love, is not absent: "Franckly each paramour his leman knowes" (xli. 7). This is not unexpected, since Amoret is to be "lessoned — In all the lore of love", not of Platonic love, but of married love. To place Amoret in a purely pagan "earthly paradise", though it created an atmosphere of innocence, was not sufficient. But Ovid's "golden age" was commonly identified with "Adams tyme in Paradyse"[108]. The identification eminently suited Spenser's allegorical purpose. Love, begotten by heaven, "his owne perfection wrought" (*Colin,* 1.805) in the garden of Eden, styled garden of Adonis for the sake of the mythological fable[109]. But Amoret is not only Love, she is a maiden; and she is to be joined one day to Scudamour, a knight of the court of Gloriana. For the sake of the story, the Garden had to be a *present* Garden, not a former Eden. The difficulty lay in reconciling the moral allegory with the tale or fable. Moreover, since the natural growth of Love was to take place in the Garden, the process of generation and growth in Nature was to be emphasized. Now, the only way of harmonizing the fable and the

---

[106] C.S. Lewis's interpretation in *The Allegory of Love;* p. 345. Woodhouse thinks that Amoret fell captive to the enchanter Busyrane and the Court Cupid through her own frailty because the lesson taught in the Garden of Adonis — that is the mere natural instinct — is "insufficient for life on the human level" (*ELH* 16, p. 219). Amoret's womanhood, no doubt, must be perfected in the Temple of Venus, but there is not the least indication that she is responsible for her captivity: she endures this trial because of her faithful love to Scudamore: see III. vi. 53, xi. 9-11.

[107] *F.Q.* III. vi. 9. 2.; cf. I. i. 37. 6.

[108] *Golding's Ovid,* Epistle, 1. 470; noted by Bennett.

[109] The current etymological confusion Adonis-Eden has been pointed out by *Bennett: PMLA* 47 (1932), p. 48.

moral and cosmological allegories was to make of the Garden "the first seminarie of all things, that are born to live and die" (xxx. 4-5). That is, in Augustinian tradition, the storehouse of seeds in which all living beings were preformed from the first day of Creation: a garden both of pre-existence and continued generation, where creatures as yet unclothed "with sinfull mire", and nevertheless truly existent, live sinlessly until they are "sent Into the world" (xxxvi. 1-2).

For, according to Augustine, God created all things, present and future, simultaneously [110]. All living beings not fully developed in the first act of creation — whether plants, beasts or the bodies of men — were preformed in the *rationes seminales,* or invisible germs, not to be mistaken for the eternal "ideas", which were not created, but preexisted in the divine mind or World from all eternity:

> Nam illa quae in Verbo Dei ante omnem creaturam sunt, non utique facta sunt; haec autem facta sunt, cum factus est dies, sicut Scriptura verba declarant: sed tamen antequam essent super terram, antequam exorirentur, quod de viridibus ex foeno agri dictum est [111].

All the things created at once through the Wisdom of God — the Sapience of the *Hymne of Heavenly Beautie* — are brought to blossom, as it were, at proper intervals and "according to their kinds" out of those hidden *rationes* which "God has scattered like seeds" [112]. Such was the Neoplatonic exposition called forth by those verses in *Genesis*:

> These are the generations of the heavens and of the earth when they were created, in the day that the Lord God made the earth and the heavens.
>
> And every plant of the field *before it was in the earth,* and every herb of the field *before it grew;* for the Lord God had not caused it to rain upon the earth, and there was not a man to till the ground. (*Gen.* 2. 4-5; my italics.)

I therefore agree with Professor Bennett in considering the Garden as "the meeting-place of temporal and eternal reality" [113]. But I think the Augustinian account of *Genesis* a safer parallel than any Ficinian hierarchy of graded worlds. Augustine himself, of course, was influenced by Plotinus and the very notion of *rationes seminales* came to him through the *Enneads* [114]. But it was closely adapted to an exposition of the Biblical account of Creation in the *De Genesi*

---

110 *De Genesi ad litt.,* I. i-iii and *passim.*

111 *De Gen. ad litt.,* V. iv. 8: "For the ideas that are in the Word of God before every creature, have not been made, whereas the preformed creatures have been made all at once when Day had been made, as Scripture teacheth us (cf. *Gen.* 1. 5), and before they were on the earth, before they grew, as is said of every green herb and the hay that grows in the field".

112 *De Genesi ad litt.* IV. xxxiii. 51: "... ut hoc quod nunc videmus temporalibus intervallis ea moveri ad peragenda quae suo cuique generi competunt, *ex illis insitis rationibus veniat, quas tanquam seminaliter sparsit Deus in ictu condendi,* cum dixit, et facta sunt, mandavit, et creata sunt". Cf. Gilson, p. 261: "Grâce à ces germes latents qui contiennent toutes les choses que la suite des temps verra s'en développer, on peut dire que le monde a été créé par Dieu gros des êtres à venir".

113 *PMLA* 47, p. 74.

114 The notion was originally Stoic. Plotinus sought to remove its fatalistic character (*Enneads* III. i. 7 sq.) and Augustine integrated it to the Christian notion of creative Providence: cf. Gilson, *Saint-Augustin,* p. 269, n. 5.

and in various hexaemerons composed by other Church Fathers[115]. Ficino may have felt he was writing in the Augustinian tradition and his *seminariae vires* undoubtedly claim kinship with the *rationes seminales* in the chapter of the commentary *In Parmenidem* cited by Dr Bennett[116]. But, on the one hand, this disquisition on the nature of ideas and their descent from the universal to the particular deals with problems with which Spenser is not concerned in the Garden of Adonis. On the other hand, it does not touch upon the point emphasized in the poetic myth: the *creation* of an everlasting store of pre-formed beings and their gradual coming to existence in orderly succession.

The Augustinian theory of Creation and pre-existent seeds best explains why all living beings that replenish the world are "fetch" by Nature from the Garden of Adonis, where they still grow "as they created were", but in a state of pre-existence (see sts 30,1-6; 34.3,35,36.1-2). It also accounts for their coming into actual being in a temporal succession[117] ordained by "eternall fate" (st. 32.6), that is to Spenser as to Boethius and Golding "the order which is set and stablished in things By Gods eternall will and word". It may further account for details which hardly fit into either Bennett's or Stirling's exposition such as the lines:

> No doe they need with water of the ford,
> Or of the buds to moysten their roots dry;
> For in themselves eternal moisture they imply (vi. 34. 7-9).

This "eternal moisture" is not satisfactorily explained by Ovid's "moysture", neither eternal nor intrinsic[118]. The lines are based on *Genesis* 2.5 as Dr. Bennett acknowledges. But the verse must have first received an Augustinian interpretation: parallels with Plutarch are irrelevant[119]. In the *De Genesi,* the seeds are said to be essentially moist:

---

[115] Cf. *L'Hexaéméron de Saint Basile,* ed. Stanislas Giet, Introduction, pp. 28-31.

[116] *PMLA* 47, p. 52. Ficino, *In Parmenidem,* XXXIII. As the whole chapter cannot be quoted, I only reproduce excerpts concerning the "seminal forces": "Quinto, nantes ideas, speciesque sunt in tali natura, seminalis videlicet formarum corporalium rationes in natura quidem & naturalis animae, & in naturis animae superiorum atque nostrarum... In quinto particularium jam, & membrorum corporis seminariae vires" (ed. 1576, II. 121). A clearer statement, I think, is found in the Commentary *In Timaeum,* cap. X. The definition of the last three worlds may be quoted: "Post archetypum hoc mundum quarto gradu sequatur corporei mundi anima. Mundus jam rationalis ex intellectuali mundo progenitus quasi splendor ex lumine. Quintus huic succedat gradus, ipsa videlicet natura rerum, *mundus jam seminarius,* ex rationali anime mundo, quasi calor splendore resultans. Sexto tandem gradu mundus hic corporeus collocetur, *ex seminario,* ita proxime ductus, sicut rerum generatio ex calore" (*Opera,* ed. 1576, p. 1442). None of Ficino's images, it will be noticed, are echoed by Spenser.

[117] *De Gen. ad lit.,* V. xxiii. 45. I translate: "For, just as in the seed was enclosed whatever developed into a tree in the course of time, so must we believe that the world when God created all things together held together within itself whatever was made in it and with it when day was made; not only the sun, moon and stars ... but also whatever the water and earth produced in a potential and causative way, before the course of time had made them appear such as we see them now, in the works of God, through the divine operation that has never ceased to the present day."

[118] That "moysture mixt with equall heate all living things createth" was a commonplace (Golding's *Ovid,* p. 31).

[119] Bennett, *PMLA,* 47, p. 59.

Omnia quippe primordia seminum, sive unde omnis caro, sive unde omnia frutecta gignuntur humida sunt, et ex humore concrescunt [120]

The "uncouth formes which none yet ever knew" (st. 35.2) cannot be the monsters bred by the earth in former ages, but creatures to come; the "creatures yet unknown" of the *De Genesi* [121]. That the Garden should hold the seeds of men as well as the seeds of plants or animals is not surprising since Augustine maintained that in the first act of creation, the body of man and the bodies of all animals were created like grass *antequam exorirentur* [122]. But the soul of man was created apart, to be later joined to the body [123]. Human souls do not grow in the Garden, since it is "the first seminary of all things that are borne to live and die" (st. 30.4-5). Any theory implying that Spenser meant human souls to be mortal may be rejected outright: it is obviously inconsistent with the poet's sincere Christianity. The Pythagorean theory of the transmigration of souls, therefore, cannot be read into the cyclic process of the babes in stanzas 32-33: some other explanation must be and will be sought. To the author of the *Hymne in Honour of Beautie,* "soule is forme" (1.133), but, whatever the "babes" may be, the "shapes" and "formes" bred in the Garden of Adonis do not include rational souls. They are only the forms of bodies which souls later assume:

Some fit for reasonable soules t'indew,
Some made for beasts, some made for birds to weare. (st. 35, 5-6)

Chaos, which Augustine and Spenser identify with both the Timaeic *hyle* and the Biblical *materiam informam* [124] supplies matter for the seeds when they "invade the state of life" (st. 37.4). The creation of the reasonable soules is not described, but since they neither grow in the Garden nor come from Chaos, it is sufficiently clear that they are of "supernatural" origin, as they would be to any Christian [125].

---

[120] *De Gen. ad Litt.*, V. xvi. 20: "For all the primordial seeds that give birth either to all flesh or to every kind of shrub are moist and grow out of moisture."

[121] *Ibid.*, V. xviii. 36: "Creatures plures nobis ignotae."

[122] *Ibid.*, VI. i-iv.

[123] *Ibid.*, VI. vi. 10; t. 34, c. 343.

[124] Cf. Gilson, *Augustin,* p. 255 and note (2). Augustine also identifies the "materiam informam" of the Book of Wisdom with the Chaos of the Greek poets: *De Gen. ad. litt. imp. lib.* IV, 12; t. 34, col. 224. Cf. *H.L.* 11.57 sq.

[125] The Neo-Platonic interpretation of the Garden of Adonis would ascribe to Spenser several of the "Erroneous Opinions of the Creation of Souls" reviewed by Sir John Davies in *Nosce Teipsum:*

Then neither from eternity before,
Nor from the time when Time's first point begun,
Made He all souls, which now He keeps in store,
Some in the moon and others in the sun:

Nor in a secret cloister doth He keep
These virgin spirits until their marriage-day.
Nor locks them up in chambers where they sleep
Till they awake within these beds of clay:

Nor did He first a certain number make,
Infusing part in beasts, and part in men,
And, as unwilling further pains to take,
Would make no more than those He framèd then:

Spenser was at least as likely to know the *De Genesi* as Ficino's abstruse Commentary *In Parmenidem*. Further signs of Augustinian influence will be disclosed in the following chapters. Besides, no more than a general knowledge of the Augustinian interpretation of *Genesis* 2.5 was required, and this knowledge may have come to the poet through various channels [126]. This interpretation had been anticipated or adopted by various Church Fathers in their accounts of Creation. If the fourth and fifth centuries were the Golden Age of Hexaemerons, the sixteenth century was their Golden Age Restored [127]. The Greek and Latin works early won the praises of such humanists as Erasmus, were eagerly printed and widely influential. Their revival was directly responsible for the poetic versions of *Genesis* which Bartas, Tasso, Avecedo and others published by the end of the sixteenth or the beginning of the seventeenth century [128]. Though some of the Church Fathers were satisfied with an interpretation of Genesis more literal than Augustine's, the best known hexaemerons were agreed on the instantaneous creation of all things. Not as they would be unfolded in time, but in a state of pure potentiality, yet already actuated by a "seminal power" which could of itself develop without any new Divine intervention whatever was virtual in the world and bring all beings to existence in a fore-ordained temporal succession according to the first command of God [129]. Thus, when God said "Let the earth bring forth grass, the herb yielding seed, and the fruit tree yielding fruit after his kind, whose seed is in itself, upon the earth" (*Gen.* 1.11), "his Word became as it were a law of nature, and remained in the earth, imparting to it the power of bringing forth all beings and yielding fruit in the future" [130].

For the Platonic reflection of the changeless ideal in the ever changing phenomenal world Christian thought had substituted the temporal unfolding of a timeless Creation. And though his deeper allegiance may be blurred by the puzzling "transmigration" of the babes, Spenser's thought, as in the Muta-

---

> So that the widow Soul, her body dying,
> Unto the next-born body married was,
> And so, by often changing and supplying,
> Men's souls to beasts and beasts to men did pass.

In my interpretation, on the contrary, there is nothing in the Garden of Adonis that may not agree with the orthodox Christian view, as set forth by Davies:

> But as God's handmaid, Nature, doth create
> Bodies in time distinct and order due,
> So God gives souls the like successive date,
> Which Himself makes, in bodies formèd new:
> ....
> Nor He in this doth Nature's service use,
> For though from bodies she can bodies bring,
> Yet could she never souls from souls traduce,
> As fire from fire, or light from light doth spring.

[126] The channels are so various, including sermons and works of vulgarization, that an exhaustive enquiry on this single point could not be undertaken within the scope of the present study.

[127] See Maury Thibaut de Maisières, *Les Poèmes inspirés du début de la Genèse à l'époque de la Renaissance* (Louvain, 1931), chap. II and III.

[128] *La Sepmaine* (1578), *Sette Giornate* (1608), *Creacion del Mundo* (1615).

[129] Gregory of Nyssa, *In Hexaemeron*, 77 D (quoted in *L'Hexaéméron de saint Basile*, p. 28).

[130] Basilius, *Hexaemeron*, V. i. 40: *Hexaéméron*, p. 279.

bilitie Cantos, is once more in harmony with the Christian point of view. The very influence of the traditional expositions of *Genesis* may explain why the rule of Time is felt in the Garden of Adonis. To account for the havoc wrought in what she takes to be a Platonic world of pure form, Dr Bennett had to make an unwarranted assumption: Time may mar and spoil whatever grows in the Garden "because he [Spenser] believes that the world of forms furnishes the pattern for the world of matter, and therefore he must expect to find in the original whatever he finds in the copy" [131]. To my knowledge there is no precedent for this odd twisting of the Platonic philosophy and Dr Bennett offers none. Now Spenser's mind was not discriminating: he could blend several notions, associate several traditions with little regard for philosophic consistency. But if he meant, indeed, to keep within the Neoplatonic tradition, as Dr Bennett claims, he would be unlikely to fly in the face of tradition by introducing mortality in the realm of pure form. On the other hand, if the poet was writing, as I think, in the tradition of the *Hexaemerons* and the *De Genesi,* death and change would be spontaneously associated in his mind with the temporal unfolding of the timeless act of Creation through the gradual and mysterious working of some seminal power. For, in the words of St Basilius, God having called upon the earth to bring forth living creatures "the nature of all beings, impelled by this one command, moves steadily through the whole creation *subject to birth and death* and ensures the continuity of species, through the resemblance of individuals, to the very end of time" [132]. The "flowring herbs and goodly things" mown by the scythe of Time (vi. 39) in Spenser's Garden, of course, cannot be the pre-existent seeds but the actual beings they produced. Yet, since the *rationes seminales* were not changeless ideal models but latent germs involved in a temporal process of development, when the mortal beings that had arisen out of those germs eventually died, their "causes" ceased to be as well. The distinction between the "seeds" and whatever grew out of them could not but be blurred in the poetic myth. But the rule of Time, in both the gradual unfolding and the death of all things, was undoubtedly to be shown as extending to "the first seminary Of all things that are borne to live and dye".

The transmigration of the babes, I admit, remains unexplained, though not unexplainable, in the light of the hexaemeral tradition. The *rationes seminales,* once they had developed into actual beings, were not supposed to grow afresh in the "first seminary" for "some thousand yeares" and be once more

> .... sent into the chaungefull world againe,
> Till thither they returne, where first they grew:
> So like a wheele arownd they ronne from old to new. (v. 33. 7-9)

In the very allusion to the "thousand yeares" this seems to be reminiscent of the Platonic *animorum orbis.* The notion was widely disseminated and, without tracing it to its source, Spenser could have found it, for instance, in Landino's *Disputationes*:

> Invenies igitur apud Platonicos cum mille annos apud inferos fuerint animi hominum ad corpora illa redire / atque idem vicissim ad inferos remeare. Idque toties facere donec duodecim annorum milia transierint [133].

[131] *PMLA* 47, p. 68; the argument is taken up again on p. 77.
[132] *Hexaemeron* IX, 2, 81; *Hexaéméron,* p. 485.
[133] *Disputationes,* p. LXXXV.

Yet I have shown that the babes cannot be human souls. On the other hand they cannot be mere "substrates"[134]. This is hardly consistent with the special emphasis on their sinlessness (st. 32.7) before being attired "with fleshly weeds" (32.5). Only two closely related solutions are left: the babes *must* be the "seeds" of human bodies or pre-existent vegetative souls of human creatures. Both interpretations are in agreement with the part allotted to Old Genius as the Porter who letteth in or out "All that to come into the world desire" (31.5-9, 32). In his association with both generation and Nature in the Garden of Adonis Genius may be traced to Alanus and Jean de Meung through Gower's *Confessio Amantis* and Lydgate's *Reson and Sensuallyte*[135]. He is not only different from the Socratic daemon of Apuleius and Plutarch[136] but also divested of his Neoplatonic associations with Jove and the World Soul in Varro and Augustine[137]. Even the rôle ascribed to him by Bernardus Silvestris and Alanus in the coming of all things into being is described by Spenser as a more immediate and natural operation — the clothing of babes with fleshly weeds — than the calling forth of fleeting images as a painter or scriptor causing shadowy and changing reflections of the eternal Ideas to appear and vanish in the phenomenal world[138]. In the *De universitate mundi* and the *De planctu Naturae* Genius ensures the conformity of earthly beings to ideal heavenly forms; in the Garden of Adonis the pre-existent forms are not transcendent: they are *rationes seminales* immanent in Nature from the first act of Creation.

Yet Alanus might have suggested the association of Genius with a cyclic process. He used the word "transmigrate" to describe the passage from the truth of essence to phenomenal life and Genius was said to call back to life again by some new birth whatever was laid asleep by death[139]. This cycle, it

---

[134] Stirling, *PMLA*, 49, pp. 517-8.

[135] See H.A. Kahin, *ELH*, 8, pp. 266 sq.

[136] See the *De Deo Socratis* of Apuleius and the *De genio Socratis* of Plutarch.

[137] See *De Planctu Naturae*, ed. Migne, *Patrologia* CCX, col. 479 C - 480 B; *Roman de la Rose*, 11. 12249 sq., 19505 sq.; Varro *apud August. Civit.* VII. 13; Augustine, *De Civitate Dei*, VII. 16. On the various conceptions of Genius in Antiquity and in the Middle Ages, see *Alain de Lille* by Raynaud de Lage, pp. 89-90. The Renaissance mythographers were aware of them and Natalis Comes offered several interpretations (*Mythologia*, p. 293), but Spenser only retained the un-metaphysical and mediaeval idea that the gods entrust to the care of Genius whatever is to be procreated.

[138] Bernardus, *De mundi universitate*, II. 3 (ed. Barach & Wrobel, p. 38): Nature meets Oyarses (identified with Genius) in heaven: "Illic Oyarses quidem erat et genius in artem et officium pictoris et figurantis addictus. In subterjacente enim mundo rerum facies universa coelum sequitur sumptisque de caelo proprietatibus ad imaginem quam conversio contulit figuratur. Namque impossible est formam unamquamque alteri simillimam nasci, horarum et climatum distantibus punctis. Oyarses igitur circuli quem pantomorphon Graecia, Latinitas nominat multiformem, formas rerum omnes omnibus et associat et ascribit."

Alanus, *De planctu Naturae* (Migne, *Patr.* CCX, 479 C): "Ille vero calamum... manu gerebat in dextra; in sinistra vero morticinii pellem... in qua, styli subsequentis subsidio, imagines rerum sub umbra picturae ad veritatem suae essentia transmigrantes, vita sui generis munerabat. Quibus deletionis morte sopitis, novae nativitatis ortu aliae revocabat in vitam."

[139] *De planctu*, Migne CCX, c. 479 C, quoted above. Though the *De Planctu* was only available in MS in Spenser's day, this does not imply that the text could not have been accessible. Spenser's own reference to Alanus in *F.Q.* VII. vii. 9 is ambiguous, but cannot be taken to mean that the work "sought" could not be found. Whether the poet himself had found it or not is left uncertain.

will be noted, applied to whatever lives and dies, but not to human souls. There are differences, though; Spenser seems to be only concerned with human beings in the stanzas relating to the "babes", and he introduces an interval of "some thousand years" between death and re-birth. We must therefore assume that the poet felt free to avail himself of the Platonic doctrine of transmigration for his own purposes. This was the kind of poetic myth in which he could indulge, for it no longer endangered the very foundation of Christianity when transferred from souls endowed with a moral sense and responsibility to the seeds of human bodies or to merely vegetative and sensitive souls.

The former hypothesis is more consistent with my general interpretation of the Garden myth. But I wish to show that the latter might suit as well the description of the babes' progress and would not appear unduly fanciful in the light of contemporary philosophy. I must first remind the reader that it would not affect my earlier rejection of the parallel with Plutarch's account of the transmigration of souls, for Spenser's souls of growth and sense cannot prove virtuous or wicked, are not subject to reward or punishment. Whereas each rational soul was held to be created by God and not "traduced" from parent to child, the vegetative and sensitive souls were said to be educed from the actual bodily seed in the act of generation [140]. Since all future bodies pre-existed in the *rationes seminales,* their souls of sense and growth might be described as pre-existent too. This need not even imply that the immortal souls had also been created all at once from the beginning of the world, an opinion rejected by Sir John Davies as by Saint Thomas and most Christian theologians [141]. But it seems to require a plurality of souls in man. This was at the time a definitely Platonic (or Paracelsian) tenet when the souls were held to be distinct [142]. Aristotle and Saint Thomas had disproved it [143] and despite the influence of Platonism over the Renaissance mind, this opinion does not seem to have been *seriously* entertained by Spenser's contemporaries when they spoke as philosophers [144]. But poets freely alluded to their several souls for the sake of an argument [145]. The notion was in the air and Spenser might not have felt that

---

[140] See St Thomas, *Summa,* Ia, q. 118, art. 1.

[141] See Thomas, *Summa,* Ia, q. 118, art. 3; Davies, *Nosce Teipsum,* sts 149-50 quoted on p. 79, n. 125).

[142] See *Republic* IV. 434 e-441 c and X. 611b-612a; *Timaeus,* 69c-72d. The theory was well known throughout the Middle Ages. Cf. St Thomas, *Summa,* Ia, q. 76, art. 3, Resp.: "Plato posuit diversas animas esse in corpore uno...". Later developments are sketched by Burton in the *Anatomy of Melancholy:* "Some therefore make one *soul,* divided into three principal faculties: others, three distinct *souls* (which question of late hath been much controverted by *Piccolomineus,* and *Zabarel*): *Paracelsus* will have four souls, adding to the three granted faculties a *spiritual soul:* which opinion of his *Campanella,* in his book *De Sensu Rerum,* much labours to demonstrate and prove" (ed. Shiletto, vol. I, p. 177). Campanella was a late Renaissance Neoplatonist.
Writing in a more scientific and materialistic spirit, Telesius had reduced the plurality of souls to a duality: the animal soul, *educta ex semine,* and the divinely created soul. But the *De Rerum Natura* was only completed in 1586 and was hardly influential in England before Bacon hailed Telesius as a philosophical reformer. See *The Philosophical Works of Francis Bacon,* ed. J. M. Robertson (London, New-York: 1905), pp. 29-32, 492-3, 645-6.

[143] *De Anima,* lib. 2, cap. 2, *Summa,* Ia, q. 76, art. 3.

[144] To sir John Davies "This soul of ours / Being only one... Doth use on divers objects divers powers": *Nosce Teipsum,* st. 234. He even avoids the three-fold division, which most easily led to the distinction of three souls.

[145] Cf. Donne's *Valediction: of my name in the window,* st. V. Yet the *Second Anniversary* shows that Donne did not think of the three souls as distinct: see

he departed from orthodoxy. Saint Thomas himself, after all, had to assume that the human embryo in the early stages of its development in the mother's womb has a soul of its own, nutritive and sensitive, for which a more perfect soul, both intellectual and sensitive, was substituted in a later stage [146]. Although a merely naturalistic interpretation of Spenser's myth proves unsatisfactory, we may be sure that the thought of the human embryo and its vegetative life in the womb or even in the "fleshly seed" [147] was not off the poet's mind and may have suggested the presentation of the pre-existent beings, whether souls of growth or *rationes seminales* ,both as babes and plants.

I am aware that I have reintroduced into the scheme of the Garden some of the inconsistencies that Stirling sought to remove: but only such inconsistencies as were allowable in a poetic myth and reconcilable with the Christian tradition. They mostly stem from the twofold requirement I have earlier noticed. The Garden had to be sinless, therefore, since it could not be Eden, a world of creatures as yet unborn. But Amoret being already born and in the world, it had to be an actual garden of generation and growth and not a mere pattern-world of form. Augustine had wondered where all the creatures preformed were to be found: "ubi ergo?" Of course, no location in space could be assigned to them; they existed *causaliter* [148]. But the seeds were immanent, not transcendent causes, bound to unfold themselves on earth at the appointed time. The "first seminary", in a way, is not *in* the world, and yet *of* the world. To remove this paradox either through a sheerly naturalistic or a purely Platonic interpretation would amount to removing the moral significance of the allegory. It would compel us to misconstrue the love-making frankly displayed in this "delightfull Garden":

> And sweete Love gentle fits emongst them throwes,
> Without fell rancor, or fond gealosy;
> Franckly each paramour his leman knowes,
> Each bird his mate, ne any does envie
> Their goodly meriment, and gay felicitie. (vi. 41. 5-9)

II. 159-62 and Grierson's *Commentary* II. 198. The best reference, however, is not *Summa*, Ia, q. 76, art. 3, but Ia, q. 118, art. 2, ad 2um. Close comparison will show that Donne, in phrasing at least, does not exactly follow St Thomas when he describes the rational soul as feeding upon and drawing into itself the two souls of sense and growth which had earlier appeared in the embryo. Such language implies, as it were, the merging of three souls into one, while St Thomas assumed that the sensitive soul of the embryo was in due course displaced by a human soul endowed with its own powers of sense and growth (see note 146).

[146] *Summa*, Ia, q. 118, art. 2, ad 2um: "anima praeexistit in embryone, a principio quidem nutritiva, postmodum autem sensitiva, & tandem intellectiva"; Ia, q. 76, art. 3, ad 3um: "prius embryo habet animam quae est sensitiva tantum; qua abjecta, advenit perfectior anima, quae est simul sensitiva et intellectiva."

[147] In the *Hymne in Honour of Beauty,* 1. 114, the soul il described as enraced "in fleshly seed". This is the actual *semen* out of which the human body is generated, not the *ratio seminalis*. The "babes" are only clothed in "fleshly weeds" when they are sent out of the Garden into the world. But the ambiguity of *semen* invited the imagination to move constantly to and fro across the borderland between the virtual and the actual. To some extent, Spenser may even have pictured to himself the *rationes seminales* as hidden seeds lying underground in the "griesly shade" (st. 37. 5).

[148] *De Gen. ad Litt.*, V. iv. 9-10.

This is *natural,* not Platonic love, indeed, but it takes place in a *sinless* world. The love-making which man might have enjoyed in Paradise, according to Augustine, is not improperly assigned to creatures pre-formed that know not as yet "fleshlie corruption" [149]. The myth served a twofold purpose. It allowed the poet to suggest that love, when it has generation for its end, answers the very command of God and *within the natural order,* is blameless. To Spenser as to Alanus, Nature is the vicar of God, but Venus is her "subvicar" in her prime operation, which means that the sexual instinct and all the impulses connected with it are normally called into play for the fulfilment of God's design and are fundamentally honest when curbed by temperance and modesty [150]. Yet this is only the point of view of Nature, which has not to take original sin into consideration in the *De Planctu* as in the Garden [151]. But the Christian poet never forgets that man does not belong to the natural order only and is clothed with sinful mire when he comes into the world (*F.Q.* III.vi.32.7). Accordingly, Spenser has made the picture of natural love innocuous by describing the Garden of Adonis as a Paradise and a world of pre-existence distinct from the actual world of human experience. But he also means to show that the innocency of love may be unsullied in this very life. To the Protestant author of the *Epithalamion* wedded love is spotless and his closing apostrophe to Genius should not be ignored (as it usually is) in any interpretation of the Garden of Adonis:

And thou glad Genius, in whose gentle hand,
The bridale bowre and geniall bed remaine,
Without blemish or staine,
And the sweet pleasures of theyr loves delight
With secret ayde doest succour and supply,
Till they bring forth the fruitfull progeny,
Send us the timely fruit of this same night.

That is why actual love-sports in the Temple of Venus or even in the *Hymne in Honour of Love* may also be described as "devoid of guilty shame" [152]. In the Garden of Adonis wedded love is also implied when Amoret is to be "lessoned In all the love of love and goodly womanhead" (st. 51,8-9). On being brought forth to the world's view, she will straight away link fast her loving heart to Scudamore, "In faithfull love, t'abide for ever more" (52.3-4). Her stay in the Garden had not merely ripened in her the natural powers of growth and generation required for womanhood. Genius was the porter but she had been committed to the care of Psyche (st. 51). And Psyche, "after long troubles and unmeet upbrayes" (50.3), was now living with Cupid "in stedfast love and happy state" (50.6), a description which suggests wedded love. With the myth

---

[149] *F.Q.* III. vi. 33. 4. Augustine thought that sexual love would have taken place in Paradise had Adam and Eve remained in it: *De Gen ad. litt.* IX. iv. Milton later assumed it had.

[150] *De Planctu,* Migne, CCX. col. 453 sq., 456 CD; cf. *Alain de Lille,* pp. 48, 83-4.

[151] *Alain de Lille,* p. 84: "la notion de péché originel est absente de l'œuvre, et cela n'est pas très surprenant puisqu'on ne s'y place qu'au point de vue de Nature; pour tout ce qui la dépasse... elle renvoie son interlocuteur à la théologie". Spenser's awareness of the traditional distinction between the order of nature and the order of grace is unquestionable though Woodhouse's exposition of the *Faerie Queene* in the light of this principle may be challenged on several points: see *ELH* 16, 194-228.

[152] *F.Q.* IV. x. 1-2, 28. 5-6; *H.L.* 280-91.

of Cupid and Psyche the poet was moving away from the realm of cosmological allegory, but instead of passing into the metaphysical or mystical with the Neoplatonists, he was content with imparting to the story, enjoyed for its own sake, a moral significance in accordance with the individual bent of his nature[153].

In its general trend and spirit, therefore, the philosophy, of the Garden, as embedded in the story of Amoret, cannot but appear thoroughly un-Platonic. As to the notions involved, though they may be of Platonic descent, they need not imply any great familiarity with Renaissance Neoplatonism. Golding's Ovid, Bartholomew or Bartas may have inspired the conception of the form-substance relationship. Every Elizabethan had heard about the Pythagorean theory and the transmigration of souls, notions which Spenser, in my interpretation, does not adopt but adapts to his own ends. And, in my interpretation again, the pre-existence of the creatures found in the Garden must be explained in the light of the Augustinian and hexaemeral tradition. The Venus-Adonis myth has not yet been considered, but it will not alter these conclusions. T. P. Harrison may be right in pointing out a difference between the Garden subject to Time and death, and the Mount on which Adonis "liveth in eternal blis, / Joying his goddesse, and of her enjoyed" (st. 48). As he first noticed, Adonis, presented as "eterne in mutabilitie" within the phenomenal world (st. 47) is now beyond the reach of death and change (48.3-9), and this pattern heralds the close of the Mutabilitie Cantos, the simultaneous assertion of a law of cyclic change and of divine eternity[154]. But T. P. Harrison does not take into account the very requirements of the myth as myth; Adonis is now among the gods and the immortal gods cannot but live in "eternal blis". The Mount is obviously reminiscent of Mount Olympus, since "many of the gods in company... thether haunt" (49.2-3), I do not think it should be identified with the "heavenly hous" of Venus (st. 12) which has other connotations, Platonic and astrological[155]. The comparison with Mount Acidale, on the contrary, is justified (see *F.Q.* VI.x), but once again the associations are mythological rather than metaphysical or even cosmological. The Venus-Adonis myth, of course, has a cosmological significance but it does not extend beyond the natural order, and the philosophy of the Mount is on a level with the philosophy of the Garden.

Since the house of Venus was described as "the house of goodly formes" (vi.12.2) and her beloved was said to be undying though "Transformed oft, and chaunged diverslie" (vi. 47.7), Adonis was sometimes equated with matter[156]. But matter, to Platonists and Aristotelians alike, was traditionally feminine. Besides Adonis is only "by succession made perpetual" (47.6), whereas Spenser's substance is "eterne, and bideth so" (37.6), never "changed nor altered "but only in "outward fashion" (38.1-2). Lastly matter cannot be

---

[153] To Apuleius and the Neoplatonists the myth of Cupid and Psyche was a symbol of the soul's union with the divine.

[154] *Univ. of Texas Studies in English* (1934), pp. 58, sq., 70-73. On Mutabilitie see pp. 68-70 above.

[155] See p. 89 below. The "house" of Venus is undoubtedly in heaven and probably denotes the planet. The Mount cannot and need not be distinctly located. But it would not have been described as rising in the midst of a Garden set on earth if Spenser had meant it to be "identified with the house of Venus". In Bennett's interpretation the Mount would be in the sphere of the Moon. I take it to be a purely mythical but helpful symbol to present the immortal life of Adonis hid from the world and from the envy of Stygian gods (st. 46. 5-6).

[156] See the various theories set forth in *Variorum F.Q.* III.

described as "the Father of all formes" (47.8). Yet Stirling's identification of Adonis with form and of Venus with matter or Chaos [157] must be rejected as well. Venus is too closely associated with form and the bestowing of form and beauty at the beginning of the Canto (vi. 12) for such an unprecedented allegory to be plausible [158]. Both these contrary interpretations rest on the unjustified assumption that the Adonis-Venus myth merely parallels the earlier described form-substance relationship. But this allegorical reiteration of a plain statement would be pointless. Since Spenser usually follows the Renaissance mythographers, the traditional explanations of the Adonis myth are likely to prove the safest key to the poet's symbolism.

Besides a full account of the myth based on Ovid and Theocritus, Natalis Cómes offered two cosmological interpretations. One saw in the dying and reviving hero an image of the fate of corn, which stays six months underground with Proserpina and enjoys Venus, that is the mildness of the air, for the remaining months [159]. The myth could be extended to the general cycle of vegetation. But far more space was devoted to another interpretation. Adonis was identified with the Sun, "father of germination", and the boar with Winter [160]. Comes traced this symbolism to the Orphic Hymns. A more elaborate exposition could be found in the *Saturnalia* of Macrobius. It had been reproduced in the *De Genealogia Deorum* of Boccaccio and commended for its ingenuity [161]. This consensus of opinion among his favourite authorities could not but impress Spenser. Though his own adaptation of the Adonis myth could be referred to the cycle of vegetation in general outline, some statements imply that a sun myth was intended. The Sun, indeed, "may not — For ever dye, and ever buried bee — In balefull night" (st. 47.2-3), but is "by succession made perpetuall", for "needs mote he live, that living gives to all" (47.6,9). The boar is the emblem of Winter for, in the words of Macrobius, "Winter is as a wound to the Sun, whose light and heat it lessens, which happens through death in all living beings" [162]. That the boar should now be imprisoned in a rocky Cave hewn underneath the Mount (st. 48.5-9) agrees with the earlier description of the Garden, since "There is continuall spring, and harvest there Continuall, both meeting at one time" (st. 42.1-2). This would be a simple explanation of the *stable* immortality there enjoyed by Adonis: the Sun always shines over Eden and all Earthly Paradises [163]. Adonis would be set in the "thickest cover" (44.1) of a "gloomy grove" (41.3) because such Paradises are

---

157 *PMLA* 49, pp. 534-37.

158 Venus is linked with Chaos in *H.L.* 57-70, but not in a way that supports Stirling's theory: since she lends Cupid light to guide him through Chaos, she herself obviously cannot be identified with Chaos (see 11. 71-75).

159 *Mythologia,* p. 527.

160 Comes, *Mythologia,* pp. 527-28 (cited by Lotspeich, *Mythology in Spenser,* pp. 32-3): "Sensit tamen Orpheus in hymne in Adonim illum esse solem, cum illum rebus omnibus praebere nutrimentum, & esse germinandi autorem ... ea de causa illum ait Orpheus modo esse apud superos, modo apud inferos...". This interpretation of the myth was also adopted in Cartari's *Le Imagini de i Dei de gli Antichi* (Lyons, 1581, p. 462), as J.W. Bennett discovered: *SP* 30, p. 165.

161 *De Genealogia,* II. liii: "Dicit enim Adonem solem esse, quo nil pulchrius...".

162 *Saturnalia,* I. xxi.

163 Stanza 47, which describes Adonis as dying and reviving, would not refer to his life in the Garden, but in our world. Stanzas 41-42 show that spring and summer may be continual in the Garden though the plants, animals and men living in it are subject to time.

"hid from the world" (46.6) of our experience, because Adonis must be shown to be alive even when out of our sight and because privacy is required for the love sports in which "fayre Venus" and "the wanton boy" indulge "in secret", "Lapped in flowres and pretious spycery" (46.4-5). The emphasis on voluptuousness in stanzas 46 and 49 is in keeping with both the literary treatment of the myth and another allegorical interpretation recorded by the Renaissance compiler Equicola together with the Sun myth. The text deserves quotation since it has not yet been noticed and is not easily available:

> Plutarch scrive che in Siria Venere da gli habitanti è chiamata Giunone, laquale dà principio a tutte le cose che nascono. I poeti dissero essere stata innamorata di Adone, il quale significa il Sole secondo la religione de gli Assiri, osservata da Fenici ... La terra è divisa in due hemisperii. Questo superiore, c'habitiamo noi, si dice di Venere: nell' inferiore de gli Antipodi, secondo li antichi habita Proserpina. Sei mesi piange Venere, cioè quel tempo che'l Sole è nel altro hemisperio. Il porco ciguale, il quale ammazzo Adone, intendono la vernata.
>
> Altri dicono, che Adon nacque di Mirrha cosa grata a Venere, appropriata al coito, & como Petronio dice incitamento di Venere. E ammazzato Adone; cioé la libidine, laquale cessa con l'età, & non risorge. Leggiamo in Platone, e in Plinio, che Adone da' suoi horti significa suavità [164]?

Spenser obviously echoes the latter legend when he surrounds Adonis with "mirtle-trees" (43.3) and repeatedly calls attention to "sweet gum" (43.7), "dainty odours" (43.9), "spicery (46.5) and the "sweetnesse" (46.9) of the wanton boy. Yet he obviously does not abide by the merely erotic interpretation [165]. With his usual lavishness and vagueness of imaginative reference, he probable seeks to work it into the dominant solar myth, since the sun "living gives to all" (47.9). This was the easier since Venus, or the act of generation, was thought to require "the force of the sun" [166].

Though my approach is different from hers, I therefore agree with Dr Bennett when she writes: "Adonis represents the principle of life as it expresses itself in the world through the phenomenon of generation, in the

---

[164] *Di Natura d'Amore,* pp. 107-8. On Equicola, see pp. 108-10.

[165] It might be tempting, though, to trace an allegory of the anatomical "mount of Venus" in the description of the Mount on whose round top

> *A gloomy grove of mirtle* trees did rise,
> Whose shady boughes *sharp steele did never lop*
> ....
> And from their *fruitfull sydes sweet gum did drop.*
> ....
> And in the *thickest covert* of that shade
> ....
> *With wanton Yvie-twine entrayld athwart,*
> And Eglantine and Caprifole emong,
> Fashioned above *within their inmost part.*

The traditional association of Adonis and myrtle with eroticism makes the reference likely, whether conscious or unconscious. Even if conscious, it would not be so surprising. Jean de Meung had set a far bolder precedent in his description of the plucking of the Rose.

[166] Comes, *Mythologia,* Lib. IIII, Cap. XIII, "De Venere": "Hanc Deam jure Adonim amasse dicunt, qui Adonim solem esse arbitrati sunt: quoniam sine vi Solis, nulla esset Venus."

vitality of the seed, and in the life-giving power of the sun" [167]. But I fail to see why an unprecedented Neoplatonic construction should be put upon this straightforward Nature myth. There is not a shred of evidence to show that Adonis was connected in Spenser's mind with "Jove, in whose garden the Ideas are planted like trees, according to Pico" [168]. I am not even sure that "Platonic form" is intended, as even Harrison maintains [169], when Adonis is styled "the Father of all formes" (47.8). The phrase turns out ot be his only title to Platonic significance. But that title rests on his giving life to all (47.9), therefore to the "variable" and decaying "formes" of all things earlier mentioned (38.6). The Sun had been styled "Great Father ...of generation" (III.vi.9.1). Whether Spenser meant any thing more than this or not depends on the significance ascribed to **Venus.**

Venus has earlier been associated with transcendent or, at least, heavenly form (st. 12). Adonis, therefore might be expected to beget transcendent form as well as phenomenal shapes. This would imply two very different activities, but there might be two Adonises as there are two Venuses, one in the Angelic Mind, the other in the World-Soul [170]. The trouble is that no such duality is intimated. Were Adonis meant to be in the Angelic mind, would he be described as a "wanton boy"? Venus herself, in Spenser's relation of the myth, never once appears in her "heavenly" character, nor even as the bestower of form and beauty, but only in her mythological and erotic character. Had the poet intended to depict Adonis as the begetter of Platonic form, he could hardly have set about it more awkwardly. The very Cupid with whom Adonis plays (st. 49) is the mediaeval god untouched with Platonic speculation.

In the circumstances, one may wonder whether the earlier description of the "heavenly hous" of Venus has been so deeply influenced by Neoplatonism as is commonly thought. Let us read it over:

> The house of goodly formes and faire aspects,
> Whence all the world derives the glorious
> Features of beautie, and all shapes select,
> With which high God his workmanship hath deckt; (III. vi. 12. 2-5)

Is this the distinctive note of *Renaissance* Platonism? We notice, first, that Spenser abides by the traditional "Timaeic" and mediaeval conception of the work of creation followed by "the work of adornment" [171]. He ignores the processions and emanations described by Plotinus and his Renaissance disciples, such as Ficino, to account for the diffusion of Divine beauty [172]. Besides, his language is both untechnical and inaccurate if meant to convey

---

[167] *PMLA* 47, p. 74.

[168] *PMLA* 47, p. 72. On the garden of Jove see p. 75 above and p. 93 below.

[169] *Univ. of Texas Studies in English,* 41, pp. 63-4.

[170] Cf. Ficino, *In Convivium,* II. vij: "To sum it all up, Venus is twofold: one is clearly that intelligence which we said was in the Angelic Mind; the other is the power of generation with which the World-Soul is endowed" (Jayne's translation, p. 142).

[171] Cf. Gilson "La Cosmogonie de Bernardus Silvestris", p. 7.

[172] Cst. Ficino's conception of Beauty as the Radiance of Divine goodness diffusing itself through four circles (*In Convivium* II. iii-iv). The Timaeic idea of "workmanship does not **intervene.**

notions borrowed from the Renaissance Neoplatonists[173]. Indeed such words as "aspects", or even "house" have an astrological meaning, which suggests that the planet Venus rather than the Angelic Mind, or the abode of ideas, was foremost in the poet's mind. The rôle "of that goodly Parangon" as the dispenser of features of beautie" was acknowledged by the more popular Neoplatonists, like Equicola[174], and seems to have been in Spenser's mind whenever he speaks of the bright star of the Cyprian Queen[175].

Mutabilitie and the Garden of Adonis had to be discussed fully. The Temple of Venus need not detain us. About the many philosophical conceptions involved in the allegory and Spenser's wise indifference to intellectual consistency, C. S. Lewis has written with a keen insight into the workings of the poet's imagination:

> In IV. x we can find, if that is our interest, the following: (1) Love as friendship; (2) Venus distinct from Love (or Cupid) as mother from son; (3) Love (Eros) as the brother of Hate (Eris) derived ultimately from Empedocles (32); (4) the hermaphroditic Venus whose obscure origins have been studied by Miss J.W. Bennett (41); Love naturalistically conceived in lines adapted from Lucretius (44 et seq). But Spenser did not set out by collecting these concepts, still less by attempting a philosophical synthesis of them. His theme is courtship and his model medieval erotic allegory. How a gentle knight found the island fortress of true love and overcame its defenders and won meek Amoret — that is the substance... The philosophical matter merely adds a suggestion of depth, as if shadows of old thought played about the Temple: just as fugitive memories of Donne or Dante or Patmore or Meredith might play about our own minds during a real love affair. I do not mean that Spenser thought of it quite in that way. He was too serious and too syncretistic. Everything that the wise had said about Love was worth attending to. He would not have said 'Let us shade in here a little Platonism and there a little Epicureanism'. He would have said 'Proclus in *Timaeum* doth report... Orpheus hath it thus ... read the like in that place of Ficinus'. But the result is much the same. It produces that depth or thickness which is one of the excellences of the *Faerie Queene*[176].

As literary criticism this is admirable. But I doubt whether Spenser ever thought of Proclus or Ficino when writing this Canto. Besides, out of the blending of philosophical conceptions, manifold as they are, a general colouring must result, an intellectual approach or attitude must emerge, and I think that they could be characterized as both naturalistic and ethical, but not at any time Platonic and metaphysical. The story, ending in marriage, implied that Spenser should be mainly concerned with the earthly Venus. Her function and power were, of course, acknowledged by the Neoplatonists whose philosophy of love involved love as generation. But when a poet takes her for his theme and leaves out the heavenly Venus and love as contemplation, the characteristic note of

---

[173] "Forms" are placed by Ficino in the last circle: "species illas in mente, ideas; in anima rationes; in natura, semina; in materia, formas appellare solemus" (*In Convivium*, II. iii). Aspect" has no Platonic meaning, unless it is an awkward translation of "species".

[174] Equicola devotes several pages to the star called Venus and its influence: "Fa gli huomini amabili, belli..." (*Di Natura d'Amore, Di Venere*, p. 110). The idea was mediaeval: cf. Bartholomaeus, *De Propr. Rerum*. VIII. xxvi: "disponit ad pulchritudinem".

[175] Cf. *H.B.* 54-6 and Chapter VII below.

[176] *English Literature in the 16th Century*, pp. 387-88.

Platonism is not sounded, and Platonic influence cannot be detected, even though he has availed himself of material derived from the disquisitions of the Neoplatonists on the cosmic and earthly effects of love. Now, the Temple of Venus does not reverberate any *distinctive* echo of the Neoplatonic philosophy. Just as Spenser took "medieval erotic allegory" for his model, as C. S. Lewis observed, he retained the medieval Venus adding the Lucretian hymn and borrowing from Macrobius and Plutarch, or later mythographers [177], the idea that Venus "hath both kinds in one, Both male and female, both under one name" (IV.x.41.6-7). Plutarch and Macrobius, I agree, conveyed to the Renaissance mind some of its more corrupt notions of Platonism. But the hermaphroditic Venus is to be associated with actual religious cults and the Isis myth rather than with any development of the Platonic philosophy in Antiquity or in the Renaissance [178].

Nor do the other characters in the Temple of Venus imply an allegiance to any other philosophy — be it Plato's or Empedocles' — than the "widely prevailing generalizations of the cosmology and physics of the period" [179]. Concord was a stock figure of Elizabethan pageants [180]. The opposition of Love and Hate, or Love and Strife, has been shown to be "a mediaeval commonplace" and the cosmological rôle ascribed to Love has been traced in typical contexts offered by mediaeval authors [181]. Well may the historian add:

> That Spenser presents the same generalizations in similar contexts and with similar coloring or imaginative "machinery" of figures and setting, is indicative of a closer relationship than we commonly recognize between his thought and that of the mediaeval period. The Cambridge education of Spenser's day was still a mediaeval as well as Renaissance education; a sixteenth century poet must still have been influenced in his ideas of a Christian philosophical poetry by the literature and philosophy of the age which had preceded him [182].

It is not surprising, therefore, that the influence of the *Timaeus,* a mediaeval classic, should be the only Platonic influence distinctly traceable in the cos-

---

[177] Lotspeich cites *Saturnalia* 3. 8. 1, and Servius, *ad Aen* (*Mythology,* p. 115). But Plutarch is as likely, since Isis is described as male and female (*De Iside* 43). Isis is identified with Nature by Plutarch (*ibid.* 53; pp. 165-6), with Venus by Equicola, *Di Natura d'Amore,* pp. 107-9.

[178] See note 177 on Isis. To J.W. Bennett this hermaphroditism is proof that Spenser never loses sight of the relationship of the Earthly to the Heavenly Venus: *SP* 30, p. 165. It is, indeed, a Neoplatonic commonplace that every emanation is both masculine and feminine (Bennett, *PMLA* 47, p. 72). But the emanation was "male in its contemplative function, female in its active and creative function" (Bennett, *SP* 30, p. 169; based on Ficino, *Opera,* Basle 1576, p. 570). Now Spenser obviously refers both the male and female principles to generation alone, without any allusion to contemplation:

> She syre and mother is herselfe alone,
> Begets and eke conceives, ne needeth other none (IV. x. 42. 8-9).

The poet must have either misconceived Ficino's meaning (a gratuitous assumption) or simply followed Macrobius whose account of the old religious cults was uninfluenced by speculations on Neoplatonic emanations (*Saturnalia* III. 8). Besides, it should be noticed that there is no allusion to hermaphroditism in Ficino's account of the double nature of Venus: Cupid is "the consort of Venus" and three must needs be as many Cupids as there are Venuses (*In Convivium,* II. vii).

[179] R. Tuve, *SP* 30 (1933), pp. 133-47.

[180] See C.G. Smith, *SP* 32, pp. 158-69.

[181] Tuve, *SP* 30, pp. 133-47.

[182] Tuve, *SP* 30, p. 147.

mology of the *Faerie Queene*. Spenser even proves more conservative than some allegorists of the Middle Ages in his avoidance of Platonic intermediaries. He is satisfied with God and Nature [183] and does not need the Noys, or Mind, Endelecheia or World-Soul, Imarmene, or temporal order, Urania and Physis of Bernardus Silvestris, nor the *aeternalis Idea* of Alanus and her reflection, *Iconia* [184]. Even more remarkable, perhaps is the absence of the Neoplatonic daemons in his "fairy land", which should have proved hospitable to their airy tribe. C. S. Lewis has seasonably reminded us that to an Englishman of that period Platonism would not only mean a philosophy of love and beauty but a system of daemonology [185]. Since Platonic daemonology must have been early known to Spenser, if not through the Alexandrian and the Florentine Platonists, or through Paracelsus and the dabblers in magic from Agrippa to Dr. Dee, at least through Apuleius and Plutarch, the absence of *aëros daemones* in his cosmology must betray a conscious choice and a personal disinclination, whether dictated by religious scruples, or common sense, or an aesthetic preference for classical mythology and native fairy lore.

Besides the *Faerie Queene* the main instances of cosmological poetry are found in *Colin Clouts Come Home Again* and in the *Fowre Hymnes*. The *Hymnes* are to be considered separately. Colin's speech on love in *Colin Clout* is transitional ,for the influence of the *Symposium* is for the first time distinctly traceable in poetry published by Spenser before 1596. Now, that definition of love is obviously a set speech, introduced as an addition — or afterthought. In support of this opinion, Dr Bennett has pointed to Melissa's remark [186]. But the clearest proof is furnished by repetitions and contradictory accounts of the birth of Cupid. He is first described by Colin in terms that closely recall the Temple of Venus and Garden of Adonis episodes in the *Faerie Queene*:

> For him the greatest of the Gods we deeme,
> Borne without Syre or couples of one kynd,
> For *Venus* selfe doth soly couples seeme,
> Both male and female, through commixture joynd.
> So pure and spotlesse *Cupid* forth she brought,
> And in the Gardens of *Adonis* nurst:
> Where growing he, his own perfection wrought,
> And shortly was of all the Gods the first.
> Then got he bow and shafts of gold and lead,
> In which so fell and puissant he grew,
> That Jove himselfe his powre began to dread,
> And taking up to heaven, him godded new. (*Colin,* 11.799-810).

The hermaphroditic Venus, we know, comes from Macrobius or Plutarch and has no genuine connection with Platonism [187]. It is commonly thought that Spenser substituted his own Garden of Adonis for the Platonic "garden of Zeus" in *Symposium* 202. But had the poet *first* thought of the Garden of

---

[183] Venus and Love are mythological characters or represent the generative forces in Nature. Venus and Nature are nearly represented alike as J.W. Bennett pointed out: *SP* 30, p. 165.

[184] See Gilson, "La Cosmogonie de Bernardus Sylvestris", pp. 5-24; Raynaud de Lage, *Alain de Lille*, pp. 77-8, 92. Cf. J.M. Parent, *La doctrine de la création dans l'Ecole de Chartres,* Paris-Ottawa, 1938.

[185] See *English Literature in the 16th Century*, p. 10.

[186] See *SP* 28, p. 53.

[187] See notes 177 and 178 above.

Jove, identified with the Angelic Mind by Ficino and Pico[188], why should he have departed from the Platonic myth? I can think of one explanation only and it would make him a conscious rebel against the Neoplatonic philosophy: assuming he had the earlier myth in mind, he must have meant to substitute an "earthly paradise "for a heavènly garden of Ideas. For no doubt can be entertained: the Garden of Adonis is not a place *above* the earth, since Cupid, once he has grown to "his owne perfection", has to be *taken up to heaven* to be "godded new". Confirmation of my interpretation may also be found in Spenser's mythical account of the creation of man by Prometheus and that man's first encounter" in the gardins of Adonis" with "a goodly creature... th'author of all woman kynd" (II.x.71). Though that man, for the story's sake, has to be "the first author of all Elfin kynd" and the woman to be called a Fay, it is obvious that the Garden of Adonis is not associated in Spenser's imagination with the Platonic theory of ideas but with generation through sexual union between man and woman.

Now, in Colin's next speech, Love is no longer nursed in the gardens of Adonis, but "bred *above* in Venus bosome deare" (1.840). As in the *Hymne in Honour of Love,* "By his powre, the world was made of yore"[189]. These ideas were commonplaces which could have been found in the *Mythologia* of Natalis Comes[190]. But there are indications that Spenser was now following a passage in the *Symposium* or a fuller exposition of it than Comes afforded. The *Mythologia,* for instance, did not contrast brutish love and human love with arguments based on the desire for beauty and immortality. Those arguments must have been borrowed either from *Symposium* 206 b — 208 b, or from commentators such as Ficino or Le Roy[191]:

> But Man that had the sparke of reasons might,
> More then the rest to rule his passion,
> Chose for his love the fairest in his sight,
> Like as himselfe was fairest by creation.
> For beautie is the bayt which with delight
> Doth man allure, for to enlarge his kynd, (*Colin,* ll. 867-72).

For the first time therefore, we find it necessary to appeal either to Plato or the more scholarly Renaissance Platonists to illustrate Spenser's meaning. It is significant that the necessity should arise in connection with lines composed not earlier then 1951, and probably as late as 1594 or 1595. For, whereas the hermaphroditic Venus and the gardens of Adonis in Colin's first account of Cupid's birth belong indeed with the cosmological myths of Books III and IV of the *Faerie Queene,* the set speech, though retaining a mainly naturalistic conception of love, plays upon Platonic themes further developed and idealized in the *Hymnes.* Since there are good reasons to believe that it was a late insertion[192], it is one more indication that Spenser's interest in Platonism reached a peak in the later years of his life, after the completion of the first six books of the *Faerie Queene* recorded in the *Amoretti*[193].

---

188 See Ficino, *In Conv.,* VI. vii; Pico, *Commento,* II. xi.
189 Cf. *Colin,* 1. 841 and *H.L.* 1. 75.
190 See the chapter "De Cupidine (IIII. xiii), pp. 398-408.
191 Cf. *In Convivium* III. ii; VI. xi; *Sympose,* ff. 107 r°, 120 v°, 124 v°.
192 Reasons stated above and prosodic reasons: see Appendix II.
193 That is, in the Spring of 1594.

CHAPTER V

A REVIEW OF SPENSER'S PLATONIC SOURCES UP TO THE PUBLICATION OF THE « FOWRE HYMNES »

> The waies, through which my weary steps I guyde,
> In this delightfull land of Faery,
> Are so exceeding spacious and wyde,

And the undergrowth of criticism so luxuriant that, whatever haste was made, the "wished scope" could only be reached after "a paineful pilgrimage". The wide field of Spenser's poetry has been travelled over from end to end — leaving out the *Fowre Hymnes.* The revaluation of the amount and nature of Platonic or Neoplatonic influence over his inspiration may now be followed by a reconsideration of the likeliest sources. This line of proceeding was dictated by the very profusion of "parallels" and the scarcity of unmistakable "borrowings". There is no means of ascertaining which author or treatise, if any, determined the poet's thought. Only by following the poet's own line of thought, as disclosed in his works, may we trace the authors he knew best or liked most.

Lodowick Bryskett has made Spenser a reputation for Greek scholarship [1]. Whether that reputation was deserved or not, remains a controverted issue [2]. If the translation of the *Axiochus* were indisputably attributed to the poet, it would be decisive proof that his knowledge of Greek was very slender since the translator availed himself of the Latin parallel version without even taking the Greek text into consideration [3]. Yet, since Spenser's authorship, strongly supported by F.M. Padelford and by the *Variorum* Editor of the *Prose Works* [4],

---

[1] See *A Discourse of Civil Life* (London, 1606), p. 25.

[2] Cf. Padelford, "Note on the *Axiochus*", *PMLA* 50 (1935), p. 912, and C.S. Lewis, *Engl. Lit. 16th Century*, p. 355.

[3] *Axiochus*, ed. Padelford, Introduction, pp. 17-25.

[4] See *Prose Works,* Appendix II, for a survey of the whole controversy. The editor, Rudolf Gottfried, ascribes the *Sweet Speech* and the dedication to Munday but thinks that the translation "may be by Spenser" on account of the number of striking parallels in phrasing with the *Faerie Queene* and the *View: Prose Works,* pp. 495-6. The verbal evidence is strong, if not decisive, in my opinion. Though published in 1592 the *Axiochus,* if Spenser translated it, was "presumably one of the pamphlets written before the poet's 'departure' overseas in 1580" (*Prose Works,* p. 490). As the work was then ascribed to Plato, the translation might point to an early interest in his philosophy. But this dialogue on death happens to have little affinity with Platonism or Neoplatonism. Spenser's choice might have been influenced by Mornay's *Discours de la Vie et de la Mort* translated into English by Sidney and the Countess of Pembroke (*ibid.,* p. 490). The translation of the *Axiochus* was in harmony with Protestant devotion rather than Renaissance Platonism.

is still in doubt[5] and no other decisive evidence is available, the question whether Spenser was "perfect in the Greek tongue" is likely to remain a matter of controversy and conjecture. It need hardly be raised for our present purpose since the poet could have availed himself of the Latin translations of Ficino or Serranus[6].

Yet, leaving out the *Fowre Hymnes* for the time being, I fail to discover any proof that the poet was acquainted with the Platonic philosophy at first hand. There is even evidence to the contrary. Out of three references to Socrates in the whole of Spenser's works, one is vague and devoid of interest (*F.Q.* I.ix.48.1-2), the other two contain grievous blunders[7]. Whether Spenser was taking his knowledge at second-hand from Cicero's *De Oratore* and the first book of the *Tusculans,* or whether he was misled by an illustration in Achille Bocchi' *Symbolicarum Quaestionum Libri Quinque*[8], it must at least be acknowledged that his memory of the *Phaedo* and the *Phaedrus* was "not very clear"[9]. A. E. Taylor was even more positive and observed: "If Spenser had ever read Plato for himself, there is nothing in these passages to prove it, and the blunder about the incidents of Socrates' last day could not well have been made by any one who knew the *Phaedo.* Yet if Spenser was unacquainted with the *Phaedo,* is it likely that he knew any Platonic work at first-hand? Here is a question that deserves investigation..."[10].

The proem to Book IV of the *Faerie Queene* was written after 1590, and there are reasons to believe it was composed shortly before publication. Thus, a serious doubt hangs over Spenser's acquaintance with Plato as late as January 1596. Yet Taylor's generalization is too hasty. That the author of Book II was unacquainted with the *Phaedo,* and that the poet who wrote the proem to Book IV had not read the *Phaedrus,* seems beyond doubt. But neither the *Phaedo* nor the *Phaedrus* were the more popular and more easily available dialogues by the time Spenser wrote. Even in the Renaissance period, Plato was still usually depicted holding the *Timaeus* in his hand as his masterwork[11]. The *Symposium* might have been placed in his other hand, as the dialogue on which poets and writers on love drew most heavily. Both were available in separate editions and translations. Spenser may have shrunk from the heavier

---

[5] C.S. Lewis still rejects it: *Eng. Lit. 16th Century,* p. 378.

[6] According to Jayne the translation of Plato's works by Serranus was actually more popular in England than Ficino's.

[7] In *F.Q.* II. vii. 52, Socrates is said to have "Pourd out his life and last Philosophy To the faire *Critias,* his dearest Belamy." This implies a confusion of Critias with Alcibiades, and Socrates with Theramenes: see *Variorum F.Q.* II. 263-4. Besides, when the poet recalls that Socrates "to his *Critias* shaded oft from sunne. Of love full many lessons did apply (*F.Q.* IV, Proem, 3), the allusion to the plane-tree in *Phaedrus* 229a-b is obvious, and Critias this time must have been mistakenly substituted for Phaedrus (whose name would fit as well into the line).

[8] See A.E. Taylor, *MLR,* 29, pp. 208-10, and T.M. Gang, TLS, August 3, 1956, p. 463. Gang's explanation is the simplest and likeliest.

[9] T.M. Gang's cautious assertion only applies to the *Phaedo,* and even Taylor does not insist on Spenser's ignorance of the *Phaedrus.* Yet, I think it very unlikely that any one familiar with the *Phaedrus* should have chosen to mention Critias rather than Phaedrus in this context. And any one who had read the dialogue once could not have forgotten the boy's name when it happened to be the very title. Commentators may have suggested "shaded oft from sunne".

[10] *MLR* 29, p. 210.

[11] *Timée, Critias.* Trad. A. Rivaud (Paris: Belles Lettres, 1949), pp. 3-4. Cf. Klibanski, *Platonic Tradition,* p. 28; Taylor, *Platonism,* p. 16.

folios and never plunged into the *Opera Platonis,* but he is more likely to have read isolated dialogues and the commentaries they had inspired. A list of editions and translations will be found in Appendix III.

With the *Phaedrus* and the *Phaedo* ruled out, the only dialogues for which some influence may be claimed over the poems considered in the previous chapters are the *Timaeus,* the *Republic,* the *Ion,* and the *Symposium.* Yet, not the Renaissance but the mediaeval interpretation of the *Timaeus* proved dominant in the poet's cosmology. Spenser may well have read the *Republic,* a favourite with the earlier English humanists, but he did not follow Plato's views on temperance and justice. What ideas he may have derived from the *Ion* may have been fetched more readily from Minturno, Castiglione and other courtly or literary Platonists. Whether he knew the *Symposium* at first hand remains doubtful, though there are clearer signs of influence, as might be expected since it was the most popular dialogue in literary circles [12]. Yet the Platonic conception of love received at the poet's hands a Christian as well as a naturalistic colouring. Identifying ideal love with married love, he moved away not only from the original philosophy but even from its various Renaissance adaptations with few exceptions. Lastly, the claim that more is meant than meets the ear in a poem like the *Faerie Queen* hardly increases the probability of Platonic influence for no consistent Platonism or Neoplatonism can be read into its allegories. Even its ethics are a blend of classical, mediaeval and Elizabethan commonplaces, into which Platonic notions enter only in a state of dilution.

Such conclusions will shock only such scholars as still seek to vindicate Spenser's own scholarship. But only Gabriel Harvey would take the poet to task for not having read Plato further than Montaigne [13]. Many other Renaissance poets, besides Spenser, had echoed the dialogues at second-hand. An interesting parallel is afforded by Sidney. The pupil of Languet asserted he had read Plato in one of his sonnets (XXV). We may well believe him. Yet, in *Astrophel and Stella,* the only clear reminiscence of Plato is the following:

> The wisest scholler of the wight most wise
> By Phoebus doome, with sugred sentence sayes:
> That Vertue, if it once met with our eyes,
> Strange flames of Love it in our soules would raise (XXV).

The lines allude to a passage of the *Phaedrus,* but do not imply direct acquaintance with it, for it had been earlier translated by Cicero:

> Formam quidem ipsam, Marce fili, & tanquam faciem honesti vides, quae si oculis cerneretur, mirabiles amores, ut ait Plato, excitaret Sapientiae [14].

It is impossible to tell whether Sidney echoed Plato or Cicero. But the fact that he should have especially noticed in Plato what Cicero had earlier pointed out is noteworthy and significant. And the explanation is obvious: he may have read the *Phaedrus* once (though we have only his word for it),

---

[12] See Appendix III. Cf. Cassirer, *Die platonische Renaissance,* p. 72.

[13] Harvey was not always satisfied with Spenser's scholarship: cf. *Marginalia,* ed. Moore-Smith, pp. 162-3.

[14] *De Officiis,* 1.5.

but, as a school-boy, he certainly had pored over the *De Officiis*. "The first Impressions are immortall all".

Spenser too, from his youth, must have been familiar with Cicero and Seneca. As an Elizabethan he must have known the *Consolatio* of Boethius and the *Zodiacus Vitae* of Marcellus Palingenius, whether in the original or in Googe's translation [15]. As an allegorist, he became acquainted, through Chaucer with "the school of Alanus", if not with Alanus himself. As a Renaissance poet,

---

[15] The *Zodiacus* was included in the statutes of St Bee's Grammar School. See F. Watson: *The Zodiacus Vitae of Marcellus Palingenius Stellatus: An old school-book,* London, P. Wellby, 1908. Spenser's probable indebtedness has been traced by J.W. Bennett in *PMLA* 47, pp. 46-80, and R. Tuve, in *JEGP* 34, pp. 1-19. No clear instance of actual borrowing has been offered. The more convincing parallels are the more general: "strife and friendship as the chief beginnings of the world... Love as the principle which keeps the elements in harmony, brings order in the world and thus growth and continuity, ... God as the "workeman" of the world, ... chance and law and mutability, ... seeming change but real stability, ... inspiration through God's "sacred spright" inflaming the mind with "heavenly love" and causing it to mount up through the spheres to join itself to the divine, ... Urania who helps the poet to 'disclose" Dame Nature's face'" (Tuve, *JEGP* 34, p. 17). Parallels in setting and motif — e.g. the Paradise of Voluptuousness in *Gemini* and Spenser's House of Pride and Bower of Bliss (Tuve, *JEGP*) — are vague and inconclusive. As regards Neoplatonism, Bennett's parallel between the Garden of Adonis and the temporary abode of souls on the moon in "Sagittarius" 150-63 (*PMLA* 47, pp. 50-54), must be rejected in my interpretation (see Chapter IV, pp. 74-75). Palingenius drew heavily upon Cardan and Agrippa for his astrology and daemonology: Spenser's poetry, we know, is free from the airy and fiery daemons of the Neoplatonists, which the translation of Googe turned into "Angels" (see *Zodiake,* ed. 1588, pp. 115-19). What the English poet may have retained from the Platonism of Palingenius therefore does not extend beyond the commonplaces listed by Tuve, that is the divine nature of poetic inspiration and cosmological notions already widespread in the Middle Ages. Palingenius, in fact, was one of the least scholarly Renaissance Platonists: he lumped together transcendent forms and the Divine Ideas in the abode of the saints ("Pisces". 11. 169-94: see Bennett, *PMLA* 47, p. 52). The very imprecision of his philosophy and language in a way brings him closer to Spenser (the imprecision was increased by Googe's awkward translation). Yet, in his works published up to 1595, the English poet hardly reproduced or echoed any of the more distinctly Platonic notions set forth in the *Zodiacus:* the elaborate contrast between the intelligible, archetypal world and the vain shadows of the sensible world (*Zodiacus,* "Libra"; ed. 1581, pp. 182-3), the discussion on God's motives for creating the world ("Aquarius", p. 334 *et seq.*) and the exposition of a Neoplatonic "theology of light" (Pisces"; pp. 348-50). On the other hand, however daring in the field of astronomy and daemonology, Palingenius does not introduce the Plotinian entities dear to Ficino and Pico: Mind, World-Soul, etc. In this, he and Spenser are at one. If affinity is a test of influence, the most interesting parallels are those which have not been advertised. Spenser must have applauded the defence of earthly Venus, whose God-appointed task is to "repair the losses of Nature". What God ordained, Palingenius argued, cannot be damnable ("Cancer"; ed. 1581, p. 75; cf. *F.Q.* IV. x. 47. 2). He may have been impressed, too, by the awe-struck acknowledment of the eminence of Nature only excelled by God, in accordance with the mediaeval tradition; Nature as the law of God directing the union of form and matter out of which all things arise. I give my translation of the Latin original (ed. 1581, p. 327):

"For Nature indeed is of greater might than any other mover. Only God surpasses Nature and, but for Him alone, there is no better nor greater thing than Nature in the universe. What I call Nature, indeed, is the Law that the Almighty Father imposed on all things from the very beginning of the world, a law to be kept inviolably as He commanded, as long as the world would last. For this same law has God assigned to the forms of things. Hence, when they give being to things, forms willingly carry out God's injuctions and cannot evade that law, since the things generated out of their forms are no doubt such as He who established those very forms wished them to be. Truly and properly speaking, Nature is that law and

he would know Minturno's *De poeta,* and be familiar with Petrarchan sonnet-sequences and the French Italian poetry of his age. As a would-be courtier, he must have been interested in Castiglione's *Cortegiano.* Lastly, as a lover of mythology, he appears to have thumbed Conti's *Mythologia* and Boccacio's *Genealogia* over and over again, and the *Faerie Queene* shows clear indebtedness to Plutarch and Macrobius [16]. Of all these influences, we may be sure, and of these alone. They have been noted in the foregoing chapters and there is no Platonic notion in any of Spenser's poems, but for Colin's speech on Love, for which they could not fully account. I do not wish to deny the poet any acquaintance with other Platonic or Neoplatonic works, but the outstanding fact is that he borrowed nothing from the more scholarly Renaissance Platonists but what he could have obtained through more popular or mediaeval channels. Up to 1595, in his published poetry at least, his Platonism was both conservative in spirit and loose in expression. Again, it cannot be proved that he was not already acquainted with Ficino, Pico and their like. But when acquaintance is unaccompanied by influence, it is of little interest in the history of a poet's inspiration.

"A poet, Renwick wrote, is not a passive body impinged on by external forces, and Spenser was a man of positive mind, who chose his own way. The mark of an "influence" is the record of an affinity; the exploitation of a "source" in an indication of taste or reason, or both" [17]. The remark is wise and timely. And it points the way to a new method of exploration for our present purpose. Concerned with "sources" we are, but not merely for sources' sake. The elucidation of Spenser's meaning is our main design. And, when decisive evidence fails us, we are entitled to illustrate that meaning by means of parallels, even though we have no proof of influence. Thus we may reach, though not the certainty of "science", at least the probability required by Plato in the realm of "opinion". For, if Spenser had read *all* the Neoplatonic treatises, as Renwick surmises [18], he must have especially cherished the authors with whom his mind and temper best agreed, and therefore borrowed more readily from them than from less congenial writers. And if he had read only a few, the number of parallels recorded should point to the books he was acquainted with. Affinities, in the first hypothesis, would especially denote the poet's own selection; in the second hypothesis, they would betray as well a high sensitiveness to external suggestions.

Whether it happened to answer best Spenser's previously formed conceptions, or whether the reading of it moulded the poet's own thinking, the commentary on the *Symposium* composed by the French humanist Louis Le Roy undoubtedly shows the clearest affinity with the Platonism of the *Faerie Queene,* and *Colin Clout.* And it probably affords the largest number of parallels. Besides, it is, in a way, an epitome of earlier commentaries on love, for it

---

superior to either form or matter, which some have maintained her to be. The latter, indeed, are rather the principles of all things, either their first causes, or first elements, but are not Nature ..."

These lines throw more light on the meaning of the Garden of Adonis or Spenser's conception of Nature in the Mutabilitie Cantos than Pico's disquisitions on the Angelic Mind and the Garden of Jove.

[16] Chaucer's *Parlement of Foules* would have called Spenser's attention, if need were, to the *Somnium Scipionis.*

[17] *E. Spenser,* p. 5.

[18] *Ibid.,* p. 165.

reproduces (without acknowledgment) passages of Ficino's *Sopra l'Amore,* Pico's *Commento* and Bembo's *Asolani* [19] — a noteworthy feature, for the lines quoted from Ficino by some critics to illustrate Spenser's portrayal of true love in Britomart had been translated by Le Roy [20]. The parallel therefore is not only vague; it is far from being unique, and yields no proof of acquaintance with the Ficinian treatise.

More interesting still is Le Roy's own selection of illustrations, for it discloses a deliberate rejection of the more abstruse and far-fetched interpretations in which Pico, and occasionally Ficino, had revelled. After giving the latter's metaphysical disquisition on Love as the youngest of the gods, he adds:

> Ceste exposition ne me satisfait pour estre trop esloignee du subject comme aussi une autre qu'admene Picus Mirandula, & me semble qu'il n'est seant d'imaginer telz songes, & rechercher de si hault les Allegories [21].

Since none of the more metaphysical notions of Renaissance Platonism have passed into Spenser's poetry, as they did into Benivieni's, Palmieri's or Nesi's [22], we may assume that, like Le Roy, he regarded the Neoplatonic First Intellect, World-Soul and other entities as mere "dreams". He was interested in mythological "fables" and myths mainly for their own sake, and must have heaved a sigh of relief with the Frenchman, when, after transcribing once more Pico's allegorical interpretation of the birth of Venus, the latter ironically declared:

> Apres tant d'Allegories nous raconterons en peu de paroles la *fable,* pour donner plus d'intelligence à ce passage [23].

Spenser and Le Roy are also at one in reading Plato in the light of Cicero, Seneca, Plutarch and both classical and Renaissance poets, rather than by the fuliginous candle of the cabalists, or in the mystical spirit of Plotinus. Le Roy quotes Ovid, Virgil and Lucan on chaos [24], Cicero on Venus, on the nature of beauty, on the contemplation of Ideas, the doctrine of reminiscence, etc. [25]. Seneca is quoted for his explanation of the theory of ideas [26], Plutarch for the presence of inhabitants in the moon [27], Theophrastus on the beauty of wisdom [27 bis], Pontanus for mythological and astronomical enlightenment. The commentator is more concerned for poetic than for philosophical agreement in his choice of illustrations. For a description of "l'ardant desir es bestes brutes",

---

[19] Le Roy, for instance, translates Pico's and Ficino's interpretations of the birth of Love and Venus. He gives a summary of Pico's exposition of the Platonic *scala* (cf. *Sympose* ff. 158 r°-v° and *Commento* ff. 64 r°-65 r°). In the Epilogue to the first Book, he reproduces Bembo's description of cosmic and civil love (cf. *Sympose,* f. 66 r°-v°, and *Gli Asolani* pp. 129 ff.).

[20] Cf. *In Convivium* II. vii. end (Jayne, p. 49) and *Sympose* f. 22 v°. Ficino's text is quoted in another connection on p. 28 above.

[21] *Sympose,* ff. 64 v° - 65 r°.

[22] On Palmier and Nesi, see Robb, *Neoplatonism,* pp. 137-59.

[23] *Sympose,* f. 63 v°.

[24] *Sympose,* f. 11 v°.

[25] Respectively ff. 23 r°; 108 v° and 171 r°; 144 r° - 148 r° and 167 v° - 68 r°. Also on virtue (168 v°; 157 r°), immortality (154 r°), intellect (152 r°, v°), and the divine origin of the soul (155 r°).

[26] *Ibid.,* ff. 144 r° - 45 v°.

[27] *Ibid.,* f. 48 r°.

[27 bis] *Ibid.,* f. 148 r°.

he refers the reader to Lucretius, Columella, Virgil, Cicero and Pontanus [28]. The mention of Lucretius, here and on other occasions, is interesting since Spenser translated the Lucretian hymn to Venus [29]. Le Roy quotes several lines of it in Bellay's translation [30].

Not only Lucretius, but Empedocles occasionally [31], and Aristotle time and again [32], are quoted by Le Roy to elucidate Plato's meaning. He shows little sense of disagreement between his authorities, and his exposition of the *Symposium,* accordingly, is far from being unalloyed Platonism. The same is true of Ficino or Pico, but whereas the latter chose Neoplatonic illustrations of a metaphysical or mystical character, Le Roy has a more naturalistic bent. He neglects the Neoplatonists and ignores the Cabalists. He quotes the physical and physiological treatises of Aristotle far more frequently than his metaphysics. On the other hand, he repeatedly brings the *Timaeus* into his exposition of the *Symposium* [33], for he considered it as "le plus accomply" of the Platonic dialogues [34]. The spirit of his commentary therefore is both realistic and (perhaps unwillingly) conservative. His interpretation of Plato has greater kinship with mediaeval Platonism, on the one hand, and Renaissance naturalism, on the other hand, than it has with the more mystical and metaphysical theories of Renaissance Neoplatonism as represented by Pico and Ficino. It is therefore best suited to illustrate Spenser's own philosophy in the *Faerie Queene* and *Colin Clout.*

Spenser's cosmogony, as I have shown, was woven out of mediaeval or Renaissance commonplaces. None of his notions therefore can be securely traced to any single author. But that Le Roy's commentary should offer them all, is, at least, noteworthy, since no other treatise, not even Conti's *Mythologia,* afford such completeness of illustration. More important still is the agreement in temper.

Among the commonplaces Spenser could have found anywhere, I list: original Chaos, the birth of Love, conceived as "the creator of the world" [35], "a natural virtue", establishing concord between the elements [36] and diffusing itself in all things [37]. But of greater interest is Le Roy's opinion on the Cupid-Venus relationship:

> Il convient disputer s'il est né de Venus, ou avec Venus: Or ont estimé les anciens Theologiens qu'Amour estait né de Vénus... [38]

Le Roy here departs from Plato (*Symposium* 178, 203). So does Spenser. Any poet would, is the reader's first thought. Not *any* poet, since Benivieni did

---

[28] *Ibid.,* ff. 113 v° - 115 v°.
[29] See *F.Q.* IV. x. 44-47.
[30] *Sympose,* f. 23 r°-v°, and appended translations. Ficino had twice mentioned Lucretius in the *Sopra l'Amore,* but only for a physiological explanation (VII. v.) and a realistic piece of advice: "how to get out of love" (VII. xi.).
[31] See ff. 29 v°; 108 r°.
[32] See 32 v°; 105 v°; 107 v°; 120 v°, etc...
[33] See 32 v°; 105 v°; 107 v°; 120 v°.
[34] *Le Timée de Platon,* sig. A ii r°.
[35] *Sympose,* f. 30 r°.
[36] *Ibid.,* ff. 11 r°; 29 v° - 32 v°. See also f. 108 r°; where Empedocles is quoted.
[37] *Ibid.,* f. 30 r°.
[38] *Ibid.,* f. 23 r°-v°.

not[39]. This is but one more proof that Spenser treated myths as myths, not as philosophy.

Le Roy's epilogue to the first Book of his commentary also deserves quotation, for, although it contains nothing but commonplaces, it presents them in compact form and in the order in which they occur in *Colin Clout*:

> Toutes les choses de ce monde dependent d'Amour, & tiennent de luy leur estre & conservation (*Colin,* 11. 841-2). En premier lieu ceste machine ronde, grande & belle n'auroit point de durée & ne pourroit consisted en son entier sans l'amitié qui est en ces parties inférieures & superieures, & qui retient les elements en concorde discordante (*Colin,* 11. 843-52). En apres si nous considerons de quantes diversitez elle est capable, combien il y a de sortes d'animaux en la terre, en l'eau & en la mer: nous ne trouverons rien qui ne se sente de l'amour, & ne recongoisse de luy sa naissance, procreation & continuation (*Colin,* 11. 853-60). Lequel s'il ne conjoignoit deux corps à engendrer leurs semblables, il ne se produiroit ny naistroit aucune chose sur la Terre (*Colin* 863-4). Le poisson cherche entre les undes sa femelle, qu'il desire, & elle d'autre part le quiert... Les oyseaux s'entre-suyvent en l'air. Les bestes sauvages se cherchent parmy les foretz (*Colin,* 865-6)[40].

I am not claiming Le Roy's epilogue as a source for Colin's speech on love: for similar claims could be made for Natalis Comes[41] and for Bembo, whom Le Roy closely follows here, though he changes the order of the arguments[42]. Yet it is worth noting that neither Comes nor Bembo afford *all* the materials used by Spenser in *Colin Clout*[43], whereas Le Roy's *Sympose* does, since the commentary preceeding the first epilogue also accounts for the mythological birth of Love (*Colin,* 11.839-40) and the lines on "the Suns life giving light"[44].

Le Roy's exposition of the *Banquet* may also have been responsible for the introduction of stanzas on the form-substance relationship in the story of Venus and Adonis told in the *Faerie Queene*. Describing the birth of living beings as the result of a love-relationship between heaven (meaning the sun) and earth (cf. *F.Q.* III.vi.6-8), he refers to Pontanus who had described the same relationship in terms of the Venus-Adonis myth[45]. Immediately after this, he adds:

> Il y a Amour de la matiere premiere ditte par Platon mere de l'univers, & nourrie de toute generation, envers toutes les formes qu'elle reçoit & entretient, l'une survenant au lieu de l'autre incessamment. Aristot. au premier de la Phisiq. chap. 8 & 9 & Plat. au Timée.

The same passage therefore may have furnished the poet with the mythological and cosmological couples upon which his imagination played in the Garden of

---

[39] See *Canzone*, stanzas III-IV; *Opere*, p. 43.

[40] *Sympose*, f. 66 r°.

[41] See chapter IV, p. 93.

[42] Cf. *Asolani*, pp. 129-32.

[43] The desire for immortality and the contrast between men and animals is not in Comes, and only implied by Bembo (p. 131). The reconciliation of the elements is not in Bembo, and the order of the arguments different, the cosmological rôle of Love as a "discordevole catena" being mentioned last (p. 132). The ideas are in Ficino's *Commentarium in Conv.*, but disconnected, and mixed with metaphysical considerations (*Comm.* II. iv; III. i-iv; VI. xi) absent in Spenser, Bembo and Le Roy. Lastly, neither Ficino nor Bembo mention the part played by the Sun in the generation of living beings — an Aristotelian idea emphasized by Le Roy (30 v° - 32 v°; 48 r°).

[44] *Colin,* 11. 861-2; cf. *Sympose,* f. 48 r°.

[45] *Sympose* ff. 31 r° - 32 v°; Pontano, "De Adonide & Venere" in his *Urania* (*Opera,* IV. 2900).

Adonis Canto: sun-earth, form-matter, Adonis-Venus[46]. Further, it may have suggested the picture of forms as transient "l'une survenant au lieu de l'autre incessamment", in contrast with the abidingness of "substance". Le Roy, like Spenser, and like mediaeval commentators on the *Timaeus,* combines the Aristotelian doctrine of immanent forms with the Platonic doctrine of intelligible forms. Lastly, his words on the ceaseless engendering of all things through love, "recevant tousiours la matiere nouvelles formes: dont ce monde demeure fourni & embelly"[47], recall Spenser's "infinite shapes" the stock of which is never "lessened nor spent", even though the argument is different (*F.Q.* III.vi. 35-6).

Le Roy and Spenser, therefore, are in full agreement in their conceptions of love as a cosmic force. But more remarkable still is their agreement on the nature of human love. Spenser, as we have seen, rejects in the *Faerie Queene* the Platonic notion of love unaccompanied by fruition[48]. To him, as to any Christian, the consummation and perfection of love between man and woman is generation[49]. But, highly susceptible to the purity and nobility of the Renaissance ideal of Platonic love, he worked out a compromise, which, on the human level, for instance in Britomart, practically identified Platonic love with virtuous love, married love[50]. It is the kind of compromise that could have grown out of Spenser's own temper without any exterior suggestion. But it is interesting to notice the same fusion of the Platonic and Christian ideal in Louis Le Roy, since he alone presents it in Spenser's manner. Among all the other Neoplatonists that the poet is supposed to have known, some condemned sexual love altogether, most condoned it, some even pronounced it good. But none of them, to my knowledge, identified Platonic love with married love[51]. Among the more orthodox Platonists, Ficino comes nearest to Spenser, yet even he fails to fuse sexual love and the higher love[52]. For he draws the line between love as a desire of generation and love as a desire of contemplation. Now, contemplation transcends itself and leads away from the beloved object to God. Thus human love, in a way, is impoverished and reduced to the desire of generation, while the more contemplative activities of the lover — visual and auditive delights — are taken up into heavenly love. But instead of a *metaphysical* distinction which cuts human nature in two, Spenser retains the religious distinction between human love and the love of God. And, within human love, he stresses the ethical distinction between "love" — the whole affection uniting sense and soul — and "lust", or mere sensuality.

---

[46] Respectively, *F.Q.* III. vi. 9; III. vi. 37-8; III. vi. 46-7. In *F.Q.* III. vi. 9, the Sun's "faire sister for creation" is the Moon, but this again was a traditional couple, introduced by Le Roy a little later, with an illustration from Pontanus: "Le Soleil & la Lune en la generation ... font office l'un de pere, l'autre de mere" (f. 48 v°). Cf. Macrobius, *Saturnalia* I. xix, ad fin. The sun und moon preside at the birth of man. The sun because he is the life-giver. The moon, because bodies are in her charge. That is why she "ministreth matter fit for creation" (III. vi. 9. 4), a puzzling phrase which led some to identify the sun's fair sister with the earth.

[47] *Sympose*, f. 64 v°.

[48] See Chapter II, pp. 35-6.

[49] The Platonic conception is, of course, retained for love between friends: *F.Q.* IV. x. 26. 5.

[50] See Chapter II, pp. 35-6.

[51] See Chapter VIII, pp. 144-6.

[52] *In Convivium,* II. vii; see chapter II, pp. 27-8.

Now, in his running commentary on the *Symposium,* often a paraphrase of Ficino, Pico or Bembo, Le Roy is rather confused. But in his own prefaces and epilogues, as well as in the general division of his work into three books, he gives a clear pictures of his design. The first two books are devoted to cosmic and human love, the third book to divine love. Since Platonic heavenly love in Le Roy's epilogue turns out to be traditional Christian love, as in Spenser, it will be considered in the examination of the *Fowre Hymnes.* For my present purpose I need only emphasize his insistence on marriage. In the first *Preface,* he makes Plato responsible for recommending married love. Addressing François II and Mary Stuart, he tells the kingly pair:

> ... j'ay mis le Sympose ou Banquet de Platon en François pour vous le presenter: estimant le subject du livre fort convenable à vostre heureux mariage, à vos aages, à vos espritz, & voluntez. Auquel il recommande *l'honneste Amour qui consiste principalement en mariage...* [54]

The identification of Platonic love — on the human level — with married love is followed, in the second *Preface,* by a warm praise of generation, grounded on God's own words "increase and multiply" so willingly echoed by Spenser [54]. He further praises the institution of marriage and moralizes on lechery [55].

If source ascription were my main concern, I could point out many more parallels [56]; suggest, for instance, that Spenser's imitation of Moschus — Venus' quest for Cupid — may have been due to Le Roy's full insertion of *L'Amour fugitif de Mosque mis en françois par Clement Marot* into his exposition of the *Symposium* [57]. But, since definite proof of influence is not available, the survey of the parallels may end here. The interest of the comparison lies in the main affinities. My contention in the preceeding chapter was that the poet played with Renaissance Platonism like a poet, in the light of Christian faith, mediaeval philosophy and popular ethics. It may satisfy those whom this interpretation of Spenser's thought may surprise, to find the same characteristics in a Renaissance commentator of Plato, who, for his dismay at Pico's subtleties, was none the less a scholar, had little reverence for the Middle Ages and was confident of human perfectibility [58].

A prominent French humanist [59], Le Roy was well known in England by the end of the sixteenth century. A translation of *Aristotle's Politiques* from

---

[53] *Sympose,* sig. a ii r°. Platonic love was commonly called "l'honneste amour"; cf. the title of La Boderie's translation.

[54] *Ibid.,* 68 v° - 69 v°.

[55] *Ibid.,* 69 v° - 71 r°.

[56] On love eldest and youngest of the gods (10 v°); on Chaos (11 r°); on love as a "fury" (12 r°; cf. *H.L.* 28) or a desire for immortality (107 r°; 120 v°; 124 v°; 126 v°). But these were Platonic commonplaces. The interesting thing is that Le Roy offers *all* the commonplaces *together* with a number of characteristics *not* found in other Neoplatonists.

[57] *Sympose,* f. 83 r° sq.

[58] See A.H. Becker, *Un humaniste au XVI*e *siècle. Loys le Roy* (Paris, 1896), p. 258 ff.

[59] Le Roy translated several Platonic dialogues (*Timaeus, Phaedo, Republic, Symposium*], Aristotle's *Politics,* and works by Demosthenes, Isocrates and Xenophon. He wrote a life of Guillaume Budé and several treatises: *Considération sur l'Histoire française et universelle de cet temps* (1562), *De l'origine et excellence de l'Art politique* (1562), *De la vicissitude et variété des choses en l'Univers* (1576). In 1572 he was appointed to a Greek professorship in the Collège Royal. He had earlier travelled in Italy, England and Germany. He died in 1577.

the French of "Loys Le Roy called Regius" appeared in 1598. Norden's elegiac poem *Vicissitudo Rerum,* published in 1600, was modelled on his *De la Vicissitude et variété des choses en l'univers* [60]. Since Le Roy found evidence of Divine purpose and of progress in change, Spenser may have been prompted to write his Cantos of Mutabilitie by the publication of an English translation as early as 1594 [61]. Yet it might be asked why the English poet should have gone to the pains of reading a French commentary on the *Symposium* when Ficino's commentary was available in both Latin and Italian versions. The objection cuts both ways. What if French was easier reading to Spenser than Italian or even Latin? Was he not the translator of Marot and Du Bellay? In early life, at least, he seems to have had a better command of the French than of the Italian language since his *Visions* of Petrarch were not translated from Petrarch's third Canzone in his *In Morte di Madonna Laura,* but from Marot's earlier French version [62]. His knowledge of Italian certainly improved when Ariosto and Tasso became his favourite reading. But the next chapter will show that he probably read Ficino's commentary *In Convivium* in a French translation. Besides, personal preference or proficiency are not alone to be considered: French works of scholarship were more easily obtainable at the time than Italian or Spanish [63]. That Spenser should have availed himself of Le Roy's commentary in preference or in addition to other works would not be surprising in the least. I do not claim influence as certain. My only claim is that Le Roy's *Sympose* is the only commentary on Plato in Renaissance literature that could have affected Spenser's inspiration — prior to the *Fowre Hymnes* — more profoundly than as a mere treasury of Platonic myths and philosophical notions [64]. It may have moulded his very conception of Platonism if he read it early. Affinities are conspicuous. Influence is at least likely.

What of the other Renaissance treaties? Influence — if not acquaintance — will be highly improbable whenever such affinities are wholly lacking. For Pico and Benivieni — apart from the *Fowre Hymnes* — J. W. Bennett herself makes only one modest claim. I do not think it can be retained [65]. The following chapters will further show how different in spirit Spenser's Platonism was from Pico's and Benivieni's even in the *Hymnes.*

The English poet certainly had more in common with Ficino than with Pico. Yet the influence of the *Commentary on the Banquet* is not distinctly traceable in his poetry prior to the *Fowre Hymnes.* The parallel on Concord offered by G. C. Smith is a mere commonplace [66]. In his interpretation of Britomart as the

---

60 Cf. Bush, *English Literature in the 17th C.,* p. 278.

61 *Of the interchangeable course of things in the whole world.* Trans. by R. Ashley. London: C. Yetsweirt, Esq., 1594. The first twelve books record all instances of change in the elements and in the revolutions of the planets.

62 See E. Koeppel's articles in *Englische Studien* 15 (1891) and 27 (1903), summarized in *Variorum M.P.* II. 616-7.

63 See Schoell, *Etudes sur l'humanisme &c.,* p. 139 *et seq.:* "il y avait plus d'Anglais sachant le français que d'Anglais sachant l'italien, et en tout cas, vers la fin du siècle, l'Angleterre semble avoir acheté plus de livres français que de livres italiens" (p. 140).

64 The only mention of Le Roy in connection with Spenser occurs in a list of possible sources given by Renwick without any comment or analysis: see *Daphnaida,* p. 209,

65 See my discussion of the parallel between the Garden of Adonis and Pico's Garden of Jove in Chapter IV, p. 75.

66 See *Variorum, F.Q.* IV, p. 330. To illustrate Spenser's idea that there is *but one soul* in friendship (cf. Cicero, *De Amicitia* XXV), Lemmi quotes a passage

embodiment of Earthly Venus. C. W. Lemmi quoted a passage from Ficino on the two Venuses as "pertinent to the inquiry". I have rejected this interpretation, but even if it should be retained, the quotation is no more than an illustration, not even a parallel [67]. Since J. W. Bennett's introduction of the Neoplatonic hierarchy into the Garden of Adonis and the *Mutabilitie* Cantos is not supported by an examination of the text, her quotations, too, become irrelevant [68].

The Neoplatonic character of Spenser's symbolism has also been urged by M. Y. Hughes, and grounded on the allegorical interpretation of the *Aeneid* by Ficino's disciple, Cristoforo Landino. The theory is attractive, but its promoter's own argument leaves room for doubt:

> In all of Belphoebe's appearances we have seen that there is something *faintly and ambiguously* recalling a scene in which Venus figures in the *Aeneid*. The ressemblances to Venus were — it is clear — *not intentional and perhaps* not even conscious, but they *may not have been altogether fortuitous.* If for any reason the Virgilian Venus was attached to Spenser's conception of Belphoebe, these strange reminiscences of her would be less mysterious. Now it is *just possible* that — in an altogether unexpected way — the Virgilian Venus *may* have hovered on the fringe of his consciousness whenever he brought Belphoebe into his story. The key to the mystery lies, *perhaps,* in the allegorical interpretation of the *Aeneid* which passed current in the Renaissance [69].

Whether Spenser knew the *Disputationes Camaldulenses,* for lack of evidence I will not dispute. If he did, the dialogues may have afforded him part of his Platonic information: poetry as a "divine fury" [70], love as the creator of the world [71], Platonic first matter or *Hyle* [72], the wheel of being [73], the distinction of two Venuses and two loves [74], and ethical commonplaces [75]. These are analogues, not even parallels. They would be of interest only if affinities in spirit were disclosed. An earlier chapter has shown that a Neoplatonic meaning should not be fastened on the allegories of the *Faerie Queene.* If Landino exerted any influence on Spenser, beyond the supply of Platonic raw materials, it can only have been through his attempt at reconciling the claims

---

from the *Sopra l'Amore* (II. viii). Ficino explains how the lover, though undergoing one death, gains two lives when he is loved in return, for he lives again in the loving contemplation of the beloved and is resurrected once more when he himself recognizes himself in his beloved. I fail to see how this applies to the deaths of Priamond and Diamond, and the transference of their souls to the *third* brother, Triamond (*F.Q.*, IV. ii. 41 ff.).

[67] See *Variorum F.Q.* IV, p. 318.

[68] *P M L A* 47, pp. 52-3, 61; and *S P* 30, pp. 162, 169.

[69] *Variorum, F.Q.* III, p. 245 (my italics). See also *P M L A* 44 (1929), pp. 696-705.

[70] *Disputationes,* III, f. XXXVII r°.

[71] *Ibid.*, III, f. XLII r°.

[72] *Ibid.*, IV, f. LVIII, f. LXXI v°.

[73] *Ibid.*, IV, f° LXXXV.

[74] *Ibid.*, III, f° XLI r°-v°.

[75] Reason-passion: *Ibid.* III, f. LII r°. Also the imagery of wings, IV, f. LXXII r°-v° and the distinction of Providence and Fate, attributed to the Platonists: IV, f. LXXIII.

of the active and the contemplative life: a Renaissance commonplace that will be given further consideration [76].

Leone Ebreo and Bembo have sometimes been mentioned in the roll-call of the Renaissance Platonists Spenser may have known, but no examination of the poet's possible debt to them has ever been attempted. Yet the *Dialoghi di Amore* and *Gli Asolani* might have deserved more attention, since they seem to have been more popular than any other treatise with the exception of *Il Cortegiano* [77]. The probable influence of the *Dialoghi* on Spenser's *Hymne of Heavenly Beautie* will be discussed at length in Chapter XI. In the earlier published poems it is not distinctly traceable.

Gli Asolani will prove of interest when the relation of earthly love to heavenly love is discussed [78]. Besides, the various views on love set forth by different speakers in Bembo's dialogue may have offered material more attractive to Spenser than pure Platonism. Perotino's oration on the bitterness of love introduced the despised lover, a prominent figure in Spenser's early poetry. The description of his woes was done after the manner of the sonnetteers. Gismondo's reply, urging the sweetness of love, only claimed that the pleasure of seeing and hearing his mistress should be a perpetual feast to the lover and rank higher than the grosser pleasures afforded by the other senses. But his idealisation of love retained a distinctly Petrarchan colouring since the lover was not invited to proceed beyond the enjoying of his lady's sight along a ladder leading up to the contemplation of the heavenly beauty [79]. Gismondo rests satisfied with an "amore umano" tempered by sweet reasonableness and contrasted with the sensual perturbations. When praising "temperance" in love he even seems to have Aristotle in mind rather than Plato [80]. Yet inspiration is found in the *Symposium* for the praise of love as a cosmic force binding all creatures and a social bond between friends, relatives and citizens. Whereas Ficino's exposition of the *Symposium* sought to bring all the orations into a single philosophical system through far-fetched allegorical interpretations and Plotinian metaphysics, Bembo clearly perceived that the orations of Phaedrus, Pausanias, Eryximachus, Agathon and Aristophanes should only be used to support a defence of love on natural or civil grounds. And this, to my mind, is the dominant view in the *Faerie Queene* and in *Colin Clout.* But even the spokesman for the truly Platonic conception of love in *Gli Asolani* will largely ignore the subtleties of the Neoplatonic *scala.* The Hermit who advised Lavinello did not rely on a process of abstraction and introversion but on the contemplation of God's handiwork to discover the "bellezza sopra ogni bel-

---

[76] In Chapter XII, pp. 208-9. Ficino had another uninventive disciple Francesco Cattani da Diacceto. His works appeared in English Libraries in the "period of Platonic poetry" (Jayne, *Comp. Lit.* 4, p. 232), but would not have brought anything new to one who had read Ficino: see Robb, *Neoplatonism*, pp. 182-3. Diacceto's only originality was to emphasize the Christian character of the Ficinian philosophy (see Tonelli, *Rinascimento,* pp. 275-6). This trend, I own, might have appealed to Spenser, but Diacceto's insistence on Divine Goodness in preference to Beauty is not reflected in the *Faerie Queene* nor in the *Hymnes.*

[77] On Leone see Chapter XI, and Savino, *Trattati d'amore,* pp. 102-4. As regards Bembo, Savino (*Ibid.,* 322-5) lists 22 Italian editions up to 1593, a Spanish translation in 1551 and a French translation in 1545. The latter had run into 8 editions by 1572.

[78] See Chapter VIII, pp. 150-51.

[79] See especially lib. II, pp. 135 ff.

[80] E adunque... naturale affetto de gli uomini nostre Amore, & per questo di necessita & buono & ragionevole & temperato" (*Asolani,* p. 117).

lezza"[81]. There are considerable divergences of opinion between Bembo and Spenser on the subject of human love[82]. Yet the former's exposition of contrasted conceptions, suffused with the earlier courtly and Petrarchan ideals, unburdened with metaphysics but indebted to Christian tradition as regards heavenly love, should have proved congenial to the poet. On the whole, *Gli Asolani* are less distinctly, "technically" Platonic than the speech attributed to Bembo in Castiglione's *Cortegiano.* Unfortunately, no clear evidence of Bembo's influence on Spenser is available up to the *Fowre Hymnes.* I have quoted part of Le Roy's Epilogue inspired by Gismondo's praise of love: whether Spenser had the original or the paraphrase in mind when he wrote *Colin Clout* cannot be ascertained, although Le Roy seems more likely[83]. To suggest a connection between Lavinello's Hermit and the Hermit of the Mount of Contemplation would be a highly dubious conjecture, for hermits have no copyright[84].

Bembo's *Asolani* have been described as "the great prototype of the courtly Neoplatonic treatise"[85]. Throughout the sixteenth century countless authors of *Trattati d'Amore* rang the changes on familiar themes[86]. To a poet who had read Castiglione, Bembo and Le Roy's *Sympose,* not to speak of Ficino and Leone Ebreo, they would bring nothing new in the way of Platonic information[87]. Their standpoint is usually more psychological and concrete; Sperone Speroni, for instance, discusses jealousy at length[88]. A later chapter will show that Spenser's attitude to human love, despite some superficial likeness, differs from the compromise worked out between Platonic idealism and the claims of the body by Betussi, Varchi and Sperone Speroni in the circle of Tullia d'Aragona[89]. In other respects a detailed examination seemed to be the less necessary as these minor writers do not appear to have been widely known outside Italy[90].

More attention must be devoted to an earlier treatise, by Mario Equicola, secretary to Isabella d'Este. Though unoriginal and uninspiring, his *Libro di Natura d'Amore* went through 13 editions from 1525 to 1589 in Italy and two different translations into French were published in Paris (1574, 1589) and in Lyons (1597, 1598). This farrago of mythological, poetical, historical, philosophical and medical information on love was widely used as a "treasury" or commonplace book by later writers[91]. Spenser, who seems to have often taken

[81] Libro III, p. 222.

[82] See Chapter VIII.

[83] For reasons stated above, p. 102.

[84] The comparison is interesting only in so far as it brings out the *essential* duality which both Bembo and Spenser recognized between even the purer love for woman and the love of God. See *F.Q.* I. x. 62. 6-9 and chapter VIII.

[85] Robb, *Neoplatonism,* p. 184.

[86] For a survey see Savino, *Di alcuni Trattati e trattatisti d'amore* (1909-14); Tonelli, *L'amore nella poesia e nel pensiero del Rinascimento* (1933); Robb, *Neoplatonism* (1935), ch. VI.

[87] After Bembo, Leone and Castiglione, Savino pointed out, the *Trattato d'amore* underwent a change becoming less philosophical and more personal: "L'amore, invece di essere oggetto di speculazione teorica, é un emanazione della vita pratica dell' autore e della sua cerchia" (X. 164).

[88] See ff. 9 v° et seq. in *Dialogi di M.S. Speroni,* ed. 1543.

[89] See Chapter VIII, pp. 142-46.

[90] Translations are not recorded.

[91] See Savino, vol. X, pp. 99 et seq.; Robb; *Neoplatonism,* p. 189.

his mythology at second-hand from Natalis Comes, may not have been above taking a hint from Equicola's encyclopaedia. Now, the *Libro di natura d'Amore* furnishes one more proof of the usual absence of any dividing-line in the Renaissance mind between the older philosophy of love and the new metaphysics of the Neoplatonists. The first book lumps together mediaeval and Renaissance "scrittori d'Amore": Jean de Meung, Calandra, Guittone di Arezzo, Boccaccio, Cavalcanti, Dante, Petrarch, Ficino, Pico the elder and his nephew, Bembo, Diacetto, etc. Throughout the six Books, syncretism prevails; not the esoteric syncretism of a scholar and a metaphysician like Pico, but the wide and undiscriminating sympathies of a Renaissance mind. Equicola himself has given a convenient summary of his eclectic philosophy at the end of his work:

> Tra le Filosofiche sette eleggemmo la Academica. La verità Christiana sempre abbracciamo, l'ordine di Aristotele, che distintamente procede, mi piaque. Platone mi insegno ornar i principii con qualche digressione... Vedrassi adunque in questa nave, benche debile, & piccola sia quanto in me è stato, Platone con Dionisio governare il timone, Aristotele con Aurelio Agostino ministrar le vele & i remi mover M. Tullio, da historici & Poeti aiutato [92].

Aristotle, Plato, Cicero, Dionysius, Augustine, the historians and the poets: such a mixture exactly suited Spenser's taste, and further opportunities of quoting from Equicola will arise in the exposition of the *Fowre Hymnes*. A clear instance of borrowing fails us once more, but the parallels are illuminating [93]. With regard to earlier poetry, it should be noticed that Equicola is at one with Conti, Le Roy and Spenser in rejecting the more metaphysical allegories to retain only the physical or ethical explanations. Describing the birth of Love from Porus and Penia, he discards the metaphysics:

> Di si alta fittione lasciamo star i sensi metafisici che Venere sia l'anima del mondo [94].

The chapter *Di Venere* emphasized all the mythological, cosmological and astrological characteristics noticed in the Venus of the *Faerie Queene*. Spenser could introduce the classical Venus, whose "delight is all in joyfulnesse, in beds, in bowres, in bankets, and in feasts" (III.vi.22) into a Canto which presented Venus as a cosmological symbol. This many-sidedness was primarily due to his poetic temperament as Lotspeich observed [95], but the eclectic attitude of the poet was countenanced by the eclecticism of compilers like Equicola, who constantly fused astrology and mythology and saw no inconsistency in addressing Venus now as "natura antichissima, madre & origine principale de gli elementi & di tutto il mondo" [96], now as the Aphrodite "laqual ami riso & giuoco; ami le notturne vigilie... de' conviti & feste ti allegri... gioconda ne i liti" [97]. This Janus-faced Venus was also described as hermaphroditic by both the Italian writer and the English poet [98]. The similarity may be due to common

---

[92] *Di Natura d'Amore*, pp. 407-8.

[93] See Chapter X, p. 177.

[94] *Di Natura d'Amore*, p. 120.

[95] *Mythology in Spenser*, p. 23.

[96] Di *Natura d'Amore*, p. 115; cf. *F.Q.* IV. x. 47. 1-2.

[97] *Ibid.*, p. 118.

[98] *Ibid.*, p. 111: "In Cipri era il suo simulacro barbato. L'une, & l'altro sesso le attribuiscono; perche senza l'uno, & l'altro sesso non si genera animale perfetto" (p. 111). That "the Poets many times speaking of the Gods, meddle the kindes together" (Castiglione, *Courtier*, p. 199) was, I own, a Renaissance commonplace.

sources, Plutarch and Macrobius, but Spenser may well have borrowed hints from a compiler who gave special prominence to the myth of Venus and Adonis [99]. Lastly, it is not uninteresting to note that Equicola offered a mainly Aristotelian exposition of ethics and psychology, and, discussing the moral virtues, numbered them twelve like the author of the *Faerie Queene* [100].

Though he must have been out of sympathy with Equicola's personal inclination "towards a utilitarian view of love" [101], if he perceived it, Spenser may owe more to the pedestrian, uninventive and syncretistic *Libro di Natura d'Amore* than he owes to the daring, novel, enthusiastic philosophy of Giordano Bruno. Yet no better opportunity for influence could be dreamt of. Bruno wrote and published his most constructive philosophical works in quick succession during his stay in England: *La cena de le ceneri, De la causa, principio et uno, De l'infinito universo et mondi, Spaccio de la bestia trionfante* in 1584; *Cabala del cavallo pegaseo* and *De gl'heroici furori* in 1585. Both the *Spaccio* and the *Heroici Furori* had been dedicated to Sir Philip Sidney, Spenser's patron and friend, and should have clamoured for attention. But I failed to detect any borrowing, and, beyond the commonplace notion of love as a divine fury, there is no real analogy between Spenser's imaginative flights up to the heavenly beauty and Bruno's strained and intense yearning to achieve intellectual illumination and self-surrendering union with the divine One [102]. As to the earlier claims made for Spenser's indebtedness to Bruno in the *Mutabilitie Cantos* and in his conception of eternal substance, they may likewise be discarded in the light of recent criticism [103]. Even the astronomy of the *Faerie Queene* was unaffected by the revolutionary theories of *La Cena* and *De l'Infinito* [104]. While claiming some influence for the *Spaccio,* Elton had wisely admitted that the poet's and the philosopher's tempers were poles apart. [105]. From the preceding pages, it is clear there were two types of Renaissance minds. The one progressive, resolutely breaking with the past in his eagerness to build a new earth and new heavens, a new social, scientific, religious or metaphysical order. The other conservative, though alive to modern ideas, interpreting the new in terms of the old, reading Renaissance theories in the light of his mediaeval inheritance. Bruno obviously belongs with the first; I have shown, and will further show, that Spenser belongs with the second.

---

[99] *Di Natura d'Amore,* pp. 107-8, quoted in Chap. IV, p. 88.

[100] Aristotle "in tutti i suoi libri morali divide le virtu in dodici morali & cinque intelletuali" (p. 77) "...I labour to pourtraict in Arthur ... the image of a brave knight, perfected in the twelve private morall vertues, as Aristotle hath devised" (*Variorum,* I, p. 167). On *Spenser's Twelve Virtues According to Aristotle and the Rest,* see the decisive evidence adduced by V.B. Hulbert (*Variorum, F.Q.* I, pp. 353-6), showing that from the time of Aquinas "there is an interpretation of the virtues of the *Nicomachean Ethics* which numbers them twelve".

[101] According to Robb, *Neoplatonism,* p. 190: perhaps a slight overstatement.

[102] Cf. P.H. Michel's Introduction to *Des Fureurs Héroïques,* pp. 42-4.

[103] As regards the Mutabilitie Cantos, Levinson's arguments (*PMLA* 43, pp. 675-78) have been refuted by Allbright (*PMLA* 44, pp. 747-9). The notion of eternal substance in *F.Q.* III. vi. 37-8, should not be traced to Bruno, but to mediaeval sources: see Chapter IV, pp. 70-3. Lastly, a parallel on friendship has been shown to be inconclusive: see C.G. Smith, *SP.* 32, p. 116.

[104] See Chapter IV, pp. 64-5.

[105] In *Modern Studies,* p. 28.

CHAPTER VI

THE DEBATE ON THE « FOWRE HYMNES » AND LA BODERIE'S TRANSLATION OF FICINO'S « SOPRA L'AMORE »

1 — THE DEBATE

Spenser's *Fowre Hymnes* have been lavishly and variously commented upon. Source-hunting has even been carried to such an extent that the danger of "flooding" the text has by now become obvious. The Platonism of the *Hymnes* has been illustrated by means of profuse quotations from Ficino, Bruno, Benivieni, Pico and Castiglione. Out of various parallels conflicting interpretations of the key stanzas within each hymn have been evolved by different scholars. But the main controversy has raged round the problem of unity of composition. The more conservative critics abide by the sharp distinction which Spenser's dedication professes to draw between earlier written profane hymns and the later compositions, meant for a recantation. Other scholars have attempted to read into the *Fowre Hymnes* a continuous and consistent exposition of the Neoplatonic philosophy of love and beauty. Of late, the contention for unity of inspiration has been boldly reversed and the three stages of Christian mysticism substituted for the Neoplatonic ladder[1]. Moreover, the major issue is further complicated by the minor, but acute controversy concerning the Christian or Platonic character of Spenser's Sapience in the fourth hymn. Suggestions of a Cabbalistic influence, as well as divisions among those who favour a Christian interpretation, have made "confusion worse confounded". One is hardly surprised that the more sober critics should have discarded as futile all attempts to pin down the poet's philosophy to any single source of inspiration. Concerning the Platonism of the first two hymns, W. L. Renwick wrote warily:

> The works of Plato were available to him with the useful Latin version of Ficino, and he was certainly acquainted with the classics of Renaissance Platonism, Ficino's Commentary on the *Symposium*, Benivieni's *Canzone d'Amore* with the commentary of Pico della Mirandola, Bembo's *Asolani*, the third book of Castiglione's *Corteggiano* translated by Hoby... There are other treatises which he may have known such as Leone Hebreo's *Dialoghi di Amore*, Sperone's *Dialogue*, Bruno's *Degli Heroici Furori*, Loys le Roy's commentary on the *Symposium*, and so on, not to mention what he would find in his Cicero. The difficulty of "sources" here, indeed, is like that of the *Amoretti*, that much

---

[1] All the theories will be fully discussed in the following chapters.

of the matter is common to several authors all of whom Spenser probably knew [2].

This is the voice of sanity. Both earlier and later critics when they indulged in source-hunting were not unnaturally tempted to thrust their own findings or "candidates" into the limelight and leave their rivals out of the picture, at best lumping them all in the background. But, in his anxiety not to overstate the influence of any single author, Renwick may have been carried to another — though safer — extreme. No one is unduly left in the background, no one unduly obtruded in isolation, but all are crowded in the foreground, as in mediaeval pictures. The canvas remains a flat one, without the proper distribution of lights and shadows, without any *perspective*. The lack of discrimination is especially felt in his pregnant essay on Spenser [3]. In his Commentary on the *Fowre Hymnes,* Ficino and Castiglione are allowed to stand out and perspective is introduced, but mainly for practical purposes and without any serious justification. The only reasons offered for the selection are that Ficino's treatise was "the most readily available" and "the best representative of the common conception of Platonism circulating among those who were not professed philosophers" [4]. It may readily be agreed that Renwick was right in giving prominence to Ficino and Castiglione, but it may be regretted that his choice was left unsupported by an appeal to internal evidence. In the following pages, an attempt will be made to supply such evidence for the direct influence of several Neoplatonic treatises on the *Fowre Hymnes*. The main task will be one of discrimination. On the one hand, the poet will be discharged of his alleged debt to Plato, Bruno, Benivieni and Pico; on the other hand, his debt to Ficino will be examined in a new light, and the influence of Leone Ebreo and other Neo-Platonists for the first time stressed and studied. All the materials that went to the building-up of Spenser's philosophy of love will be set in perspective, both according to their importance and to chronological acquisition, since a line of development has emerged from a general consideration of Platonic notions in the poet's works. Lastly, the careful sifting of evidence will make it possible to take a firm stand in the controversy concerning the dominantly Christian or Platonic character of the heavenly hymns.

But to find out the true perspective, a "perspective glass" is required. Not the glass of the critic's own bias, but the glass of Spenser's own mind. It is easy to read Plato, or Pico, or Calvin, into the *Fowre Hymnes* and put upon them each time a brand-new construction. But obviously the proper method would be to read Plato, Pico and Calvin through Spenser's own mind. We could not attempt to do it before we had discovered the bent of the poet's mind through a study of *all* his works. The safest approach to the *Fowre Hymnes* was not through any alleged "source", but through the *Faerie Queene,* through *Colin Clout,* through the *Amoretti.* Within each hymn, likewise, the safest interpretation of any stanza or group of stanzas will be reached by bringing out its significance in relation to the whole poem, rather than by fastening a "parallel" from outward upon each sentence. Spenser admittedly shows little precision in his use of philosophical terms, and when he strays into metaphysics, various

[2] *Daphnaida,* p. 209.
[3] *Spenser,* p. 165.
[4] *Daphnaida,* p. 209.

— if not contradictory — meanings can be and have been "educed" out of his words when taken out of their context — not to speak of the different parallels "superinduced". Nevertheless, even when his language is at its loosest, the poet's *meaning* is not as inconsistent as baffled critics have occasionally assumed. Provided the reader follows the chain of argument instead of focusing his attention on a single stanza or a single line, that meaning will emerge clearly enough. Only then should parallels be brought in for illustration: their choice will be guided by the meaning, once it has been ascertained in the light of Spenser's own intentions. Too many critics have been tempted to obtrude upon the poem the meaning that suited best the parallels they offered. And they were further tempted to extend their partial conclusions to the whole of Spenser's poetry. This is an inversion of the right process. Since the *Fowre Hymnes* are the last of Spenser's published poems, previously written poetry had to be interpreted first, on its own merits, and the *Hymnes* approached chronologically. A poem is a self-contained whole from an aesthetic standpoint; but neither its full historical meaning, nor its place and significance in the history of the poet's mind, can be fully revealed when it is considered in isolation. The parts are known through the whole, and no stage of development, in a living whole, has any significance apart from the whole process. The psychological and the chronological approach are linked. Once the *Fowre Hymnes* had been isolated, Benivieni's *Canzone* was read into the poems taken out of their context in the poet's mind. And once the *Hymnes* had been construed into a Neoplatonic significance, that significance was read back into earlier poetry, especially the *Faerie Queene* [5]. Inversion of the right process could not but breed perversion of the true meaning.

Although the interpretation of the *Fowre Hymnes* should not be made to rest on mere source-ascription, however likely, a bird's eye view of the whole field of debate may be obtained from the first and external testimony offered, provided any initial assumption be fully borne out by an *independent* examination of internal evidence. Before we try to edge our way through the thick growth of contending opinions, it may be wise to take a broad survey from some safe *vantage-ground*, lest we might later fail to see the wood for the trees in our plodding exploration. And once the ground has been cleared, avenues of meaning laid out and currents of thought traced back to their fountainhead, we shall again ascend the earlier "mount of contemplation", survey from it an ordered landscape and more securely meet the many challengers. For the selection of a safe vantage-ground is of paramount importance in the debate on the Platonic or Christian character of the last two hymns. Most critics, having pitched their tents either on the Christian or on the Platonic watershed, saw the stream of inspiration flowing wholly from a Christian or a Platonic fountainhead. Let us select the dividing-line for our own viewpoint: we may thence command both prospects and descry on which side the stream flows faster and fuller. That vantage-ground is offered by the Epistle Dedicatory to a translation of Ficino's *Sopra l'Amore* by Guy Le Fèvre de la Boderie.

---

[5] The process is especially clear in J.B. Fletcher's article (*P M L A* 26, pp. 452-75) on the *Fowre Hymnes*, which closes on the identification of Sapience with Gloriana (pp. 474-5).

2 — The Germ

La Boderie's translation of Ficino's *Sopra l'Amore* was first published in 1578. The work was re-issued in 1588, augmented with a translation of the first two books of Pico's *Commento* on Benivieni's *Canzone* [6]. Both editions were prefaced with an Epistle *Dedicatory* to the "Serenissime Royne de Navarre Marguerite de France." The general intention and the very themes of Spenser's *Hymnes of Heavenly Love* and *Heavenly Beautie* are so vividly called to mind by this address that it deserves close scrutiny. Not only do we find in it the usual rejection of sensual love, the "far too common theme of poets", in favour of "les plus douces et savoureuses viandes de l'âme" [7], but from the very first we meet with a deliberate supersession of Platonic love by Christian love, of Platonic philosophy by Christian dogma — an attitude which, to my mind, answers Spenser's real intention in his religious *Hymnes*. I print the relevant passages with italics of my own:

> Madame, le divin Platon duquel la memoire est celebrée en ce Banquet Philosophique, estant quelquefois interrogé jusques à quand il se faudrait arrester à ses sentences & graves enseignemens, respondit en ces termes : Jusques à tant qu'en la terre apparaisse quelcun plus sainct & plus sacré ; qui enseigne la voye de verité que tous ensuivent. Ce que Marsile Ficin autheur du présent discours a interpreté comme Oracle Prophetique se devoir entendre de *nostre Seigneur Jesus Christ qui de toute eternité a esté & est la Sapience eternelle de Dieu le Pere, & qui en la plenitude des temps par le sacré mystere de l'amour eternel & divin a voulu vestir le manteau de nostre humanité,* laquelle il a prise au Sacraire & Tabernacle de la trois fois heureuse Vierge MARIE, de laquelle le beau nom retourné ne sonne rien que AYMER.
>
> "C'est bien raison", La Boderie proceeds, "que nous *apprenions de luy plustot que de Platon,* ny de quelconque autre Philosophe *les discours du vray, sincere & parfait Amour, & le moyen de bien aymer... C'est de luy proprement, & de sa doctrine sainte, qui n'est qu'amour & charité inspirée de l'Amour mesme, qu'on doit puiser les enseignemens pour devenir vrais et loyaux amoureux.*
>
> Et veuille Dieu, que non plus en memoire de la naissance & du Trespas de Platon jadis vrayment digne, si quelque autre Philosophe l'a esté de tant honnorable tesmoignage : mais bien *en souvenance & recordation du parfait autheur d'Amour & de Vie,* se puisse à jamais perpetuer ceste louable façon de discourir, *non de l'origine d'Amour à la Platonique seulement, ny des quatre sortes de ravissement dont est faite mention en ce Traité mais de l'origine eternelle & temporelle naissance du vray Amour à la Chrestienne & de la parfaite extase & ravissement de Pensee,* par lequel les Ames fideles enamourees sont abstraites & eslevees jusques au baiser sacré du parfait Amant... [8]

After this mystical flight, La Boderie stoops for a while to a less exalted but no less essential aspect of Christian love, love to one's neighbour:

> Hommes mortels heureux si d'amour mutuelle
> Debonnaires & doux ils se vouloyent aymer.

Yet he soars again, this time to praise cosmic Love, the love God bears to his own creatures, the life and bond of the universe:

---

[6] See the titles in the Bibliography.
[7] *Discours*, sig. iiij r°
[8] *Ibid.*, sig. A ij r°, A iij r°-v°.

C'est cet Amour, ce Dieu triple en son unité
Qui par tout est diffus : l'Amour tout lie & serre,
Il meut le Ciel, le Feu, l'Air, les Eaux & la Terre,
Tout-puissant, le Repos des hommes & des Dieux
Qui confit tout en miel, & n'a rien d'odieux.

And before ending with a compliment to Marguerite, he stresses again the love relationship within the Trinity in Unity:

... *l'Amant, l'Aymé, l'Amour mesme*
Qui est le Dieu unique en trois.[9]

It will be seen at a glance that nearly all the themes of the *Hymne of Heavenly Love* are touched upon in the *Epistle*: The Trinity of the Lover, the Beloved and Love, the eternal generation of the Son, and his love-inspired Incarnation as Christ, his appeal to the answering love of man, a love to be directed first to God and next to our neighbour, and lastly the consummation of love in ecstasy[10]. Occurring in such a context, the identification of the God-Christ with the "Sapience" of the Father, otherwise a commonplace of Christian theology, takes on greater significance. If Spenser did read the *Epistle Dedicatory* of La Boderie, this stray remark is likely to have been the first seed of inspiration which grew and blossomed into the Sapience of the *Hymne of Heavenly Beautie.*

Can we prove that Spenser knew the French translation of the *Sopra l'Amore*? There is nothing, as least, to disprove it. He may have had access either to the 1578 or to the 1588 edition. Books travelled rapidly and these were handy volumes, more attractive than the heavy folios of the Latin *Opera.* We have no evidence that Spenser knew any other work of Ficino besides the *Commentary on the Banquet,* and, as I have shown, there are reasons to doubt whether he had any first hand acquaintance with the dialogues of Plato, even in the Latin translation of Ficino. If so, he is more likely to have read the *Commentarium in Convivium* in either the French or Toscan separate edition, and we know that he would not hesitate to choose the French[11].

Hoping to light upon decisive evidence, I have compared the three versions of the *Commentarium,* examining all passages clearly echoed in the *Hymne in Honour of Beautie.* Unfortunately, the Toscan and French translations keep very close to their originals, and a comparison yields a mere handful of gleanings. Nevertheless, one departure at least from both the Latin and the Toscan phrasing is of keen interest. When Spenser writes:

How vainely then doe ydle wits invent,
That beautie is nought else, but mixture made
Of colours faire, and goodly temp'rament
Of pure complexions, that shall quickly fade
And passe away, like to a sommers shade,
Or that it is but comely composition
Of parts well measured, with meet disposition. (*HB,* ll. 64-70)

---

[9] *Ibid.*, sig. A iij v° - A iiij r°.
[10] Cf. in the same order *H.H.L.* 11.29-49; 29-42; 127-47; 175-88; 190-96; 197-217; 258-288. The idea that Love is diffused throughout the creation, as a life-giving and binding power, had been developed in *H.L.* 85-98.
[11] See Chapter V, p. 105.

he is obviously echoing word for word a passage which reads in the French rendering:

> Il y en a d'aucuns qui ont opinion que la Beauté est une certaine assiette de tous les membres, ou vrayment une symmetrie & proportion avecque quelque gratieuse meslange de couleurs. L'opinion de ceux-cy nous ne recevons pas : ... La même raison nous enseigne que nous ne soupçonnions que la Beauté soit une gratieuse temperature de couleurs... [12]

Now, if we turn to the Latin and Toscan versions, we notice that the French "gratieuse meslange de couleurs" stands for "quadam colorum suavitate" and "qualche soavita di colori" [13]. Again, "gratieuse temperature" is the translation of "soavità di colori" and "colorum suavitatem". This is not unimportant since it is the only slight change of meaning introduced by La Boderie [14]. Spenser's "mixture of colours faire" is obviously closer to the French "gratieuse meslange" than to the Toscan "soavità" or Latin "suavitas". Moreover, "goodly temp'rament" may have been suggested by "gratieuse temperature". The idea of "mixing" and "tempering" do not appear in any but the French version. It might be objected that Spenser had in mind another phrase of Ficino: "elementorum quattuor temperata complexione" [15]. But it occurs in a different context: not in a definition of beauty, but in a description of the preparation required for the "informing" of matter. Moreover, there is no mention of colour. Yet I do not wish to deny that this particular phrase may have strayed into Spenser's mind as he was composing; but, if it did, it may have been through unconscious association with the word "temperature", which occurs only in the French translation.

If Spenser, as I will show, was following Ficino in the much fought-over stanza "And then conforming it into the light..." (*HB* 218), he was again closer to the French "s'y conforme" "than to the Latin" quadret & undique consonet". The Toscan "si confà", I admit, is almost identical with the French [16].

I could also have pointed out slight verbal analogies in the *Epistle* and in the fourth hymn. "Le sacré mystère de l'amour éternel et divin" [17] might have suggested the "sacred mysteries... of that faire love of mightie heavens king" (*HHB* 11.234-5). La Boderie's "ravissement de pensée" reminds us of the poet "rapt with the rage of [his] own ravisht thoughts" (*HHB* 1.1). But I place little

[12] *Discours,* V. iii, f. 68 v°

[13] *Opera,* vol. II, p. 1336. *Sopra l'Amore,* p. 91.

[14] An earlier French version of Ficino's *Commentary* by J. de la Haye did not depart from the original:

"Outre, aulcuns sont d'opinion que Beauté est une certaine situation de tous les membres, ou (affin que nous usions de leurs parolles mesmes) mesure & proportion avec quelque souefveté de couleurs". (*Commentaire*, f. XLII r°).

Besides, on several occasions, where it differs from La Boderie's version, it also differs from Spenser's paraphrase e.g.:

— *la Matiere mal convenable* (f. LXII r°) instead of *matiere inepte* (f. 102 r°) and *unaptnesse in the substance found* (*H.B.* 114)

— *convient et de toute part s'accorde* (f. LXII r°), instead of *conforme* (f. 102 r°) and *conforming* (*HB*. 218).

[15] *Commentarium,* V. vi., in *Opera* II, 1338.

[16] *Discours,* VI. vi. f. 102 r°. *Opera,* vol. II, p. 1344. *Sopra l'Amore,* p. 137.

[17] *Discours,* sig. A ij. r°.

trust in such coincidences, and think it safer to abide by the two earlier mentioned parallels.

Such evidence, I own, is slender evidence. I would not have stressed the parallels, but that Spenser, in all other borrowings, shows no clear indebtedness to any single version among the three. These mostly concur word for word. For instance, when the poet wrote "through unaptnesse in the substance fownd" (*HB*, 144), he may have had in mind either the "propter materiae ineptitudinem" of the Latin, or the "materia inetta" of the Toscan, or again the "matiere inepte" of the French version [18]. Therefore, though no absolute certainty can be reached, the odds are that Spenser used the translation of La Boderie, and the assumption that he was acquainted with the *Epistle Dedicatory* is further strengthened.

Another objection might be raised. In the sentence in which "Sapience" is mentioned, La Boderie acknowledges he is stating Ficino's interpretation of a supposed saying of Plato. May not Spenser have found directly in Ficino what I assumed he had found in the *Epistle Dedicatorie?* He hardly may, for Ficino, in the passage quoted, does not even allude to Sapience, nor to the Incarnation; the relative clause mentioning them is a development added by La Boderie. In the *De Christiana Religione* we simply read:

> Plato quoque interrogatus quatenus in praeceptis ejus quiescendum esset : traditur respondisse, quatenus in terris appareat sacratior aliquis, qui fontem omnibus veritatis aperiet, quem denique sequantur omnes [19]

Sapience is not mentioned either in the *Epistle to Marcellus*:

> Neque vero praetermittenda est aurea sententia illa Platonis academiae ducis, eatenus acquiescendum esse, dicentis, praeceptis suis, donec sacratior aliquis, quam homo in terris appareat, qui fontem omnibus veritatis aperiat, quem denique sequantur omnes [20].

In view of the conformity of the "heavenly" *Hymnes* to La Boderie's recommendations and the closeness of the profane *Hymnes* to the French translation, it might be assumed that Spenser had read Ficino's *Commentarium in Convivium* in La Boderie's version and was influenced by the Dedicatory Epistle. The granting of this assumption would have the following consequences:

1) The main source of Spenser's Platonism in the first two *Hymnes* was Ficino's treatise. This recognition deeply affects the interpretation of the controverted stanzas in the second hymn.
2) Spenser did mean a distinction to be drawn between Platonic love and Christian love, and if a structural unity is discovered in the *Fowre Hymnes*, it will be the unity of a diptych with parallel but contrasted themes on each leaf, not the continuous ascent of a Platonic *scala*.
3) Spenser must have meant the Sapience of the fourth Hymn to be identified with the Second Person of the Christian Trinity.

---

[18] *Discours* VI. vi. f. 101 v°, *Opera*, vol. II, p. 1343. *Sopra l'Amore*, p. 137.
[19] *Opera*, vol. I, p. 29. Sapience is mentioned in cap. XXXI, and in both the *De Christiana Religione* and the *Commentarium in Convivium* (VII. xviii) the word is used to denote the Second Person of the Trinity, but the identification is not *expressly* made and it occurs in a context different from the themes of Spenser's *Hymnes*.
[20] *Opera*, vol. I, p. 867.

Now, to my own mind, the evidence offered for Spenser's acquaintance with La Boderie's translation cannot, in itself, warrant any such assumption. Yet, it is of far reaching interest in itself, since it shows how the mind of a Renaissance Christian reacted to Platonism. But the full value of La Boderie's *Epistle* in connection with the *Fowre Hymnes* can only be ascertained if we deliberately leave it out of consideration for the time being. Let us turn to internal evidence with an unprejudiced eye. Should the latter reveal that Spenser did follow Ficino, rather than Benivieni, Pico or even Castiglione in the trend of his argument, should it show that the contrast between the earthly and the heavenly hymns is not the Platonic contrast between Earthly and Heavenly Venus, and leave it beyond doubt that the last hymns are dominantly Christian; should it point to the identification of Sapience with the Second Person of the Trinity, then, indeed, such a perfect agreement between *a priori* assumptions and *a posteriori* conclusions will be invested with its full significance. Then, and only then, will conviction be reached — so far as conviction is attainable in so nice a question — and the contention urged that the *Fowre Hymnes* originally sprang from La Boderie's Epistle *A la Serenissime Royne de Navarre.*

Yet the place of the *Fowre Hymnes* in the chronological development of Spenser's interest in Platonism must first be marked out. From a survey of his earlier published poetry definite conclusions have emerged concerning the character of the poet's Platonism. From an examination of his sources only tentative conclusions could be reached as to the degree of his acquaintance with the Renaissance Platonists. The results of both investigations should now be compared and brought to bear upon the present object of study, the *Fowre Hymnes,* and the initial problem that confronted us, the date of composition.

3 — The Date

I will point out presently that Spenser's mythology and cosmogony in the hymns of earthly love and beauty shows little advance on his earlier published poems. His "sources" for Colin's speech on love and the Garden of Adonis, whatever they were, could have furnished him as well with the Platonic materials needed for his account of the birth of Love and the creation of the world. With ethics, the first two *Hymnes* are not concerned beyond the ethics of love, which fall within the province of what I called, for distinction's sake, aesthetic Platonism; and Castiglione could supply them. But in the philosophy of love and beauty developed in the *Hymnes,* three things strike us as entirely new in Spenser's poetry: the definition of ideal beauty, the account of the soul's descent from its native planet to take a body on earth, and the recognition of the identity of the lover's souls through the process of abstracting and idealizing the image of the beloved (*H.B.* 64-133; 190-230). These ideas are clothed in a language of unusual technicality and for the first time, the English poet shows unmistakable indebtedness to Ficino as well as probable indebtedness to Benivieni. Two questions are raised:

> Could an early date of composition be consistent with these *facts*?
> Could an early interest in Ficino's *Commentarium in Convivium* be consistent with a late date of composition for the first two hymns?

Had the first two hymns, as they now stand, been written in Spenser's youth, we should have to assume that, after giving a full and precise account of the

Ficinian philosophy of love and beauty, the poet showed no further sign of interest in the more characteristic and refined notions of the Neoplatonic theory he had developed. It might be argued that he felt he had exhausted the subject. But Spenser was far from averse to repeating himself. Colin's speech on love must have been a paraphrase of the hymns on love and beauty, if the latter were extant. Would Spenser have deliberately left out the more metaphysical arguments? He might have done so, since the pastoral setting lent itself best to a more naturalistic description. But when the two accounts of creation are compared, it is difficult not to believe that the description of the *Hymne in Honour of Love* was an improvement upon *Colin Clout*. And if we turn to the *Amoretti*, we are struck by the looseness and generality of their occasional Platonism, in comparison with the precise notions expressed in the *Hymnes*. If we assume, on the contrary, that the Platonic sonnets herald the composition of the *Hymnes*, the whole evolution of Spenser's interest in Platonism becomes clear and consistent. The *October* eclogue of the *Shepheardes Calendar* marks the first flush of enthusiasm in a young man discovering the Platonic theories, but interested as yet in the more general notions only. He appears to have lived on these early notions, as regards "aesthetic" Platonism, throughout the six books of the *Faerie Queene*. The writing of sonnets seems to have sharpened his interest in the metaphysics of love. The foreign sonnetteers he imitated had all been Platonists to some extent. He may have felt necessary to extend or brush up his own knowledge of Plato and the Neoplatonists. And when circumstances called for the composition — or revision — of two hymns on love and beauty, he largely made them a paraphrase of Ficino's *Sopra l'Amore*, which he seems to have been reading for the purpose.

Reading, or re-reading? It is not easy to say, but a number of circumstances make a late acquaintance with the *Sopra l'Amore* at least probable. First, there is the absence of any precise parallel in the poetry written before the *Hymnes*. This is not decisive, for unmistakable echoes are rare. Yet, that Spenser, for ten or fifteen years, should have made no use of the Ficinian theories on love born of 'starres concent', or the soul's descent into the body, would be surprising if he knew them well. We must at least suppose that they had not deeply engaged his interest. And the absence of any allusion to them would be explained if Spenser relied at the time on Bembo, Castiglione and Le Roy for Platonic information. For the theories just mentioned were not developed either in *Gli Asolani, Il Cortegiano*, or Le Roy's *Sympose*. The Neoplatonic ladder, I admit, was used by Le Roy and Castiglione, and yet before the *Hymnes* its various steps were never distinguished in Spenser's poetry. But I may point out that Le Roy entirely confined his exposition of it to the last Book, devoted to the heavenly Beauty, which he identified with the Christian God. He therefore passed lightly over the first steps, giving only an inconspicuous summary of Pico's own summary of them. Castiglione's account was more likely to arrest Spenser's attention. But it was again based on Pico, and, in the following chapter, I will show that Pico's conception of the steps was not congenial to the poet, It is therefore only natural that he should not have availed himself of the Neoplatonic ladder except in vague and general terms, until he found in Ficino a description of the first steps better suited to his conception of love. The Ficinian assertion of the identity of the lovers' souls, on the contrary, with its astrological support, would certainly have attracted him. He might easily have introduced it into his Legend of Friendship. But the idea was never expressed before the publication of the *Fowre Hymnes*. Should the poet have been as yet unacquainted with the *Sopra l'Amore*, his silence would not be surprising since none of the Neoplatonic treatises he seems to have early known developed the theory of love born "of starres concent". I have failed to trace the idea in Castiglione's *Cortegiano*, Bembo's *Asolani* and Le Roy's *Sympose*. Accordingly, although no certainty can he reached, a late acquaintance with the Ficinian treatise appears probable. If so, Spenser is more likely to have used the 1588 edition of La Boderie's translation than the earlier one. The point is of interest since the 1588 edition alone included the first two books of Pico's *Commento*. The influence of Pico on Spenser has been much exaggerated of late, but the *Hymnes* seem to contain echoes of Benivieni's *Canzone*. The translation of the *Commento* appended to the *Discours de l'Honneste Amour* may have first aroused the English poet's interest in the *Canzone*. The same volume, in a way, affords the key to the Platonism of the first two hymns as well as to the Christian meaning of the "heavenly" hymns.

CHAPTER VII

PLATONISM IN THE HYMNS OF EARTHLY LOVE AND EARTHLY BEAUTY

1° — TRADITION AND PLATONISM

The previous survey of Spenser's poetry has cleared the ground for a consideration of the first two *Hymnes*. Their distinctive feature is the appearance of the Ficinian metaphysics of love. But the older Platonic materials are retained, and the poet does not discard either the traditional elements of his philosophy of love, even when they seem hardly consistent with his Platonic argument.

The pageant of Love suggested in the first *Hymne* is ultimately traceable to the mediaeval classic on love, Ovid, whose popularity was undiminished in the Renaissance [1]. It may be "reminiscent of the end of Agathon's speech in *Symposium* 197", as the *Variorum* editor suggests [2], but in its emphasis on Love's cruelty, it is more clearly reminiscent of the *Elegia Secunda* in the first book of the *Amores*, and the countless mediaeval and early Renaissance embroideries upon its themes [3]. Spenser's Love, "Victor of Gods, subduer of mankynd", is Ovidian as well as Platonic [4]. In the second *Hymne,* the final invocation to Venus offers an echo of the same Ovidian elegy

> Then *Iö tryumph,* ô great beauties Queene, (*HB* 267)
> Vulgus, *Io,* magna voce, Triumphe! canet [5]

Spenser's inheritance of the mediaeval love themes is again traceable in the lover's progress to Paradise through "paines of Purgatorie" (*H.L.*, 273-9). The

---

[1] The mediaeval writers chiefly drew upon the *Ars Amatoria*, the Renaissance poets on the *Amores*. Spenser's debt to the *Metamorphoses* in the *Faerie Queene* is well known, but his indebtedness to *Amores* I. iv. for the Malbecco-Paridell-Hellenore episode in *F.Q.* III. ix. 27-31, has escaped notice. For the signs exchanged by the lovers during the meal Upton refers to *Amores* II. v. 17-20. But the episode is clearly modelled in the *Elegia Quarta of Amorum* Lib. I, which furnished not only the exchange of signs (11. 17-26), but also the characters and "argument": "Cum amica coenaturus, monet qua arte vel praesentem virum conscia amoris mutui signa possint fallere".

[2] *Variorum, M.P.I.*, p. 510.

[3] *Amores* I. ii. See especially 11. 25 ff.

[4] *H.L.* 45. Cf. *Amores* I. ii, 1. 37: "superas hominesque Deosque".

[5] *Amores* X. ii, 1. 34.

lover in the *Romaunt of the Rose* also said "Now am I raised, at my devy, / Fro helle unto paradys" [6]. And old allegorical figures lurk in the description of "The doubts, the daungers, the delayes..." [7].

The idea that the eyes carry messages to the heart (*H.B.* 235-6), or that Cupid's darts pierce to the heart through the eyes (*H.L.* 121-6) are as old as mediaeval poetry [8]. But the introduction of a psycho-physiology of love distinguishes Spenser's account from the descriptions of Guillaume de Lorris. That psycho-physiology itself is Neoplatonic only by adoption: it was originally created by the Italian poets of the *dolce stil nuovo* [9]. As to Spenser's notion of "gentle Love that loyall is and trew" (*H.B.* 176), even when occurring in a Platonic context, it still retains a touch of Guinicelli's ideal of "the gentle heart". For truth and loyalty are ethical standards irrelevant to the metaphysical ascent in the Platonic scheme.

The power of love "all sordid basenesse (to) expell" and the complaint that he should "tyrannize" most over such as serve him best [10], were already commonplaces at the time when Dante puzzled over these thoughts:

> L'uno de li quali era questo : buona è la signoria d'amore, pero ché trae lo intendimento del suo fedele da tutte le vili cose. — L'altro era questo : — Non buona è la signoria d'Amore, pero che quanto lo suo fedele più fede li porta, tanto più gravi e dolorosi punti li conviene passare [11].

Lastly, the dramatic "frame" of the first two *Hymnes* — the poet courting an "obdurate lady and suing for grace [12] — is "Petrarchan" in the worst sense: it repeats frigidly the Petrarchan commonplaces on the "enmarbled" heart of a "rebellious Dame" or the lover's "long pyning grief", but affords none of Petrarch's subtle notations of a lover's moods.

Some of the poet's themes in the *Fowre Hymnes* have an ancestry ranging from Ovid to Petrarch, through the mediaeval Courts of Love. But it does not mean that Spenser was aware of a difference in spirit between the Ovidian, courtly or Petrarchan themes, and the Neoplatonic philosophy of Love. Just as the ideal of courtly love had survived in Petrarch and Dante, though transmuted into a higher excellence, both the Petrarchan moods and the earlier psycho-physiology of love were brought into Platonic exposition by the Renaissance commentators. I have pointed out the absence of any distinction between mediaeval poets like Jean de Meung, pre-Renaissance poets like Dante, Cavalcanti or Petrarch, and the Renaissance Platonists in Equicola's popular ency-

---

[6] *The Romaunt of the Rose,* 11. 3620-21, in Skeat's *Chaucer,* p. 37.

[7] *H.L.* 262. Cf. *F.Q.* IV. xii-xvii where they are personified.

[8] See the *Romaunt of the Rose,* 11. 2915-21, in *Chaucer*, p. 30.

[9] Cf. Kristeller, *Ficino,* p. 287. Dante's "Donne ch'avete intelletto d'amore" offers a fair parallel to *H.L.* 121-6:

> De gli occhi suoi, come ch'ella li mova
> Escono spirti d'amore infiammati,
> Che feron gli occhi a qual che allor la guati,
> E passan si che'l cor ciascun retrova.
>
> (*Opera Minori,* I, p. 76.)

[10] *H.L.* 190 ff. and 158-61.

[11] *Vita Nuova,* XIII (*Opere Minori,* I. 46).

[12] See *H.L.*, I-14; 141-154; 293-307; *H.B.* 273-87.

clopaedia of love [13]. Ficino himself had discovered an epitome of the Renaissance philosophy of love in a mirror poem by Guido Cavalcanti [14]. The author of the *De Triplici Vita* fitted the astrological lore and the psycho-physiology of his age into his exposition of the *Symposium* [15]. He associated a materialistic explanation of "vulgar love" due to a transmission of "spirits" with the doctrine of ideas and the Augustinian theory of illumination [16]. He invested with metaphysical truth and significance the poetical hyperbole of the lover's death [17], and even gave the sanction of philosophy to such time-honoured themes as the lover's grief in absence and his delight in beholding the beloved. [18]

The writers of *trattati d'amore* freely borrowed from Ficino, and often seized upon the older notions he had more or less transmuted, for they proved more familiar and attractive than the brand-new and more abstruse Neoplatonic metaphysics. Both Castiglione and Bembo discarded the Plotinian hierarchy in their courtly expositions. But Castiglione echoes the Ficinian psycho-physiology; and Bembo, who even dismissed the Platonic "steps", introduced a fair amount of Petrarchan material into *Gli Asolani.* As to the "Platonic" poetry of love in the Medici circle, it freely blended the Petrarchan and Neoplatonic themes [19]. In Benivieni's *Canzone* and Pico's *Commento* alone is Neoplatonism unmixed with other traditions.

The large amount of non-Platonic material in the Renaissance treatises on love had to be stressed since the same phenomenon in Spenser's *Hymnes,* has been described as the incorporation of *older* material, but in a wrong sense. [20] Older material from the standpoint of the history of ideas, many of his notions undoubtedly are. But it is unsafe to assume that they belong to an earlier period of inspiration, and represent fragments of earlier poems inserted into the Platonic framework of the *Hymnes.* If Spenser had outgrown courtly love and Petrarchism by the time he wrote the distinctly Platonic stanzas of the *Hymne in Honour of Beautie,* he need not have retained the older material. If he wished to emulate Benivieni's *Canzone,* he should have discarded it as irrelevant to his design. To save her Neoplatonic interpretation of the *Hymnes,* J. W. Bennett does injury both to Spenser's intellectual consistency (though her own interpretation requires it far more than any other) and to his

---

[13] See Chapter V, p. 109.

[14] *Discours,* VII. i. f. 155 v° — J.B. Fletcher's translation of the poem is reproduced in *Jayne,* pp. 239-40. From now on, page references for parallels will be given to the French translation that Spenser probably used, but the indication of Part and Chapter will enable the reader to find out the text in any edition since Ficino's chapters are very short.

[15] He fused the Socratic "daemons" and the Neoplatonic median spirits" with the "influences" of each planet. The planet Venus, for instance, is said to inspire love through Venerian daemons (*In Convivium,* VI. iii-v). Earthly love is explained by means of the psycho-physiology of his age, combining classical and mediaval notions (*In Convivium,* VII. iii-xii).

[16] *Discours,* II. viii, ff. 164 r° - 169 r°: VI. vi, ff. 101 v° - 104 v°; VI. xiii, ff. 136 r° - 137 r°.

[17] *Discours,* II. viii, ff. 29-32.

[18] *Discours,* VI. vi, f. 104. On Ficino's relation to "Amour courtois" see also W. Moench, *Die italienische Platon-renaissance,* III. 3, p. 123 ff.

[19] See Robb, *Neoplatonism,* Chapter IV. Even Benivieni's *Canzoniere* is characterized as "Petrarchan-Neoplatonic" (p. 112).

[20] J.W. Bennett, in *SP* 28, pp. 31; 35; 55.

artistic competency (which she means to vindicate), since the alleged adaptation cannot but appear "awkward" [21].

It is much more reasonable to assume that Spenser was not aware of any disharmony — whether intellectual or aesthetic — between the older" and the newer materials. Indeed, he could not have been, since he found them both in the Renaissance expositions of the Neoplatonic philosophy of love. The psycho-physiology of the *Hymnes* [22], ultimately traceable to mediaeval sources, was directly borrowed from Ficino or Castiglione [23]. The description of the lover's woes and delights is in harmony with the Petrarchan colouring of Bembo's *Asolani* in the first two orations, and parallels might be fetched as well from the *Sopra l'Amore* and the *Cortegiano* [24]. Le Roy even appealed to Ovid to illustrate the *Symposium* [25].

Though Ficino, Castiglione and the various trattatisti undoubtedly afforded the materials used in the *Hymnes,* it was necessary to emphasize the mediaeval or pre-Renaissance ancestry of these notions, for in the discussion of Spenser's philosophy of love, the fundamental question is: did he adapt the old to the new, or the new to the old? Did his adoption of the Neoplatonic theories fully inform his conception of love, transmuting the courtly and Petrarchan notions? or did the earlier inheritance command his own interpretation of Neoplatonism, to the extent of smoothing away or altering the sharper features? This is the psychological problem I will attempt to solve. And a first point has been made. In retaining themes of pre-Renaissance origin, Spenser is at one with the earlier and more conservative Platonists, such as Ficino, and the courtly and "aesthetic" Platonists, such as Castiglione and Bembo. This recognition already sharply distinguishes the Petrarchan Neoplatonism of the *Hymnes* from the pure Neoplatonism of Benivieni's *Canzone* and Pico's *Commento.* And the further remark that the Petrarchan convention furnished the dramatic framework of the first two hymns, with their personal appeal to a personal lady, not to impersonal beauty, already suggests, the adaptation of Neoplatonism to an earlier convention rather than a mere survival of the older tradition in a consistent Neoplatonic scheme. Such a process is likely to be accompanied by distortion of the new to fit it into the old.

A further point will be made in favour of the conservative interpretation when the cosmogony of the *Hymnes* is considered. *The Hymne in Honour of Love* develops the earlier account of the birth of Love and the creation of the world given in *Colin Clout* [26]. The later description is more clearly indebted to the *Symposium* and its commentators. But Natalis Comes might have supplied the mythology as well as Ficino. Spenser paradoxically introduces the Porus-Penia myth while retaining his favourite conception of Love as the son of Venus: in this he may have been influenced by Comes, as Lotspeich argued [27].

---

[21] *S P* 32 (1935), p. 151.
[22] *H.L.* 120-7; *H.B.* 71-2; 232-45.
[23] Ficino, *Discours,* VII. 4, f. 167 r° — R.W. Lee, in *P.Q.* 7 (1928), p. 69, quotes as Spenser's immediate source Castiglione's *Courtier* (*Everyman,* p. 247).
[24] Lee (pp. 70-71) quotes Castiglione's *Courtier* on *H.L.* 127-33 and *H.B.* 246-52 (See *Variorum M.P.* I, pp. 516, 536). The same themes had been handled by Ficino in his description of the "passions of lovers": *Discours,* VI. vi. ff. 112 r° - 120 r°.
[25] *Sympose,* f. iii r°.
[26] *H.L.* 50-98. *Colin,* 839-63.
[27] See *Mythology,* p. 101.

And although the idea was a commonplace, Le Roy may have suggested the lines on Love:

> ... elder then thine owne nativitie;
> And yet a chyld, *renewing still thy yeares;*
> And yet the eldest of the heavenly Peares.
> (*H.L.* 54-6; my italics)

The French humanist had rejected the highly metaphysical interpretations of the paradox propounded by Ficino and Pico, giving a simpler explanation of his own, with which Spenser's lines agree:

> Amour est tousiours jeune pour ce que les choses jeunes par son moyen, sont incessamment engendrées [28].

The important fact is that Spenser deliberately steers clear of metaphysical implications and does not even hint at the Neoplatonic significance of the myth, clearly marked by Benivieni and laboriously worked out by Pico in his *Commento* on the *Canzone* which Spenser has been supposed to emulate [29]. He shares Le Roy's distrust of far-fetched allegories. It should be noted, too, that Natalis Comes, in his interpretation of the birth of Love, has dismissed the Porus-Penia myth as relevant to ethics rather than cosmogony [30]. The metaphysical allegory, he ignored altogether, and he must have taught Spenser to read into such "fables" a physical or moral meaning only. Le Roy's distrust of excessive subtleties, his naturalistic tendencies [31] could only confirm the poet in his rejection of the Neoplatonic allegories. Instead of the descent of the Ideas into the Angelic Mind and the raying down of beauty, awakening love, through a series of emanations, we have here, as in Natalis Comes a "myth" followed by a physical description of Love ordering chaos [32]. Spenser modifies his earlier account of creation in *Colin Clout* on two points: when he describes Love borrowing light from Venus, and the reconciliation of the elements. [33] The part played by Venus, as J. W. Bennett suggests, paves the way for the *Hymne in Honour of Beautie* [34], and the Platonic Venus, or Idea of Beauty, is clearly intended. Here, and here only, Spenser may have taken a hint from Benivieni who said that Love always followed the light of Venus [35]. But he adapted the idea, if he did borrow it, to his own physical account of creation. In the latter, Love, which in *Colin Clout* was described as a natural force inherent to the elements, takes on the character of a transcendent power "compelling" the elements. The reason for the change is in part artistic; Love is personified, as Beauty will be, both being balanced against the central figures of Christ and

---

[28] *Sympose,* f. 64 v°.

[29] By J.B. Fletcher and J.W. Bennett. See the so-called parallels in *Variorum M.P.* I, pp. 509-12. See also Benivieni, *Opere,* ff. 42-3, 52-5.

[30] *Mythologia,* p. 408 "... quod de Poro & Penia *fabulose* dicitur... etsi potest ad has ipsas res accomodari, tamen ad mores magis videtur spectare".

[31] His explanation of the Platonic myth is followed by a physiological description of generation, taken from Aristotle, the *Timaeus* and Hippocrates (*Sympose,* ff. 105 v° *seq.*). Physics, thoughout his illustrations, bulks larger than metaphysics.

[32] *H.L.* 57 ff. Contrast Benivieni, *Canzone,* sts. iii-v, in *Opere* ff. 42-43, and Ficino, *Discours* I. ii, ff. 3-8; VI. vii, ff. 104 v° - 109.

[33] *H.L.* 70-74; 78-91.

[34] Bennett, *S P* 28, p. 30.

[35] *Canzone,* st. iv.; *Opere,* f. 42 v°.

Sapience in the last two *Hymnes*. But there is also a strong suggestion of the activities of the Demiurge in the *Timaeus* [36]. The lines on Love taking the elements "and tempering goodly well Their contrary dislikes with loved meanes" may allude to the Platonic idea that God joined the elements by introducing "means" — that is water and air — between the extremes of earth and fire. Spenser's insistence on the indissoluble order of the elements thus "Together linkt with Adamantine chaines" (*H.L.* 87-89), may also be reminiscent of *Timaeus* 32 b-c [37].

The *Timaeus* again is responsible (ultimately at least) for the second account of Creation:

> What time this worlds great workmaister did cast
> To make al things, such as we now behold,
> It seemes that he before his eyes had plast
> A goodly Paterne to whose perfect mould,
> He fashioned them as comely as he could, [38]

Neither account of creation, therefore, would have struck a mediaeval poet like Jean de Meung as something new. He had combined them when he versified the *Timaeus* in the *Roman de la Rose*:

> Cil Deus qui de beautez abonde,
> Quant il trés beau fist ce beau monde,
> Don il portait en sa pensee
> La bele fourme pourpensee
> Toujourz en pardurableté
> Ainz qu'ele eüst dehors esté.
> Car la prist il son essemplaire,
> E quonque li fu necessaire;
> ....
> E le fist au comencement
> Une masse tant seulement,
> Qui tout iert en confusion,
> Senz ordre e senz distinction.

The French poet went on to speak of: "La bele chaeine doree Qui les quatre elemenz enlace..." [39]. But he would have been horrified at the vagaries of Spenser's imagination:

> That wondrous Paterne, wheresoere it bee,
> Whether in earth layd up in secret store,

---

[36] It should be noted that the transcendent activity of a Demiurge is not required by Ficino's conception of love as an immanent force drawing like to like (*In Conv.* I. xi).

[37] *Opera Platonis*, f. 254. I translate: "But as the world was to be solid and as solid bodies are always joined, not by one mediate body, but by two, the god set air and water between fire and earth and as far as could be done, paired these elements with each other in the same proportion, in order that air should be to water what fire was to air, and water should be to earth what air was to water. Out of which conjunction the world was so framed that it became visible and tangible. In that way was the world's body fashioned out by means of four things assembled in proportion as I said. Wherefore, united by friendship, it makes up one whole and holds together so aptly that it cannot be dissolved but by him who first bound it together."

[38] *H.B.* 29-33. Cf. *Timaeus* 28-9, a *locus classicus.*

[39] *Roman*, 11. 16728-16787.

Or else in heaven, that no man may it see
With sinfull eyes, for feare it to deflore,
Is perfect Beautie which all men adore, (*H.B.* 36-40)

Commenting on these lines, a scholar writes:

> On one point he [Spenser] diverges from the Platonic to the Neoplatonic. Plato makes Beauty one of several archetypal Ideas. Spenser, like Pico, and the Renaissance Platonists generally, makes it the sum of the Ideas [40].

Whether Spenser diverged from Plato, or agreed with Pico, is no doubt a profound issue, but we hesitate to fathom the depths of his meaning when we stoop to notice that our sage and serious poet suggests that the Idea of Beauty may be "in earth layd up in secret store". Besides, if we read further down, we find the description of the raying down of Beauty strongly reminiscent of the current astrological conceptions attributing "influence" to the stars [41]. And the "bright starre" of the Cyprian Queene is not the Intellectual Sun of Beauty, but either the visible sun or the planet Venus [42].

The cosmogony of the *Fowre Hymnes* therefore calls for two observations. First, it is very largely made up of commonplace notions, some of which were borrowed from the *Timaeus* (or its mediaeval and Renaissance commentators), while others are traceable to the *Symposium,* read in the light of Natalis Comes and Louis le Roy rather than in the spirit of Pico, Ficino standing half-way. Secondly, though he never so much as suggests the Neoplatonic scheme of emanations, the poet gives a fuller and more distinctly Platonic description of Venus, conceived as Heavenly Beauty, than he had done heretofore, but his treatment is loosely poetical. It looks as if Spenser could handle Platonic notions of mediaeval inheritance with tolerable accuracy as in the first part of his exposition of creation according to the *Timaeus,* but lost all precision and consistency when he drew upon Renaissance Neoplatonism. The reason is fairly obvious: the older notions, played upon time and again by poets and commentators, must have been familiar to Spenser from his youth; they were polished by long use and they would fit of themselves into the poet's still mainly mediaeval frame of mind. The newer notions had still to be digested.

I have traced in the Platonic *Hymnes* Spenser's continual allegiance to mediaeval love-conventions and mediaeval cosmogony. In the poet's ethics of love, too, the sway of a tradition older than Renaissance Platonism is apparent.

---

[40] Bennett, *S P* 28, pp. 31-2.

[41] Spenser uses the astrological term of "influence" (*H.B.* 44). "Infusion", "spirits", also point to the physical virtue of a star (*H.B.* 50-2).

[42] *H.B.* 55-57. The "bright starre may be the sun, since the sun, source of light and "Lively spirits" (cf. "lifefull spirits, 1.52) is later spoken of as "that fayrest starre" (110-12). On the other hand Equicola had described the "star" of Venus (*Di Natura d'Amore,* 109) and "reverently saluted it (*Ibid.*, p. 117). He had declared it to be, not only the largest star, but "da suoi cognomi emula del sole & della luna" (*Ibid.*, p. 109). That star might well pour "lifefull spirits" since "par la natura di questa ogni cosa si genera in terra". I believe Spenser fused the Sun and its "emulator", Venus or Lucifer, into the "bright starre" of "Beauties Queene", no more minding the contradiction than when he telescoped into one the two myths on the birth of Cupid (*H.L.* 52-3). The Planet Venus seems to be uppermost in his mind in *H.B.* 50 ff., but the star "which lights the world forth from his firie carre" can hardly be anything but the sun (112). Light to Spenser is the cause of beauty: see Ch. XI, note 54.

The desire for immortality in man and beast was a Platonic commonplace, developed by all Renaissance commentators, and particularly emphasized by Le Roy [43]. But the contrast between the kinds of immortality achieved looks like a variation of Spenser upon the usual theme [44]. Had he followed the Renaissance interpreters, he would have contrasted the immortality attained through propagation of the species with the immortality conferred by the productions of the mind or the love of virtue [45]. Le Roy had devoted pages to that typical ambition of the Renaissance man: "laisser memoire eternelle" [46]. But Spenser's lines can hardly be construed into the like meaning:

> Thereby they all do live, and moved are
> To multiply the likenesse of their kynd,
> Whilest they seeke onely, without further care,
> To quench the flame, which they in burning fynd:
> But man, that breathes a more immortall mynd,
> Not for lusts sake, but for eternitie,
> Seekes to enlarge his lasting progenie. (*H.L.* 99-105)

On this, Renwick quotes Ficino:

> Dimandate voi che cosa sia lo amore degli uomini, & a che giovi : egli è appetito del generare nel subbietto bello per conservare vita perpetua nelle cose mortali. Questo è lo Amore delli uomini viventi in Terra [47].

Renwick adds: "It will be noticed that Spenser does not go beyond this". That he did not go beyond this in *Colin Clout* is certain [48]. And the next stanza shows that he had still in mind his earlier argument; the contrast between mere lust, and love awakened by "Beautie, borne of heavenly race". But this is insufficient to justify his assertion that man seeks to enlarge his progeny "for eternitie", as well as his insistence on man's "immortal mynd". The latter ideas would rather point to immortality achieved through the mind, but for the parallel insistence on "progenie". Did Spenser fuse — and confuse — two contradictory notions, as in his account of the birth of Love? I believe the explanation lies in an unnoticed parallel afforded by the *Epithalamion*:

> And ye high heavens, the temple of the gods,
> ....
> Poure out your blessing on us plentiously,
> And happy influence upon us raine,
> *That we may raise a large posterity,*
> Which from the earth, which tney may long possesse,
> With lasting happinesse,
> Up to your haughty pallaces may mount,
> And for the guerdon of theyr glorious merit
> *May heavenly tabernacles there inherit,*
> *Of blessed Saints, for to increase the count.* [49]

---

[43] See *Sympose,* ff. 107 r°, 120 v°, 124 v°, 126 v°.
[44] The contrast itself is in the *Symposium* (208). See Winstanley's quotation in *Variorum M.P.* I, p. 514.
[45] *Symposium,* 208-9.
[46] *Sympose,* ff. 124, v° - 126 v°.
[47] *Daphnaida,* Commentary, p. 215; *In Convivium,* VI. xi.
[48] *Colin,* ll. 863-70.
[49] Ll. 409-23; *Variorum M.P.* II. 252 (my italics).

The *Epithalamion* and the *Hymnes* were fairly contemporary in composition, and I believe Spenser implicitly introduced the Christian idea of immortality into the first hymn. Man "seekes to enlarge his lasting progenie", that is, to give birth to more souls, more "immortall mynd(s)". And he does so "for eternitie", not merely to perpetuate his species on earth, for brutes do it as well, but "of blessed Saints for to increase the count". Thus, at the very heart of Spenser's Platonism lurks a Christian ideal, quite irrelevant to the Platonic conception of immortality.

Again, Spenser's treatment of the heroism inspired by love into the lover's breast, though perfectly in agreement with the *Symposium* and its commentators [50], is strangely reminiscent of the chivalric ideal in spirit and language:

> Then forth he casts in his unquiet thought,
> What he may do, her favour to obtaine;
> What brave exploit, what perill hardly wrought,
> What puissant conquest, what adventurous paine,
> May please her best, and grace unto him gaine. (*H.L.* 218-222)

It may be noted incidentally that the poet includes Orpheus among the noble lovers, whereas Plato had waived him aside disparagingly [51]. Critics have not observed that Ficino silently placed Orpheus with the other types of true love [52], while Le Roy showed surprise at Plato's blame, and for once dismissed his usual distrust of far-fetched allegories in an attempt to rescue Orpheus from condemnation [53]. This suggests that Spenser followed the commentators, siding with them against Plato's own words.

Spenser's praise of the ennobling power of love, a Renaissance commonplace, with pre-Renaissance as well as Platonic origins [54], becomes distinctly Platonic in formulation when the process of abstraction and the mirror image are introduced (*H.L.* 190-97). But it is characteristic of the ethical outlook of Spenser, that the contrast stressed time and again in the *Hymnes* should be the contrast between "loiall" love and "disloiall lust" [55]. Had he been a Platonist at heart, he would have insisted on the distinction between the gross pleasures of touch — or sexual love — and the pure delights of sight and hearing: a distinction which made no call on the personal "loyalty" of lover to lover [56]. The fact is that both the earlier chivalric ideal and the Christian ideal of married love inform his very apprehension of the Neoplatonic philosophy of love and beauty.

I have traced as yet in the *Fowre Hymnes* only such features as recall Spenser's treatment of Platonism in the poetry written before he became interested in the more metaphysical notions of the Platonic "scala". These notions he will now develop, chiefly in the *Hymne in Honour of Beautie,*

---

[50] See *Variorum, M.P.* I. 518-9.

[51] *Symposium* 179 d.e. Previously noted by Winstanley and Renwick (*Variorum, M.P.* I. 518-9).

[52] *In Convivium,* I. iii; *Discours* ff. 10-12.

[53] *Sympose,* f. 15.

[54] See for instance Guinicelli's *Al cor gentil,* and Dante's *Vita Nuova* quoted above, p. 122.

[55] *H.B.* 176, 170.

[56] On this distinction, see Ficino, *Discours* V. ii, ff. 64 v° - 66 r°; Castiglione, *Courtier,* pp. 304-7; Bembo, *Asolani,* p. 147.

borrowing them mainly from Ficino. But the preceding pages have made it clear that the poet's mind would be propossessed by earlier notions, earlier convictions, earlier emotional tendencies. They further showed that the notions of Christian and mediaeval inheritance were rooted in the deeper layers of the poet's sensibility. Whether Renaissance Platonism went so deep, there will be further occasion to debate. The examination of the Neoplatonic stanzas, defining spiritual beauty and retracing the soul's descent into the body, as well as the birth of love in the lover's mind, should throw some light on the subject since they take us to the core of the Neoplatonic doctrine.

2° — FICINO AND OTHER SOURCES

Recent interpretations of the first two *Hymnes* have been commanded by the assumption that Spenser intended to reproduce the Neoplatonic *scala* described in Pico's *Commento* and Castiglione's *Cortegiano*. But no agreement has been reached on the number of degrees ascended. The key-stanzas of the *Hymne of Heavenly Beautie* have been variously interpreted as marking the attainment of the second, third, fourth and fifth steps. [57] My own contention is that Spenser was little preoccupied with the "steps" of either Pico or Castiglione for a twofold reason: 1) the Platonic ladder was not congenial to his mind and temper and 2) he closely followed a chapter of Ficino which did not imply the notion of ascent. As usual, I will draw my arguments from a consideration of the text and I will not attempt to read parallels into the poem before the poet's own intention has been ascertained.

Much comment has been spent on the stanzas of the second Hymne describing the abstraction and idealization of the image of the beloved in the lover's mind. Unfortunately those three formidable stanzas have often been considered in isolation of both the preceding and following stanzas. Once we have noticed that the chain of argument is continuous from:

> But in your choice of Loves, this well advize,
> That likest to your selves ye them select,
> The which your forms first sourse may sympathize, (*H.B.* 190)

down to:

> Which seeing now so inly faire to be,
> As outward it appeareth to the eye,
> And with his spirits proportion to agree, (*H.B.* 225)

we perceive that the emphasis throughout is on the *identity of the lovers' souls*. The description of the process of abstraction is incidental or parenthetical. It is introduced to explain how this identity comes to be recognized. Now, this is exactly the trend of argument followed by Ficino in a chapter of his *Commentary on the Banquet*. The parallel has been noticed by Harrison and Winstanley [58]. But since later emphasis on Benivieni, Pico and Castiglione has unduly overshadowed the influence of Ficino, it is necessary to re-assert it.

---

[57] Respectively by Renwick (*Daphnaida*, pp. 210-11), Bennett (*SP* 28, pp. 18-48), Lee (*P.Q.* 7, p. 7), Fletcher (*M P* 7, p. 557). Padelford (*S P* 29, p. 212) finds that "the third and fourth steps are thus treated as one".

[58] Harrison, *Platonism*, pp. 115-16: Winstanley, note on the *H.B.* 183-238.

Let us keep out of mind for the time being the "steps" of Pico, which have been read into the second *Hymne.* Here are the "arguments" we discover in Spenser's own relation, exactly parallel to Ficino's account:

1. — Those only love each other, whose souls were born under the same planet[59].
2. — Therefore the cause of love is not beauty alone[60].
3. — But the true lover, "abstracting the image of the beloved", conforms it to the "idea" that originally informed his own soul, and, beholding the image "fashioned" accordingly, he now admires in fact a reflection of his own "idea"[61].
4. — This image he perpetually holds in his imagination counting it fairer than it is indeed (=than the lady is), yet no fairer than the "idea" informing the soul of the beloved actually is[62].

This is a perfectly clear, continuous and straightforward argument. There would be no difficulty but for apparent echoes of Benivieni, Pico or Castiglione in the stanzas amplifying the process of abstraction and idealization. I will not attempt to decide which — if any — Spenser was following. One thing is clear: he did not go beyond the second step. The formation of a concept of universal beauty out of various beauties is nowhere stated nor even suggested, whereas it is essential to the third step, not only in Castiglione, but also in Benivieni and Pico[63]. The fourth step does not appear either. When Spenser

---

[59] *H.B.* 197-203, *Discours* VI, V (fol. 101); souls "ayment souverainement les hommes qui sont nez soubs les Estoilles mesmes".

[60] *H.B.* 204-210: "For all that like the beautie which they see streight do not love..." (208-9).

Discours, VI. vi. (fol. 102 r°, v°) "Dont il advient que chacun aime principalement, non quiconque est très beau, mais aime les siens, je dy ceux qui ont eu nativité semblable..."

[61] *H.B.* 221-224. *Discours*, VI. vi. (fol. 102 v° - 103 r°): "... ceux qui sont nez sous une mesme estoille sont disposés en telle manière que l'*image du plus beau d'entr'eux entrant par les yeux en l'âme de cest autre s'y conforme entièrement avecques une certaine image formée dès le commencement de la génération* tant au voile céleste de l'âme comme au sein de l'âme. *L'âme de cestuy ainsi frappée, recognoist comme chose sienne l'image de celuy qu'elle rencontre:* laquelle est presqu'entièrement telle qu'elle la contient en soy-mesme dès le commencement et qu'elle avoit ja voulu l'engraver en son corps, mais elle n'avoit peu. *Laquelle soudain elle fiche en son image intérieure et si quelque partie luy manque et defaut reformant elle la rend meilleure* à la parfaite forme du corps jovial [in the instance chosen, the two souls had descended on earth "in the reign of Jupiter"]. *Et depuis ayme cest image ainsi reformée, comme son ouvrage propre...*" (my italics). To avoid ambiguity the image formed both in the celestial body and in the inner part of the soul from the beginning of generation will be called throughout "idea". Ficino calls it so when he speaks of an image "remade by the soul according to the likeness of its own Idea", *ad ideae suae similitudinem* (VI. vi; Jayne, pp. 82, 188; see also note 62).

[62] *H.B.* 225-31 *Discours,* VI. vi (103 r°): "... de là vient que les amants sont tant engainez et trompez, qu'ils jugent la personne aymée estre plus belle qu'elle n'est. Parce qu'à trait de temps ils ne voyent point la chose aymée en la propre image parcette par les sens, mais ils la voyent en l'image ja formée de leur âme à la semblance de leur Idée."

[63] See Castiglione, *Courtier*, p. 317. Benivieni, *Canzone* ll. 123-26. Bennett's contention that universalization was not required by Pico cannot be retained in the face of such clear evidence as the following:

"El terzo grado è quando l'anima nostra... ne *piu à la propria imagine di uno solo corpo, ma alla universale bellezza di tutti i corpi insieme* si volge" (*Commento*, III. x; Benivieni, *Opere*, f. 64.)

"*... et multitudine di tutti e particulari corpi begli nella unita della bellezza in se reduce...*" (*Ibid.*, III. x, fol. 71 r°; my italics).

describes the lover as fashioning out of his idea of the beloved "*An* heavenly beautie to his fancies will", he cannot mean *the* Heavenly Beautie for two reasons:

— (1) The article "an" points to the apprehension of beauty in a particular, not in a collective or universal object.

— (2) This beauty is still apprehended in the "fancy" or "fantasy". If Spenser is speaking with any degree of precision, this means that we have to do with an "image" as in the second step, not with a pure "idea" as in the third and fourth steps [64]. Spenser simply means that the lover fashions out of the image abstracted a more perfect image agreeable to his own idea, the image of "an heavenly beautie".

If we turn to Benivieni, we observe that the conclusion of the whole process described by Spenser has its counterpart in the Canzone *before* the third step is taken:

> Indi qual'hor dal sol ch'en lei ne sculto
> Scende nell'altrui cor l'infusa stampa
> Seglie conforme advampa
> L'alma qual poi ch'ense l'alberga assai
> Piu bella à divin rai
> Di sua virtu l'essinge, & di qui nasce
> Ch'amando el cor d'un dolce error si pasce [65].

We have already reached Spenser's twofold conclusions

> The mirrour of his owne thought doth admyre
> ....
> Counting it fairer then it is indeede... [66].

I agree the earlier lines "And then conforming it unto the light..." may echo Benivieni's language: "Talhor voi reformando, Quell'al lume divin che'n lui n'impresso..." [67]. But Spenser's lines cannot have been meant to denote Pico's third step, unless he was putting the cart before the horse. Either we must believe with Professor Padelford that the poet was thinking very loosely indeed, or we must admit that he was using the language of Benivieni to express the

---

[64] Cf. Ficino's account of the formation of images, in the same chapter:

"... Mais l'âme estant presente à l'esprit en toute partie, voie légèrement *les images des corps reluisants en l'esprit ainsi qu'en un miroir...* Et pendant qu'elle y *regarde, par sa vertu elle conçoit en soy images semblables à icelles, et encore plus pures.* Et telle conception se nomme *imagination*". (*Discours* VI. vi, fol. 103 v° - 104 r°.

[65] *Canzone*, 11. 102-10, 43 r°, I give Fletcher's translation in *MP* 8, 545-68:

> Whence sometimes from the sun that in her shines
> Into other heart sinks her imprinted form,
> There, if well-matched, to warm
> The soul that meetly lodging it displays
> It fairer in the rays
> Of her own potency, whence is decreed
> That loving hearts on a sweet error feed.

[66] *H.B.*, 11. 224, 280.

[67] *Canzone*, ll. 111-12; f° 43 v°.

notions of Ficino [68]. In either case, it implies that he was not primarily interested in the steps as nicely distinguished by Pico.

This should have been expected, for Pico and even Benivieni described the process of "enamoration" from a metaphysical standpoint, whereas Spenser was much more intent on the *psychological facts,* as they were experienced by the lover. Now, in the chapter under consideration Ficino shows an understanding of human nature. In returning to "fleshes frail infection" after flapping his wings for a flight to higher beauty, the poet is countenanced by the shrewd psychology of the philosopher. It has not been observed that the falling-off from the pitch of Platonic idealism in the closing stanzas has a counterpart in the *Sopra l'Amore.* Since Spenser was in the main following Ficino's argument he need not be branded with inconsistency; nor need we assume any "incorporation of older material", however inferior in thought the remaining stanzas may appear. After explaining how the lover deceives himself while beholding, not the image of the beloved, but the image already printed in his own soul, Ficino whose purpose, like Spenser's, is to describe the psychological processes of love, goes on to explain why the lover cannot rest satisfied with the ideal image, but craves the presence of the body whence it was abstracted:

> Ils désirent aussi continuellement voir ce corps duquel ils ont prinse telle image. Car bien que l'âme (encore qu'elle soit privée de la présence du corps) en soy neant moins conserve l'image d'un tel: & bien que quant à elle elle luy soit à suffisance: toutefois les esprits et les yeux qui sont instruments de l'âme, ne conservent pas telle image... Donques à l'âme conservant l'image de l'homme beau (je dis l'image en elle une seule fois conceue) & l'ayant reformée suffiroit bien d'avoir veu quelquefois la personne aymée. Néantmoins à l'œil & à l'esprit est requise la perpétuelle présence du corps extérieur, afin que par l'illustration d'iceluy continuellement ils s'illuminent, se confortent, se délectent. Lesquels comme miroirs prennent l'image par la presence du corps et par l'absence la délaissent. Ceux-ci donc par leur pauvreté cherchent la présence

---

[68] Acording to Ficino, each soul receives from God a "seal" or "ratio" (*Discours* V. v, fol. 74 v°), an inner "form": "Ce ray divin infond en l'ange et en l'Ame la vraye figure de l'homme qui se doit engendrer toute entière...". On coming down to earth, the soul assumes an ethereal body and engraves on it a *second* figure, similar to the first "seal" and agreable to its native planet (*Discours* VI. vi, fol. 101 v°). Finding on earth a "well-tempered seed" (cf. *H.B.* 114), the soul engraves on it a *third* figure sometimes distorted *propter materiae ineptudinem* (cf. *H.B.* 144).

In the light of this account, I would thus explain the controverted stanzas. The "more refined form" is the image of the *third* figure, conceived in the fancy, and already purer than the sensuous image carried by the spirits (cf. quotation in note 64). This image is "reduced to her first perfection" that is, to the perfect image the soul had striven to engrave on its body. But it, is still an *image,* not an *idea:* otherwise, the poet need not have added that it was free from "fleshes frayle infection". This image, corresponding to the *second* figure is then conformed to the light "Which in itself it hath remaining still Of that first Sunne", that is to the spark it retains of the divine beam ("ce ray divin") which had imparted to the soul its first "seal" or "inner form", laquelle nostre âme a prinse de l'Auteur de tout, et la *retient en soi*" (*Discours*, V. v, fol. 74 v°). Ficino had spoken of this form as "l'estincelle de l'ornement divin" (*Discours* V. v, fol. 74 r°). Now, this inner form is the idea of the beloved identical with the lover's own; and the *image* of the beloved, still retained in the lover's *fancy,* is fashioned and perfected according to this *idea.* This is not a step from one beautiful image to the concept of universal beauty, but the perfecting of an image in the light of the individual idea of the lover's soul, that idea being itself a spark of the divine.

du corps et l'âme le plus souvent leur voulant servir est contrainte désirer icelle mesme [69].

Since Ficino recognized the claims of the eyes as well as of the soul, it was natural for Spenser to end the poem, as the chapter of the *Sopra l'Amore* ends, expressing the delight with which "lovers" eyes" feed on the "sweete aspect of the beloved" [70].

Not only is Spenser's description of the process of "enamoration" clearly based on Ficino, but the *Sopra l'Amore* seems to have afforded all the Platonic notions for the first time used by the poet, excepting only stray echoes of Benivieni's *Canzone.* Moreover, throughout the first two *Hymnes,* despite the cosmological or metaphysical framework, the feeling is focused on a human object, the poet's main concern being to show the power of love and the power of beauty, or "in what way men are captured by love" [71], not in what way they ascend from a lower to a higher love, from sensible to intellectual beauty.

In the first *Hymne,* the stanza describing how love

> ... the refyned mind doth newly fashion
> Unto a fairer forme, which now doth dwell
> In his high thought, that would it selfe excell;
> Which he beholding still with constant sight,
> Admires the mirrour of so heavenly light. (*H.L.* 192-6)

has been taken for a prelude to the second *Hymne* and the first step of the Platonic ladder [72]. This would be awkward since the first step is again described in the *Hymne in Honour of Beautie* (11.211-15). In fact, the relation is one of parallelism, not of development. In the first *Hymne,* the emphasis is on the effects of love on the lover, and the lines just quoted show how the lover seeks to conform himself to the image of the beloved he beholds constantly, thereby refining his own mind. In the second *Hymne,* it is just the reverse process: the image is conformed to an idea pre-existent in the lover's mind. Each description provides a metaphysical peak for each hymn. Each is complete in itself, neither of them implying further progress. In each case, the following stanzas are a development of the *human* consequences of a self-contained theory. The first two hymns offer no continuity in the sense of growth. They are conceived as a diptych.

The first hymn offers only familiar notions apart from the stanza just discussed, for which Spenser may have borrowed a hint from Ficino [73]. The poet may further have had in mind the *Sopra l'Amore* for a great many details, but parallels are hardly noteworthy since they occur in Castiglione and Le Roy as well; such ideas had long been part and parcel of the poet's Platonic stock-in-trade.

---

[69] *Discours* VI. vi, ff. 103 v° - 104 v°.

[70] *H.B.* 232-59.

[71] *In Convivium,* VI. vi: "Quomodo capiantur amore".

[72] Bennett, *SP* 28, p. 21 ff.

[73] Ficino explains how "a lover imprints a likeness of the beloved one upon his soul, and so the soul of the lover becomes a mirror in which is reflected the image of the loved one" (*In Convivium* II, viii). This is a paraphrase of the *Phaedrus* (255 d), but it suggests that the lover becomes in Shelleyan phrase "like that it contemplates".

But in the second hymn, reminiscences of the *Sopra l'Amore* stand out clearly, so clearly as to suggest actual translation. Moreover, from the definition of beauty onward, the poet follows the arguments of the *Sopra l'Amore* in chronological order, as if he had turned the leaves of the volume as he was composing. Most of the parallels have already been pointed out [74]. I only wish to illustrate briefly the continuity of the argument and to show once more how nearer in language and spirit Spenser stands to Ficino than to Pico.

In the *Hymne in Honour of Beautie,* the trend of the argument runs closely parallel to Ficino's exposition of the fifth and sixth orations. The parallelism starts with the definition of Beauty. Spenser, like Ficino, rejects from the first the idea that beauty might be due to proportion and colour:

> How vainely then doe ydle wits invent,
> That beautie is nought else, but mixture made
> Of colours faire, and goodly temp'rament
> Of pure complexions, that shall quickly fade
> And passe away, like to a sommers shade,
> Or that it is but comely composition
> Of parts well measured, with meet disposition. (*H.B.* 64-70)

> Il y en a d'aucuns qui ont opinion que la Beauté est une certaine assiette de tous les membres ou vrayement une symmetrie & proportion avecques quelque gratieuse meslange de couleurs. L'opinion de ceux-cy nous ne recevons pas [75].

The distinction is clear, the rejection emphatic. Pico, on the contrary, reverts to the peripatetic definition of beauty as a *discordia concors,* thereby excluding beauty in God and all simple things, such as light [76]. A consideration of the heavenly hymns will show that Spenser unmistakably places beauty in God, and his aesthetics, both in the *Hymnes* and in the *Faerie Queene,* are dominated by a "Licht-Metaphysik" which practically equates beauty and light. Moreover, the trend of Pico's argument in his definition of beauty is quite different from Ficino's and Spenser's.

Pico starts from "the wide and common signification of the word "beauty", and, instead of rejecting it, he will use it as a stepping-stone to reach a definition of Beauty proper:

> Ce vocable beauté se peut prendre selon une ample et commune signification, & se peut prendre proprement. Selon la première manière, toutes les fois que plusieurs choses diverses s'assemblent à la constitution d'une troisième laquelle naisse de la *convenable mixtion & temperament fait de ces choses diverses, cest harmonie & temperance qui resulte & procedde de ceste proportionnée mixtion s'appelle beauté* [77].

Beauty *proper* is *visual* harmony. Vision itself must be distinguished into *corporeal* and *intellectual.* The reasoning throughout is much more scholastic

---

[74] See *Variorum, M.P.* I, pp. 523-36.
[75] *Discours,* IV. iii, f. 68 v°.
[76] Beauty is "une amiable inimitée, & une accordante discorde" "Et suyvant ceste (définition), aucune chose simple ne peut estre belle, dont s'ensuit qu'en Dieu ne soit la beauté". (*Commentaire* II. vi. in *Discours,* f. 223 v°. Cf. Ivanoff, *Humanisme et Renaissance,* III, p. 17).
[77] *Commentaire* II. iii; in *Discours,* f. 223 r°.

and abstract than in the *Sopra l'Amore.* Besides, Spenser, like Ficino in the third chapter of the fifth oration, is mainly concerned with *proving* why sensuous beauty is but an "outward show". Although he does not select the same arguments, he chooses like Ficino psychological — and not metaphysical — explanations: he appeals like him to common experience: pictures, the blossoms of the field, a lover's own experience [78]. I find nothing of the kind in Pico or Benivieni [79].

From a rejection of vulgar beauty, both Spenser and Ficino proceed to an account of the celestial origin of the beauty seen on earth. Both describe the descent of the soul from its native planet and the informing of matter. But Benivieni himself had followed Ficino [80]. It will be noticed that he devotes one single line to the "unaptness" of matter, and without transition, turns to the birth of love in the lover's soul. Spenser is more leisurely. He will dwell first, as Ficino does in a later chapter, on the identity of beauty and vertue. The body is the image and shadow of the soul, "de sorte que tirant conjecture de cest image nous estimons qu'en un beau corps soit une ame belle" [81]. Faced with the problem of accounting for vertuous souls in ugly bodies, he develops a hint of Ficino:

> Ceste splendeur ne descend point en la matière ni premièrement, elle n'est fort cointement préparée [82].

Now, this argument is taken up again and developed in the sixth chapter of the sixth Oration. Spenser would naturally turn to that chapter, and here he found both the explanation sought for and a theory of love born "of starres concent". Ficino explains how each soul has a "seal" or "form" and how, on leaving its native planet, it engraves on its ethereal body the figure of a man, corresponding to the planet of his birth.

> Et si pareillement elle trouve en terre une semence tempérée, en icelle aussi elle dépeint la tierce figure fort semblable à la seconde & à la première. Il avient souvent que deux ames seront descendues, Juppiter regnant, combien qu'en

[78] *H.B.* 78-91; cf. *Discours,* V. iii, f. 69 r°-v°.

[79] There is an interesting definition of beauty in a psychological treatise published in 1601 by Thomas Wright. He associated the scholastic conception of the nature of Beauty and Bounty (meaning Goodness): "And what was this beauty which so fed their appetites? It could not be certainly any other thing then the apt proportion & just correspondence of the parts & colours of visible bodies which first delighted the eie, & then contented the mind, not unlike the harmony of proportionable voices and instruments, which feed the eare; and health which issues from the just proportion & temper of the foure humors, & some dainty tast, which ensueth from the mixture of divers delicate meats compounded in one. Beauty is the rinde of bounty, & those creatures are more beautifull which are most bountifull" (ed. 1630, pp. 199-200).

But Wright was not so optimistic as the Neo-Platonists were concerning human creatures for "here, alas, in humane corps it falleth out contrariwise...", "Bounty then and beauty", he concluded, "by nature are linked together though perverse soules, like stinking corps lie buried in beautiful sepulchres...". The Christian moralist had laid his finger on the main difficulty of the Platonic theory of beauty. Il could account for the presence of a beautiful soul in a misshapen body. It could not explain whence the body could derive its beauty when the soul it lodged had none, or had lost it.

[80] *H.B.* 106-33. Benivieni, *Opere,* f. 43 r°-v°; *Canzone* ll. 91-108. Benivieni acknowledged his debt to Ficino: see Robb, *Neoplatonism,* p. 118.

[81] *Discours,* VI. xi. f. 132 v°.

[82] *Ibid.,* V. vi. f. 77 v°.

> divers temps, l'une d'icelles estant escheuë en terre à semence accomodée aura son corps parfaitement figuré selon les Idées de la première. Mais l'autre *ayant trouvé matière inepte,* aura bien encommencé la même ouvrage, mais ne l'aura pas accomply avecques si grande similitude à l'exemple de soy mesme. Ce corps là est plus beau que cestuy-cy. Mais tous les deux par une certaine ressemblance de nature se plaisent mutuellement [83].

Disentangling the two threads of argument here twisted together by Ficino, Spenser first explains how:

> Yet oft it falles, that many a gentle mynd
> Dwels in deformed tabernacle drownd,
> Either by chaunce, against the course of kynd,
> *Or through unaptnesse in the substance fownd,*
> Which it assumed of some stubborne grownd, (*H.B.* 141-5)

With a characteristic love of symmetry and moralization, the poet adds the converse truth, and a warning to fair Ladies: Beauty may be abused and defaced by lust. "Gentle love" on the contrary, will enhance it, and display the essential likeness of the lovers' souls, which the poet expresses in an image reminiscent of Ficino's explanation of Cavalcanti's poem:

> Like as two mirrours by opposd reflexion,
> Doe both expresse the faces first impression [84].

This is followed by a natural transition on the necessity of choosing wisely one's lovers. Spenser then takes up Ficino's main argument in the chapter under consideration: "De la Manière de s'enamourer" [85]. Thus is he led to introduce the stanzas describing the recognition by the lover of a soul fit "with his spirit's proportion to agree" through a process of abstraction and idealization. The identity of spirit and argument first disclosed by Spenser's handling of these notions has now been found to extend to the whole *Hymne in Honour of Beautie.*

The influence of Ficino, therefore, may safely be said to outweigh any other influence — at least so far as the newer Platonic materials are concerned. R. W. Lee has rightly called attention to Spenser's debt to Castiglione [86], but the debt is limited to the Petrarchan passages [87] or to stray verbal echoes in distinctly Ficinian developments [88]. The *Courtier* says nothing of the descent of the soul from her heavenly bower and of love born "of starres concent". The definition of beauty offered by Castiglione stresses the notions of colour and proportion which the second *Hymne* emphatically rejects [89], and Spenser's description of the soul framing her heavenly house is closer in language and

---

[83] *Ibid.*, VI, vi, f. 102 r°.
[84] *H.B.* 181-2; cf. *Discours,* VII. i, f. 155 v°.
[85] *Discours,* VI, vi, f. 101 v°.
[86] *P.Q.* 7 (1928) 65-77.
[87] e.g. "fancy engendered in the eyes" (*H.L.* 120-6; *H.B.* 231-45: *Courtier* 246-7). Other analogues on the contemplative pleasures of love (*H.B.* 246-52; *Courtier*, 313-14) and the sufferings of the lover (*H.L.* 127-33; 252-64; *Courtier* 305; 311; 317) are vague. The close of *H.B.* opens with a clearer reminiscence of Bembo's *Asolani* (see Ch. VIII, p. 142).
[88] e.g. "through the virtue of imagination, hee shall fashion with himselfe that beautie much more faire than it is in deede" (*Courtier* 317: *H.B.* 230).
[89] Cst. *H.B.* 64-70 and *Courtier* 304.

imagery to both Ficino and Benivieni [90]. Moreover the trend of argument throughout is quite different. The process of abstraction is introduced as a remedy against the torment of absence and leads up, not to the recognition of the affinity of the lovers' souls, but to the contemplation of "universall beautie", whereas Spenser stops at "the particular beautie of one woman" [91]. To R.W. Lee's assertion that "Castiglione gives a human application, a concreteness to the esoteric philosophy of Ficino and Benivieni" [92], we may assent with a qualification. The Third and Fourth Books of the *Courtier,* indeed, discuss "la pratica d'amore" as well as the theorics thereof. But Bembo's oration, though free from esoterism, plays with a less "concrete" conception of love than is found in the *Hymnes* and the chapter of the *Sopra l'Amore* which Spenser closely followed. For Castiglione's ladder of love is largely modelled on Pico's seven steps, and no theory could be less congenial to the English poet's "personalized" apprehension of beauty.

Pico's *Commento,* therefore, may be ignored, even though Spenser was acquainted with it, a not improbable hypothesis [93]. There may be stray echoes of it in the *Hymnes,* but the steps of the *Commento* did not affect the first two hymns; much less should they be read into all four hymns [94]. Besides, the thought of Pico is broken up into scholastic divisions and wrapped up in a mystical obscurity quite alien to the genius of Spenser. "Tout cela exprimé en un langage abstrait et sec que n'anime point le souffle ardent du *Commentaire sur le Banquet*" [95], the true source of the *Fowre Hymnes.*

To some extent, the same remarks apply to the *Canzone* of Benivieni. The *Hymne in Honour of Beautie* probably echoes the sixth and seventh stanzas describing the descent of the soul and the birth of love [96]. But again the echoes

---

[90] *H.B.* 120-126; 134-40. The *Courtier* (310-11) does not offer Ficino's and Spenser's image of the architect framing a house (*Discours,* V. v, f. 75 r°-76 v°), nor the idea of "unaptnesse in the substance found". Lee's parallels for beauty as an emanation (*H.B.* 43-52, *Courtier* 304), the advice to love nobly (*H.B.* 161-77; *Courtier* 313) and the steps (*H.B.* 211-31: *Courtier,* 317) are extremely vague.

[91] *Courtier,* 317-8. For Spenser, see above p. 131.

[92] *P.Q.* 28, p. 76.

[93] He almost certainly knew Benivieni's *Canzone,* and the *Commento* was always included in Benivieni's *Opere.* Besides, two books were included in the volume containing the 1588 edition of La Boderie's translation of the *Sopra l'Amore.*

[94] The only parallel that might be considered a proof of indebtedness occurs in Pico's description of the third step: "Dice adunque que talhor lanima reforma quella specie universale AL LUME DIVINO CHE IN LEI NE E IMPRESSO, cioè al lume della beltà ideale ad lei participata..." Benivieni's *Opere,* f. 69 r°). But Spenser in *H.B.* 218-20, is speaking of the "refyned forme" of the beloved, not of a "specie universale", and that image is not merely *reformed* in the light of ideal Beauty, but finally *conformed* unto the own "form" of the lover's mind, his "spirits proportion", as in Ficino (quoted above, note 61). For Clotho waking Love (*H.L.* 63), J.W. Bennett (*S.P.* 28, p. 30) refers to Pico (*Commento,* II, xxi), but Lotspeich offers a clearer parallel from Boccaccio I. 5 (*Mythology,* p. 59). Both Pico and Boccaccio assign the highest part of the universe to Atropos, the middle part to Clotho. However I am not sure that this was Spenser's intention, for Love is waked as he lay "in Venus lap above" (*H.L.* 24). In his Commentary on the *Timaeus,* Le Roy assigned the higher part to Clotho (*Timée,* f. 48 r°). Spenser may have had in mind the tradition followed by Le Roy. He may even have read the *Timaeus,* like the *Symposium,* in Le Roy's translation.

[95] Festugières, *Philosophie de l'Amour,* p. 41.

[96] *Opere* f. 43 r°-v°. Noted by Fletcher, *M.P.* 8, pp. 553-4. "Fleshly seed" and "nel seme human" is not a decisive parallel since "seed" is a common Neoplatonic term. But "sua celeste spoglie prime" seems to be distinctly echoed in *H.B.* 118.

are incidental, occurring in a different argument. For Benivieni is concerned with the soul's descent from heaven to earth and its return through love to the fountain of beauty : human love has no place in the *Canzone dell'Amor Divino* and the perception of beauty in an individual object is treated only as a step towards intellectual beauty. But Spenser's first two hymns are devoted to love and beauty as they are felt and apprehended on earth. The framework is human: metaphysics are introduced to *explain* human emotions. The celestial origin of Beauty *accounts* for the wonders it works upon the minds of men (*H.B.* 71-91). The heavenly light preserved by the soul "when she in fleshly seede is eft enraced" *accounts* for the identity of outer and inner beauty in human beings (*H.B.* 134 ff.). The process of idealization in the lover's mind *accounts* for the birth of love between "likely harts" (*H.B.* 225-31). Metaphysical causes are assigned to human effects, but the human effects are in the centre of the picture, human emotions in the centre of interest. The Platonism of Spenser is "homocentric", like his "geocentric" cosmology, whereas Benivieni, travelling on a circle whose poles are heaven and earth, no sooner alights on earth — and the human heart — than he takes his flight back to heaven. We may grant, therefore, that the Platonic hymns of Spenser are occasionally reminiscent of the *Canzone,* provided we bear in mind the essential difference. And even those reminiscences should not be unduly extended, nor parallels strained, as they often were in Fletcher's over-laboured comparison [97].

The recognition of the dominant influence of Ficino — a point of little consequence if mere source ascription was involved — has a twofold interest. It enabled us to emphasize once more the conservative character of Spenser's Platonism. By the time he wrote the *Fowre Hymnes* as they now stand, the poet had long been acquainted with Castiglione and he probably knew Benivieni and Pico. Yet in the key-stanzas of the second hymn, he chose to follow a chapter of Ficino's *Sopra l'Amore.* As the reason for his choice was obvious. Ficino included the description of the soul's descent and the process of idealization in the discussion of a human, "earthly" experience: *Quomodo capiantur amore.* His metaphysics, brought to bear upon a human emotion, were recon-

---

[97] Stanzas I, II, III, V of the *Canzone* offer no parallel worth notice. If *H.L.* 1-28 is reminiscent of stanzas I-II, then we are to assume that Spenser had also the *Canzone* in mind in *F.Q.* I. Pro. 2. 9; II. x. 1; III. iii. I. 1-2, etc. (cf. Appendix I). In fact, all poets in all their invocations to Love have felt their wits to faint and have drawn upon the common imagery of wings and fire. St. IV (ll. 55-8) is a better parallel to *H.L.* 70-73, yet Spenser, admitting he remembered Benivieni, gave an original turn of his own to Benivieni's commonplace thought about Love following the light of Venus. It is characteristic that Spenser should have substituted for an aesthetic and metaphysical idea a cosmological relation: Venus lending light to Cupid as he took his flight through Chaos to make the world. The *Canzone* is metaphysical throughout: the *Hymnes* are dominantly cosmic, psychological, ethical.

Fletcher and Bennett assume that Spenser follows Benivieni when he describes the soul as taking light and lively spirits from the sun (*Canzone* ll. 91-4; *H.B.* 109-12). But Benivieni merely says that the soul departs "dalla piu eccelsa parte ch'albergi el sol" (*Opere,* f. 43 r°). If we turn to Pico's *Commento,* we find it means the sign of Cancer: "& è sententia de Platonici, liquali dicono lanima descendere per il Cancro, & ascendere per il Capricorno, & credo che il loro fondamento sia *perche il Cancro è casa della Luna la cui virtu massime domina sopra la parte vegetale vivificativa de corpi*" (*Opere,* f. 66 v°). Spenser either did not follow the *Commento,* or deliberately substituted the sun for the moon. In any case, he need not be in Benivieni's or Pico's debt for this commonplace notion also found in *F.Q.* III. vi. 8-9: see Chap. IV, p. 87.

cilable with the Petrarchan and even the chivalric ideal. I do not mean that Spenser consciously sought out a reconciliation. But coming to the Neoplatonists with a Petrarchan and chivalric inheritance, he naturally seized upon the more congenial exposition of Platonic doctrine for the framework of the hymns. There would have been no room for the earlier notions in the inflexible scheme of the seven steps. Besides, Le Roy would have taught him to consider the steps as falling wholly, from first to last, within the province of heavenly love [98]. Even Castiglione used them to describe a continuous ascent, the ultimate goal being reached by a straightforward progression, without any real inflexion or conversion [99]. Had he adopted the scheme, Spenser could not have focused his interest on human love. And he could not have managed "a conversion": a dramatic contrast between earthly and heavenly love. Such a conversion his Dedication openly states. Such a contrast is plainly perceptible in the profane and sacred *Hymnes*.

But before studying the turning away from earthly beauty to heavenly beauty, the second point of interest must be stressed. The acknowledgement of Spenser's indebtedness to Ficino was essential to my initial assumption; the origin of Spenser's *Fowre Hymnes* in the Dedicatory Epistle of La Boderie. The first confirmation of my hypothesis has been obtained. The recognition of a clear break between the two pairs of hymns will afford a second confirmation, should it appear that the contrast is not merely between a lower and a higher love in the Platonic sense, that is, between sensible and intellectual love, but between the love of woman and the love of God in the Christian sense.

---

[98] Only in the third book, devoted to intellectual beauty, are the steps of Pico introduced by Le Roy (*Sympose*, f. 158 r°-v°). They were not used in the first two books which described love as a desire for corporal or moral beauty.

[99] *Courtier*, pp. 313-19. See Ch. VIII, p. 149 and Ch. II, pp. 29-30.

CHAPTER VIII

FROM EARTHLY LOVE TO HEAVENLY LOVE

To bring out the contrast between the two pairs of hymns, we must know what Spenser intends by earthly love and earthly beauty. Throughout the hymns, beauty, no doubt, is described as a spiritual radiance. But the feeling is evoked by the beauty of *one* woman. It is perhaps more refined and less hyperbolic than in other poets who spoke of their lady as Beauty incarnate [1], for Spenser, writing a hymn in honour of Beauty, is conscious throughout that the particular beauty of each being is not its own, but a gift of a higher Beauty. Yet, that higher Beauty is described as a source, not as a goal. The lover's aim is the conquest of an earthly beauty, not the vision of Beauty's self; his heart is set on a "handmaid" of *Cytherea*, not on "great beauties Queene" (*H.B.* 26-87). To the "great Soveraine" he proffers homage, after the chivalric and classical tradition; to "*Venus* dearling", the addressee of "these fearefull lines", he proffers love. What kind of love?

The answer is given by the description of Love's "Paradize" in the first hymn. If Spenser meant to describe only the Platonic delights of eye and ear, would he have written these lines, fraught with clear suggestions of fruition?

> There with thy daughter *Pleasure* they doe play
> Their hurtlesse sports, without rebuke or blame,
> And in her snowy bosome boldly lay
> Their quiet heads, devoyd of guilty shame,
> After full joyance of their gentle game. (*H.L.* 287-91)

Moreover, that "Paradize of all delight and joyous happie rest", where the classical Gods and Cupid's daughter, Pleasure, are assembled, is clearly intended to recall Venus' "joyous Paradize", the Garden of Adonis. [2] Spenser was fond of pointing back to his own myths [3], and we know that all four hymns were written, or, at least, re-written, after the first six books of the *Faerie Queene.* Love in the Garden of Adonis has been shown to be the natural instinct, innocent so far as it is indulged in a sinless Eden, or within the sinless bonds of marriage [4]. I therefore think it not improper to read the close of the first Hymne, coming after the *Amoretti* and the *Epithalamion,* as "an apology of the

---

[1] e.g. Lorenzo in the *Selve d'Amore,* Pt. I, stanzas 27-8 quoted by Robb, (*Neo-platonism,* pp. 105-6), or Sidney in *Astrophel and Stella,* Sonnet XXV.
[2] *F.Q.* III. vi. 29. See also the paradise of lovers in the Temple of Venus, *F.Q.* IV. x. 23 sq.
[3] In *Colin Clout* (l. 804), he reminded the reader of his own "gardens of Adonis".
[4] See Chapter IV, pp. 76-7, 84-5.

marriage-bed" the interpretation scorned by Dr. Bennett[5] "Marriage", in a way, may be thought an unnecessary qualification, and, indeed, Spenser refrains from suggesting it as clearly as in the Amoret story. I have shown that the *Fowre Hymnes* were composed at a time. For the sake of the retractation, it was not amiss that a "lewd" construction might be put upon the rhymes ascribed to "greener" years. But I have suggested also that Spenser was anxious to make even the more sensuous lines unobjectionable when properly construed, in order to answer the criticisms of Burghley[6]. He therefore insisted throughout, not only on the ennobling power of love, but on truth and loyalty, feelings which, though they were called for as well by the chivalric romance of adultery, may be taken in Spenser as the ethical standard pointing to married love "devoyd of guilty shame". Besides, his description of the lover's quest is little more than a rather dull narrative of the quest of Scudamour for Amoret "through seas, through flames, through thousand swords and speares". It will be noticed that it does not end when the lover has gained his lady's *grace*, for

> He nathemore can so contented rest,
> But forceth further on, and striveth still
> T'approch more neare, till in her inmost brest,
> He may embosomed bee, and loved best (*H.L.* 247-50)

The suppressed stanzas on the meeting of Scudamour and Amoret changed into a "faire Hermaphrodite"[7] are a better comment upon the *Hymne in Honour of Love* than the fastidious Platonic interpretation of Dr. Bennett, provided we remember that chaste love, "without rebuke or blame", is implied throughout. Of such a love, not of "brutish" love, will the poet sing "An heavenly Hymne, such as the Angels sing"[8]. For such a love did "sweet Angels Alleluya sing", as the bride "before the altar (stood)"[9].

The first hymn, therefore, leaves us in no doubt that Spenser remains faithful to the conception of love we have traced in the *Faerie Queene*. Since the second hymn is devoted to beauty, and beauty is perceived by the eyes and the ears alone, it is not surprising that only the more Platonic delights should be suggested. The close of the hymn seems distinctly reminiscent of the rhapsody of Gismondo on the pleasures of love in *Gli Asolani*:

> For lovers eyes more sharply sighted bee
> Then other mens, and in deare loves delight
> See more then any other eyes can see,

Non sono, como quelle de gli altri huomini, le viste de gli amanti, o Donne...[10].

---

[5] Cf. *S P* 32 (1935), p. 151.

[6] See chapter I, p. 22.

[7] *Variorum F.Q.* III, pp. 181-2.

[8] *H.L.* 302. "Do the angels sing the praises of sensual or beastly love?" (Bennett, *S P* 32, p. 151.). Obviously not, but (1) Spenser means that he would praise Love ("my God") as the Angels praise God, a commonplace of profane love-poetry, mediaeval or Renaissance; (2) he has in mind not "beastly love", but a love "bred in spotlesse brest" (*Amoretti*, LXXXIIII).

[9] *Epithalamion*, 1.240. Hebe is present both in *H.L.* 284 and *Epith.* 1.405.

[10] *H.B.* 232 ff. *Asolani*, p. 135: "Nor is the sight of lovers like that of the other men..." See also the description of "amourous eye-glaunces": "O mirabile forza degli amorosi risguardamenti... dolcezze, che al core li passano per le luci" (p. 139) and compare *H.B.* 235 ff.

Both Spenser and Bembo give prominence to the visual and auditive delights, in accordance with both the Petrarchan and the Platonic code of love. But the English poet ends with the traditional plea for "grace", and the first hymn has shown that the lover, once "grace" is gained, "forceth further on" (*H.L.* 245-50). As to Bembo's spokesman Gismondo he praises that *amore humano,* which is content to rest in the senses of sight and hearing. Yet he allows his eyes to rove complacently on the budding charms of a lady's breast while describing the contemplative delights of a lover [11], and he humourously declines to keep up the pretence to the last. The pleasures afforded by the other senses are not utterly disclaimed. Lovers are only invited to "taste" then sparingly. And though sacrificing in speech to the fashionable convention, Gismondo smilingly confesses his own inability to restrain his appetite [12], further adding that such advice would ill apply to a bridegroom [13].

Gismondo, no doubt, is no true Platonist and will be upbraided by Lavinello. He is not given the last word. Yet many *trattati d'amore* could have afforded precedent for a toleration or even a vindication of sexual love. The uncompromising attitude of Pico and Benivieni has already been contrasted with the more moderate views of Ficino [14]. Yet, while refusing to scorn earthly Venus and the desire of generation as base and brutish, while praising marriage as a civil and religious institution, Ficino wisely avoided any attempt to fuse or associate the sexual instinct with the higher Platonic love. Paradoxically, though logically enough when the claims of human nature are considered, an easy-going and sophistical toleration of sensual love, irrespective of matrimony, often appeared among those who professed to follow the philosophy of Pico. A clear instance is afforded by *Il Cortegiano.* The last speech, ascribed to Bembo, is an outright rejection of sexual love in principle. But the speaker's asceticism, modelled on Pico's, is tempered in practice and his very contention implies a qualification since he undertakes to shew that "*olde men* may love not onely without slander, but otherwhile more happily than young men" [15]. Though the happier love is recommended to old and young alike, Bembo admits that sensual love in young men "deserveth excuse, and (is) perhaps in some case lawfull: for although it putteth them in afflictions, dangers, travels, and the unfortunateness that is said, yet are there many that to winne them the good will of their Ladies practise vertuous thinges, which for all they be not bent to a good end, yet are they good of them selves. And so of that much bitternesse they picke out a little sweetnesse, and through the adversities which they sustaine, in the ende they acknowledge their errour" [16]. This is no more than a toleration or a palliation, for the principle is maintained: "sensuall love in every

---

[11] *Asolani,* p. 138.

[12] *Asolani,* pp. 158-9. "...Quantunque io per me non mi seppi far mai cosi savio; che io a quella guisa ne conviti d'Amore mi sia saputo rattemperare".

[13] *Asolani,* p. 159: "nor would I counsel our inexperienced bridegroom that when love puts upon the board that final course which he has not tasted yet, he like one contented with his previous fare, should merely sample this before he let it be removed: he might repent his moderation afterwards" (transl. Gottfried, p. 134).

[14] See Chapter II, pp. 27-8.

[15] *Ibid.,* p. 303.

[16] *Ibid.,* pp. 306-7. Cf. p. 312: "I say therefore, that since the nature of man in youthful age is so much enclined to sense, it may be granted the Courtier while he is young to love sensually... Such love in young men deserveth more to be pittied than blamed".

age is naught", and the coveted ende", not "a good end" in itself[17]. The wiser lover will rest satisfied with "mery countenances, familiar and secret talke, jeasting, dalying, hand in hand", and "may also lawfully and without blame come to kissing", for "a kisse may be saide to be rather a coupling together of the soule, than of the body"[18]. But even that love is still subject to the miseries bred by absence and "the trouble to behold the beautie of one bodie alone"; the "not yong Courtier" is invited to press further and "beholde no more the particular beautie of one woman, but an universall, that decketh out all bodies"[19]. Love for one woman, therefore, whether sensual or Platonic, is never a satisfying self-complete experience, even on the human level.

The more fastidious writers of *trattati d'amore* treated Platonism as a beautiful aesthetic creed and a fashionable garb. The more sincere did not hesitate to vindicate the sensual love which others affected to disclaim. They derived their arguments from the Aristotelian and scholastic philosophy which denied that the human intellect could act without the instruments of the senses. But they could also appeal, whether seriously or irreverently, to the Christian conception of man. To the Platonist, the soul was the whole man, but Christianity had always insisted that "the union of body and soul makes the man"[20]. Renaissance writers in love who took that stand therefore should hardly be styled Platonists, since they opposed the very spirit of Platonism even while retaining much Platonic material. Equicola no longer let "Plato trim the sails", but was faithful to the principles of Aristotelian philosophy and Christian faith[21] when he did not admit of any separation of body and soul in the experience of love. But he went beyond this and sounded an almost naturalistic note when he argued that spiritual love by itself, when disembodied, could not endure. He who loves permanently, he concluded, must needs love both the soul and the body in the beloved, for the body ministers sensual pleasure to the senses as their own end, while the soul seeks from the soul a love answering hers[22].

An abler and more mystical defender of this philosophical position, though, was the Hebrew scholar Jehudah Abarbanel, known as Leo Hebraeus or Leone Ebreo. He argued that the union of the lovers' souls was the end of perfect love but could only be fully achieved when the bodies, too, were united: the bodily union therefore made spiritual love more perfect[23]. Not only did he approve of the function of generation, like Ficino, but he claimed that "carnal delectations", when temperate, were good in themselves and belonged with

---

[17] *Ibid.*, p. 306.

[18] *Ibid.*, p. 315.

[19] *Ibid.*, pp. 317-8.

[20] Donne's words in *Death's Duell*; *Complete Poetry and Selected prose*, ed. Hayward, p. 746.

[21] See the earlier quotation from Equicola, Chap. V, p. 109.

[22] *Di Natura d'Amore*, p. 381.

"Concludiamo qualunche si sia, che permanente ama, amar l'animo e'l corpo insieme, dico amar necessariamente & per vigor naturale l'uno & l'altro, & afferma che l'uno dall'altro in tal amore non patisce separatione: i sensi dell'amante dall' amato corpo ricercan volutta sensuale come suo fine: l'animo di vero amante dell' amato animo amor richiede, & esser riamato".

[23] *Dialoghi*, ed. S. Caramella Bari, 1921, p. 50.

"honest" love [24]. His Dialoghi d'Amore were highly praised and immensely popular throughout the sixteenth century. Their influence is traceable in the later vindications of bodily union together with the earlier Aristotelian arguments. One instance from Varchi's *Lezioni sopra alcune questioni d'amore* may suffice:

> ... è impossibile, che nell' amore umano, cio è, quando alcun uomo ama alcuna donna ancora di buono amore, che cotale amore sia perfetto, se non si congiungano ancora i corpi. Perchè tutto il composto, cioè la forma e la materia ed in somma l'anima e'l corpo sono tanti uniti mentre viviamo, che niuna cosa è piu una, che essi si siano; onde come il corpo non fa nulla da sè, non essendo il fare della materia, ma della forma, cosi l'anima, se bene è suo proprio il fare come forma, non pero si puo dire, che faccia da sè cosa niuna, ma tutte insieme col corpo per la colleganza che hanno le sentimenta e tutte le potenze dell'anima insieme. [25]

Spenser's frank acceptance of physical love, therefore, was neither new nor surprising. Yet both his approach to the problem and the compromise he evolved were different from the philosophy of the Italian *trattattisti d'amore*. The characteristic of his attitude, indeed, is that there does not seem to be any problem in his eyes. That the consummation of love between man and woman should be a physical as well as a spiritual union is quietly taken for granted and no dialectical justification is offered nor felt to be required. In a way this allows the poetic imagination to move in a more uniformly Platonic *atmosphere* than the thought of Varchi or Donne in the *Extasie,* since the poet need not introduce Aristotelian considerations on the union of matter and form, or body and soul. On the other hand, the very conception of "l'amóre honesto" suffered a sea-change when the "sage and serious Spenser" identified it with wedded love; either openly as in the *Faerie Queene,* or implicitly as in the *Hymnes.*

I have discovered so far no other instance of this identification in the Neoplatonic literature of the Renaissance but for Le Roy's prefaces to his translation of the *Symposium* [26]. And since the French humanist was addressing a newly-married pair, he could be suspected of a complimentary intention. The other Platonists often urged contradictory opinions in regard to sexual love, but they always kept apart the consideration of marriage and the Platonic philosophy of love. That duality is noticeable in Castiglione's *Courtier.* The treatise on the whole has a high ethical standard. The ideal "gentlewoman"

---

[24] *Dialoghi,* ed. 1558, f. 229 v°: FI. Di questa sorte di dilettationi non ho detto mai che fussero cattive, & solamente buone in apparentia, anzi t'affermo che sono veramente buone. SO. Sono pur dilettationi carnali, & l'amor loro e dalla parte del dilettabile. FI. Sono ben carnali dilettationi, ma non sono puramente della specie del dilettabile, anzi sono veramente di quella dell' honesto, quando, comme dissi, sono temperate quanto si richiede al bisogno della sostentatione dell' individuo, & conservatione della specie".

[25] Varchi, "Lezione Seconda, Quistione Quinta" (ed. 1880, p. 310): "it is impossible in human love, that is, when a man loves a woman even though with the right love [spiritual love], that such a love should be perfect if the bodies too be not joined. For the whole compound, that is form and matter, which are the soul and body, is of such unity as long as we live that nothing could be more one than these are together. Hence, as the body does nothing by itself since action is no attribute of matter but of form, so the soul, although her property as form is to act, nevertheless cannot be said to do anything by herself, but does everything together with the body on account of the interconnection of the sense impressions and of all the faculties of the soul."

[26] See Chapter V, p. 104.

fashioned by the Lord Julian will be truly virtuous. In case she "be not married minding to love, I will have her to love one she may marrie"[27]. Once married, she would do herself injury in loving any other beside her husband:

> Yet since not loving is not many times in our will, if this mishappe chaunce to the woman of the Pallace, that the hatred of her husband or the love of an other bendeth her to love I will have her to graunt her lover nothing els but the minde[28].

Platonic notions are not introduced into the portrait of the ideal wife, who is only required to have, with regard to her husband and children, "all those partes that belong to a good huswife"[29]. And when "love of the minde", Platonic love, is discussed, it turns out to be like *amour courtois* an ideal version of adulterous love. Loving platonically, the Courtier "shall doe no wrong to the husband... of the woman beloved"[30]. For the ethical advice of the Lord Julian, Bembo substitutes the refinements of the Neoplatonic ladder. But the purposes of generation and married love are no longer taken into consideration. In Italian courtly circles and in the language of fashion, married love and Platonic love indeed were usually contrasted. In his *Trattato del matrimonio* dedicated to the courtesan Tullia d'Aragona on her entering into wedlock, Girolamo Muzio, one of her admirers, could at the same time rhapsodize on marriage and press his own suit, assuring her "che il suo amore per lei non era di quelli volgari, che sogliono concludersi col matrimonio, ma era di quelli spirituali, che non si stancano mai di amar e contemplare la bell'anima dell'amata"[31]. Needless to say, such Platonism often proved the cloak of gallantry.

The originality of Spenser's philosophy of love lies in the association of Platonic idealism with an acceptance of bodily union limited by ethical standards. The "Englishness" of this attitude is obvious. It rejected the worldly game and mere pretence of courtly Platonism, but it also excluded the higher flights of mysticism. On the one hand, what had become a mere convention at the hands of *trattatisti* and courtiers, became again a living inspiration and a sincere creed — what it had earlier been for Ficino. Spenser's deep instinct for purity ensured sincerity in his profession of scorn for mere sensual love while the un-Platonic features of his philosophy of love, his apology of fruition, in a way infused new blood to the Platonism it modified. He introduced true passion into an aesthetic and intellectual pastime. But, on the other hand, he turned into an essentially human experience what had earlier been a reaching-out towards the divine in Ficino or Benivieni. What had only been a "step" became with him a self-contained, self-complete experience. The "happie port" was reached with the lover's possession of his mistress[32]. Scudamour wins Amoret; Spenser weds Elizabeth Boyle, and the story ends. Romantic love, contrary to Platonic love, does not transcend itself. This does not mean that it bears no relation to a metaphysical scheme. Love is of heavenly nature, but its consummation is earthly. The process of falling in love may receive a metaphysical justification, but its effects are not different from the phenomenon

---

[27] *Courtier,* p. 240.
[28] *Courtier,* p. 239.
[29] *Courtier,* p. 190.
[30] *Courtier,* p. 317.
[31] Savino, *Trattati d'amore,* t. X, p. 306.
[32] *H.L.* 298.

Stendhal later described as crystallization [33]. Such being his conception of love between man and woman, what kind of relation could the poet establish between human love and divine love?

The relation could not be conceived as a progression, for one does not progress from the enjoyment of a bride, or mistress, to the enjoyment of God. The relation could only be one of analogy or contrast, inclusion or exclusion. Spenser's poetry happens to offer both types of relation. The first is best illustrated by the second Easter sonnet in the *Amoretti* (LXVIII):

> Most glorious Lord of Lyfe that on this day,
> Didst make thy triumph over death and sin:
> and having harowd hell didst bring away
> captivity thence captive us to win:
> This joyous day, deare Lord, with joy begin,
> and grant that we for whom thou diddest dye
> being with thy deare blood clene washt from sin,
> may live for ever in felicity.
> And that thy love we weighing worthily,
> may likewise love thee for the same againe,
> and for thy sake that all lyke deare didst buy,
> with love may one another entertayne,
> So let us love, deare love, lyke as we ought,
> love is the lesson which the Lord us taught.

Christ's redeeming love has not only justified sinners; it justifies human love. The love of a bridegroom for a bride, as well as love for our brethren. Nothing could be more alien to the spirit of Platonism. For the Platonist always seeks to divest love of all earthliness. But by the mystery of the Incarnation, God has stooped to earth and consecrated earthly love. The entire contrast between the Platonic and the Christian conception lies in two words: abstraction, consecration.

If we turn now to the hymns of heavenly love and beauty, we are confronted with an uncompromising rejection of human love. The first two hymns which had praised "true" love — possibly married love in the poet's mind — are characterized as "lewd layes" (*H.H.L.* 8).

> And that faire lampe, which useth to enflame
> The hearts of men with selfe consuming fyre,
> Thenceforth seemes fowle, & full of sinfull blame; (*H.H.B.* 274-6)

Christ's redeeming love is celebrated as an invitation to love him again, "then next to love our brethren", but the poet carefully abstains from mentioning or suggesting any other love than Christian charity [34].

How shall we account for such a difference in the poet's outlook on the relation of earthly love to heavenly love? Spenser's profession of ascetic contempt in the last two hymns is naturally suspect of some exaggeration for the sake of dramatic emphasis. He meant to contrast the two pairs of hymns, and just as he emphasized the profanity of the hymns ascribed to "greener times" [35],

---

[33] *H.B.* 218-31. I have shown that the "fancy" is mainly involved in the process, the stage of pure concept not being reached.

[34] *H.H.L.* 190-217. Cst. *Amoretti* LXXII, 9-14, quoted above.

[35] In *H.H.L.* 8-21 and in the Dedication. The hymns themselves are not more profane than Colin's praise of love and other poems.

he may have overdone his *contemptum mundi* in the religious hymns. Another explanation would be furnished by a change in the poet's mood. But, on the one hand, two or three years at most had elapsed since the composition of the *Amoretti* sonnet, and at the time when he wrote the *Hymnes,* Spenser, so far as we know, had given no sign of abjuring his earlier ideal of human love [36]. On the other hand, the vanity of "ladies love" in comparison to the love of God had been emphasized as early as the first Book of the *Faerie Queene,* when the Red Cross knight asked the Hermit:

> But deeds of armes must I at last be faine,
> And Ladies love to leave so dearely bought?
> What need of armes, where peace doth ay remaine,
> (Said he) and battailes none are to be fought?
> As for loose loves are vaine, and vanish into nought. (I. x. 62. 5-9)

There is no reason to suspect Spenser's sincerity. In both cases he speaks in perfect accordance with the Christian tradition, and if his contrasted utterances disclose a paradox, it is the time-honoured Christian paradox. In a way, the poet's attitude is much more consistent, because much more true to the complexity of human nature, than it would have been without that apparent contradiction. God is love, and all pure love proceeds from God and is approved by Him. Even physical love is the result of his injunction "Be fruitful, and multiply", and the will of God is accomplished in the Garden of Adonis as in the House of Holiness [37]. Love, therefore, is to be experienced by the lovers with the full consciousness of fulfilling the designs of the God of Nature and the God of Love. Human love, not to degenerate into brutish love, must never be experienced apart from the love of God. But the Christian love of God, on the contrary, does not admit of any alloy: it must be experienced in its purity. It does not admit either of any intermediary. It is not impious for a lover to tell his bride: "love is the lesson which the Lord us taught". But it were wrong for a Christian to attempt to reach God through the love of woman, even though the woman were early left behind in the progression. Beauty in the woman is divine, and must be so acknowledged [38]. Even love in the lover is divine and should be so experienced [39]. But both the lover and the beloved, being men, are sinful creatures in the eyes of Spenser. Though love is pure, there will be in *their* love some impurity, as in *her* beauty some imperfection. Now, the mind may proceed from a lesser beauty to a higher beauty, but the heart cannot substitute a purer feeling for a less pure: the feeling of adoration may be more or less intense, but it must be pure from the first. God therefore must be adored apart from woman, though the woman is not to be loved apart from God. Human love is included in divine love, so far as it is humanly experienced; but it must be excluded from divine love, divinely experienced. It is not merely

---

[36] The sixth book of the *Faerie Queene,* probably completed in 1594, has delightful idylls. Part of Colin's praise of love seems to have been inserted before publication in 1595, and the proem to Book IV of the *Faerie Queene,* probably written before publication in 1596, is a vigorous defence of love. The *Prothalamion* composed in November 1596, though an occasional piece, affords further evidence that no marked change had come over the poet's mind since the day when he wrote his own *Epithalamion.*

[37] *F.Q.* III. vi. 34 and I. x.

[38] T'adore thing so divine as beauty were but right (*F.Q.* III vii. 2. 9).

[39] Cf. *F.Q.* III. iii. 1 and *T.M.* 387-90.

a question of being differently sincere at different times: it may be a simultaneous realization of different orders of reality.

Spenser may not have been fully conscious of the distinction I have drawn. But both his own temper and his Christian inheritance would force upon him that twofold attitude. The Platonic mode of ascent from earthly beauty to heavenly beauty through abstraction and intellectualisation did not suit the concrete mind of the poet, and it would be open to suspicion for the Christian, owing to the character of Spenser's own sensitiveness to beauty. The Italian Platonists were able, or pretended they were able, to abstract the sexual element from human love as early as the second step. Ficino's own Platonism was convincing because he was mostly concerned with love-friendship between men, which enabled him to effect a fusion of Platonic love with Christian charity [40]. But Spenser mainly conceived of love as a response to the beauty of woman:

> Why doe not then the blossomes of the field,
> Which are arrayd with much more orient hew,
> And to the sense most daintie odour yield,
> Worke like impression in the lookers view? (*H.B.* 78-81)

The argument is used as a metaphysical proof of the spiritual nature of beauty, but it affords clear psychological evidence that love to Spenser was essentially a sexual emotion. The contemporary of Montaigne and La Boëtie naturally wrote a Legend of Friendship, and gave the "Zeale of friends combyned with vertues meet" pre-eminence over "raging fire of love to womankind" (*F.Q.* I.ix.1.6-7). But it is characteristic of him that he should have failed to invest his pairs of friends with the poetry and glamour he attached to his pairs of lovers. Obviously his feelings, though sincere, are much more sober: though friends are but "another kind of lovers", he insists on "zeal" and "virtue" rather than on love. The conception is more or less Platonized, but the feeling hardly extends beyond the old chivalric sense of the personal loyalty of man to man. Friendship with Spenser is an ethical, not an aesthetic nor an intellectual emotion as with Ficino. And since he did not separate love from sex in human relations, he could idealize human love after the manner of the poets and the Petrarchans. He could declare it heavenly in his profane poetry, but he could not consider it as a step towards heavenly love in his religious poetry. No clear-sighted and healthy-minded man could treat it so.

Now, precedent for the recantation of the last two hymns will be found, not in consistent and orthodox Platonists like Ficino, Pico or even Castiglione, but in authors still influenced by mediaeval Christianity like Bembo, and beyond him, Petrarch. For orthodox Platonism does not call for a recantation, but for a process of elimination; it does not require a turning-away but a passing-beyond. The 'conversion', if any, occurs from the very start, when love is defined as a desire for beauty, and beauty declared to be incorporeal [41]: henceforth, the progression is lineal [42]. It has been contended that Pico introduces a "conversion" after the third step, when the soul turns in upon itself and finds within itself the source of the beauty formerly beheld in the sensible object [43].

---

[40] See Kristeller, *Ficino,* pp. 277-85.
[41] Ficino, *Discours,* I. iv. f. 11 r°; IV. iii. f. 66 v°.
[42] See the paraphrase of Diotima's speech in Ficino, *Discours,* VI. xviii, f. 141 v°.
[43] Bennett, *S.P.* 28, p. 24.

The process may be described as a conversion, no doubt, but a conversion of an intellectual and mystical type, not the simple religious conversion of Spenser in the *Hymnes*[44]. Besides no break is implied here. What the soul considers is not really a different object. It has turned from the effect to the cause, from the light reflected to the fountain of light, but there is no real discontinuity in the progress, for there in no change in the goal. From the first, the soul had travelled in the direction of God. We may picture it to ourselves as a man who, catching a reflection in a mirror, first moves away from the mirror with his eyes still on it and at a certain point, swings round and beholds the object itself. But Spenser in the first two *Hymnes* had not really moved away from the reflection; he had not even fully taken the second step, since the "wished scope" vas still the enjoyment of beauty in the body. In the heavenly hymns, he had to make a fresh start from the lowest stair, as Renwick observes[45]. But the start was in a new direction and from another kind of beauty than the beauty of woman. And, again, he found precedent for it in the Renaissance *trattati d'amore.*

Both Bembo and Leone Ebreo, as I will show, had adopted, instead of the Platonic ladder, the Christian and Biblical mode of ascent: the contemplation of God in his handiwork[46]. Castiglione had also used it, but for a different purpose: to prove "that whatsoever is good and profitable, hath also evermore the comeliness of beautie"[47]. For the notion of ascent he closely followed the steps of Pico[48]. Spenser's debt to Leone Ebreo will be the subject of Chapter XI. The probable influence of Bembo's *Asolani* has also been strangely neglected. It is not a mere question of source-ascription: the interest lies in the identity of spirit and composition. *Gli Asolani* did not reproduce the continuous Platonic ladder. Gismondo was concerned in his speech with the praise of love and, like Spenser, he fused the first and second steps, the beauty of the body and the beauty of the soul[49]. As in Spenser's first hymns, the feeling remained concrete and personal, not extended to a universal concept of beauty. Besides, as in the last hymns, the speech of the Hermit to Lavinello did not invite the lover merely to take a new step beyond earthly love and earthly beauty, but first to abjure them, and entertain an entirely different love by contemplating not the beauty of

---

[44] For the enlightement of the reader, I reproduce Pico's words: "El quarto grado è che lalma considerando la operatione sua, vede se conoscere la natura della bellezza universalmente, & non ristretta ad alcuna particolare, & conosce che ogni cosa che è nella materia fondata è particolare, di che conclude questa tale universita non dallo obietto esteriore sensibile, ma dallo intrinseco suo lume, & dalla sua virtù procedere, & infra se stessa dice, se nelli adombrati specchi de phantasmati materiali per vigore della mia luce mi si representa questa bellezza, certo è ragionevol cosa che nello specchio della mia sostantia dogni nube materiale spogliata riguardando, debba ogni simil cosa assai piu chiaramente vedere & cosi in se conversa vede la imagine della beltà ideale à lei dalla intelleto participata" (Benivieni, *Opere*, ff. 64 v°-65 r°).

The *Hymne of Heavenly Love* is devoted not to the turning inward of the soul, purged of all sensible representations, but to the coming down of Christ on earth to take a body. One can hardly imagine a sharper contrast.

[45] *Daphnaida*, p. 212. See also Padelford, *JEGP* 13, pp. 424-6.

[46] *Gli Asolani*, p. 211 ff. *Dialoghi*, f. 166 v°.

[47] *Courtier*, p. 309.

[48] *Courtier*, pp. 317-19.

[49] *Asolani*, p. 186: "For as that body whose members are proportionate is beautiful, so is that mind whose virtues meet in harmony. ... So virtuous love is a desire for beauty of mind no less than body; and in order to reach that end and object of its longing, love spreads and beats its wings" (Transl. Gottfried, p. 157).

woman, which awakes desire, but the beauty of the creation, which awakes love for the Creator [50].

This meant a clean break with both Perotino's and Gismondo's conceptions of love. The attribution of the speech to a hermit made the contrast the more emphatic. Like Spenser within the diptych of the *Fowre Hymnes,* Bembo within the triptych of *Gli Asolani* worked by opposition, not by continuous progression as Ficino, Pico, Benivieni and Castiglione had done in their consistent expositions of the Platonic *scala.* Each speech was self-ended, and each made a fresh start in the contrary direction to the preceding [51]. With a writer like Bembo, more concerned with art than philosophy, it is not easy to say whether the composition commanded the thought, or the thought governed the composition. Spenser, too, was a poet first. Had he hesitated between Platonic continuity and Christian duality, artistic reasons would have swayed his mind and determined his choice [52]. But was any choice offered to his mind? By temper and tradition he was bound to reject or modify the Neoplatonic ladder. He had petrarchized Platonism in the first hymns. The turning away from earthly to heavenly love was not to be described as the turning inward of the soul and the discovery of intellectual beauty. It was to be the common Petrarchan recantation of loose loves and lewd rhymes (*H.H.L.* 8-21). Not that the love earlier praised had been loose, nor the rhymes lewd [53]. The poet, like Petrarch, might even have pleaded with himself that his earthly love had truly inspired him with the love of virtue and the love of God. If he did, he probably gave himself the answer which Petrarch had received from Augustine in the *Secretum*:

> Thou hast perverted the order, for, whereas thou oughtest to have loved the creature for the sake of the Creator, captured by the charms of the creature, thou hast loved the Creator, but not in the way thou shouldst have loved him [54].

---

[50] On the contrast between love and desire see pp. 173-4. On the revelation of God in his handiwork, see p. 176.

[51] Perotino had discoursed on the bitterness of (vulgar) love. Gismondo extols the pleasures of love (Petrarchan, with Platonic overtones). Lavinello and the Hermit repudiate human love to praise divine love, both Christian and Platonic.

[52] Spenser was partial to symmetrical arrangements, and symmetry invites contrast or identity rather than development.

[53] Padelford has observed, (*S.P.* 29, p. 214), that Spenser in the *Dedication* styled the two sisters, his patrons, "the most excellent and rare ornaments of *all* true love and beautie, *both in the one and the other kinde*", that is, both of earthly and heavenly love and beauty. This had been a strange compliment, had the first hymns been seriously considered "lewd".

[54] *De Contemptu Mundi, Opera,* t. 1, pp. 355-6.

Chapter IX

THE HEAVENLY HYMNS: CHRISTIAN OR PLATONIC?

> The problem of Ficino's reconciliation of Platonism with Christianity may be stated in this way: Is Ficino a Platonizing Christian, or a Christian Platonist? The nearer of the two to the correct answer is the latter [1].

Substitute Spenser for Ficino and "former" for "latter": you have again the correct answer [2]. J. W. Bennett had described the last two hymns as basically Platonic, with just an "additional Christian coloring" [3]. F. M. Padelford, insisting on their "Calvinism", showed them to be "basically Christian with a mere coloring of Neoplatonism" [4]. J. W. Bennett renewed her contention, but gave some ground, insisting on the fact that Renaissance Platonists like Ficino and Pico were Christian Platonists and that the antithesis of Platonism versus Christianity was a false one [5]. Of late, J. B. Collins again asserted the Christian character of the hymns. Rejecting both the Calvinistic interpretation of Padelford and the Neoplatonic interpretation of Bennett, he traced in all four hymns the three stages of Christian mysticism [6]. One hesitates to take up again a question which has been thrashed out so many times. But overstatements are conspicuous in the theories advanced and a revaluation should be attempted.

It is true that there is no *historical* antithesis between Platonism and Christianism; true that the Renaissance Platonists were Christians. But it is no less true that there were wide gaps between Platonism and Christianity, both in *doctrine* and in *spirit.* Those gaps, the Christian Platonists variously sought to bridge. But it cannot be maintained that they were unaware of the basic difference. Even in the hey-day of Renaissance Platonism, a large number of texts would give the lie to any such assumption. I have quoted in the opening chapter an Epistle of La Boderie which sharply distinguished between Platonic love and Christian love. Even the author of the *Theologia Platonica* time and again reminds us that Plato was but a foreshadower and had not

---

[1] *Jayne,* p. 22.

[2] Even in the case of Ficino, I cannot accept Dr Jayne's answer without reservations. Ficino is a Christian Platonist in his "commentaries" on the Platonists. In his own *Theologia Platonica* and in his letters, he is a Platonizing Christian.

[3] *SP* 28 (1931), p. 26.

[4] *SP* 29 (1932), p. 207.

[5] *SP* 32 (1935), p. 131.

[6] *Christian Mysticism in the Elizabethan Age,* p. 204 ff. The extravagance of the contention as regards the first two hymns should not blind us to the many judicious remarks on the traditional and Christian character of Spenser's ideas.

known the Christian Trinity[7]. The Plotinian trinity, indeed, read in the light of St. John and Dionysus, was sometimes thought to be a figure of the Christian Trinity[8]. But the central mystery of Christianity, the outgoing of God to man through the Incarnation of the Son, was acknowledged to have no parallel in Platonic doctrine[9]. Other differences were recognized, even by the most enthusiastic Platonists. In his *Apology for Plato against the philosophers of Paris,* "Diacceto admits that there are basic differences between Platonic and Christian doctrine: the former assumes as a first principle the One that is above all number, the latter teaches that God is both One and Three. The former assumes that Heaven, the angels and the souls have no beginning, whereas the latter teaches that they were created in time"[10].

Still more important than the differences in doctrine, acknowledged by the Platonists themselves, is the difference in spirit which they may not have clearly perceived. Platonism has sometimes been contrasted with Christianity as an aristocratic and intellectual doctrine with a popular creed, both ethical and mystical. That contrast is true only if we go back to the earliest days of Christianity. For our present purpose, the contrast between universality and personality will prove more serviceable. The tendency to abstraction and generalization, already noted in the Platonic philosophy of love, culminates with the conception of God as the One, or the Idea of the Good, whereas personality, not universality, nor mere "oneness", is the dominant character of the Christian God[11]. Among the Christian Platonists, therefore, those who stress universality may be expected to find Platonism more congenial than Christianity[12]. But no such suspicion can be entertained when personality in God is emphasized, however Platonic the terminology may be. That main distinction will command further distinctions, notably in the mode of ascent. Moreover, it affects the whole conception of divine love.

The creation of the world "out of meer love" had only been faintly foreshadowed by Plato in the *Timaeus*[12]. "Absence of envy" was the motive given for bringing order into chaos. Plato and all true Platonists conceived love as a "want", an imperfection, which they never thought of ascribing to the self-sufficient Idea of the Good. Plotinus substituted for the Platonic demiurge the overflowing of divine goodness into matter[13]. In the hierarchy of being, he attributed to the superior care for the inferior, but the circle described only became a circle of *love* with Dionysus, under Christian influence[14]. In Plotinus,

---

[7] See *Opera,* t. I, p. 956. Ficino assumes that later Neoplatonists borrowed hints from St. John and Dionysius.

[8] Cf. Ficino, *De la Religion Chrestienne*, xiii, pp. 89-90.

[9] The classical reference was St. Augustine's "sed quia verbum caro factum est et habitavit in nobis" (*Confess.* VII. ix.).

[10] *Opera* (Basilea, 1563), pp. 332-37. Summarized by Kristeller in *Francesco da Diacceto and Florentine Platonism,* pp. 289-90. See also F. Pico's exposition of the "imperfections" of Platonic philosophy from the Christian point of view in *De Amore Divino,* II. v, ff. 15 r°-16 v°.

[11] This note of personality is sometimes subdued in rational theologies, like that of Aquinas. It was most forcefully expressed in the theologies least influenced by Greek philosophy, for instance in Scotus. But it is always *present* in any Christian theology, and always *dominant* in Christian devotion, as in the Gospel.

[12] The *locus classicus* is *Timaeus* 29 e.

[13] *Enneads,* III. ii. 2, IV. viii, 6.

[14] *Enneads* IV. x. 4 (cf. Cassirer, *Platonische Renaissance,* p. 69). Dionysius, *De Div. Nom.,* cap. IIII; *Opera,* p. 455.

I discover little more than a phenomenon of transmission and attraction, which is characterized as "love" only in the *upward* movement[15]. To Plotinus, as to Plato, love only means a desire for the beautiful and the good. There is no love in God, save for himself[16]. Neither Platonism nor Neoplatonism would allow that outgoing of God to man that calls for the *answering* love of man as an *immediate* response to a *personal* appeal. They suggest at best the participation or diffusion of divine goodness; and the love by which the soul ascends through *successive* degrees of abstraction or *successive* grades of being is an aspiration to an ultimate and *impersonal* reality, never an answer to the prevenient love of God. To read all Christian ideas and emotions into Platonism does injury to Platonism as a philosophy, to Christianity as a religion. Accordingly, whenever a Christian Platonist presents love between God and man as a personal relation, we may be confident that he is at heart far more of a Christian than a Platonist.

Now, in the *Hymne of Heavenly love,* Spenser emphasizes the very dogmas which the Renaissance Platonists acknowledged to be basically different from Platonic doctrine: the Christian Trinity and the Incarnation. And the Christian characteristic of personality is throughout present, in the fourth as well as in the third hymn. For the Platonic One or Good the poet substitutes a Christian — and popular — "God Almighty"; for the Idea of the Beautiful, a Biblical and personified Sapience. It cannot be doubted that he thought and felt like a Christian. But it will be objected that he may nevertheless have intended to convey a Platonic meaning, and may have introduced Platonic notions. The first objection must be dismissed. The second may be granted — and qualified.

To assume that the *Hymnes* express "the basic conceptions" of Benivieni's *Canzone* and Pico's *Commento,* with only "an additional Christian coloring", would mean that Spenser consciously expounded Platonic philosophy by means of Christian symbols. The assumption would have horrified him, and horrified Benivieni and Pico as well. Not so much on account of its impiety as on account of its absurdity. The "characters" in the last two hymns are Christian "characters": God, Christ, the Holy Ghost, the Biblical Sapience. And, to Spenser, they had real existence whereas the Demiurge or the Heavenly Venus of the Platonists existed in his mind only as philosophical or poetical symbols of Christian realities. In the *Faerie Queene* Jove, for instance, is often used as a symbol of the Christian God, and Renaissance poets did not hesitate to compare Christ to Orpheus and other mythological heroes[17]. Spenser might have used the Heavenly Venus of the Platonists as a figure of the Christian Sapience. But he would never have dreamt of turning the Christian Sapience into an allegory of Venus Urania. The real could not be used to symbolize the unreal, Christian truths to signify Platonic tenets; which were true only in so far as they agreed with those Christian truths. Had the poet purposed to express those tenets, he would have refrained from introducing Christian notions inconsistent with them. In his Platonic *Canzone dell'Amor Divino,* Benivieni finds no room for Christian love. In his *Commento,* Pico declares from the first that his intention is to

---

[15] Cf. his treatise on love, *Enneads* III. v.

[16] *Enneads,* VI. viii. 15. The Good loves himself because his beauty is his own and he has it in himself. Love in God, as in man, is a desire for beauty. As to Plato, according to the Renaissance Platonists themselves, he had maintained that God is unaffected by love (cf. Leone Ebreo, *Dialoghi*, f. 132 v°).

[17] See chapter IV, p. 68. Pico the nephew compared Christ to Ulysses and Orpheus, in his purely Christian *Hymni... ad Trinitatem, Ad Christum et Ad Virginem.*

expound the philosophy of Plato, not Christian theology, "which alone is true" [18]. Another method for the commentator was to show how close to Christianity the Platonic writings were: Ficino and Le Roy could afford many instances. But Christian dogmas were never used to figure or express Platonic philosophy.

Spenser, therefore, cannot have given the heavenly hymns a Platonic *meaning*. This alone sharply distinguishes the hymns from Benivieni's *Canzone*. But the poet may have transferred Platonic notions to the Christian theology of the hymns. So Ficino had done in his *Theologia Platonica,* and before him Dionysius, Augustine and countless Church Fathers. Moreover, Spenser when he wrote the hymns certainly knew the purely Neoplatonic scheme. He must have been conscious of substituting the Christian truths for the Neoplatonic allegories. Sapience, for instance, was certainly not meant to stand *for* Heavenly Venus, but she must have been purposely depicted so as to remind the reader that she stood *in lieu* of Heavenly Venus. Platonism could not afford "basic conceptions", but a fitting language and decorative illustrations, just as mythology would on other occasions. "Thunder and lightning" are to be found underneath the feet of the Christian God as under the feet of Jupiter: but no one has ever thought that Spenser's conception of God was "basically" mythological [19]. It may even be granted that Platonism was used, to some extent, as a philosophy, to illustrate Christian dogmas. Christian truth is the centre of reference. The poet is not harmonizing dogmas with a full-blown philosophy, but importing fragments of Platonic philosophy into Christian theology. And the importance of those fragments has been much exaggerated by various critics [20]. They will be briefly reviewed as they occur in the hymns, so as to escape any suspicion of exclusion or specious arrangement.

The Trinity described by Spenser in the *Hymne of Heavenly Love* is obviously the Christian, not the Neoplatonic Trinity. The Son, begotten by the Father "like to it selfe and "with equall honour crownd" is not the *prima prole* or *Angelica mente* of Benivieni and Pico [21], but the Christian Son of God, "coequal" with the Father, of whom He is the perfect "Image" [22]. The Holy Ghost proceeds from *both* the Father and the Son and all three reign together [23]. It will be noticed that Spenser does not even avail himself of the Johannine conception of the Word, closest to the Neoplatonic Logos. In his description

---

[18] *Commento,* I. iii; *Discours,* f. 197 v°.

[19] *H.H.B.* 180-82.

[20] Notably by Winstanley, J.B. Fletcher and J.W. Bennett.

[21] Fletcher's assumption in *M P* 8, p. 549. See Benivieni, *Opere,* f. 42 r° and f. 52 r°-v°. "La summaria sententia di tutta la stanza è questa, che quando da Dio descende nella mente dello angelo PRIMA PROLE, cioè prima creatura di Dio, la copia delle Idee, desiderando langelo la perfettione di quelle, à Dio si rivolge & da lui conseguita piena possessione di quello che lui desidera, il che quanto piu pienamente ha in se, tanto piu lo ama ardentemente".

How this argument can be discovered in *H.H.L.* 29 ff. "and the *begotten* Son (l. 30) identified with the "prima creatura di Dio", I fail to see.

[22] This is the meaning of "like to it selfe"; cf. 1.171. The Christian notion of the Son as the Image of the Father is entirely opposed to Neoplatonism, for the Mind, which is already a multiplicity, cannot be the perfect "image" of the One: cf. Plotinus, *Enneads* VI. iv. 4; V. ix. 2; Ficino *In Convivium,* II. iii.

[23] Again irreconcilable with Benivieni's *alma* despite Fletcher's contention (*M P* 8, 549), for the World-Soul is not derived from *both* the first and second Neoplatonic hypostases. Successive emanations are not processions from equal to equal within the Godhead.

of the processions and the persons, he is more orthodox than many Church Fathers had been. The Son to him is first and foremost a person and the image of the Father, not the mind of God, much less the intelligible world [24]. Platonic notions are used only to account for the generation. They provide a philosophical justification for a Christian truth:

> It lov'd it selfe, because it selfe was faire;
> (For faire is lov'd;) and of it selfe begot
> Like to it selfe his eldest sonne and heire, (*H.H.B.* 29-31).

It may be agreed with Dr Bennett that this is "good Renaissance Platonism", though her quotations from Ficino are irrelevant and she herself admits that the idea is not in either Pico or Benivieni [25]. It will be further noticed that Spenser, contrary to Pico and Benivieni, places "il primo amore" and "la prima bellezza" in God ,not in the Angelic Mind or "prima prole". In so doing, he stands closer to Plotinus [26], and chiefly to Leone Ebreo whose *Dialoghi* offer the clearest and likeliest parallel [27]. But it should be noted that the ideas that God loves himself and Himself is fair are Christian commonplaces [28]. Since Plato had taught Spenser that love was a desire of generation in beauty [29], it was only natural to ascribe the generation of the Son to God's love of his own beauty. It afforded an explanation for Christian dogma, but did not alter it. Theologians may disagree, but I find the explanation in a way much more consistent with the characteristic Christian affirmation that God is love than is the current doctrine according to which the Son is begotten, not through God's self-love, but through His self-knowledge [30].

Thoughout the third *Hymne,* as might be expected, love will be the attribute most emphasized in God. Not Platonic love, even when the definition is Platonic — for Plato did not impart to God the "daemonic" love of generation in beauty. Not even Plotinian love; for to Plotinus, God is both the source and goal of love, but He is not love. Only with John and Dionysius did love become an attribute — the main attribute — of God [31]. Naturally Ficino read Plotinus in the light

---

[24] As in Ficino, *In Convivium,* I. iii, II. iii, and Pico, *Commento,* I. iv. v.

[25] *SP* 28, p. 37. The first quotation is traditional theology with the intellectual procession of the Word and the spiration of the Holy Ghost. (*De Christ. Relig.* cap. XIII; cf. Aquinas, *Summa Theol.* Pt. I. q. xxxii). The major part of the second quotation is found in Augustine and Aquinas: "... dicit augustinus super joann, (tract. 110, a med. aequivalenter): omnia diligit Deus quae fecit et inter ea magis diligit creaturas rationales et in illis eas amplius, quae sunt membra Unigeniti sui, et multa magis ipsum Unigenitum suum" (*Summa Theol.* pt. I, q. xx, a. 3). Hardly more Platonic is Ficino's addition: "... Si Deus sibi ipse placet, si amat seipsum profecto imagines suas et sua diligit opera" (*Theol. Plat.* lib. II, cap. XII). Neither quotation is a good parallel for *H.H.L.* 29-31.

[26] *Enneads,* VI, viii. 15. The Good is at once lover, beloved and self-love, because it is fair and has its beauty *from* itself and *in* itself.

[27] Leone reproduced the Plotinian argument and linked it like Spenser with the generation of the Son. See Chap. XI, pp. 190-91.

[28] See for instance Aquinas, *Sum. Theo.* pt. I, q. xxvi; Augustine, *In Psalm.* lxxxiv, in 8; t. 36-7, c. 1075; *Confess,* t. I, c. 795.

[29] *Symposium,* 206 e.

[30] As in Ficino and Augustine quoted above, note 25. Cf. Aquinas, *Summa Theol.* Pt. I, q. 34, art. 2; q. 27, art. 1.

[31] I. John. 4.8. Dionysius, *De Div. Nom.* iiii.

of Saint John and Dionysius [32]. I am not attempting to prove that Spenser departed from the Renaissance Platonists when they spoke like Christians. I am attempting to show that he borrowed from them either traditional ideas which had long been denizened in Christianity, or incidental notions which did not affect Christian dogma, whereas he discarded the Neoplatonic system as a whole.

The description of God as "the fount of love and grace — still flowing forth his goodnesse unto all" (*H.H.B.* 99-100) may be styled Neoplatonic if we choose to trace the image back to Plotinus [33]. But it had been at home in Christianity from the days of Dionysius to the days of Dante [34], and "grace" is a distinctly Christian addition. Besides, it was the natural language of poetry. That Spenser should speak of the Son as the Father's "eldest sonne" (*H.H.B.* 31) and of the Angels as his "second brood" and "next offspring" (*H.H.B.* 53,92) is no proof that he substituted Neoplatonic emanations for the Christian creation of angels. He had precedent in Scripture for the metaphors, since St. Paul characterized the Son as "firstborn among many brethren" and "the first-born" of every creature" (*Romans* 8.29; *Colossians* I.15). Should the critics that favour the Neoplatonic interpretation insist on giving the language of the poet a literal meaning, they would be defeated on their own ground, for Spenser described the Angels as the "off-spring of the *Makers* love", "glistering glorious in their *Makers* light" (*H.H.B.* 92,56). "Maker" clearly points to creation, not to emanation. The more distinctive Platonic feature is again the "reason" afforded for their creation: "love, that loves to get — Things like himselfe, and to enlarge his race" (*H.H.B.* 51-2). Spenser applied to Christian dogma the principles of the *Timaeus* and the *Symposium* concerning the nature of the Good and of love [35]. *Timaeus* and *Genesis* are again blended in the account of the creation of man [36]. But, to preserve the proper perspective, the reader should be reminded that Creation out of love is not Platonism, but Christian Platonism; and Christian Platonism not of the Renaissance alone, but of all ages [37]. Besides, *Timaeus* and *Genesis* had been harmonized by mediaeval as well as Renaissance writers. Indeed, thinkers like Ficino and Pico, drawing more upon Plotinus than Plato for their hierarchy of emanations had little use for the *Timaeus* in their exposition of the grades of being. A Timaeic account of the creation of man was conservative Platonism in Spenser's age [38].

---

[32] See for instance *In Convivium,* II. ii, where the Dionysian circle of love is brought into Platonic exposition.

[33] As Bennett does in *S P* 28, p. 37.

[34] *De Divinis Nominibus,* II (*Opera,* p. 433): "... patrem quidem esse fontanam... deitatem". — *Divina Commedia,* "Paradiso", Canto XXIX.

[35] The *Timaeus* (29 e) provided the idea that God being good, wished all things to be as like him as could be. The *Symposium* insisted on love as a desire of generation in men and beasts. Spenser logically extends the idea to divine love. Both ideas agree with Scriptural teaching (*Genesis* I. 26).

[36] Noted by Winstanley; cf. *Variorum, M P.* I. 542.

[37] See Dionysius, *De Div. Nom.* iiii (*Opera,* p. 455):

Ipse enim benefactor, existentium amor in optime per excellentiam ante subsistens, non sinit ipsum infoecundum in se ipso manere. Movit autem ipsum in agendum juxta omnium genitivam excellentiam".

[38] Ficino's and Pico's accounts of the origin of the world or the soul's descent into the body are Plotinian, not Platonic: cf. *Commento* I. vi (*Discours* 200 v°-202 v°); *Discours* I. ii, ff. 3-8; II. iii, ff. 16-20; VI. vi, f. 101 v°. They are irreconcilable with the description of creation in the *Timaeus*: "Ce mode de production, raisonné et prévoyant, contredit le genre de causalité des hypostases plotiniennes qui agissent

However deep the influence of the *Timaeus* proved on Spenser as on mediaeval poets, it was always subdued to Christianity. The Lord of Love which "him [man] at first Made of mere love, and after liked well" (*H.H.B.* 127-8) is obviously the Christian Son of God, not the Platonic Demiurge, since the same descends out of Heaven "In which he reigned with his glorious syre" to redeem fallen man (*H.H.B.* 134-40). To ascribe the creation of man to the Son is no "distinct piece of Platonism" [39], but current Christian theology. We read in St. Augustine that "Deus hominem sicut caetera per Verbum suum fecit" [40]. Besides, it was argued from the plural "Let us make man" that all three persons of the Trinity had taken part in the making [41]. Spenser ascribes the creation of man first to "that eternall fount of love and grace" (*H.H.B.* 98-120), God the Father, [42] and next to God the Son (*H.H.B.* 127-8). This clearly shows that he had in mind the traditional Christian Trinity, "distinguisht undistinct", for whatever the Father does, the Son also does [43].

The account of the Incarnation and the Crucifixion are so obviously, so characteristically Christian that no Neoplatonic interpretation has been urged, though a desperate attempt has been made to find at least one stray echo of Plato. The line on Christ's death, — "And slew the just, by most unjust decree" (*H.H.B.* 154) — has been thought to disclose a "strong reminiscence of Socrates in the *Republic*" and to add "one more item to the mass of evidence that Spenser was... steeped in Platonism" [44]. Whether the poet ever read the *Republic* is doubtful, but the line certainly adds one more item to the mass of evidence that he was steeped in Scripture, since it is an echo of the *Acts* [45]. The characters of personality and immediacy which distinguish Christian love from Platonic love are conspicuous at the very core of the *Hymne of Heavenly Love.* These central stanzas, over one third of the poem, cannot be dismissed as a "devotional "interruption [46]. It is just this ultimate proof of the outgoing "ecstatic" love of God for man which affects and informs Spenser's whole conception of heavenly love, whether in God or man:

> And give thy selfe unto him full and free,
> That full and freely gave himselfe to thee. (*H.H.L.* 265-6)

Christian love is not merely an impersonal desire for beauty: it is a desire of self-surrender. The Platonic conception of love seems to be dominant, I own, in the last stanzas. But they certainly do not represent the fourth and fifth steps of the Neoplatonists [47]. The meaning remains devotional, though the language

---

par *rayonnement sans calcul*" (Bréhier, *Plotin*, VI, p. 43). Spenser's God who "cast" to create man (*H.H.L.* 103) after a pattern "fashioned in his wise foresight" is the God of *Timaeus* and *Genesis*, not of the *Commento* and the *Sopra l'Amore,* the God of mediaeval Platonism rather than Renaissance Neoplatonism.

[39] Bennett, *S P* 32, pp. 135-36.

[40] *De Genesi ad litt.* VI. xii; t. 34, c. 347.

[41] Aquinas, *Summa Theol.* pt. I, q. 91, art. 4; Augustine *De Genesi* III. xix (t. 34, c. 291).

[42] "He" (l. 109) refers to "that eternal fount" (l. 99).

[43] A commonplace of Christian theology: cf. Augustine *In Joan.* CX. iii (t. 35, c. 1921-2).

[44] Bennett *S P* 32, pp. 137-8.

[45] *Acts* 7.52: 3.14. Noted by Landrum in *P M L A* 41, p. 542.

[46] Bennett, *S P* 28, p. 37.

[47] Bennett, *S P* 28, p. 38. Cf. Pico. *Commento,* 64 v°-65 r°; Castiglione, *Courtier*, pp. 318-9.

is philosophical. The transition from the Gospel story to Platonic notions is especially clever and curious. For literary reasons of symmetry and antithesis, Spenser wished to parallel the process described in the *Hymne in Honour of Love* [48]. He had invited the heavenly lover to meditate on Christ crucified. He further invites him — devotional advice again — ever to bear in mind His blessed image, just as the earthly lover's mind was "affixed wholly" on the image of his mistress (*H.L.* 204). And, just as the profane lover beheld in his mind, not the image of the earthly body only, but a "fairer forme", a truly "ideal" image, so the divine lover will behold "Th'Idee of [Christ's] pure glorie" (*H.H.L.* 284). Now, I have pointed out that Spenser, hostile to the process of generalization or universalization, substituted for the Platonic concept of beauty in all beautiful bodies the individual "idea" of the beloved, that is, in his vague Platonic terminology, the heavenly form which the soul first receives from God [49]. Again ,in the *Hymne of Heavenly love,* he holds out for ultimate contemplation a personal "Idea" of Christ. It should be noted, first, that the Idea of Christ is captured at a leap, from the sensible image of Christ, whereas "la celesta Venere" was only attained through rising from a particular to a general concept. The only way of reading the Platonic steps into the third hymn without glaring inconsistency, would be to assume that Spenser started again from the *lowest,* substituting from the first a sacred love for a profane. Thus presented, the theory might not prove irreconcilable with my contention, for it would emphasize a duality between the two pairs of hymns, not a progression from first to last. But it would not make Spenser a true Platonist either, since the capture of the Idea at one bound is distinctly un-Platonic.

In fact, if we look closer, we discover that the poet merely meant to express in fashionable Platonic language the traditional Christian — and mystical — distinction between the man-Christ who is the first object of contemplation for beginners in devotion, and the God-Christ, God the Son, as he stands in the bosom of the Father. "That celestiall beauties blaze" (*H.H.B.* 277) is not the radiance of the Heavenly Venus, but the "splendor" of the Son, which is "the brightness of [the Father's] glory" [50]. Saint Augustine had commented on Hilarius' distinction of what is proper to each Person within the Trinity: "Aeternitas, inquit, in Patre, species in Imagine, usus in Munere". And he had explained that the Son was characterized by "species" on account of his Beauty [51]. The notion was a commonplace of Christian theology and Spenser was fully orthodox, and probably aware of his orthodoxy, in emphasizing beauty in the Son after characterizing him throughout the hymn as the "Most lively image of [his] fathers face" [52].

The Christocentric Hymne of Heavenly Love [53] has been acknowledged to be at core un-Platonic, despite an occasional admixture of Platonism. It illus-

---

[48] *H.L.* 210. See Chapter VII, p. 131.

[49] *H.B.* 211-24. Cf. discussion in Chap. VII, p. 131 sq.

[50] "Fillius Dei... splendor Dei ipse est" (Augustine, *De Videndo Deo,* XVIII). The origin is *Hebrews* I. 3.

[51] *De Trinitate* VI. x. 11. Cf. Aquinas *Summa Theol.* Pt. I., q. xxxix, art. 8: "Species autem, sive *pulchritudo* habet similitudinem cum *propriis* Filii".

[52] *H.H.L.* 171. Cf. Aquinas, *Summa Theol.* Pt. I, q. xxxv.

[53] I adopt Collins's distinction of the two religious hymns as "Christocentric" and "Theocentric", (*Christian Mysticism,* p. 210) ,though I believe artistic reasons (parallelism with the hymns in honour of love and beauty) rather than mystical "methodology" commanded the poet's choice.

trates a Christian love widely different from the Platonic Eros. The *Hymne of Heavenly Beautie* might have been, at core, indifferently Christian or Platonic since it illustrates only the upward aspiration, lifting the soul through love to the contemplation of heavenly beauty. Such an aspiration had been taught by the Platonists before and after Christianity: they may claim copy-right from the point of view of the philosopher. But, historically, love as a desire for beauty soon became one aspect of Christian love — not, indeed, the most characteristic. Yet, though the Christian and the Platonist have the aspiration and the goal in common, the way of ascent and the nature of the ultimate object of contemplation may be widely different. And the difference may to some extent modify the motive and qualify the feeling itself.

The opening invocation of the fourth hymn has undoubtedly a Platonic ring. J. W. Bennett has pointed out parallelisms to the *Hymne in Honour of Beautie* [54]. But though the fourth hymn was certainly intended to "parallel" the second, the symmetry being one of antithesis, only the full significance of the hymn will reveal whether the poet meant to contrast earthly and heavenly Venus, or profane beauty and the beauty of the Christian God. One thing is already clear: contrast, not continuity is emphasized. The antithesis was familiar to the Platonists. But in the next stanzas its terms prove entirely different. For Platonism contrasted sensible and intellectual beauty. Having earlier praised beauty in woman, Spenser now turns to a consideration of beauty in nature. If we remember that he had earlier contrasted the feeling stirred by the beauty of woman with the impression worked "in the lookers vew" by the beauty of natural objects [55], then granting the name of "love" only to the former, we instantly perceive that the contrast between the second and the fourth hymn is at root ethical and emotional, not metaphysical. The poet does not oppose intellect to sense, but a non-sexual to a sexual emotion.

Within the profane hymns Spenser, unlike the Platonists had fused the higher and the lower Eros, not separating fruition from contemplation in earthly love. Accordingly, the contemplation of beauty in woman and the contemplation of beauty in God disclose the ethical duality of Christianity, not the intellectual duality of Platonism. The distinction which the Platonists drew from the first between sex and contemplation, the poet draws only now, for only now is disinterested contemplation attained. Just as the earlier hymns would have been judged impure by the orthodox Platonists, so would the Neoplatonic mode of ascent, starting from the beauty of beautiful bodies even when "abstracted" by the Mind, appear dangerous, if not impure, to a Christian of Spenser's type [56].

Renwick has justly characterized the progress from "th'easie vew — Of this base world, subject to fleshly eye... To contemplation of th'immortall sky" as "the method of the preacher, not of the philosopher" [57]. The poet takes a fresh start from sensible beauty and his progress to heavenly beauty is described in spatial terms, inconsistent either with the Platonic dialectic or the Neoplatonic intellectual and mystical ascesis. The description, no doubt, is Platonized, but neither the Platonism of Plato nor the Neoplatonism of Plotinus and Ficino prevail: the cruder mediaeval conception of a local abode of the blest in a heaven beyond the visible heaven is still uppermost in the poet's mind. *The*

---

[54] *S.P.* 28, p. 38.
[55] *H.B.* 78-81. See Chapter VIII, p. 149.
[56] He may also have been aware that an improper construction had been put upon Platonic or Socratic love: see Robb *Neoplatonism,* p. 181.
[57] *Daphnaida,* p. 212.

Zodiacus Vitae, "an Elizabethan schoolbook", is probably responsible for the ascription of "infinity" to the higher heaven, a current astronomical as well as metaphysical concept by Spenser's time [58]. The idea of dividing the Empyrean into nine heavens duplicating the visible heavens is a rather naïve piece of Platonism which has no warrant either in Plato, Plotinus or the Renaissance Platonists. It bears the stamp of the current passion for correspondences and was directly suggested by the traditional angelology echoed by Le Roy:

> Au premier monde Dieu préside à neuf ordres d'Anges... Au moyen, le Ciel préside à neuf Spheres [59].

If Spenser had grasped the Platonic theory of Ideas, he would hardly have "enraunged" them above the blessed souls and below the angelic orders. This is certainly not in keeping with Christian theology, for, to the Christian, Ideas are in God: Ficino himself acknowledged it [60]. But it is not consistent either with Neoplatonism which placed them in the Angelic Mind or First Intellect [61]. This is again *naïve* Platonism of the poet's own mint, like the "pattern" of the second hymn (*H.B.* 36-8). Intellectual notions are substituted for spatial notions only when the "Highest" is reached and his "essentiall parts" are to be described (*H.H.B.* 106-119):

> Those unto all he daily doth display,
> And shew himselfe in th'image of his grace,
> As in a looking glasse, through which he may
> Be seene, of all his creatures vile and base.

Not the language of Plato, this, but the language of Paul, if not of Calvin. The Scriptural sources of the following stanzas have been fully established [62].

---

[58] On Spenser's debt to Palingenius, see Chapter V, p. 98, n. 15. Beyond the visible heavens, Paligenius placed an archetypal world:

"Menti consimilem mundi qui continet in se
Res veras, stabiles, puras, immateriales"
(*Zodiacus* "Libra", p. 182)

in an infinite heaven of immaterial light:

Quippe extra coeli fines non ponimus ullum
Corpus: sed puram, immensam, & sine corpore lucem"
("Pisces", p. 347).

On the other hand, the astronomical conception of an infinite universe had gained ground from Nicolas of Cusa onward: "By 1500 the evidence indicates that the infinity themes, and particularly that of an infinite universe, had achieved noticeable prestige" (Mc Colley "The Seventeenth Century Doctrine of a Plurality of Worlds", *Annals of Science,* 1936, p. 406). Copernicus urged the hypothesis and Digges reproduced it in England (Mc Colley, "N. Copernicus and an Infinite Universe", *Popular Astronomy* 44, pp. 525-33). We may notice that Spenser abides by the more familiar and mediaeval conception, that of Palingenius, retaining the *primum mobile,* and making only the heaven of God infinite (cf. Mc. Colley, *Annals of Science,* 1936, p. 402).

[59] Le Roy, *Sympose,* f. 165 r°. Le Roy brought the correspondence into Platonic exposition, but it had been a commonplace throughout the Middle Ages: cf. Bartholomaeus, *De Propr. Rerum,* II. vii-xviii.

[60] In the theology of Ficino "Ideas are identical with the divine essence" (Kristeller, *Ficino,* p. 249), for "Ficino's concept of God contains the essential attributes both of the Plotinian one and of the Plotinian Mind" (*ibid.,* p. 282).

[61] Plotinus, *Enneads,* VI. iv. 4. In Pico (*Commento* I. v.) and Ficino (*In Convivium* I. iii), Ideas "are collected together in the Angelic Mind", but they were first in God whence they descended into the Mind. The theory was evolved to reconcile Christian orthodoxy with Neoplatonism.

[62] See Padelford, *JEGP* 13, p. 428; Osgood, *S.P.* 14, pp. 166-77; Landrum, *PMLA* 41, pp. 540-44, and Renwick's notes in *Daphnaida,* pp. 223-4.

Parallels offered out of Bruno, Ficino or Benivieni, on the contrary, are extremely general ,if not irrelevant [63]. The God of Truth and Righteousness has been shown to be Biblical and Calvinistic, and, apart from Scriptural parallels, the description of his throne offers only classical reminiscences [64]. The poet's ethical conception of God and divine light is so obviously irreconcilable with either the Platonic or the Neoplatonic conception that one feels inclined to apologize for pointing out so glaring a contrast [65].

It is more interesting to note that Spenser is at variance not only with Christian Platonism, but with his own *Hymne of Heavenly Love.* The God

> [Whose] scepter is the rod of Righteousnesse,
> With which he bruseth all his foes to dust, (*H.H.B.* 155-6)

hardly recalls "the eternall fount of love and grace". The Old Testament has been substituted for the New; or, within the New, St. Paul for St. John. I find the duality regrettable, not only on religious, but on artistic grounds. But we are not to believe that Spenser was insincere either in the third or the fourth hymn, for the duality was in him. The gentle Spirit "breathing from above... Thoughts halfe devine full of the fire of love" (*T.M.* 360-2) dwelt in the breast of the man who recommended the extermination of all irreconcilable elements in the Irish population [66]. To the poet's discharge, it must be said that, as he had placed "Osyris" under "Isis' feet" [67]

> To show that clemence oft in things amis,
> Restraines those sterne behests, and cruell doomes of his (V. vii 22)

---

[63] Winstanley's parallels from Bruno and Ficino are commonplaces on the intellectual vision of God and the gradation of beauty (*Fowre Hymnes*, pp. lxix ff. and Notes). Renwick's quotation from Ficino V. iv (*Daphnaida*, p. 222) is also a commonplace, and hardly relevant, for Spenser substitutes the traditional Christian gradation for the Neoplatonic hierarchy: *Materia mondana, Animo, Angelo.*

Lastly *H.H.B.* 113-15 alludes to the *single* Scriptural "glasse" (I. *Cor.* 13.12) not to the "*tre* fulgidi speculi" of Benivieni (*Opere*, f. 43 v°; quoted by Fletcher, *M.P.* 8, p. 558).

[64] Of Jove: cf. *H.H.B.* 180-2.

[65] It is not merely a matter of language or imagery but a fundamental opposition between an ethical conception of the judment-seat of God and a metaphysical conception of the Good or One. The light which environs the throne of God "farre exceeding" the light of the visible sun is again both crudely and ethically conceived. It need not be reminiscent of Ficino's quotation from the *Republic* VI (Renwick, *Daphnaida*, p. 223), for the Sun-God analogy was a mediaeval and Elizabethan as well as a Neoplatonic commonplace: cf. Dionysius, *De Div. Nom.* iiii; Boethius, *De Consol.* V, metre ii; Bartholomaeus, *De Propr. Rerum*, VIII, lxxxiii r° (Bartholomaeus quotes Macrobius, Ambrosius and Plato's *Timaeus*). See also Tillyard, *The Elizabethan World-Picture*, p. 81.

Like St Augustine the Renaissance Platonists attributed a metaphysical function to divine light; it bestowed upon the human mind the power to think as the sun bestowed upon the eyes the power to see (Ficino, *Commentarium*, VI. xiii: *In Anima est Veritatis Lumen*). But Spenser merely held it to be the medium:

> Through which to God all mortall actions here,
> And even the thoughts of men, do plaine appeare (*H.H.B.* 172-3).

This is not the Augustinian and Ficinian theory of *illumination*, but the bare idea that we can hide nothing from God, and the significance is ethical.

[66] *A View*, p. 134. Judgson pleads extenuating circumstances (*Life*, p. 136).

[67] Noted by C.S. Lewis, *Allegory of Love*, p. 349.

so he divides, as it were, the divine attributes between "mightie God' and Sapience. And, though God retains precedence, not the frown of Jehovah, but the lovelier face of Sapience arrests our attention.

Who, then, is Sapience? That the poet described her with the Book of Wisdom in his mind, no one can doubt [68]. But the Scriptural Wisdom in his mind, no one can doubt [68]. But the Scriptural Wisdom has been variously identified and Neoplatonic as well as Christian sources and interpretations of Spenser's Sapience have been offered [69]. Probable sources will be reviewed in another chapter. The safe method, now as ever, is to ascertain the poet's meaning first from internal evidence alone, so far as we may.

The first striking fact is the symmetry between the apotheosis of Christ at the close of the third *Hymne,* and the apotheosis of Sapience at the close of the fourth. The parallel points to identity, not to contrast, since exactly the same language is used to describe the same experience in the divine lover and emphasize the same attribute in the object of contemplation:

That in no earthly thing thou shalt
[delight,
But in his sweet and amiable sight.
(*H.H.L.* 272-3)

Thenceforth all worlds desire will in
[thee dye,
And all earthes glorie on which men
[do gaze
Seeme durt and drosse...
(*H.H.L.* 273-5)

And thy bright radiant eyes shall
[plainely see
Th'Idee of his pure glorie present still,
Before thy face, that all thy spirits
[shall fill
With sweete enragement of celestiall
[love,
Kindled throught sight of those faire
[things above.
(*H.H.L.* 283-7)

And letteth them her lovely face to see
Whereof such wondrous pleasures they
[conceive,
[that no] idle thought of earthly things
[remaine,
(*H.H.B.* 255-6, 268)

Cf. the stanza begining:
"Ne from thenceforth doth any fleshly
[sense,"
and the next proclaiming all pomp and
[riches "drosse".
(*H.H.B.* 267-80)

And looke at last up to that soveraine
[light,
From whose pure beams al perfect
[beauty springs,
That kindleth love in every godly
[spright,
Even the love of God...
(*H.H.B.* 295-7)

These are not chance repetitions for the God-Christ in the third Hymne is spoken of as "*celestiall beauty*", *Blinding* the eyes and lumining the spright" (*H.H.L.* 280), just as Sapience "Whose beautie filles the heavens with her light, And darkes the earth with shadow of her sight" (*H.H.B.* 228-9).

---

[68] See Osgood, *S P* 14, (1917), 166-77.

[69] The following theories have been advanced:

Winstanley (*Fowre Hymnes,* p. 74): the Platonic Idea + reminiscences of the Virgin Mary.

Fletcher (*P M L A* 26, 457 ff.): Heavenly Venus + the Holy Ghost.

Padelford (*J.E.G.P.* 13, 418-33): the Logos.

Osgood (*S P* 14, 167-77): the Scriptural Sapience.

Saurat (*Rev. Litt. Comp.* 1926, 5-15): the Schekhina of the Cabbalists.

Bennett (*S P* 28, 43-7: *S P* 32, 140 ff.): "la celesta Venere" of Pico.

Collins (*Christian Mysticism,* 222-6): a personified attribute of the Christian God

From the Holy Ghost, Professor Osgood observed, "all gifts of wit and knowledge flow". From Sapience flow all "heavenly riches" [70]. Therefore the Holy Ghost, the "most wise", should be Sapience [71]. But those "heavenly riches" are not "gifts of wit and knowledge". These are only required as a means of gaining "heavenly riches", that is, the sight and fruition of heavenly beauty. The assistance of the Holy Ghost is besought by the poet in order that he may show

> Some little beames to mortall eyes below,
> Of that immortall beauty, there with thee, (*H.H.B.* 12-3).

Spenser could not have made his meaning clearer. Here is plainly declared that the Holy Ghost is not Beauty, but the revealer of Beauty. Now, Sapience is Beauty; and the God-Christ, in the last stanzas of the third *Hymne,* is also Beauty [72]. Sapience therefore and the God-Christ are one in essence. But whereas the third *Hymne* stressed the relation of God to man, in the person of Christ, the fourth *Hymne* stresses the inner relationship of the first and the second persons within the Trinity.

Yet, some of the characteristics of the second person as "mediator" were retained in the portrait of Sapience. The dispensation of "heavenly riches" comes from the *Book of Wisdom,* but the rôle well becomes the Son, who is the Mercy of the Father and the giver of eternal life. The best commentary on the 36th stanza is found in Paul's *Epistle to the Ephesians*:

For she out of her *secret threasury,*
Plentie of riches forth on him will [powre,
Even *heavenly riches,* which there [hidden ly,
Within the closet of her chastest [bowre,
Th'eternall portion of her precious [dowre,
Which mighty God has given to her [free,
and to all those which thereof worthy [bee.
None thereof worthy be, but those [whom shee
Vouchsafeth to her presence to receive...

(*H.H.B.* 246-54)

(my italics)

Unto me is this grace given, that I should preach *the unsearchable riches* of Christ.
And to make all men see what is the fellowship of the mystery *which from the beginning of the world hath been hid in God,* who created all things by Jesus-Christ. (*Eph.* 3. 8-9.)
That he might shew the *exceeding riches of his grace* in his kindness towards us *through Christ Jesus.* (*Eph.* 2. 7.)
For by grace are ye saved through faith; and that not of yourselves: it is the gift of God. (*Eph.* 2. 8.)
In whom we have boldness and access with confidence *by the faith* of him [Christ]. (Eph. 3. 1.)
For *through him we have access* unto the Father. (*Eph.* 2. 18.)

---

[70] *H.H.L.* 39,44; *H.H.B.*, 9. Cf. *H.H.B.* 248. That the Holy Ghost should be styled "most wise" does not imply that he is Sapience for, although "Sapientia nomine Filius potissimum insinuetur in Scripturis", yet "et Pater et Spiritus sanctus sit Sapientia (Augustine, *De Trinitate,* VII. i; t. 42, c. 936).

[71] Osgood, *S.P.* 14, p. 175.

[72] Critics have asserted that Christ is love in the third *Hymne.* This must be qualified. He is the "Lord of Love" (La Boderie's "parfait autheur d'amour"). But he is distinguished by love only *in relation* to mankind, only as he is Christ. Within *the trinity,* the name of love belongs properly to the Holy Ghost according to both traditional and Ficinian theology. When Spenser wished to mark off the Son (not Christ) from the other persons of the trinity, he always stressed his *beauty* (*H.H.L.* 277) or his being the perfect *image* of the Father (*H.H.L.* 31, 171), a character which connoted beauty in Augustinian theology (*De Trinitate,* VI, x; t. 32, c. 931).

The Biblical verses are not quoted as parallels. But I believe they illustrate the meaning of Spenser: the riches of eternal life out of God's "secret threasury" (that is, his foreknowledge and election) are gained only through Christ and by a special grace. In other words, "no man knoweth the Father save the Son, and he to whomsoever the Son will reveal him".

"God created all things by Jesus-Christ" wrote Paul (*Eph.* 3.9). And John had declared: "all things were made by him" (I.3). Spenser had described the creation accordingly in the third *Hymne,* emphasizing the part played by the Son in the creation of man. In the fourth *Hymne,* he stressed the part played by Sapience: one more proof that Sapience and the Son are one [73]. The phrasing of St. John may even be echoed in the words: For of her fulness which the world doth fill, They all partake, (*H.H.B.* 199-200). "And of his [the Son's] fulness have we all received" declared John (I.16). And he went on to say: "No man hath seen God at any time; the only begotten Son, which is *in the bosom* of the Father, he hath declared him" (I.18). Likewise, Spenser, after describing God as "hid in his owne brightnesse from the sight of all", shows us Sapience sitting in his bosom, a phrase not to be lightly dismissed, for the poet here for once departs from the *Book of Wisdom* where Sapience is described as sitting "by the throne" of God (*Wisd.* IX.4).

The last quotation raises the question whether Sapience is created or begotten. Since I have shown her to be identical with the Son of the third *Hymne,* the answer is obvious. Yet it has been contended that Sapience is not the uncreated Word of Christian Theology, co-essential with the Father, but "the Word or Logos of the Neoplatonists, the "first created intellect" of Pico. But I fail to discover in the *Hymnes* any evidence that Spenser considered Sapience as a creature, even were it "the first and noblest Angel God has produced" [74]. This could only be argued from a single line, when her beauty is said to be "Sparkled on her from Gods owne glorious face" (*H.H.B.* 207). But the poet adds: "And more increast by her owne goodly grace". This cannot apply to the "angelica mente" of Ficino and Pico, for it has no light or beauty of its own but what it receives from God. Both lines agree, on the contrary, if we take God to mean God the Father, as in the verse of St. John quoted above (I.18), and Sapience

---

[73] Professor Bennet's Neoplatonic interpretation of the stanza (*S.P.* XXXII. 141) cannot be retained for the line "As their great *Maker* did at first ordaine" (*H.H.B.* 201) refers to God the Father, not to the Lord of Love (*H.H.L.* 127) Compare:

"So that next off-spring of the *Makers* love" (*H.H.L.* 92) and even

"As their Almightie *maker* first ordained" (*F.Q.* IV. x. 35),

where the Maker is undoubtedly God.

Besides, as we have seen, the Lord of Love is not the Platonic demiurge but the Son of God. To identify him with the Maker would therefore make the stanza meaningless. For a clarification of the respective parts played by God and Sapience (the Father and the Son) in the work of creation, see further down the quotations from Julian of Norwich and R. Bostocke ch. IX, p. 167 and Ch. X, p. 181.

[74] Bennett, *S P* 28, pp. 44-5. Pico, *Commento,* I. iv.

[74 bis] Both Giles Fletcher and Milton described the Son as Spenser had described Sapience:

"Full of his Father shines his glorious face".

(*Purple Island,* xii. 81)

"Beyond compare the Son of God was seen
Most glorious, in him all his Father shon"

(*Paradise Lost,* III, 138-9)

God the Son. For the radiance and glory of the Son, though streaming from the Father ("lumen de lumine") are yet *his own,* since He is coessential with the Father[74 bis].

The insistence on Sapience as Beauty and her love-relationship with God make no difficulty either. The first has led to a Neoplatonic interpretation; the second, to various hypotheses as to Gnostic and Cabalistic sources. Spenser may have been aware of all these implications; but the core of his meaning is simply the traditional characterization of the Son as "Beauty" and the no less traditional love-relationship between the Father and the Son. St. Augustine and all Augustinian writers had rung the changes on the theme of *pulchritudo Christi* or *pulchritudo Filii*[75], and Dr Bennett herself characterized as a commonplace the male-female relationship between the first and second persons of the Trinity[76]. That a poet should have painted the second person as a heavenly queen can shock only the modern mind, unaccustomed to these mystical symbols. The mediaeval mind was not dismayed at the apparent incongruity of calling the Son "Mother" as he was called in the *Revelation of Divine Love,* recorded by Julian of Norwich:

> ... I understood that the high Might of the Trinity is our Father, and *the deep Wisdom of the Trinity is our Mother,* and the great Love of the Trinity is our Lord[77].
>
> Our high Father, God Almighty... willed that the second Person should become our Mother. *Our Father* (*willeth*), *our Mother worketh, our good Lord* the Holy Ghost confirmeth...
>
> ... All the *fair working* and all the sweet natural office of Motherhood is impropriated to the second Person[78].
>
> *Our Kind Mother, our Gracious Mother* [=our Mother by Nature, our Mother in Grace]... He took the Ground of His Works full low and full mildly in the Maiden's womb[79].

To Julian the Second Person is Wisdom and "our Mother of Mercy", God *working* in Nature and Grace, whereas the First is "endless sovereign Truth". "God Almighty" *willing* from all Eternity that which the second Person *works* in time. This is the distinction suggested by Spenser: he stresses Truth and Might in God (*H.H.B.* 155-82), Mercy and Grace in Sapience. The latter appears as a world-pervading influence, incessantly active, whereas God "ordained" all things from the first[80]. This comparison was not meant to suggest an influence, but only to show once more that the poet remained "in the channel of accepted Christian thought".

More light is thrown on Sapience when the symbol is considered, against the larger background of Spenser's poetry. J. B. Collins has pointed out the

---

[75] See *In Psalmum XLIV,* 3; t. 36, c. 495-6.

[76] *S.P.* 28, pp. 44-5.

[77] *Revelations of Divine Love,* Chap. LVIII; ed. G. Warrack, p. 145 (my italics).

[78] Ibid., Ch. LIX, p. 148.

[79] *Ibid.,* Ch. LX, p. 149.

[80] *H.H.B.* 197-203. The first person was characterized as Truth in the 44th Chapter of the *Revelations*: "God is endless, sovereign truth, endless sovereign Wisdom, endless sovereign Love" (p. 93).

insistence of Spenser on Wisdom as a divine attribute in the *Teares of the Muses*[81]. The most interesting parallels are:

> But they, whom thou great Jove by doome unjust
> Didst to the type of honour earst advaunce;
> They now, puft up with sdeignfull insolence,
> Despise the prood of blessed Sapience. (*T.M.* 69-72)
>
> For God himselfe for wisedome most is praised,
> And men to God thereby are nighest raised. (*T.M.* 89-90)

But the contention that Spenser, in the *Fowre Hymnes* "took Sapience out of his catalogue of attributes and personified it" is not satisfactory despite the weight of mystical and mediaeval evidence which supports it[82]. On the one hand, it does not fully account for the part played by Sapience as a Mediator (*H.H.B.* 249-59). On the other hand, "as an intelligent churchman Spenser must have been utterly inattentive of eye, ear and mind, not to know the traditional identification, both Catholic and Protestant, of the attribute Wisdom with Christ"[83]. Collins argues that Augustine insisted that Wisdom was a divine attribute[84]. But St. Augustine acknowledged that "Sapientiae nomine... Filius potissimum insinuetur in Scripturis"[85]. The Father, no doubt, is Wisdom as well as the Son, but in a poem so clearly of "Scriptural" inspiration, is it astonishing that the Son should be "insinuated" under the name of Sapience? Yet, at the same time, it may be granted that the object of contemplation is no longer the "Idee of Christ" as in the third *Hymne,* for even that "Idee" retained a twolfold nature, human and divine. The soul now contemplates God the Son in his divine essence; which is the *one* essence of the trine Godhead. The Son-Sapience equation, therefore, does not prevent us from acknowledging the contemplation of Sapience to be of the Theocentric type.

Of a quite different nature are the parallels suggested by J. W. Bennett between the Sapience of the fourth *Hymne,* the Nature of the Mutabilitie Cantos. and the Venus of the Fourth Book of the *Faerie Queene*:

> In the super-celestial world Venus is identical with Sapience, the personification of the divine Wisdom or Mind of God. There is an account of earthly Venus in the fourth book of the *Faerie Queene* (x. 39 ff.). Nature is evidently the Venus principle of the intermediate, or celestial world[86].

This is an extremely ingenious hypothesis, but it rests on the Neoplatonic distinction of a hierarchy of worlds which Spenser never expressly made and, in all likelihood, never intended. Besides, according to J. W. Bennett herself, "evidently he did not think of the three stages in the Venus emanation as distinct and independent deities". Sapience includes the created universe, i.e. both Nature and earthly Venus under her dominion. On the other hand, earthly Venus, like Sapience, is said to have created the world. The explanation afforded is that "the conception of a single emanation from the deity, which is represented in several worlds or degrees, by several divinities who differ in name but telescope

---

[81] *Christian Mysticism,* pp. 223-4.
[82] *Ibid.*, pp. 222-4.
[83] Editor of *Variorum, M.P.* I, p. 564.
[84] *Christian Mysticism,* p. 224, *De Trinitate* VII. iii.
[85] *De Trinitate,* VII. iii. *Opera,* f. 72 r°.
[86] *S P* 30, p. 163.

in function, is a commonplace of Renaissance Neoplatonism" [87]. But not a single reference is offered in support. Nature and the World Soul are sometimes hardly distinguishable in the Neoplatonic hierarchy [88], but I am not aware that the Angelic Mind and the World-Soul ever "telescoped in function". In fact, the statement should be reversed: distinct emanations of the deity may receive the same name though they differ in function. The Neoplatonists distinguished two Venuses: "one is clearly that intelligence which we said was in the Angelic Mind; the other is the power of generation with which the World-Soul is endowed" [89]. Contemplation and generation are not, I believe, identical functions. Besides, it is clearly stated that "the Angelic Mind is completely foreign to any relationship with corporeal matter [90]. In fact, the Mind is a transcendent intelligible world of Ideas [91]. It is the formal cause of the material world, not an immanent power still active in it (*H.H.B.* 197-203). On the other hand, I have shown that Sapience is not the Neoplatonic Mind, but God himself, in the person of his Son. Both transcendence and immanence are characters of Sapience, as of the Christian God:

> That high eternall powre, which now doth move
> In all these things... (*H.H.L.* 28-9)
> For of her fulnesse which the world doth fill
> They all partake... (*H.H.B.* 199-200)

But though any Neoplatonic systematization is spurious, the recognition of a single divine principle in Sapience and Nature is essentially right, provided it be thought out in a Christian way, and mainly in mediaeval terms. Behind the veil of Nature in Mutabilitie there hides the Creator-God of revealed religion, and perhaps more especially God the Son, as the allusion to the transfiguration of Christ suggests. In the *Hymne of Heavenly Beautie,* we are beyond the veil, face to face, not with an emanation of the Deity, but the Deity itself. The ascription of the creation of the world to the Lucretian Venus of the fourth book may be merely a literary *cliché,* authorized by Natalis Comes [92]. If a relationship between Venus and Sapience is required, the simplest explanation is that Spenser substituted a Christian for a pagan account, as he substituted the "eternall fount of love" for the Love waking in Chaos of pagan cosmogony.

Was Spenser a Platonizing Christian or a Christian Platonist? Time and again the former has proved the right answer. The hymns of heavenly love and heavenly beauty are purely Christian in spirit since love is presented either as an immediate answer to the personal love of God, or as the desire of enjoying, not the vision of the Idea of the Beautiful or the Good, but the beauty of a *personal Christ* and a *personal* Sapience [93]. They are dominantly Christian in substance, since Christian dogmas are throughout intended and respected, even when the language is Platonic. What Platonism has found its way into the *Hymnes* is thoroughly subdued to Christianity.

---

[87] *Ibid.*, p. 164.
[88] e.g. in Ficino, *Comment. in Conv.* II. iiii (*Jayne,* p. 137).
[89] *Ibid.*, II. vii, p. 142.
[90] *Ibid.*, II, vii, p. 142.
[91] *Ibid.*, I. iii, p. 127. Pico, *Commento,* I. v-vi.
[92] "Hanc unam denique mundum procreasse & procreatum nutrire & conservare crediderunt" (*Mythologia,* IIII. xiii, p. 386).
[93] As a poet, it will be objected, Spenser was bound to personify the Neoplatonic entities. But Benivieni did not: the sun, the angelic mind are hardly

Since profane hymns of a pre-eminently Platonic character were followed by sacred hymns of a dominantly Christian character, I further believe that the substitution of Christian themes for Platonic themes was conscious. Patches of Platonism were retained, for Spenser no more sensed any *antagonism* between Platonism and Christianity than many Church Fathers had. But he knew the shortcomings of Plato, which even Ficino had exposed [94], and he may have remembered the words of Jean de Meung:

> N'en sot pas Platons jusque la;
> Ne vit pas la trine unité
> En ceste simple trinité,
> Ne la deïté souveraine,
> Afublée de pel humaine [95].

---

personifications. Should it be argued that the difference is due to a different poetic genius, Spenser's being more concrete, it might be answered that the difference in poetic genius implies a different cast of mind, which made one poet, for a time at least, a Platonist, whereas the other never was anything but a Christian.

[94] See his letters in *Opera*, I. 956.

[95] *Roman de la Rose*, ll. 19140-44.

CHAPTER X

RENAISSANCE PLATONISM AND THE AUGUSTINIAN TRADITION IN THE HEAVENLY HYMNS

An examination of the text has revealed that the poet consciously substituted Christian themes for Platonic themes in the last two hymns and clearly identified Sapience with the Second Person of the Christian Trinity. Since it had already been recognized that he mainly followed Ficino's *Sopra l'Amore* in the profane hymns, full agreement has been reached between conclusions based on internal evidence alone and the earlier assumption that La Boderie's Epistle to the Queen of Navarre determined the composition of the *Hymnes*[1]. Only a qualification must be introduced, for it may be objected that Spenser does not contrast Platonism and Christianity; he simply makes the former subservient to the latter. But La Boderie had not invited the poet to banish "le divin Platon" altogether. He had only advised him to write, not in memory of Plato, but "en souvenance & recordation du parfait autheur d'Amour & de Vie"; not of Platonic love *alone* ("non de l'origine d'Amour à la Platonique *seulement*") but of Christian love: "de l'origine éternelle & temporelle naissance du vray Amour à la chrestienne"[2]. Plato had only foreshadowed Christian truth, but, as Diacceto claimed, Dionysius had shown that Christian theology could avail itself of Platonic philosophy[3]. Even with the conscious purpose of writing of Christian, not merely Platonic love and beauty, Spenser could make use of Platonic notions. But is it not characteristic that he should have mentioned "le divin Platon" only in the description of the Ideas "which *Plato* so admyred" (*H.H.B.* 83)? I have earlier suggested that the collocation of the Platonic Ideas in the Christian heaven, just below the angelic hierarchies was a piece of naïve Platonism[4]. I may have done injustice to the Christian poet, though not to the inconsistent Platonist. May not Spenser have intended to show that the Greek philosopher had risen no higher than the fringe of divine truth, the region of "Intelligences" (*H.H.B.* 84), beyond which lies the vision of God obtained by "grace" alone (*H.H.B.* 239 ff.)?

Most — if not all — Renaissance Platonists agreed on this point with Spenser and La Boderie whenever they gave their opinion on the relation of Platonism to Christianity[5]. But the distinction I wish to draw is not between men of different opinions but works of a different nature or intention.

---

[1] See Chapter VI, *ad. fin.*
[2] See full quotations, ch. VI, p. 114.
[3] Kristeller, *Diacceto and Florentine Platonism,* p. 290.
[4] See Chapter IX, p. 162.
[5] Cf. quotations from Diacceto, Ficino and Francesco Pico in Ch. IX, p. 154.

Renaissance treatises or poems of Platonic inspiration roughly fall into three categories":

1° expositions of Platonic philosophy *per se.*

2° expositions of Platonic philosophy in the light of Christian doctrine.

3° expositions of Christian doctrine in the light of Platonic philosophy.

The heavenly *Hymnes* belong with the third kind of exposition, with the Christian works of Ficino, not with his commentaries on Plato and Plotinus. Among the Renaissance expositions of Platonism, they discover affinities with the commentary of Le Roy on the *Banquet,* and the treatises of Equicola and Leone Ebreo rather than the *Sopra l'Amore* or even the *Cortegiano*; for the former emphasize the Christian (or Scriptural) aspects of Platonic doctrine, whereas the latter only suggest them. Lastly, they stand out in sharp contrast to such expositions of Platonic philosophy as Benivieni and Pico gave, confining themselves to Neoplatonic notions in a Neoplatonic scheme [6]. Renaissance commentaries and treatises of Christian inspiration, therefore, offer by far the largest number of parallels to the Christian *Hymns* of Spenser. Not for the sake of source-ascription (a hopeless and thankless task) will such parallels be recorded, but for the sake of illustration, the better to bring out the characteristic features of the hymns. These are the conception of divine love, the contemplation of God in his handiwork, the insistence on the necessity of grace and the identification of Sapience with God the Son.

Benivieni's *Canzone dell'Amore Divino* and Pico's *Commento* were only concerned with divine love in the creature, not in the Creator; with Eros, not with Agape. Pico, as a Christian, naturally attributed love to God, but he himself declared that it would not be considered in his Commentary, for the Platonic definition of love he had given was "repugnant" to it:

> ... estant l'amour duquel nous parlons un desir de posseder la beauté d'autruy, n'estant en Dieu le désir d'aucune chose hors de luy, comme celuy qui est en tout tresparfait, & n'a faute d'aucune chose, cet amour ne pourrait d'avantage luy repugner: pource que celuy duquel il ayme les creatures, procede justement d'occasion opposite [7].

The *Hymne of Heavenly Love* therefore clearly falls outside the province of "Amor Divino" as treated in the *Canzone* and the *Commento.* And, though he introduced the Dionysian circle of love into his exposition of the *Symposium,* Ficino, throughout his *Commentary,* abided by the conception of love as a desire for divine Beauty:

> Et ceste espece divine, c'est à dire la Beauté, a procrée en toutes choses l'Amour c'est dire, desir de soy. Par ce que si Dieu ravit le Monde & le Monde est ravy de luy il y a un certain continuel attrait entre Dieu & le monde qui commence de Dieu & passe par le monde & finalement se termine en Dieu [8].

---

[6] Pico, *Commento,* I. iii (*Discours,* f. 197 r°-v°). Pico mentions the ecstasy of St. Paul (*Commento,* II. xxv) and the fall of the Angels (Ibid. III.iv), but occasional Christian references do not alter the purely Neoplatonic nature of the argument and scheme.

[7] *Commento* II. ii (*Discours,* f .217 v°).

[8] *Discours,* II. ii, f. 14 r°.

However close to Christian love this definition may be, it is still insufficient to account for the *Hymne of Heavenly Love,* and throughout the *Commentary* Eros, not Agape is discussed. Only in the beautiful closing invocation when Ficino no longer speaks as the expositor of Plato, but as a Christian calling on the Christian Trinity, do we meet with the characteristic conception of Christian love: love that "runs to meet us before we seek Him" [9]. This alone, not the circle revolving from good to good, fully accounts for "le sacre mystere de l'amour eternel & divin" which La Boderie wished to substitute for the Platonic teachings [10]. This, indeed, Spenser illustrated in the key-stanzas of the third hymn. It will be noticed that Ficino identifies Love with the Holy Ghost, as a consistent Christian Platonist necessarily would [11]. La Boderie insists on Christ as "parfait autheur d'Amour", so does Spenser on the "Lord of Love" [12]. For the conception of love as a *universal* bond, they substitute love as a personal relationship.

Next to La Boderie's Epistle, the close of Le Roy's Commentary on the *Banquet* offers the best illustration of the *Hymne of Heavenly Love.* Affinities between Spenser and Le Roy, if not direct influence, have already been traced in their philosophy of human and cosmic love [13]. They are as conspicuous in their conception of divine love. In the running commentary on the *Banquet,* Le Roy mainly reproduces the arguments of Pico and Ficino. But at the close he devotes several pages to pure Christian doctrine:

> Nature est le commencement de grace, la philosophie de religion, ny doit estre estimée Philosophie celle qui retire l'homme de religion [14].

There follows an account of the fall of man, the Incarnation and the life of Christ on earth:

> Car ne se contentant d'avoir créée le monde de rien, avoir fait l'homme à son image, luy mesme [Dieu] a vestu l'espece humaine... Donques l'unique filz de Dieu qui est Dieu pere devant les siècles, & qui a crée toutes choses [15], nostre humanité prise, a esté faict homme, & par ce moyen a accomply nostre salut. Pour tous lesquels benefices il ne demande sinon que nous l'aymions de tout nostre cœur... Aussi qu'aymions nostre prochain comme nous mesme... & non seulement qu'aymions nostre prochain amy, mais aussi que ne hayons nostre ennemy [16].

Only to show that Platonic philosophy had not affected traditional Christianity, and was, indeed, considered by many as the mere "beginning" of religion, were these devotional commonplaces quoted. If we turn from the commentaries to the *trattati d'amore,* we find again that followers of Pico like

---

[9] *Discours,* VII. xvii, f. 189 r°.
[10] *Discours,* sig. A i j r°.
[11] In the trinity of the Christian Neoplatonists, the Father (the One) and the Son (the Mind) remain transcendent, But the Holy Ghost, reminiscent of the World-Soul, is conceived as pervading the world. Love, therefore, was best equated with the Holy Ghost, both proceeding from God and returning to God *through the world.*
[12] *Discours,* sig. A. iij. r°; *H.H.L.* 128.
[13] See Chap. V, p. 100 sq.
[14] *Sympose,* f. 177 r°.
[15] Cf. *H.H.L.* 128; *H.H.B.* 203.
[16] *Sympose* ff. 178 v°-179 r°. Cf. *H.H.L.* 190 ff.

Castiglione, and even Bembo [17], only offer the Neoplatonic conception of divine love. Castiglione, indeed, places love in God [18], but insists on the *universal* bond, the "meane betwixt heavenly and earthly thinges", which "bendest the high vertues to the government of the lower", notions which apply to the Neoplatonic intermediaries not to the Christian mediator [19]. Leone Ebreo, in his reconciliation of Platonic and Hebraic doctrine comes nearer to the conception of a personal love of God for his creatures. It is of interest to note that he asserts the presence of love in God, in conscious opposition to Plato, on the authority of Scripture. His position, like Spenser's, is religious *before* being philosophical:

> la sacra Scrittura dice che Iddio è giusto, & ama i giusti & dice che Iddio ama i suoi amici, & dice che i buoni huomini sono d'Iddio figliuoli, & Iddio gli ama come padre. Come vuoi dunque tu ch'io nieghi che in Dio non sia amore ? [21]

Equicola, in a chapter "Dell'Amore di Dio", speaks of divine love in the Christian sense, quoting from Augustine and Dionysius:

> ... Dio in se stesso si diletta: da che debbiamo intendere che nella natura di Dio è amore. Ama dunque le cose create.
>
> ... io con Agostino acconsento che i due Padre & Figliuolo s'amino vicendevolmente [22].

Plotinus had taught that the Good loved itself, but the love of the Father for the Son (the love of God for Sapience in Spenser's *Hymnes*) is distinctly Christian. Indeed Plato is said to have taught that God created the world out of love:

> Non solamente l'Hebrea & Christiana Academia, ma quel grande opinatore Platone afferma, che amore è stato causa, che Dio habbia fabricato il mondo [23].

But Equicola immediately added that the identity of divine providence and divine love had only been perceived "per velo & per ombra" by Plato and Plotinus, whereas

> Noi Christiani in chiaro, e rilucente giorno diciamo che Dio amando provede al tutto, & provedendo ama [24].

This is not the first time that Spenser is found to be in closer agreement with Equicola than he is with Pico or Ficino [25]. Their agreement is the more suggestive as it manifests itself on various and unconnected points concerning both human and divine love. Suggestive of direct influence? Perhaps, but source-

---

[17] Bembo followed the scholastic divisions of Pico. Cf. J. Festugière, *La philosophie de l'Amour de M. F.*, p. 43.

[18] "Thou (holy love most beautifull, most good, most wise, art derived of the unitie of the heavenly beautie goodnesse and wisedom, and therein dost thou abide, and unto it through it (as in a circle) turnest about". *Courtier*, p. 321.

[19] *Courtier*, p. 321.

[20] He produces Scriptural authority first, and next, on Sofia's request, philosophical arguments: "So. Le tue auttorita sono buone, ma non satiano senza ragione" (f. 133 r°).

[21] *Dialoghi*, f. 133 r°.

[22] *Di Natura d'Amore*, p. 172.

[23] *Ibid.*, p. 173.

[24] *Ibid.*, p. 174.

[25] See Chapter V, pp. 100 sq., 108 sq.

ascription is of little consequence. The important thing is that the minds of both men should have reacted to Platonism in the same way. Both were eclectic in their philosophy, yet they maintained Christianity at the centre of reference. Both were conservative, even in their Platonism. They both distrusted far-fetched metaphysics and in their highest raptures never forgot practical issues. Both of them had the "common-sense" that cabalists like Pico sadly lacked. Of both, it may be said that the mediaeval as much as the Renaissance spirit permeates their writings. Their common reaction to Platonism may therefore be judged characteristic of a conservative, un-metaphysical type of mind, imbued with Christian traditions. Rather than substitute a new frame of thought for an older one, both merely fitted the Neoplatonic picture of the world discovered by the Renaissance into the extant mediaeval frame. The process often involved distortion.

Confirmation of my thesis is offered by Spenser's choice of the visible fabric of the universe as the means of beholding the beauty of the Lord. In their orthodox expositions of the Neoplatonic philosophy, Pico and Benivieni chose the metaphysical "scala" leading from the beauty of human bodies (not nature) to conceptual beauty and, lastly, intellectual beauty, attained by mystical experience [26]. But when Benivieni wrote a poem of purely Christian inspiration, he almost inevitably reverted to the Christian way of "declaring" the glory of God:

> Ammonitione dello Huomo, A l'anima per la quale demostra come lei passa par el mezzo delle creature conoscere & conseguemente amare el suo creatore [27].

Ficino, naturally, describes the ascent to God in Neoplatonic terms when he speaks as a commentator [28]. In his own *Theologia Platonica,* meant to reconcile Platonic doctrine and Christian dogma, he gives both methods of ascent but from a philosophical and general standpoint, not from the standpoint of personal religious experience [29].

Castiglione's invitation to "Behold the state of this great Ingin of the worlde..." has been noted as a parallel to the *Hymne* of Heavenly Beautie [30], but it was only offered as a proof of the identity of goodness and beauty. The ascent is later made by means of the Neoplatonic ladder [31].

---

26 Benivieni, *Opere,* ff. 43 v°-44 v°. Pico, *ibid.,* ff. 64 r°-65 r°.

27 *Opere,* f. 159 v°. Padelford (*S P* 29, p .225 ff.) has pointed out several interesting parallels to *H.H.B.* in the *Ammonitione.* If Spenser knew the *Canzone,* he probably knew the *Ammonitione* as well, and there can be little doubt which had the greater influence on the composition of the fourth hymn.

28 *Discours.* VI. xviii. Cf. 149 v° seq.

29 Kristeller record three modes of ascent (*Ficino,* p. 251):

1° from the objective form through the innate formula to the Idea and from there to the divine essence (*Theol. Plat.* XII. i; *Opera,* p. 265);

2° from the lowest causes to God as the highest cause (*Theol. Plat.* IX. vi; *Opera,* p. 218), or from lowest species to highest genera (*Th. Pl.* VIII. iv; *Op.* 192);

3° from the spheres of the world through the hierarchy of the angels to God (*Th. Pl.* VIII. xvi; X. viii; *Opera,* 201-236).

The first two modes are philosophical (only the first being Platonic); the third is Christian and purely theological.

30 Renwick, *Daphnaida,* p. 222. *Courtier,* p. 309.

31 *Courtier,* pp. 318-19.

We are hardly surprised on the contrary to find the traditional Christian ascent in Bembo's *Asolani.* "The method of the preacher" proved to be also the method of the hermit who taught Lavinello the higher mysteries of divine love. Why did Bembo resort to the contemplation of the creation rather than use the Platonic ladder? Not that he feared lest the gentlewomen he addressed should find the ascent too arduous since he did not spare them slippery scholastic divisions on will, love and desire [32]. Probably because he felt it, whether consciously or not, to be more in harmony with the Christian setting, the religious character of the speaker. I have traced at least one clear reminiscence of the *Asolani* in Spenser's profane hymns [33]. He may have had the exhortations of the hermit in mind when he wrote the heavenly hymns. Let men behold the sun and moon and stars, and hear what they declare unto them:

> Voi ciechi d'intorno a quelle vostre false bellezze occupati a guisa di Narciso vi pascete di vano disio, & non v'accorgete, che elle sono ombre della vera, che voi abandonate. I vuostri animi sono eterni : perche di fuggevole vaghezza gl'inebriate ? Mirate voi como belle creature ci siamo : & pensate quanto dee esser bello colui, di cui noi siamo ministre [34].

The Hermit invited Lavinello to consider the visible fabric of the world as the temple of God, the heavens and the spheres of the planets, the regions of fire and air, then the earth "in middle centre pight" [35]. The creation was first described, contrary to Spenser's hymn, from the point of view of the Creator, but the description was perhaps even more purely mediaeval than Spenser's own [36]. The point of view now changed and Lavinello was urged to pass beyond the visible heavens and behold true Beauty:

> Ma vie maggior diletto ti sarà & piu senza fine maraviglioso ; se tu da questi cieli che si veggono, a quelli che non si veggono passerai, & le vere cose, che ivi sono, contempierai d'uno ad altro sormontando, & in questo modo a quella bellezza, che sopra essi & sopra ogni Bellezza, è, inalzerai Lavinello i tuoi desii [37].

This is the progress described in the *Hymne of Heavenly Beautie,* but the notable difference is that Spenser's ascent culminates with the vision of the Christian Sapience whereas the Hermit turns out to be a Neoplatonist and introduces Lavinello into the intelligible world of Plotinus [38]. But in the *Dialoghi* of

---

[32] See note 17 above.

[33] See Ch. VIII, p. 142.

[34] *Asolani,* pp. 211-12: "In your blind preoccupation with your false beauties, you like Narcissus feed yourselves on vain desire and never understand that they are merely shadows of true beauty, which you neglect. You have immortal souls: why fuddle them on passing charms? See what fair creatures we are, and consider how fair must be that One to whom we minister" (Gottfried's translation, p. 180).

[35] *Asolani,* p. 221.

[36] It seems to be reminiscent of the account of creation in the *Timaeus,* a mediaeval classic.

[37] *Asolani,* pp. 222-3: "But your delight and wonder will be even greater, Lavinello, if you can pass from heavens which you see to those which are unseen and contemplate the things which are actually there, ascending from one to another until you raise your desires to that beauty which surpasses them and every other beauty" (Gottfried, p. 189).

[38] *Asolani,* p. 223. Gottfried's translation, p. 189: "There lies another world which is neither material nor evident to sense but completely separate from this and pure; a world which turns around the one and is both sought and found by

Leone Ebreo, although the intelligible world is duly discussed, the contemplation of God in his handiwork ultimately leads to the vision of the divine Sapience, common to "Mosaic" and Christian theology. A full chapter will be devoted to that important parallel. The Hebrew philosopher and the Elizabethan churchman had, at least, a deep reverence for Scripture in common.

Equicola and Spenser, too, once more display affinities that arise out of the Christian and chiefly Augustinian tradition. The compiler had given an account of the various theories of love, including Pico's, in the first book of the *Di Natura d'Amore.* But when he spoke in his own name, he substituted Augustinian teaching for the Neoplatonic ladder, the beauty of the Christian Creation for the Heavenly Venus [39]. And though we could hardly expect a description of any other ascent than the Platonic progression in a commentary on the *Symposium,* it is characteristic of the Christian bias of Le Roy's Commentary, that he should have prefixed to his exposition of the Platonic *scala* the words of St. Paul: "For the invisible things of him from the creation of the world are clearly seen, being understood by the things that are made" [40]. The quotation hardly applies to the Platonic ascent and had best be read in connexion with the Christian close of the commentary, which substitutes the revelation of God in his creation for the Platonic dialectics:

> Or puis qu'Amour est desir de beauté, & que toute nostre felicité dépend d'aymer où trouverons nous plus de beauté qu'en Dieu qui est la ıontaine de toute beauté ? Sans doubte toute beauté procede de Dieu, & n'est nature autre chose que l'art & instrument du souverain Dieu, ornant tousjours toutes choses, & faisant incessamment leurs belles convenances que voyons... en la machine de l'univers, au ciel, aux elemens, aux animaux, aux herbes & arbres, aux metaux : espandant sur tous les rayons de sa beauté. Car Dieu prenant au commencement la nature de toutes choses confuse & desordonnée, la reduit de confusion en ordre, & en feit ce monde tant beau & bien orné : afin qu'en le contemplant & admirant, nos espritz soyent eslevez, & apprennent à eslire & aymer les choses belles & bien ordonnées... [41]

No less remarkable is the insistence of Le Roy on "grace and faith" in his exposition of Platonic doctrine;

> *Dont concevant la vraye vertu & la nourrissant, luy adviendra d'estre amy de Dieu, & rendu immortel. L'une felicité est par nature; l'autre par grace.*
>
> Vie eternelle est cognoistre Dieu seul & Jesus Christ *donnée de grace* par luy aux parfaitement croyans & vrayment prians comme dit l'escriture ?
>
> Prions-le donc [Christ] qu'il nous face *grace* par la congnoissance de sa parole & par *vive foy* de remplir nostre ame de verité & probité. [42]

---

it, wholly divided from it and wholly abiding in each part of it; a world divine, intelligent and full of light, itself as much beyond itself in size and virtue as it draws nearer to its final cause". Cf. *Enneads,* VI. vii. 12-15.

[39] *Di Natura d'Amore,* p. 147.

"Se la compositione del cielo è bella, se le stelle fisse, se i due gran luminari & gli altri cinque erranti pianeti sono bellissimi: qual sia la bellezza del Fattore & fabricatore di questi solo a quelli imaginabile, i quali elevati al cielo, calcano dispreggiando la terra...".

[40] *Rom.* I. 20. Le Roy, *Sympose,* f. 165 r°. Cf. *H.H.B.* 113 ff.

[41] *Sympose,* f. 179 v°. Again reminiscent of *Timaeus,* 30 a.

[42] *Ibid.,* ff. 174 r°, 178 v°, 179 v°.

"Grace" does not play a conspicuous part in Neoplatonism. Ficino has even been thought to have maintained "that man can attain to God without grace" [43]. This is a wrong interpretation of Ficinian philosophy, for Ficino, like Pico, taught the necessity of grace [44]. But he did not avail himself of the notion of grace in his exposition of the *Symposium,* and though Pico suggested it in the *Commento,* the word itself was not used. Besides, the "illuminative" grace of Pico and Ficino is philosophical rather than Scriptural. Next to Le Roy, Leone Ebreo will again offer the best parallel [45].

A full delineation of divine Sapience answering Spenser's own portrait will also be afforded by the *Dialoghi* and the *Dialoghi* alone. Leone's Sapience remained Hebraic, not Christian, but La Boderie and Ficino, if need were, would have reminded Spenser of the traditional identification of Sapience with Christ [46]. Besides theological tradition, Spenser had literary precedent. He is not unlikely to have known Pontano's *Urania,* a Renaissance classic, and he may have remembered the description of the triune Godhead, distinguished into God "ipse" (the Father), Sapience (the Sun) and Amor (the Holy Ghost):

> In medio sedet ipse, astat Sapientia dextra,
> Hinc Amor, & solio resident tria numina in uno.
> Sub pedibus natura potens, tempusque locusque,
> Et varians fortuna, atque immutabilis ordo [47]

---

[43] *Jayne,* p. 25.

[44] Cf. *Theol. Platonica* XVIII, viii (*Opera,* pp. 411-2): "Ad hoc autem ut mens divinam induat substantiam, quasi formam, non propria virtute dicitum, sed divina trahitur actione... Ut intelligamus mentem non posse ad divinam substantiam per ipsamet perspiciendam attoli per solum naturalis virtutis & hominis augmentum... sed opus esse nova quadam virtute, novoque lumine, an altiori principio descendente. Quod quidem & *gratiae & gloriae lumen* appellant..."

Yet Ficino maintains that man has merits of his own, whereas Spenser, like Calvin, considers that man is justified by grace alone. Ficino, in the *Commentary on the Banquet,* characterizes God as "Just, when He finishes according to the desert of each thing" (II. i; *Jayne,* p. 133). Cst Spenser's God of Justice, *H.H.B.* 148 ff., 253 ff.).

[45] See Chapter XI, p. 189.

[46] See Chapter VI, p. 114.

In the *Sopra l'Amore,* Ficino implicitly identified the Son with Sapience when he distinguished Power, Wisdom and Love within the Godhead (*Discours,* VII. xviii, f. 189 v°, noted by Fletcher, *P M L A* 26, 461-2). In another treatise he developed at length the identification of the "Judaic" Sapience with Christ, offering it as a proof of the Trinity:

"In iis patet, quod sapientia hujusmodi ab aevo non modo concepta erat, sed & parturiebatur... & tanquam suo quodam pacto a generante distincta, cum illo erat, & cuncta componens tanquam ipsa sit Deus. Quae quidem licet à patre gignatur semper tamen cum patre simul extitit..." (*De Christ. Rel.* XXXI; *Opera,* ed. 1641, t. I, p. 57).

There is no evidence that Spenser had read the *De Christiana Religione,* but it is obvious that the Ficinian Sapience *which is God,* is a better illustration of the Spenserian Sapience than the Neoplatonic Intellect or Sapience of Pico, which is "created", not begotten (*Commento* I. iv; quoted by J.W. Bennett in *S P* 28, p. 45).

[47] Pontano, *Urania* (p. 2912 in *Opera*): "He in the midst and Sapience on His right, Love hence: three gods are seated in one throne. Under whom mighty Nature stands, time and space, And fickle fortune and unchanging order". Cf. Dante, *Inferno* III, ll. 5-6:

> Fecemi la divina Potestate,
> La somma Sapienza, e'l primo Amore.

Milton followed the tradition: cf. *Paradise Lost,* III, ll. 168-170.

Spenser consciously substituted the Christian and Biblical Sapience for the Heavenly Venus of the Platonists as the object of contemplation. I have shown that the identification of Sapience with Beauty follows in a way upon its identification with the Son[48]. Yet, supposing Spenser had first to seek a Christian equivalent for the Heavenly Beauty of Plato, he had every chance to select Sapience. Besides the full reconciliation worked out by Leone Ebreo, he had met with one hint at least in Ficino[49]. But a clearer identification than Ficino afforded, was offered by Equicola. To prove that the good and the beautiful were one, that the highest beauty is the beauty of Sapience or that the love of beauty is sister to the love of wisdom, the compiler was not satisfied with the philosophy of Plato and the Academy. He brought up an array of patristic and scholastic authorities: Augustine, Thomas and Scotus[50]. His syncretistic mind was not aware of the differences I had to point out in an earlier chapter.[51] His impressive roll-call of Church Fathers and Doctors shows that he meant to follow Christian tradition. And he was not mistaken if the tradition is traced back to Augustine. May not Spenser, too, have caught the spirit of Augustinian love and wonder in his admiration for the heavenly Beauty?

Indeed, the best way to read the *Hymnes of Heavenly Love,* and *Heavenly Beautie* in the spirit in which they were written, that is in a Christian spirit, would be to read first some chapters of the *De Trinitate*. All the religious themes of the *Hymnes* could be illustrated with quotations from the first, sixth, seventh and eight chapters of the Augustinian treatise[52]. Moreover, the opening stanzas on

---

[48] See chapter IX, pp. 164-67.

[49] "Resouvienne toy, Socrate, que ceste unique lumiere de l'unique sapience est la beauté de l'Ange, laquelle tu dois honorer sur la beauté de l'ame" (*Discours,* VI, xviii, f. 152). Earlier quoted by Fletcher in *P M L A* 26, p. 461.

[50] *Di Natura d'Amore,* pp. 147-51:

"Conosceremo somma bellezza esser degli animi nostri la cognitione della verità & vera sapientia. Platone nel Cratilo vuole che pulchro, cioè bello sia proprio cognome della prudenza. Il medesimo consente nel Fedro". (Note that Spenser, besides sapience, emphasized the light of truth in *H.H.B.* 174.)

"Questo è quel bello del quale gli Stoici dissero che solamente i savii lo possedevano: di che Agostino si maraviglia con quali sensi corporei, con quali occhi habbiano potuto conoscer la bellezza e'l decoro della sapientia. questa è quella bellezza, che da Platone è creduta un risplendente lampo del sommo bene...".

"E consuetudine della scrittura chiamar buoni i belli del corpo. San Thomaso afferma che bello è il medesimo che buono, Scoto disse il buono e'l bello esser un medesimo, quantunque sia differente il nome: & che le cose divine si chiaman belle in quanto sono certo bene, che diletta. L'un & l'altro tolse da Augustino la sua sententia, il quale nel libro della citta, & in altri suoi libri disputa della bellezza dell' universo, & chiama Dio bellissimo. Credette, che *philokalia,* cioè amor di bellezza & *philosophia,* cioé amor di sapientia fossero sorelle, ne gli Academici..."

[51] See chapter II, pp. 25-27.

[52] See especially *Lib.* I, *cap.* VI: on the creation of the world, *ex Patre, per Filium, in Spiritu sancto* (t. 42. c. 827): *Lib.* II, cap. iiii; *personae invicem quomodo se glorificent* (cf. *H.H.L.* 35); *Lib.* VI and *Lib* VII: *quomodo dictus sit Christus ore apostolice, Dei virtus et Dei sapientia* (cf. *H.H.B.*); *Lib.* VII, cap. iii: love of God and love of one's neighbour as the only way to the knowledge and contemplation of God — the lesson taught by *H.H.L.*

Lib. VI, cap X, offers a series of interesting parallels to *H.H.B.* The Son is characterized as "sapience", "beauty", "life" and "intellect". The "embrace" of the Father and His own image is described in nearly erotic imagery as in Spenser:

"Ille igitur ineffabilis quidam complexus Patris et imaginis non est sine perfruitione, sine charitate, sine gaudio" (t. 42, c. 932).

the contemplation of God in his creation, with their insistence on beauty, even more than order or providence, and with their reaching out towards infinity, have a distinct Augustinian ring[53]. I am aware we are dealing with commonplaces, and I do not claim any direct influence although we sometimes seem to catch echoes of the *Enarrationes in Psalmos*. Both the poet and the saint describe the upward flight to God through the degrees of the Creation[54]. Both behold the beauty of the Lord, shining ont in the beauty of his works:

> Undique pulchritudo operis, quae tibi commendat artificem. Miraris fabricam, ama fabricatorem... Respice innumerabilitatem stellarum; respice tanta genera seminum, tantas diversitates animalium... omnia ista, quam magna, quam praeclara, quam pulchra, quam stupenda[55].

Professor Padelford had suggested that Spenser's conception of nature as an approach to the divine was inspired by a chapter of Calvin's *Institutes*: "*The knowledge of God displayed in the fabric and constant government of the universe*"[56]. Spenser certainly knew the *Institutes*. But, even though Calvin were his source, he is closer in spirit and language to the saint: Calvin is *arguing*, Augustine and Spenser are *hymning* God. Further, Calvin was steeped in Saint Augustine, and referred to the *Enarratio in Psalmum* CXLIV. Might not Spenser himself have drunk from the well-spring as well as from the stream? There is nothing in Calvin to suggest the soul's ascent to God on wings of wonder, described by both the poet and the saint. Augustine, not Calvin, offers a fusion of the Platonic feeling for beauty with the Christian yearning for infinity[57].

Yet it is hardly necessary to assume that the heavenly hymns were directly reminiscent of the *De Trinitate* and the *Enarrationes*. The popularity of St. Augustine had reached its peak in England by the end of the sixteenth century.

The chapter ends with an invitation to contemplate God in his creation, as in a mirror: (cf. *H.H.B.* 127 ff., 115):

> "Oportet igitur ut Creatorem, per ea quae facta sunt intellectum conspicientes, Trinitatem intelligimus... qui videt hoc... *per speculum et in aenigmate* (I *Cor.* XIII, 12) gaudeat cognoscens Deum" (t. 42, c. 932).

Augustine had insisted in all his works on the creative activity of divine Sapience, on its power to awake love, and on the Son-Sapience equation. See especially: *In Psalmum* CIII, Sermo iv (t. 37, c. 1378), *Confess.* XI, ix. Cf. *In Joan Evang.* III. iv. (t. 35, c. 1398), where the Word is identified with Sapience and with Life.

[53] "Pulchritudo mundi" is an ever-recurrent theme in the works of Augustine, Cf. *Sermo*, CCXLI, ii; t. 38, c. 1134; *In Psalm.* CXLV, 6, 12; t. 37, c. 1887, 1892; *De vera relig.* XXIX, t. 34, c. 145; *Sermo* LXVIII. i; *In Psalm.* CXLVIII. 15.

[54] *In Psalm.* LXXXV. 12 (t. 37, c. 1090). I translate: "God is ineffable. Easier it were to say what He is not than what He is. You think of the earth: this is not God. You think of the sea; this is not God. ... You figure to yourself whatever shines in the heaven, the stars, sun and moon: this is not God — the heavens themselves: this is not God — Virtues, Powers, Archangels, Thrones, Dominations: this is not God". Cf. *H.H.B.* 36-105. It may be noticed that Augustine, like Spenser, is unmindful of the Dionysian hierarchy in his roll-call of Angelic orders. And yet the poet is taken to task for it!

[55] *In Psalm.* CXLV. 5, 12 (t. 37, c. 1887, 1892); "On all sides appears the beauty of the work, revealing to you the Artificer. You admire the creation: love the Creator then! ... Behold the innumerable host of stars; consider so many kinds of seeds, so many different species of animals ... how great are all these things, how bright, how beautiful, how stupendous!"

[56] Cf. *M. P* 12, pp. 3-9; *J E G P* 13, pp. 425-30. *Institution* I. v. 1, 9, 11, 13; pp. 11, 17-22.

[57] Calvin's line of argument is that the revelation of God in his handiwork makes atheism inexcusable. Spenser's argument and purpose is very different.

Various miscellanies and collections of prayers had been compiled out of his works [58]. These manuals are the background of Christian devotion against which the last Hymnes should be set. They are often, indeed, hortatory and of a calvinistic trend (these characters are by no means entirely absent in Spenser either), but they reproduce in the original words and spirit the great Augustinian themes echoed by the Poet. Witness these few quotations, selected at random:

> This is thy heaven O Lord... The heaven of heavens, in comparison whereof all other heavens are but earth... In comparison whereof the verie fierie heaven it selfe is but earth [59]
>
> How then came I by the knowledge of thee which art highest above all the earth and above all heavens. Whom neither the Cherubins nor the Seraphins do know perfectly, but are faine to shadow their faces with their wings [60].
>
> And to know thy face is to know the power of the father, the wisdome of the sonne, the mercifulness of the Holy Ghost [61].

Augustinian influence also pervades a curious little treatise written in defense of Paracelsian medecine by the end of the century [62]. Parts of "*The Authors Obtestation to Almightie God*" are worth quoting as a comment on Spenser's fourth *Hymne*:

> O God, the father almighty, the true light, *O Christ, the light of the light, the wisedome mysterie and vertue of God.* O holy Ghost that knittest all thinges together in one, which sustainest and quicknest all thynges by this divine power and givest strength to live and to move, and also to continue and to be preserved and nourished... [63]
>
> *Thou (O God the Sonne) by whom all thynges are made, and without whom nothing is made, art the flood or river running from the Father — the fountaine:* thou art the light of the world: *for by reason of thee all worldly thinges live:* thou art the Image of the Father, *the worke, the wisedome of the father, and the vertue and power of operation and working...* All fulnesse doth inhabite in thee. [64]
>
> *For it is not to be understanded that God the Father did create all thynges without the wisedome, word and vertue, that is to saie, without the onely begotten of God our Lorde Jesus-Christ.* For so God saied of the person, of the wisedom, viz. I was with him making all thynges... *For the workes of the sonne be the workes of the father: and the father worketh in the sonne...* [65]

Since the Paracelsian Bostocke plainly identified the Wisdom of the Hebrews with the "*only begotten of God* our Lorde Jesus-Christ", why should we assume

---

[58] *Certaine select prayers gathered out of S. Augustines meditations,* published by R. Daye in 1565, by John Daye in 1574, ran into several editions (*anr. ed.* 1575-77-85-86). Other compilations were:
An introduction to the love of God (T. Purfoote, 1574)
A precious booke of heavenlie meditations (H. Denham, 1581)
A right Christian treatise, entituled S. Augustines praiers, etc. (H. Denham,, 1581).
S. Augustine's manuel (H. Denham, 1581).

[59] *Certaine select Prayers,* sig. 83 v°. Compare *H.H.B.* 64-105, and especially 64-5.

[60] *Ibid.* sig. 54 v°. Cf. *H.H.B.* 99-105 and 118-9.

[61] *Ibid.,* sig. 71 v°.

[62] *The difference betweene the auncient Phisicke ... and the latter.* By Richard Bostocke. The full title, stressing the idea of "concord" (see Bibliography), may have attracted Spenser.

[63] *Op. cit.,* fol. 5. My italics throughout.

[64] *Ibid.,* fol. 18-9. Cf. *H.H.B.* 203; *H.H.B.* 295-6; *H.H.L.* 99-100; H.H.B. 199-203.

[65] *Ibid.,* ch. XXI. Cf. *H.H.B.* 200-203.

that the no less Christian Spenser meant his Sapience to be taken for the "first created intellect" of the Neoplatonists? The equation of Sapience with the Son both agrees with contemporary testimony and satisfies all the requirements of internal evidence. Yet one more point has to be cleared, for it may appear from our first quotation of Bostocke that Spenser has invested the Second Person of the Trinity with some of the usual attributes of the Third in the lines:

> For of her fulnesse which the world doth fill
> They all partake, and do in state remaine, (*H.H.B.* 199 ff.)

It we turn to St Augustine himself, we read in the *De Trinitate* how from the embrace of the Father and the Son the Holy Ghost proceeds and overflows into the creation:

> Illa ergo dilectio... est in Trinitate Spiritus Sanctus, non genitus, sed genitores genitique suavitas, *ingenti largitate atque ubertate perfundens omnes creaturas pro captu earum, ut ordinem suum teneant et locis suis acquiescant* [66].

The parallel is striking. What then? Did Spenser mean the Holy Ghost after all? Our alarm is unjustified, for the apparent contradiction is easily explained. Sapience is the Son indeed, but her all-pervading "fulnesse" manifests the "effluence" of the Holy Ghost, forever proceeding from the Son as well as from the Father. The whole Trinity — "distinguisht undistinct" — was present in the work of creation. All things were made *ex Patre per Filium* [67], the "fulnesse" of whom, overflowing into a world created *in Spiritu sancto,* is the power and pervasion of the Holy Ghost. Indeed, the distinction between the second and the third Person in so far as they operate in the world is not easy to make in the earlier quotations from Bostocke.

In conclusion, a survey of the Neoplatonic treatises of the Renaissance on the one hand, of Augustinian manuals or works of Augustinian inspiration on the other hand, has once more brought to light the essentially traditional, conservative, Christian character of Spenser's *Hymnes,* both in spirit and substance. Apart from occasional decorative "motifs", he borrowed nothing from the more characteristic Neoplatonic doctrines, abiding by earlier themes, undoubtedly of Platonic descent, but fully christianized from the days of Augustine. Spenser's Sapience, the subject of so many controversies, had been identified with the second Person of the Trinity on internal evidence. Since Pontano, Ficino, Equicola and contemporary Augustinian literature afford clear instances of a similar identification, no further proof might be required. But though the "meaning" is beyond doubt, none of the authors quoted affords a full portrait of Sapience containing all the elements of Spenser's own delineation. That portrait no doubt could be found in Scripture. But it was also offered by the *Dialoghi di Amore* of Leone Ebreo, together with a number of interesting features which call for closer consideration.

---

[66] *De Trinitate,* liv. VI, cap. x. t. 42, c. 932: "That love, therefore, is in the Trinity the Holy Spirit, which hath not been begotten but is the sweetness of the Begetter and the Begotten and pours his overflowing abundance and liberality upon all creatures in proportion to their capacity, so that they keep their stations and rest in their proper places."

[67] "Ex" here does not denote the material cause, but the "principium et habitudinem causae efficientis" (Aquinas, *Sum. Theol.* Pt. I, q. xxxix, a. 8). It may apply therefore to the "Maker" (*H.H.B.* 201).

CHAPTER XI

SPENSER'S SAPIENCE AND LEONE EBREO

No attempt has been made as yet to trace the influence of Leone Ebreo on the *Fowre Hymnes*. Yet, his *Dialoghi di Amore* had enjoyed as wide a popularity as Ficino's *Sopra l'Amore* in the sixteenth century [1]. Ronsard presented King Charles IX with a copy and the following poem:

Je vous donne pour vos estreines
L'amour chanté par un Hebrieu;
Les cieux et les terres sont pleines
De la puissance de ce Dieu.

Ils sont (ce me semble) deux frères
Nature doubles les a faits;
Ils ont aussi deux doubles meres,
Contraires en divers effaits.

. . . .

L'un pousse les âmes guidées
Aux belles contemplations,
A l'intellect et aux idées
Purgeant l'esprit des passions.

L'autre à nature est serviable
Nous fait aimer et desirer
Fait engendrer notre semblable
Et l'estre des hommes durer. [2]

That the *Dialoghi* were available in England by the end of the century is beyond doubt. In his *Apologie of Poetry,* prefixed to his translation of Ariosto (1591), Sir John Harington, a courtly poet and a former Cambridgeman like Spenser, filched from Leone Ebreo his fivefold allegorical interpretation of the story of Perseus, coolly translating it word for word out of the Italian [3]. The *Fowre Hymnes* unfortunately do not afford clear verbal parallels to the *Dialoghi.* Yet the Sapience of Spenser bears a striking resemblance to the Sapience of Leone Ebreo.

---

[1] For a full bibliography, see Gebhardt, pp. 111-22. In the sixteenth century there were 11 Italian, 2 Latin, 6 French and 5 Spanish editions. On the popularity of the *Dialoghi,* see Gebhardt, pp. 35-6.

[2] *Odes, Cinquième Livre, Ode VII* (1573). Spenser may have known the poem. On Ronsard's acquaintance with the *Dialoghi,* see J. Festugieres: *La Philosophie de l'Amour de M.F.*, p. 138.

[3] *Dialoghi,* f. 61 r°-v°. Cf. Harrington's *verbatim* rendering in Smith's *Elizabethan Critical Essays*, II. 202-3.

Throughout the comparison I shall discard merely "pictorial" parallels as of little significance. Since Sapience was depicted as a heavenly queen, such accessories as "Royall robes", a throne, a sceptre, a crown of gold, jewels — and even light-imagery — were bound to occur. Further, the queenly character was inevitable, once the poet had chosen to impart a feminine nature to the divine person represented, The points that really matter in the characterization, and call for an explanation, are the following:

1° Sapience is not a personified attribute of God, but a divine person.

2° Yet she is not actually separate nor *essentially* distinct from God. She sits "in his bosom" (*H.H.B.* 183) and not "by his throne" as the Wisdom of the Hebrews did (*Wisdom,* 9, 4).

3° Sapience is a creating power by whose "behest" all creatures "were made and [are] still increast". (*H.H.B.* 199, 203)

4° She rules both heaven and earth, and keeps all things "in state" (*H.H.B.* 190-200).

5° She is true Beauty (*H.H.B.* 204-31).

6° She is God's "Owne Beloved" (*H.H.B.* 184, 235, 291).

7° She has the dispensation of heavenly gifts, and "None thereof worthy be, but those whom she vouchsafeth to her presence to receave" (*H.H.B.* 246-56).

8° The contemplation of Sapience carries the soul into an extasy and is the highest vision of the divine that men may obtain (*H.H.B.* 260 ff.).

Professor Osgood has made out Spenser's portrait of Sapience to be nothing but a mosaic of Scriptural phrases from the *Proverbs, Ecclesiasticus,* the *Book of Wisdom, Sirach* and *Baruch* [4]. Professor Saurat has objected that Spenser was unlikely to hunt through the Bible for widely scattered phrases and nicely fit them together [5]. Now, it might be argued that out of some forty parallels given in the Variorum edition, the only significant ones occur in the *Proverbs,* chapter VIII, and the *Book of Wisdom,* chapters VII and VIII [6]. Therefore, even had his acquaintance with the Bible been superficial (and it was not), Spenser might well have derived his characterization of Sapience directly from Scripture. The real difficulty does not lie in the gathering of texts, but in the weaving out of them of a description on the whole more definite and "metaphysical" than anything in the Bible. The *Proverbs* and the *Book of Wisdom* only faintly imply that Sapience is essential Beauty and God's "fair love". Besides, though immortality is pro-

[4] *S P* 14, pp. 166-77.

[5] *Rev. de Litt. Comp.*, 1926, pp. 5-15.

[6] Significant parallels are: *H.H.B.* 183-4; *Prov.* 8. 30 and *Wisdom* 8. 3. 4. *H.H.B.* 190-8: *Wisd.* 8. 1, and *Prov.* 8. 14, 31. *H.H.B.* 200-3: *Prov.* 8. 27-30. *H.H.B.* 238-52: *Wisd.* 8. 2, 7. 11, 7. 14 and *Prov.* 8. 21. *H.H.B.* 239-255: *Wisd.* 8. 21 and *Prov.* 8. 7.

Other references are often mere repetitions of ideas and phrases already found in these verses Spenser, therefore need not have had in mind *Wisd.* 9. 4. and 9. 10 (*Wisd.* 8. 3, 4), *Prov.* 3. 19 (=*Prov.* 8. 14), *Wisd.* 9 (=*Prov.* 8. 27-30), *Wisd.* 6. 12, 16 (= *Prov.* 8. 17).

We might also dismiss all parallels relating to jewels, attire and light-imagery as devoid of significance. But all of them occur in *Wisdom,* chapter VII and *Proverbs* chapter VIII, but for *Prov.* 3. 13-5 which repeats *Prov.* 8. 10-19.

Prov. 4. 9. in connexion with *H.H.B.* 190 is irrelevant.

Lastly I fail to see any necessary connexion between *H.H.B.* 183-4 and *Sirach* 24. 5, *H.H.B.* 199-200 and *Wisd.* 1. 7 or *Sirach* 24. 5. 7. *H.H.B.* 238-52 and *Baruch* 3. 15. (See rather *Prov.* 8. 21). *H.H.B.* 271-2 and *Wisd.* 8. 15-8. *H.H.B.* 277-80 and *Wisd.* 7. 8-9 or *Job* 15-19.

mised to her lovers, there is no white heat of ecstasy about it. On the whole the "Sapiental" books might be called "prudential", moral rather than mystical [7].

The emphasis on contemplation and beauty as well as on the love-relationship between God and Sapience is easily accounted for if Sapience is identified with God the Son, as I have shown. But Spenser's first concern, when he composed the *Hymne of Heavenly Beautie* as a parallel to the *Hymne in Honour of Beautie,* must have been to find a Christian substitute for the Heavenly Venus of the Platonists. Instead of selecting first the Second Person of the Trinity for an apotheosis, deducing therefrom both "sapience" and beauty, he may have reasoned first from beauty to sapience before identifying Sapience with the Second Person of the Trinity. Now, Renwick facilely admits that "In Ficino he found Heavenly Beautie identified with Sapience, and he found Sapience in his Bible and Apocrypha" [8]. I have given quotations not from Ficino alone but from Equicola [9]. Both identified Sapience with heavenly beauty, and the latter far more clearly than the former. But neither of them introduced the *Scriptural* Sapience, personified and traditionally identified with God the Son. Neither of them suggested any of the characteristics and attributes either of the Hebrew or of the Christian Sapience. The single quotation from Pico offered by J. W. Bennett is not more helpful, for "sapience" is only mentioned once and incidentally among the many other names given to God's "first and only creation", which Pico usually calls "first intellect" or "angelic mind" [10]. Nor is it described in Scriptural terms. Are we to suppose that Spenser's imagination was fired by an occasional hint and that he turned to Scripture to fill in the portrait of Sapience? What if a composite portrait of the Biblical Sapience as the Heavenly Beauty was already at hand? Such a delineation was offered by Leone in his third *Dialogue,* mainly devoted to a reconciliation of Neoplatonic philosophy with Mosaic theology. The *prima bellezza* of the Platonists is identified at length with the Sapience of the *Proverbs* and the Apocrypha. It is further identified with the female figure of the Canticles as "the fair love of mightie heavens King" (*H.H.B.* 235). And Biblical quotations are lavished in support. Besides, a detailed study will bring out further characteristics of Leone's Sapience with which Spenser's delineation is in close agreement.

Why is the world filled with beauty? This interrogation on the Creation will lead to the Creator:

> Che cosa è adunque questa bellezza che cosi si sparge per tutto l'universo... [11]

---

[7] I am aware their "meaning" is mystical or has been so interpreted; I am speaking of the "tone".

[8] *Daphnaida,* p. 212.

[9] See Chapter X, p. 178.

[10] *S P* 28, p. 45 — For the reader's enlightenment I reproduce the "parallel" offered:

"Ceste premiere intelligence crée est dicte par Platon & ainsi par les anciens Philosophes mercure Trismegiste & Zoroaster, ore fils de Dieu, ores esprit ou entendement, ores *sapience,* ores raison divine, ce qu'aucuns interpretent aussi verbe. Que chacun advise bien & diligemment à ne croire que ce verbe soit celuy qui est dit de noz Theologiens fils de Dieu" (*Commentaire* I. iv; *Discours,* f. 197 v°).

Sapience must indeed have had a fascination for Spenser if an incidental mention was enough to arrest his attention. And he did take care to identify sapience unmistakably with "him who is said by our theologians to be the Son of God". A strange way, this, of following Pico!

[11] *Dialoghi,* fol. 209 r°. Quotations in this chapter are too numerous to allow the insertion of both text and translation. The reader is referred to the French trans-

It is noteworthy that the themes of Spenser's fourth Hymne should occur in almost chronological order in this portion of the *Dialoghi*. This opening is the more remarkable since the more orthodox Neoplatonists who were supposed to have inspired Spenser had not mentioned the beauty of the natural world in the ascent from human to divine beauty through the well-known steps. For Leone Ebreo, as for the Christian Spenser, "The meanes therefore which unto us is lent — Him to behold is on his workes to look" (*H.H.B.* 127-8). Both paraphrase Psalm 19, "The heavens declare the glory of God". "Dice il santo, alzate al cielo gli occhi vostri, & vedete chi creó questi, chi produsse & ammoveró l'essercito loro; e tutti chiama per nome" [12].

The whole *Hymne of Heavenly Beauty* seems to be built on the distinction of "li tre gradi del bello, Dio, Sapientia & mondo", in the ascending order. Human understanding cannot comprehend the "infinite beauty" of the Creator, but it is allowed to catch a reflection of it in the "finite beauty" of the creature, as "in a looking-glass" [13]. Yet we are reminded that this is "come vedere il lucido corpo del Sole in acqua o in altro diafano; che cosi il nostro intelletto humano nelle corpore vede l'incorporee" [14]. Only angels may behold, not the essence of the Godhead, but his streaming beauty, as eagles behold the splendour of the Sun, though the substance thereof remains unknowable [15].

Yet, "gathering plumes of perfect speculation", Filone, who is Leone's spokesman in the dialogue, will declare to Sofia "the first and true Beauty" [16] that lights both the world of sense and the world of intellect. Beauty is spiritual; each thing is beautiful owing to an Idea, and the sensible world as a whole owes its beauty to the Idea of the World. This Idea of the World is not merely contained in the divine Intellect but is one with it, one with Sapience, "the principle of Creation":

> ... la Idea del Mondo e *la Somma sapienza, per laquele il mondo fu fatto,* et la sapientia divina è il verbo, & l'Intelletto suo, et la sua propria mente [17].

Filone will first describe the nature and functions of Sapience according to Platonic philosophy, and then show how the description agrees with "Mosaic theology". Sapience, in the above quoted lines, had appeared as a creative power. She next appears as "sovran" (or heavenly) beauty:

> ... *la somma bellezza è la prima sapientia*, & quella participata ne l'universo tutto, & ogn'una de le sue parti fa belle, si che *nessuna altra bellezza è che sapientia* participabile, overo participata [18].

The peripateticians assert that God and his own Sapience are one [19]. But Filone chooses to believe with the Platonists that Sapience is *personally,* though not *essentially,* distinct from God:

> che l'intelletto, *e sapientia divina* (*che è il verbo ideale*) *non sia propriamente il sommo Iddio, ne manco in tutto altro, e distinto da lui;* ma che sia una sua

---

lation by Pontus de Tyard, published in Lyons by Jean de Tournes in 1551, and to the English translation by F. Friedeberg Seeley and J. H. Barnes (London, 1937).

[12] *Ibid.*, fol. 167 v°; cf. *H.H.B.* 50 ff.

[13] *Ibid.*, fol. 166; cf. *H.H.B.* 115.

[14] *Ibid.*, fol. 168 r°.

[15] *Ibid.*, fol. 169 r°; cf. *H.H.B.* 138.

[16] *Ibid.*, "la prima vera bellezza" (*Dialoghi,* fol. 212).

[17] *Ibid.*, 215 v° - 216 r°.

[18] *Ibid.*, 216 v°. Italics mine in all quotations.

[19] *Ibid.*, 217 v°.

cosa dependente, & emanante da lui, e non separata ne distinta da lui realmente, come la luce del Sole [20].

God is beyond his own sapience, beyond his own beauty. Here indeed, Spenser as a Christian, differs from Leone. In the third hymn, he clearly places beauty *in* God (*H.H.L.* 29) and in the fourth, since Sapience is God, beauty is still in God. But considering beauty more especially in God the Son, he is led to describe God the Father, like Leone, as the fountain of beauty, not in the Neoplatonic, but in the Christian sense. Sapience is *lumen de lumine, pulchritudo de pulchritudine,* whereas Leone asserted:

> *Sai che'l sommo Iddio non è Bellezza,* ma prima origine della sua bellezza, e la sua bellezza, cioè quella che da lui prima emana, è la sua somma sapientia... *Non è bellezza ne sapientia, ma fontana onde emana la prima bellezza, e somma sapientia* [21].

But the imagery, though not the meaning, is the same in Spenser, for whom the beauty of Sapience is "Sparkled on her from Gods owne glorious face" (*H.H.B.* 207).

Filone's reason for siding with Plato against Aristotle was his religious creed:

> Conciosia ch'io sai mosaico, nella theologale sapientia mi abbraccio con questa seconda via, però che è veramente theologia mosaica, e Platone come quel che maggior notitia haveva di questa antica sapientia che Aristotele, la seguitò [22].

It will be noticed that Leone Ebreo subordinates philosophy to theology, whereas Pico, from the first, in his *Commento,* courteously bows Christian dogma out of the way and declares his intention to unfold "the common sentence and opinion of Plato and Aristotle" [23]. In his *Hymnes* Spenser, as I have shown, adopted such notions only as did not clash with Christian dogma. He and Leone alike speak to "the faithful" [24]. The Neoplatonic description of Sapience is valid only in so far as it agrees with Scripture.

Sapience was said to have made the world. This is borne out by Scripture and Scripture also identifies Sapience with Beauty:

> Le prime parole che Moise scrisse, furono, in principio, creò Dio il cielo e la terra e l'antica interpretatione Caldea disse dovo noi diciamo in principio, *con sapientia creò Dio il cielo & la terra...* Mira come la prima *cosa ne mostra che'l mondo fu creato per sapientia,* e che la sapientia fu'l primo principio creante, ma che nel sommo Dio creatore *mediante la sua somma sapientia prima bellezza creò, e face bello tutto l'universo creato,* si che li primi vocaboli del sapiente Moise ne dinotaron *le tre gradi del bello, Dio, sapientia & mondo.* & il sapientissimo Re Salomone... dichiara questa sua prima sententia nelli *proverbii* dicendo, *il Signor con sapientia fondò la terra, compose* li cieli con somma sapientia... [25]

---

[20] *Ibid.,* 218 r°.
[21] *Ibid.,* 218.
[22] *Ibid.,* 219 v° - 220 r°: an allusion to Plato's pretended knowledge of the Hebrew Scriptures. Filone ranks him among the Cabbalists (fol. 155 v°).
[23] *Commento,* I. iii.
[24] Cf. "*Tu o Sofia, che sei de fideli*" (*Dialoghi,* f. 150 r°).
[25] *Dialoghi,* fol. 220 v°. Cf. *H.H.B.* 200-3. The meaning of Spenser's lines has been controverted, and J.W. Bennett contends that "either reading puts Sapience above the creator of the world" (*S P* XXXII, p. 141). But, explaining why Sapience,

Scripture further makes it clear that Sapience is not a mere personified attribute of God:

> ... (Moses and Solomon) non dicono Dio sapiente creò, o vero saviamente creò, ma *dissero Dio con sapientia per mostrare che Dio è il sommo creatore, & la sapientia è mezzo &* instrumento, col quale fu la creatione [26].

Yet God and Sapience are not separate, but conjoined:

> *e [Salomone] dice che [la sapientia] fu appresso di lui [Iddio] per denotare* che *non è diviso essentialmente* lo emanante della sua origina ma congionti. [27]

Such is the nature of Sapience according to both Platonic philosophy and Hebrew theology. But the portrait is filled in by means of Biblical quotations, new details are touched in on the sole authority of Scripture. Leone has hitherto provided four of the characters of Spenser's Sapience recorded above: a divine person, yet not separate from God, a creating principle which is at the same time heavenly beauty. The four remaining characteristics now appear and afford stronger evidence. All, indeed, are derived from Scripture. But the coincidence is at least noteworthy, since Spenser and Leone choose to emphasize the same features. Filone, in accordance with the *Proverbs,* stresses the ruling power of Sapience: "Io son la sapientia... *io ho la fortezza: & meco li Re regnano*" [28]. He further quotes the verses in which Sapience is shown to be the dispenser of heavenly riches to her lovers:

> ... *tutte le bellezze divine ho meco degne & giuste, per participare a li miei amici assai & empire i loro thesori,* e dipoi che narrò, come vedi, a che modo dalla sapientia divina viene ogni sapere, virtù, e bellezza dello universo le quali *ella participa in gran copia a chi l'ama & sollecita...*

Nor are the verses left out that faintly imply a love relationship between God and Sapience:

> ... io alhora era appresso di lui... ogni giorno giocando in presentia sua...

But of deeper interest is the identification of Sapience with the female figure of the *Canticles,* considered as "ideal Beauty":

> ... e non solamente questo sapientissimo Re dichiarò questa emanatione Ideale principio di creationi, sotto specie & nome di somma sapientia, ma *ancora la dichiarò sotto specie e nome di bellezza nella sua cantica* onde parlando di lei dice. Bella sei tutta compagna mia, e difetto no è in te. *Mira quanto chiaro denota la somma bellezza ideale de la sapientia divina,* in porre la bellezza in tutta lei, senza mescolanza d'alcuno difetto, ciò che non si può dire d'alcuno bello par participatione... [29].

---

identified with the Beloved of the *Canticles,* is called the companion of God, Leone writes: "& la chiama compagna, perche l'accompagnò nella creatione del mondo *come ne l'arte all' opfico* (*Dialoghi,* fol. 222). This is implied throughout in the *Proverbs,* and is the meaning of Spenser. God is the "artificer" and Sapience his own "art". Speaking of God there is no reason to set the art above an artificer who brings forth from himself both the thing created and his own creating intellect.

[26] *Dialoghi,* f. 220 v°.

[27] *Ibid.*, f. 221 v°.

[28] *Ibid.*, fol. 221 r°.

[29] *Ibid.*, f. 221 v° - 222 r°.

Spenser probably had in mind the King's beloved, "fairest among women", "the only one" among queens and virgins without number, when he painted "that faire love of Mightie heavens King", "excelling" in beauty "the daughters of all womens race" [30]. And, if he had, is it not likely that the connexion was inspired by the *Dialoghi*? [31]

Both Spenser's *Hymne* and the passage of the *Dialoghi* now under consideration close with an assertion that the last end of man is the contemplation of "Heavenly Beautie", carrying the soul into ecstasy, and burning away all earthly desire. This is a commonplace ,and such had been the close of Plato's *Symposium*. But Spenser keeps closer to Leone than to any other Neoplatonist I know, by making the object of contemplation, not the face of Sapience only, but the "sacred mysteries" of the love relationship between God and her:

> *...peroche essendo il primo bello nostro progenitore, e la prima bellezza nostra genetrice* & la somma sapientia nostra patria, onde siamo venuti, il bene et beatitudine nostra consiste nel tornare in quella & adherirsi alli nostri parenti, *felicitandone in la loro suoave visione & unione delettabile* [32].

Such a sight shall "loathing bring of this vile world":

> Eche quando arrivarà la nostra cognitione alla somma bellezza, & sommo bello; il nostro amore sarà si ardente in lui, che *ogni altra cosa abbandonnarà per amare* solamente quella & quello [33].

Spenser's insistence on "saving grace" has also its counterpart in the *Dialoghi*:

> ... ne noi de l'universo, ne l'amor nostra, ne suo, sarieno mai capaci di simile unione, ne sufficienti di tanto alto grado di dilettevole *perfettione, se non fusse la nostra parte intellettualle aiutata, & illuminata dalla somma bellezza divina, & dall'amore che esso ha all'universo...* & per questo dice David, *con la luce tua vediamo la luce* [34].

The features of Spenser's Sapience have been shown to reproduce the characterization of Sapience in the *Dialoghi* but for one essential difference: the identification of Sapience with the Second Person of the Trinity. But it was easy for Spenser to make the traditional identification: all the easier since the argument and phrasing of Leone, far from forbidding it as Pico had done [35],

---

[30] *H.H.B.* 235; 204-205.

[31] J.W. Bennett has noted reminiscences of the *Canticles* in the portrait of Sapience and recalled "the mystical Gnostic and Cabbalistic idea of a male and female relationship between the first and second persons of the Trinity" (*S P* XXVIII, p. 46). But she does not quote any text showing an identification of Sapience with the Beloved. Nor is there any suggestion of it either in Pico's *Commento* or Ficino's *Sopra l'Amore*.

[32] *Dialoghi,* f. 224 v°.

[33] *Ibid.,* f. 224 v°.

[34] *Ibid.,* f. 242 r°. Cf. *H.H.B.* 239 ff. As I said earlier, Spenser's conception of grace is more purely Scriptural or Calvinistic than the illuminating grace of the Christian Platonists. But since a parallel from Pico has been offered (Bennett, *S P* 28, 41), it was worth pointing out that Leone, though not a Christian, offers a better one, since it is grounded on Scripture and introduces divine love (God's love for the world) whereas Pico stressed illumination and "communication" only (*Commento,* III, x).

[35] *Commento* I. iv; quoted in note 10.

inevitably suggested it to a Christian reader. It should be noted first that Leone, unlike Pico, never held the first emanation from God to be a "creature", never admitted of any actual distinction of essence between God and Sapience. His Sapience, therefore clearly recalled the Christian "begotten" Son whom Pico carefully distinguished from the Platonic first "created" intellect. The identification of Sapience with the creative Word of God would further have reminded Spenser of the Son *per quem omnia facta sunt*:

> ... David... dice, col verbo del Signore li cieli furon fatti, & dal spirito della bocca sua tutto l'essercito suo. Il verbo è la sapientia... [37].

These identifications, admitting Spenser ignored Pico's caution, the *Commento* could have suggested. But there is a more interesting parallel it did not offer. Leone, by distinguishing a Trinity within the Godhead itself, may have inspired the poet's account of the generation of the Son and suggested at the same time the Son-Sapience equation. Of the generation of the Son Spenser says:

> It [God] lov'd it selfe, because it selfe was faire,
> (For fair is lov'd;) and of it selfe begot
> Like to it selfe is eldest sonne and heire, (*H.H.L.* 29-31)

Sofia inquires of Filone who the first lover and the first beloved are. The answer is: God is both, for he loves his own beauty.

> FI: Il primo amante, si è Dio cognoscente & volente. *Il primo amato è esso Dio sommo bello.* SO: *Adunque il primo amore si è di Dio a se stesso.* FI: Si certamente. [38]

Hence the generation of a Son, love being, as Plato said, a desire of generation in beauty.

> ... [Dio] *amando pria se stesso desia generare in bello la sua similitudine, e genera per quello amore precedente il figlio...* [39].

This "Son", indeed, is not the Christian but the Hermetic "Son of God", the Universe. But Spenser may easily have changed the meaning: the phrasing need not be altered. Further, Leone invited a Christian interpretation, since he recognized within the divine essence a "trina reverbatione", even though he denied any real distinction of persons:

> *in lui l'amante & l'amato & il medesimo amore* è tutto una cosa: benche li numeriamo tre, e diciamo che dell'amato s'informa l'amante, & d'ambi due (come di padre & madre) deriva l'amore, tutto è una simplicissima unità & essentia [40].

A trinity of the Lover, the Beloved and Love would instantly remind a Christian reader of the Father, the Son and the Holy Ghost. And he would naturally reverse the relation: not the Beloved, but the Lover would be the first person of the Trinity, the Father. This is but one more example of the revolution Christianity brought about; and this is why Spenser is emphatically more of a

---

[37] *Dialoghi,* f. 220 v°.
[38] *Dialoghi,* f. 156 r°.
[39] *Ibid.,* f. 232 v°.
[40] *Ibid.,* f. 156 v°.

Christian than a Platonist. Now, once he had identified "l'amato" of the *Dialoghi* with God the Son, he had identified him with the "sapientia amata" that Leone discerned in God:

> perche la sua divina essentia non sarebbe di somma unità, *se ne reverberasse in se stessa della bellezza, ò sapientia amata il sapiente amante, & d'ambi due,* l'ottimo amore. [41]

This *sapientia amata,* in the *Dialoghi,* has nothing in common with the "sapientia" of the later account of creation. Leone, indeed, seems to be at variance with himself in his successive accounts. In the passage now under consideration, he distinguishes between God's "intrinsic love" (that is love within the Trinity) and his first "extrinsic love", that is his desire of generating the world in beauty. But, in accordance with the Neoplatonic hierarchy, instead of producing the world immediately, God is said to have produced the "first parents" of the world, "i primi instrumenti genitori". And these were the first Intellect, or Father of the world, produced by the "bellezza o sapientia amata", and chaos the mother of the world produced by" il sapiente amante" [42]. But in Leone's account of creation, this time based on Scripture, the world is said to be begotten by God and born of Sapience, who is at once the daughter and spouse of God [43]. Of Chaos, there is no further mention. Besides Sapience has now been identified with the Platonic first Intellect. Male and female principles have got mixed. Yet the reason for the contradiction is clear. The first account is predominantly Greek, and the beloved takes precedence of the lover: the "sapientia amata" informs the "sapiente amante", thus playing the Father's part. The second account is predominantly *Hebraic* — and therefore closer to Christianity. Leone desperately seeks to maintain the Greek principle. He notes that the Shulamite in the *Canticles* names Solomon her "beloved" whereas she herself is only called "sister or companion", which is said to mean that God's love for Sapience and the love of Sapience for God are of a different nature. But, for all these subtleties, the dominant impression given by the Scriptural texts quoted is that Sapience is, indeed, the "faire love of mightie heavens king" [44], just as in the Christian Trinity, though the Father is loved in return, the Son is best characterized as the Beloved and the Father as the Lover, since divine love begets — or creates — for itself the object of its love.

All the characters of Spenser's Sapience have been traced in the Sapience of Leone Ebreo. The Scriptural texts echoed by the poet have been found collected and interpreted alike in a few pages of the *Dialoghi.* The substitution of the Biblical Sapience for the Heavenly Venus and its identification with the female figure of the *Canticles,* both suggested in Spenser's hymn, were expressly stated by Leone. Lastly, the distinction within the Godhead of "il sapiente" and "la sapientia", "il bello" and "la bellezza", united by love, invited a Christian poet to identify that "sapience" and "beauty" with the second Person of the Christian Trinity. No other Neoplatonic treatise I have seen offers so many

---

[41] *Ibid.*, f. 156 v°.

[42] *Ibid.*, f. 158 r°-v°.

[43] *Ibid.*, f. 223 r° ff.

[44] It should be noted that English translations of the Bible have not preserved Leone's distinction since the "compagna" is called "o my love" (6. 4.). Moreover after centuries of "amour courtois", it was almost inevitable that so "chivalric" a poet as Spenser should paint the feminine figure as the beloved not as the lover.

parallels. Spenser, no doubt, may have achieved for himself the synthesis and the reconciliation of Platonic philosophy with Scripture (and not the other way round) which Leone had effected. But since he had a fair chance to read the *Dialoghi,* he may well have borrowed it ready-made. I claim probability, not certainty. But many source-ascriptions have been urged for which worse evidence has been offered.

To strengthen the case for Spenser's indebtedness to the *Dialoghi,* parallels concerning mythology [45] the cosmic power of love [46], the Empedoclean principle of strife-friendship [47], the conception of eternal substance enduing various forms [48], the notion of chaos-substance [49] and other resemblances might be brought forward. But the themes concerned have been shown to be commonplaces, many of them of mediaeval inheritance.

Leone's insistence on the dissolubility of the heavens [50] and the "sabbatical" year which will bring about "la perfetta quiete di tutte le cose" [51] offers greater interest, for such notions may have sharpened, if not awakened, the feelings that found expression in the *Cantos of Mutabilitie,* culminating in the poet's sabbatical longing:

> O! that great Sabbaoth God, grant me that Sabaoths sight.
> (*F.Q.* VII. viii. 2. 9)

Other affinities would have made Leone's treatise congenial to Spenser: a common acceptance of physical love as "truly good" when "honest" [52], a common rejection of everything artificial, contrary to life and nature, of superfluous pleasures and "apparent beauties" due to art alone [53]; a common sensitiveness to light as the cause of beauty and the sign of goodness, culminating

---

[45] Spenser seems to have borrowed his Daemogorgon from Boccaccio (Lotspeich, *Mythology,* p. 52) but the fascination the figure had for him might be due to Leone's insistence on the myth (*Dialoghi,* ff. 66 v° - 69 v°).

[46] Cf. especially the second Dialogue which develops the themes of *Colin* and *H.L.* (Dial. 42 r° - 104 v°).

[47] "La complessione delli elementi è la loro amicitia, et come posson stare gli contrarii uniti insieme senza litigio, ne contraditione, non ti par vero amore, et amicitia? alcuni chiamano questa amicitia harmonia, musica, et concordantia, et tu sai che l'amicitia fa la concordantia, si come l'inimicitia causa discordia; et per questo il filosofo Empedocles dice, che le cagioni della generatione, et corrutione in tutte le cose inferiori son sei, lo quattro elementi, l'amicitia, et l'inimicitia" (*Dialoghi,* 48 r°-v°). Cf. *H.L.* 78 ff; *Colin,* 843 ff; *F.Q.* IV. x. 32-5.

[48] "Questa, come dice Platone, appetisce, & ama tutte le forme delle cose generate, come la donna l' huomo. & non satiando il suo amore l'appettito, e'l desiderio, la presentia attuale dell'una delle forme s'innamora dell'altra che gli manca, & lassando quella piglia questa, di maniera che non potendo sostenere insieme tutte le forme in atto, le riceve tutte successivamente l'una doppo l'altra" (*Dialoghi,* 45 r°). Cf. *F.Q.* III. vi. 36-8.

[49] *Dialoghi* f. 151 r°-v°. *F.Q.* IV. vi. 36. The notion of an eternal chaos is linked by Leone with the Platonic great year and the cycle of being", eterne in mutabilitie": "furono [le cosi individuali] eterni nella successione eterna di molti mondi, cosi come esso Aristotele pone nel mondo inferiore, che nissuno delli suoi individui è eterno, & che la generatione & la prima loro materia è eterna" (*Dial.* 155 v°). Cf. *F.Q.* III. vi. 38. In vi. 32-3 Spenser used the notion of cyclic recurrence; see Chapter IV, p. 81.

[50] "So. Dunque son li cieli per dissolversi, secondo Platone. Fi. Sono." (*Dial.* 151 r°.)

[51] *Dialoghi,* f. 154 r°.

[52] See Ch. VIII, p. 144.

[53] *Dialoghi,* f. 227 v°.

in the "Licht-Metaphysik" of Leone and in the Spenserian identification of light and beauty[54]. Lastly the Scriptural quotations thickly strewn in the *Dialoghi* would make the treatise of the Hebrew philosopher the more attractive to an Elizabethan churchman. Apart from any consideration of source-ascription, parallels were worth tracing, affinities worth noting, since they once more revealed how closer in spirit Spenser stood to the more Biblical-minded as well as to the more Christian-minded among the Renaissance Platonists.

---

[54] "... & universalmente la luce in tutto il mondo inferiore è forma laquale leva la brutezza de la tenebrosità della materia deforme, e perciò quelli corpi che piu la participano, rende piu belli. ond'ella è giusto che sia bellezza vera & il sol dal quale dipende è fontana della bellezza..." (*Dial.* 201 v°).

Spenser describes the soul as borrowing light from the Sun (*H.B.* 110) and procuring the fairer body as it hath in it the more of heavenly light (*H.B.* 128). C.S. Lewis has noted the recurrent light-darkness, day-night antithesis in the *F.Q.* It may be "New Testament" symbolism (*Alleg. of Love,* p. 313), but Spenser has it in common with Leone Ebreo. Plutarch's contrast of Ormudz and Ahriman as light and darkness in *De Iside* XLVII (*Isis et Osiris,* p. 149) may also have arrested the attention of a poet so fond of contrasting "the sonnes of Day" with "Nights drad children" (*F.Q.* I. v. 23-4). But light imagery is a constant feature in Neoplatonism and such parallels should not be pressed too far.

CHAPTER XII

SPENSER'S RELIGIOUS SENSIBILITY

Spenser's religious ideas have been discussed in terms of Puritanism and Platonism, Calvinism and Catholicism, pantheism and mysticism. But it is highly doubtful whether the poet, had he been consulted, could have given a neat definition and provided clear-cut distinctions for any of these irritatingly vague "universals". Has any historian, any philosopher defined them to his own — and our — satisfaction. Or, supposing the "essence" of each is known, is there any chance of finding it unalloyed in Spenser's mind, when we know how syncretic and how unsystematic his thinking was? Shall we then reject the words altogether? Use them we must, for the sake of conveniency; but our main concern will be to bring out the inner play of thought, imagination and feeling in the poet's soul. To stick a label may be useful for ready identification; but a real understanding of the poet's response to religious impressions is only gained through an analysis of his temper and mind. Besides the psychological approach, the historical approach is relevant. For religious feelings are apt to be deep-rooted in the collective past. And when a change comes over men's minds, if often takes time before the change affects their hearts as well. Thinking, especially in religious matters, usually runs ahead of feeling. Spenser's thought has been related to the theological and ecclesiastical controversies of his age in many scholarly studies. Further enquiry in this field, or even a full review of earlier findings, would not fall within my province. The reader may be referred to the latest, and perhaps soundest contribution, Dr. Whitaker's *The Religious Basis of Spenser's Thought.*[1] But since I have repeatedly emphasized the traditional elements and the persistence of the mediaeval cast of mind in Spenser's handling of Platonic notions, the present study may be rounded off by a definition of the poet's religious sensibility that will further bring out what he owed to the Christian tradition and to the Middle-Ages.

That Spenser ever was a Puritan in the historical sense has been disproved by recent criticism. P. E. Mc Lane has shown that "except for his sympathies in the political crisis in late 1579 (where his point of view coincided with that of the Puritans) Spenser had no love for the Puritans"[2]. In his conception of

---

[1] Whitaker gives a list of previous works and opinions on pp. 5-7. It should be supplemented with the articles of A.H. Tolman, G.W. Landrum, J.F. Hankins, Beatrice Ricks and P.E. Mc Lane recorded in my Bibliography, Section D. 2.

[2] Mc Lane, *JEGP* 49 (1950), p. 33.

Church government, even in his Cambridge days, Spenser was at most a Low-Churchman.[3] The secretary to Bishop Young did not object to episcopal rule. Closer study of the *Shepheardes Calender* has disclosed that the author had "constituted himself the spokesman for a group of bishops of the Established Church".[4] Reforming bishops, no doubt, they were, and Spenser, too, was for a "purified Church" that would not be a "revolutionized Church"[5], but would "preserve as much as possible of its Catholic heritage"[6]. The strictures upon Church abuses in his poetry chiefly concern the moral evils of corruption, plundering, sloth and ignorance. They are not directed at "Church rites and monuments". His indignation at the iconoclastic zeal of the extreme Puritans could not have been greater had he been a Catholic:

> From thence into the *sacred Church* he broke,
> And robd the Chancell, and the deskes downe threw,
> And *Altars* fouled, and blasphemy spoke,
> And th'*Images for all their goodly hew,*
> Did cast to ground, whilest none was them to rew;[7]

In the *View of the Present State of Ireland,* he urged the re-building of ruinous churches:

> ... for the *outwarde shewe* asure your selfe dothe greatlye drawe the rude people to the reverensinge and frequentinge theareof what ever some of our late toonice foles saye that theare is nothinge in *the semelye forme and Comelye orders of the Churche.*[8]

Spenser may have grown more conservative in his conception of church-order and "outward shew" with advancing years[9]. But I suspect that even in his youth his deeper reason for condemning Roman ceremonies was not that they were "ceremonies", "outward shew", but that they were "Roman". His altars of iniquity in the *Faerie Queene* are abominable, not because they are altars — a sufficient reason for the narrow-minded Puritan hue and cry — but because they are, indeed, devoted to deeds of iniquity:

> And there beside of marble stone was built
> An Altare, carv'd with cunning imagery,
> On which true Christians blood was often spilt,
> And holy Martyrs often doen to dye,[10]

---

[3] Tolman's view in *MP* 15, p. 564, adopted by William P. Holden in *Anti-Puritan Satire* 1572-1642 (New-Haven: Yale University Press, 1954), p. 89. Landrum characterized him as a Precisionist: *PMLA* 41, p. 536. On the other hand, Mc Lane "goes so far as to call him a high churchman" in an unpublished thesis (quoted by Whitaker, *Religious Basis*, p. 6). This may be misleading. It would be safest to avoid any reference to "high" or "low".

[4] Whitaker, *Religious Basis of Spenser's Thought,* p. 22.

[5] Holden, *Anti-Puritan Satire,* p. 89.

[6] Whitaker, *Religious Basis,* p. 23.

[7] *F.Q.* VI. xii. 25; my italics.

[8] *Prose Works,* p. 223.

[9] Cf. J.J. Higginson, *Spenser's Shepherd's Calender,* p. 39; Padelford, *MP* 11, p. 105. This view is rejected by Whitaker (*op. cit.,* p. 7), perhaps too sweepingly.

[10] *F.Q.* I. viii. 36. 1-4; cf. the Altar of the Inquisition, also devoted to human sacrifices, in *F.Q.* V. x. 28 ff.

We must not forget that Rome and the Jesuits were the Elizabethan bugbear. Catholic worship, in Spenser's mind, was to true worship what the black mass is to the mass for any Christian: a desecration. He judged it blasphemous and corrupt, if not criminal, *in itself,* far more than in its outward trappings. These, he did not disallow, at least in his maturer years. He may have condemned them "doctrinally" in his youth. But, "psychologically" at least, even his early satire of vestments and church-service is directed far more against the clergy than against the forms of worship themselves. [11]

Despite his early association with priests, or perhaps on account of it, there is in the poetry of Spenser a definite strain of anti-clericalism which should not be slurred over. For his complaints at the greed ,ignorance and unworthiness of easy-going priests are the time-honoured grievances of the layman. The main difference between mediaeval anti-clericalism (say, Chaucer's) and Spenser's is the lack of humour and the acridness displayed by the Renaissance poet. These are Puritan features, I admit; but, on the other hand, his censure of the Elizabethan clergy is often quite alien to the Puritan temper. The protest against the suppression of everyday service, the ironical mention of "needlesse works", with its anti-Calvinistic flavour [12], recall the Catholic gibes at the easy-going ways of the Reformed clergy in England [13]. And the poet's scornful taunts at the priests that have "lying by [their] sides [their] lovely Lasses" are thoroughly mediaeval. That the "lasses" should be brides made little difference to Spenser, who constantly advocated "wilfull chastitie" among the clergy. [14]

The mediaeval reverence for hermits and monastic life also survives in the heart of the poet who wrote the *Faerie Queene*. That he should have painted false abbesses like Corceca besides saintly hermits betrays no contradiction. The psychological explanation is obvious. From his Elizabethan youth and Cambridge education, Spenser had sucked the conviction that the pre-Reformation monasteries had been dens of wickedness. But he had earlier sucked, with his mother's milk, the century-old Christian ideal of holiness. To him there was no inconsistency in detesting monasteries as they were, while praising them when he could picture them as they should have been. His abhorrence of catholicism was ethical, or political, not religious. He could at one breath, speak of the "filth and ordure" discovered in monks' cells and show reverence for "their holy heast" [15]. His ideal of priesthood is thoroughly ascetic and monastic [16]. He revered the mediaeval ideal of saintliness far more than the Puritanical and Calvinistic ideal of justification through faith. And the more deeply he revered the older ideal, the more savagely he attacked the corruptions of the present Catholic Church, not sparing the Anglican. He was a puritan, but not in the historical sense: he was concerned with ethical purity, not purity of worship. His dislike of lavish Church ornaments and vestments [17], as well as his aversion

---

[11] See *Hubberd*, ll. 361-550.

[12] *Hubberd*, ll. 448-58.

[13] Cf. Blundell's *Changes* in L.I. Guiney's *Recusant Poets* (London 1938), pp. 287-288.

[14] *Hubberd*, 11. 475-78. See Whitaker, *op. cit.*, p. 19. The bishops praised by Spenser in the *Shepheardes Calender* were not married.

[15] *F.Q.* VI. xiii. 24.

[16] Though inspired by Plutarch's *De Iside*, the priests of Isis Church are obviously described as a model priesthood: *F.Q.* V. vii. 9.

[17] A dislike voiced by Anglicans as well as Puritans in the sixteenth century, as Whitaker reminds us: *op. cit.*, p. 16.

for the gorgeous clothes and luxurious palaces of the Italianate courtier [18] sprang from a love of plainness that could be reconciled with a deep reverence for the beautiful. That feeling had nothing to do with dogma and ecclesiastical policy. "Voyons le plutôt épris de blancheur et de propreté morale", exquisitely said Emile Legouis. [19] But one may qualify a later pronouncement: "Il sera plus protestant que chrétien". Protestant? Of course, but again in the ethical, not in the religious sphere. He spiritually belongs with mediaeval satirists like Langland, pre-Reformers like Wyclif, intent on lashing Church abuses, far more than with the sixteenth-century Reformers, concerned with dogmas and worship. [20]

Some will object that Spenser was a Calvinist, in theology at least. This has been denied by several scholars of late. [21] Padelford had granted that the poet dissented from Calvin in his opinions on Church-government [22] and in the importance he attached to sacraments [23]. Whitaker has marshalled evidence for disagreement on all fundamental points [24]. Yet the distinctions he has drawn between Calvinist and Anglican teaching on the deprivation of original righteousness and the saints' perseverance in grace, however accurate, cannot but appear tenuous. [25] The consideration of his Neoplatonic ideas has not left me under the impression that Spenser should ever be taxed with some craven scruple of thinking too precisely on philosophical questions. Theological precision is hardly to be expected either from the author of the *Faerie Queene,* at least when it extends to the subtler shades of meaning. My concern is with the main outlines and the general frame of mind, not with the nicer points at issue. My approach will therefore be different from Whitaker's. On the one hand, it should be acknowledged that Spenser must have imbibed Calvinistic doctrine at Cambridge. [26] On the other hand, earlier evidence for the direct influence of the *Institutions* on Book I of the *Faerie Queene* and on the heavenly *Hymnes* cannot be lightly dismissed. [27] The Calvinistic characteristics listed by Landrum and illustrated from the works of Spenser are not all distinctive of Calvinism as

---

[18] Noticed by C.S. Lewis. P.N. Siegel makes it a feature of the poet's "Calvinist view of life": *SP* 41, p. 209 ff. That Spenser should be in agreement with the Calvinists on this point does not mean that Calvinism had dictated or inspired his "view".

[19] *E. Spenser*, p. 41.

[20] Wyclif was also concerned with dogma, but his starting-point had been ethical and political.

[21] Chiefly by Collins and Whitaker (see Bibliography, D.I.) and by Thomas P. Nelan in an unpublished thesis, *Catholic Doctrines in Spenser's Poetry* (New York University, 1943).

[22] *MP* 12 (1914), p. 17.

[23] *Ibid.*, pp. 6-7. Cf. *F.Q.* I. ix. 19; I. x. 13; I. xi. 48; *H.H.L.* 194-7.

[24] *Religious Basis*, pp. 30-58. One may add that Spenser did not share Calvin's scorn for heathen philosophy (*Instit.* I. xiii, p. 58) and for the theology of the Areopagite (*Inst.* I. xiv. 4, p. 88.)

[25] *Ibid.*, p. 36 sq, 45-6.

[26] The rebellion against Calvinistic doctrine broke out at Cambridge in 1595 only, with William Barrett's famous sermon: Cf. Frere, *The English Church in the reigns of Elizabeth and James*, (London, *Macmillan*, 1904), p. 283. On the dominantly Calvinistic character of Anglican theology in the 16th century see also C.S. Carter, *The Anglican Via Media* (London, 1927).

[27] As Whitaker does on p. 34. See Padelford's cogent articles in *MP* 12, pp. 1-18, and *JEGP* 13, pp. 418-33.

contrasted with Catholic doctrine[28]. Yet, even though some of them had only Spenser's qualified approval, in accordance with the Anglican position, the general agreement remains impressive. Nor am I certain that dissent was conscious and deliberate when the poet, in fact, departed from Calvin. His theological "statements" rather force upon me the impression that he had committed a Calvinistic lesson to memory. But I do not think he had taken it to *heart*. Religious belief does not imply intellectual assent only. It calls for the deeper response of the man's whole character and personality.

Now, Calvinism is the least compromising of theological systems. Calvinistic notions merged in a different atmosphere lose point and angularity. The last two hymns, being doctrinal, should be distinctly Calvinistic, yet their total effect is rather Augustinian. The explanation is obvious. Spenser may have had in mind Calvin's teaching on total depravity, grace and election. But, on these points, the theology of Calvin is but a cut-and-dried Augustinian theology, divested of Platonic idealism and mystical rapture. These Spenser re-introduced, clothing the bare bones of Calvinistic doctrine with Platonic radiance and poetical wonder.

This only means that the poet in Spenser may have taken precedence of the Calvinist; it does not disprove his theological allegiance. Let us scan the theological tenets more narrowly. The *Hymne of Heavenly Love* emphasizes the depravity and hopelessness of mankind after the Fall until the Redemption (*H.H.L.* 120-31). This is simply Christian dogma, as it was then understood by Catholic and Protestant alike. Chaucer's gentle Parson and the uncompromising Genevan divine were at one in dooming unredeemed mankind to hell:

> Of thilke Adam toke we thilke sinne original... And therefore be we alle born sones of wratthe and of dampnacion perdurable, if it nere baptesme that we receyven...[29]

Spenser therefore was not departing from mediaeval Christianity even though he consciously followed Calvin's theology of the Fall. But he departed from Calvin in the next lines when he dwelt on the Crucifixion in the spirit of mediaeval piety, emphasizing love and sacrifice, not faith and imputed righteousness, as a true Calvinist would have done (*H.H.L.* 141-217).

In the *Faerie Queene* the doctrine of the total depravity of man was stated uncompromisingly: "If any strenght we have, it is to ill" (I.x. I.8). But the statement was illustrated only in the Legend of Holiness. It seems to be inconsistent with the later portrayal of types of temperance, chastity, friendship, justice, courtesy, in each of which the particular virtue inhered, as it were. Indeed, the ethical scheme of the whole poem contradicted Calvinistic doctrine. For, to the Calvinist, there were no self-existing human virtues, and no isolated

[28] In *P M L A* 41 (1926) pp. 533-35. These are:
1° Confidence in Scriptures (*F.Q.* I. x. 19);
2° his definite theology in reference to the Fall (*F.Q.* I. xi. 47);
3° the depravity of man and impotence of his understanding (*F.Q.* V. ii. 42);
4° the will of God, glorified as pre-eminently just (*F.Q.* V. Pro. 10. 3-6);
5° faith in Providence;
6° the doctrine of election (*F.Q.* I. x. 57. 1-4);
7° emphasis on grace (*F.Q.* I. ix. 53. 6; *H.H.B.* 246-8; 253-5);
8° the preservation of the saints (*F.Q.* I. viii. 4.)

[29] Chaucer, "The Persones Tale," § 18; *Works,* p. 684.

virtue could exist apart from all the others, since the grace of God was the only spring of virtuous action and the elect were wholly justified. The illustration of twelve distinct virtues could only be undertaken by a poet whe was more of a "humanist" than a Calvinist.

A divorce between doctrinal theology and allegorical or mythical statements is apparent in Spenser's conception of grace and election. Again, the very planning of the *Faerie Queene,* with self-existing virtues that fight their own fights and occasionally come to each other's rescue, is hardly consistent with Calvinism. Grace, no doubt, hangs over the field, but only in the Legend of Holiness is it the grace of Calvin. In the remaining books, Spenser's conception of grace, embodied in Arthur's shield, is hardly spiritual. He conceives of it as a special providence which ensures, not salvation in the religious sense, but the triumph in battle of a chosen hero over the enemies of England and Protestantism. That nationalistic travesty of the Calvinistic doctrine of election, favoured by the Old Testament, is characteristic of English Puritanism at its lowest ebb of spirituality. But though Spenser was undoubtedly influenced by the Puritan atmosphere, his own conception of grace still retains much of the mediaeval and "chivalric" belief in the special assistance God grants ot his true servants in their battles against "paynims" and heretics. Arthur's shield belongs with the "machinery" of the "chansons de geste", or with the angels Tasso sends to the rescue of his heroes in peril — a device Spenser also used [80]. Arthur is the mediaeval champion of Christianity and the popular monster-quelling hero. As an embodiment of Calvinistic grace, he is utterly unconvincing. Even in the Legend of Holiness, it is significant that he should intervene only to slay Orgoglio and strip Duessa (*F.Q.* I,viii). For Duessa and Orgoglio stand for Mary Tudor and Philip of Spain; or, more generally, for the false Church of Rome, and the civil power that supported it. [81] Arthur's overthrow of both, therefore, is a temporal, not a spiritual victory; the release of the Red-Cross Knight a release from temporal, rather than spiritual bondage. When the knight experiences the spiritual temptation of despair, not Arthur, but Una, or the true Church, comes to his rescue. It is Una again that leads him to the mediaeval and monastic House of Holinesse (I.v). And, in his last battle with the Dragon of Sin — a battle the spiritual significance of which looms larger than the doubtful historical

---

[80] *F.Q.* II. viii. 5. Tasso, *Gerusalemme Liberata,* Canto VII, p. 195 ff. To protect Raimondi, the Angel takes a heavenly shield of diamond:

> Si vedea fiammeggiar fra gli altri arnesi
> Scudo di lucidissimo diamante,
> Grande, che può coprir genti, e paesi,
> Quanti ve n'hà fra il Caucaso, e l'Atlante;
> E sogliono da questo esser difesi
> Principi giusti, e Città caste, e sante (p. 195).

When it strikes on the shield, the sword of Argante is shivered to pieces (*ibid.* p. 198).

[81] See Padelford in *Variorum* F.Q. I, p. 470; Legouis *Spenser,* pp. 233-7. I reject Padelford's interpretation of Orgoglio as spiritual pride (*Variorum F.Q.* I. 438), for it is unsupported. Why should the Knight be attacked by spiritual pride at the time when "for the first time he yields to sensuality"? I fail to see any relation. Besides, as Legouis observed, the hero does not become proud, but helpless. The fact is, that Spenser, when unable to fuse the moral and historical allegory, treats them apart: the House of Pride is moral allegory, the dungeon of Orgoglio, historical allegory.

allusions[32] — the knight receives supernatural assistance not from Arthur's shield of grace, but from the Well of Life and the Tree of Life, from the sacraments of Baptism and the Eucharist[33]. Neither in the importance attached to the ministry of the Church in spiritual recovery nor in the efficacy attributed to sacrements is the allegory attuned to the spirit of Calvinistic doctrine regarding grace and election.

Election, no doubt, is suggested in the *Hymne of Heavenly Beautie* (ll. 253-55) and unequivocally stated in the *Faerie Queene* (I. ix. 53.4-5):

> In heavenly mercies hast thou not a part?
> Why shouldst thou then despeire, that chosen art?

That Spenser consciously believed in it is beyond doubt. But the depth of his conviction may be questioned, for it never finds indirect expression in his poetry; it never inspired his myth-making imagination. In the debate between Jove and Mutabilitie, for instance, when the poet gives veiled expression to Christian theology, he retains his conception of the will of God as pre-eminently just, but he discards predestination, since Jove offers Mutability a chance of finding favour with his "gratious Lord". The offer of Jove implies free will and suggests that the eventual decision of the "Sovereigne" depends upon the attitude of his subject:

> Then ceasse thy idle claime thou foolish gerle,
> *And seeke by grace and goodnesse to obtaine*
> *That place from which by folly Titan fell;*
> *Thereto thou maist perhaps, if so thou faine*
> Have Jove thy gratious Lord and Soveraigne.
> (VII, vi, 34.1-4; my italics)

The apparent contradiction is easily explained. Spenser was no theologian. He had an acute sense of the omnipotence of divine will and the majesty of divine justice, but he conceived of both politically rather than metaphysically: the analogy with kingly will and kingly justice was ever in his mind. And he was naturally tempted to substitute the will and pleasure of a personal ruler, apt to change his mind, for the irrevocable decrees of predestination. The favour of an anthropomorphic God, accordingly, could be lost or regained, like the Queen's favour. At the core of Spenser's conception of God is the popular notion of all ages, coloured by the feelings of a political-minded Elizabethan. If it needs must be connected with a theological system, it might best be illustrated by the theology of Duns Scot or Ockham, for both assert the arbitrary will of a personal God, whose omnipotence is not limited even by his own original decrees, but allows of variation. It is hardly surprising to find that the English poet, on

---

[32] Many commentators have identified the Dragon with Antichrist; if so, it is an awkward repetition of the sevenheaded beast on which Duessa rides (*F.Q.* I. viii). But Antichrist belongs to the historical allegory. In the religious allegory, the Dragon is original Sin. Spenser's own words leave it beyond doubt, for he says that the tree of life had no like,

> Save in that soile, where all good things did grow,
> And freely sprong out of the fruitfull ground,
> As incorrupted Nature did them sow,
> *Till that great Dragon all did overthrow.* (*F.Q.* I. xi. 47.)

[33] *F.Q.* I. x. 29 ff.; I. x. 46 ff.

this point, should agree with the "voluntarist" and the "nominalist" whose systems were England's main contribution to scholastic theology. This is the more remarkable since, unlike Ockham, Spenser inclined to stress necessity in the course of natural events, a tendency which might have favoured a predestinarian conception of spiritual life. But, despite his formal allegiance to Calvinistic theology, he failed to illustrate predestination convincingly in the allegory of the *Faerie Queene,* and even implicitly denied it in one occasion at least. This is sufficient proof that Calvinistic teaching had not deeply sunk into his imagination and sensibility.

The nominalistic trend of English religious thought from the XIVth to the XVIth century [34] could also explain Spenser's acknowledgment of the impotence of man's understanding, listed by Landrum among Calvinistic characteristics. But it is hardly necessary to claim either Calvin's or Ockham's sponsorship for such a commonplace of Christian thought, directly traceable to the Bible [35]. It should not be forgotten, indeed, that Calvinistic theology never claimed to be anything but traditional Christian doctrine, and Spenser received it as such. His assertion of God's Providence, again traced to Calvin by Landrum, would not have struck any Christian as an innovation. Besides, the poet's conception of Providence is coloured by various mediaeval influences, among which the influence of Boethius is conspicuous [36]. The awfulness of an avenging God sitting on the throne of judgment was no less vividly realized by the mediaeval author of the *Dies Irae* than by the Genevan divine and the English poet. [37] And the utter dependence of man upon the grace of God and the merits of Christ for obtaining eternal life, a Christian tenet emphasized by Saint Augustine [38], had not been questioned even by Aquinas [39].

My purpose is not to disprove the influence of Calvin on Spenser. I am convinced, on the contrary, that the description of the trembling sinner, throwing himself down before the footstool of God, "Close covered with the Lambes integrity", was directly inspired by a chapter of Calvin, the language of which it recalls. [40] But I wished to point out that his acceptance of Calvinistic theology did not imply for the conservative poet any conscious break with his mediaeval inheritance of Christian thought. For, on the one hand, he introduced into his poetry only the more traditional elements of Calvinism, never clearly stating the more rigid doctrine of predestination. On the other hand, he retained the accents of mediaeval devotion to Christ and mediaeval emphasis on the Sacraments.

---

[34] Cf. Gilson, *La Philosophie au Moyen Age,* pp. 656 ff; P. Miller, *The New-England Mind* (New-York, 1939), p. 101. In XVth Century religious poetry, constant emphasis on the divorce of faith and reason is a feature of nominalism. See *Religious Lyrics of the XVth Century*, ed. by Carleton Brown (Oxford, Clarendon Press, 1939), Nos 117-120.

[35] Landrum quotes one example only (*F.Q.* V. ii. 42), reminiscent of *Romans* 11. 13.

[36] For Spenser's Boethian conception of fate and providence, see Stirling, *S P* 30, pp. 197-203.

[37] *H.H.B.* 141-151. Cf. *Institution,* III. xii. 1-3, pp. 501-3.

[38] Quoted by Calvin, *ibid.*, p. 513.

[39] *Summa Theologica,* Part II, Sect. I. q. 109, § 5 ,and q. 114. § 2.

[40] *H.H.B.* 141-75. *Institution,* III. xii: "Qu'il nous convient eslever nos esprits au siege judicial de Dieu, pour estre persuadez à bon escient de la justification gratuite" (p. 501). Calvin, like Spenser, characterizes God as "celui qui fait *justice & vérité*" (p. 502).

Now, this did not imply on the poet's part any concession to Catholicism. It simply means that he had read Calvin with the mind and sensibility of a mediaeval Christian. Such a conservative Christian would reject, as he did, the more revolutionary aspects of Calvinistic teaching on church government or the marriage of priests. Such a Christian might adopt the Calvinistic doctrine of total depravity and saving grace, founded on Augustine, but would not dwell on the more unfamiliar themes of predestination or justification by faith. [41] Such a Christian might enjoy the opportunity of free access to the Scriptures, but would retain as well his trust in the Sacraments. I am even prepared to go further than Padelford on this point. I believe Spenser never thought he departed from Calvinistic orthodoxy in regard to the sacraments. For, on the one hand, Calvin, while rejecting transubstiantation never denied the real presence, contrary to Whitaker's assertion [42], and Spenser asserts the latter, but never states the former. [43] On the other hand, in the exchange of the diamond-box, containing Christ's blood for the Bible, the poet, contrary to Padelford's opinion, [44] at least implies that the Bible is of greater value since it is "able souls to save", whereas the miraculous liquor only cures wounds (*F.Q.* I.x.19).

I therefore believe that there was no conscious disagreement between Spenser and Calvin on points of doctrine. But the poet's acceptance of the theology of the Genevan divine throws into sharper relief the contrast in spirit, imagination, sensibility, between the two men. The doctrine he had been taught at Cambridge commanded the intellectual assent of an Elizabethan churchman; but it seldom evoked the deeper response of his personality. In the Calvinistic statements of the Legend of Holiness as in the last two *Hymnes,* one looks in vain for Calvin's depth of inward conviction, for his relentless passion and the smouldering fire of indignation that burns in his pages. Grace, election, justification by faith, imputed righteousness, these notions, which were so many living-coals on the lips of the Genevan theologian, scarcely move the English poet. Two features only appear to have called for a certain emotional response: the insistence on God's righteousness and the "absolute denial of good in any earthly thing" [45]. Both features are conspicuous in the *Hymne of Heavenly Beautie.* Yet the feelings are not unalloyed. Spenser seems to have been born a "malcontent", and a sense of frustration, in the disappointed courtier, may have given a personal edge to his sense of injustice. Insistence on giving every one his due sometimes blunts the feeling for charity, witness Artegall and Talus. If one remembers the fibre of ruthlessness in Lord Grey's secretary, one may understand why the God of righteousness was a living figure for the poet. Besides, in Spenser's conception of the justice of God, the deeper tone and statelier cadence is not heard, as in Calvin, when grace and election are discussed,

---

[41] Spenser never fully states predestination, though it may be implied in the "election" of the Red-Cross Knight. But fore-ordained damnation, he never so much as suggests. It is remarkable that Despair should not urge an argument that would admirably suit his purpose (*F.Q.* I. ix. 43-7).

[42] *Religious Basis of Spenser's Thought,* p. 33. But see *Institution,* IIII. xvii. 10 (pp. 932-3): "en prenant le signe du corps, nous prenons pareillement le corps". Cf. the Anglican *Catechism* Spenser was taught: "What is the inward part or thing signified? The Body and Blood of Christ which are *verily and indeed* taken by the faithful in the Lord's Supper."

[43] *H.H.B.* 194-6. "To feede our hungry soules" may be meant to show that the presence is spiritual.

[44] *M.P.* 12, p. 7.

[45] Padelford, *M P* 12, p. 5.

but when the political feeling of an Elizabethan is merged in the Boethian and mediaeval feeling for world-order and Providence (*F.Q.* V.ii.34-6, 39-43).

Is not the voice of all the mediaeval Christians who wrote *de contemptu mundi* as audible as the voice of Calvin at the close of the fourth hymn, or in the Red-Cross Knight's request?

> O let me not (quoth he) then turne againe
> Backe to the world, whose joyes so fruitless are; (*F.Q.* I.x. 63. 1-2)
>
> Ne from thenceforth doth any fleshly sense,
> Or idle thought of earthly things remaine. (*H.H.B.* 267-8)

Calvin's pessimistic view of the world and human nature was unqualified and consistent. Spenser's was not. The conflict in him of the Renaissance and the Reformation has often been emphasized. But was not the duality also a mediaeval inheritance? The men of the Middle Ages had not been insensitive to the glory of the earth and the fullness of life. After describing the incorruptible heavens, Bartholomaeus added:

> Non enim minus est admiranda terrae virtuosa fecunditas in productione herbarum & arborum, florum & fructuum, in generatione varia animalium et reptilium... [46]

And the mediaeval character of Spenser's conception of Nature has been disclosed by parallels with Alanus and Jean de Meung. Renaissance sensuousness and delight in beauty, no doubt, were superadded to mediaeval naturalism. But whereas the Renaissance artist did not seek to escape from the world, even when he felt it to be an "unsubstantial pageant", whereas the Calvinist, while spurning the world, made himself thoroughly at home in it, Spenser preserved the mediaeval duality. Acknowledging the "wondrous fecundity" of the earth, he remained conscious of living in a place of exile, subject to "Mutabilitie":

> Nam mundus est locus reatus & transgressionis, incolatus & peregrinacionis, doloris et lacrimacionis, laboris et fatigacionis, hororis et confusionis, motus & mutationis, fluxus et alterationis... [47]

What has prevented the basic relation between Spenser's religious attitude and the mediaeval attitude to be recognized is, on the one hand, the failure to acknowledge the "naturalism" of mediaeval Christianity, and on the other hand, Spenser's own transposition of the older dualism into Platonic terms in the last *Hymnes*. But it had been earlier stated in purely Christian terms [48], which shows that the Christian duality of mediaeval inheritance commanded the acceptance of the Platonic duality. It is characteristic, indeed, that Spenser should be nearer Plato than Plotinus. The former has emphasized the duality of appearance and reality, becoming and being, the copy and the model; the latter smoothed away the Platonic dualism by his theory of continuous diffusion and degradation in

---

[46] *De Propr. Rerum,* VIII. i (ed. 1505, sig. 1. 7. r°): "Nor should we less admire the bountiful fertility of the earth in the production of plants and trees, flowers and fruit, and in the multifarious generation of animals and reptiles...".

[47] *De propr. rerum,* VIII. i; sig. 1. 7 r°: "For the world is a place of guilt and transgression, exile and pilgrimage, grief and tears, labour and weariness, horror and confusion, motion and change, flux and mutability..."

[48] *F.Q.* I. x. 58; 62-3.

the scale of being. The Renaissance Platonists followed Plotinus rather than Plato, and, especially when they had Pantheistic leanings, stressed continuity more than duality. Spenser, therefore, in his emphatic contrast of earthly and heavenly beauty as shadow and substance (*H.H.B.* 273.291), is faithful both to Platonic and medieval dualism. But apart from the general distinction between appearance and reality, a commonplace of both Platonic and Christian philosophy, the poet showed no interest in Platonism as a system of thought and a consistent scheme for metaphysical experience. Platonism appealed to his aesthetic sensitiveness, but it could not evoke a truly religious response. For Spenser proved mainly susceptible to beauty incarnate. In the *Hymne in Honour of Beauty,* which had to be devoted to Beauty's self, I never hear the tremulousness of delight, the breathlesness of ecstasy with which the poet beheld not only the face of Una unveiled but the golden hair of Britomart unhelmeted.[49]

We could hardly expect, therefore, that the Idea of the Beautiful, or intelligible Beauty, would send him into real ecstasy; in the fourth hymn, he flaps his wings too consciously for the rapture to be wholly genuine. When a quicker throb of feeling is felt, we find it has been aroused by the vision of a *personified* Sapience. Platonism could awake in Spenser an imaginative response, which, in him as in the younger Milton, became to some extent an ethical response owing to emphasis on purity of love and the spiritual nature of beauty.[50] But it never was for him a religious, or even a metaphysical experience. On the one hand, he never could transcend the purely human feeling inspired by the beauty of woman. On the other hand, he remained faithful to the Christian conception of divine love as an answer to the personal call of a personal God. But, though I believe with C. S. Lewis that Spenser was a deeply religious man, it must be confessed that his deeper religious feelings had an ethical, or cosmological, rather than a "spiritual" character.

"Il n'a rien d'un mystique"[51]. The pronouncement of Emile Legouis can hardly be questioned. That the poet should have characterized the Holy Ghost as truth or wisdom rather than love[52] bespeaks an insensitiveness to mystical theology. He never appears to have felt the immanence of God within the soul. And the road of transcendence was closed, for negation of sense experience was utterly unknown to him. His poetry does not show the least interest in the negative theology of Dionysius, which seldom appealed, indeed, to the concrete Anglo-Saxon mind. We may, with J. B. Collins, style the third and fourth hymns Christocentric and Theocentric[53]. But even if we admitted them to be an exposition of mystical methodology, that highly doubtful contention would not make Spenser himself a mystic. Any sixteenth century poet writing of Christ and divine Sapience would have occasionally used the "language" of mysticism, which was then as conventional for religious poetry as Petrarchan diction for profane love-poetry. The sincerity of the poet need not even be impeached, for, whereas the first two hymns described earthly love as a personal and present experience, the last hymns are an exhortation to heavenly love addressed to the readers and to the poet's own soul, an invitation to a future experience. When

---

[49] *F.Q.* I. iii. 4. 6-9; IV. vi. 20.

[50] The association of a certain Puritanism with Platonism is by no means extraordinary. After Spenser and Milton, we find it in the Cambridge Platonists, notably in Peter Sterry, Cromwell's chaplain.

[51] *Spenser,* p. 36 (ed. 1923).

[52] *H.H.B.* 11. *H.H.L.* 38-49.

[53] *Christian Mysticism,* p. 210.

a description of actual ecstasy is given, it is purely impersonal, done from outward.[54]

The God of Calvin commanded only Spenser's intellectual assent. The God of Plato only called forth an aesthetic response. The God of the mystics appealed to his imagination only. Were his religious feelings shallow after all? To some extent, it may be agreed that his response to Christianity was more a traditional inheritance than a personal experience — which does not mean that it was conventional or insincere. In the devotional stanzas of the *Hymne of Heavenly Love,* he is obviously earnest, but he does not move us so deeply as in the great cosmic passages: the Garden of Adonis, the speech of Artegall to the Giant, the *Cantos of Mutabilitie.* I hesitate to assert that he himself was not so deeply moved, for subjective impressions are treacherous, especially when centuries have elapsed. But so penetrating a critic as Professor Renwick has also singled out two of the three passages just mentioned:

> One.... feels that the deeper communion of spirit was between Spenser and Lucretius, that there is a depth of the tone in the Lucretian passages of the *Faerie Queene* more moving and more heartfelt than the somewhat shrill straining of the *Hymnes* of Love and Beauty.[55]

With Professor Renwick's judgment on the *Hymnes* I fully agree. I also agree with his aesthetic judgment concerning the "Lucretian" passages of the *Faerie Queene,* but I feel bound emphatically to reject the qualification of "Lucretian". It has been shown that Lucretian influence on the passages concerned is still a matter of conjecture.[56] The Christian and mainly mediaeval character of the Garden and *Mutabilitie* has been established. That Mutability should urge atheistic arguments is no proof of Spenser's atheistic sympathies, since Mutability is identified with Sin and is a daughter of Satan.[57] The famous "sceptic' answer, "But what we see not, who shall us persuade?" (VII.vii.49.5), no more points to scepticism in Spenser than the answer of Artegall to the giant: "Of things unseene how canst thou deeme aright?" (V.ii.39.1). The same argument is urged by Mutability to question the power of Jove, and by the "righteous" knight to vindicate the justice of God. If we insist on making out Spenser to be a sceptic, we must also make him out to be a fideist:

> All in the powre of their great Maker lie:
> All creatures must obey the voice of the most hie.
> They live, they die, like as he doth ordaine,
> Ne ever any asketh reason why.
> ....
> For all we have is his: what he list doe, he may. (V. ii. 40-41)

Even if we give Mutability's answer its full "atheistic" force, it does not impeach the faith of a poet for whom, as for Shakespeare, there were more things in heaven and earth than were dreamt of in the philosophy of Lucretius. And it should be noted that the sceptic line, read in its context, calls in question, not supernaturalism, but the "secret powre" and purely physical "vertue" which

---

[54] *H.H.L.* 267-87 is in the future tense; *H.H.B.* 288-301, an exhortation to something still unachieved. The vision of Sapience (*H.H.B.* 253-87) is in the third person.
[55] *Spenser,* p. 174.
[56] See Chapter IV, pp. 65-7.
[57] See Chapter IV, p. 67.

astrology attributed to the stars. [58] The poet may not have intended, nor even realized the ultimate metaphysical implications of a limited argument.

There is not the least trace or temptation of atheism in Spenser's poetry, but his "naturalism" may be justly emphasized, provided its religious and Christian character is recognized. Not the God of Plato or Calvin, but the "God of Nature evoked his deeper emotional response. The God who claimed entire allegiance, called forth from the poet's heart the fuller flow of feeling and from his lips the statelier cadence was the God of Genesis, who bade all creatures "increase and multiply"; the God of Alanus and Jean de Meung, whose vice-gerent Nature is; the God of Boethius whose wisdom and providence rule over fate. Not with Lucretius, therefore, nor with Renaissance pantheists like Bruno does Spenser belong. For Nature "Still mooving, yet unmoved from her sted" is not to him ultimate reality, but the realization in a temporal world of the intemporal will of God. Nature is at the frontier of mutability and divine unchangeableness: beyond her lie "the pillours of Eternity", the transcendence denied by pantheism. The triumph of permanence over change is twofold. A triumph *in* time, since, by means of change, all beings work their own perfection. And a triumph *beyond* time since:

> ... time shall come that all shall changed bee,
> And from thenceforth, none no more change shall see:
> (*F.Q.* VII, vii. 59.4-5).

The first vindication would not be inconceivable in a pantheistic universe; the second obviously is. It is not even reconcilable with pure Neoplatonism, for the final dissolution of the world implies previous creation in time. it is hardly exaggerated to say that the idea of creation, essentially Hebraic and Christian [59], dominates Spenser's cosmic and religious poetry. God to him is, above all, the "Maker", and He is most frequently named as such. [60] The conception is simple, strong, popular. It will never be philosophically satisfying since it does not attempt to bridge the gap between time and eternity: you must take the leap. Hence the twofold answer of Nature, one from a temporal, the other from an intemporal standpoint. But duality here does not mean dualism, since, as C. S. Lewis emphasizes, "Change is but the mode in which Permanence expresses itself." [61] I will add: "for a time", which means here the whole of time. The duality I insist upon is not the conflict of change and permanence in the world, but the dual mode of achieving permanence, that is, fulfilling the design of God, either by ruling over change or by annihilating change. Obviously, both are compatible only in a "creationist" and eschatological scheme.

Now, I believe that the metaphysical duality commands the religions position of Christianity when it maintains the necessity of both action and contemplation, the active life seeking the temporal fulfilment of the will of God, the contem-

---

[58] *F.Q.* VII. vii. 48-9. Jove here is not the God of Sabbaoth but the planet Jupiter. A heated controversy on astrology and the influence of planets on sub-lunary matters had started with Fulke's *Pleasant Prospect* in 1563: see Allen, *The Star-Crossed Renaissance* (Durham 1941), p. 107 ff. The attack en astrology was led by Puritans like Fulke and Perkins, and Spenser was certainly aware of it.

[59] The *Timaeus* is the nearest approach to it, and therefore proved reconcilable with *Genesis*. Yet even the *Timaeus* contradicted creation *ex nihilo*. In Neoplatonism, the idea of creation altogether disappeared.

[60] Cf. *H.H.L.* 57, 92, 120; *H.H.B.* 201; *F.Q.* IV. x. 35. 5; V. ii. xl. 8, etc.

[61] *Allegory of Love*, p. 356.

plative life seeking immediate access to an intemporal mode of being. And that duality is reflected in the episode of the Mount of Contemplation (*F.Q.* I.x.54 ff.). Of course the teaching of Christianity was that action and contemplation should be combined. But, practically and popularly, either an individual or a chronological distinction was admitted: some men were recognized as more fit for contemplation, and old age was thought to be more suitable for it than youth. Spenser introduced a chronological distinction. St. George was first to achieve his temporal mission by deeds of arms, "Then peaceably [his] painefull pilgrimage To yonder same *Hierusalem* (to) bend (I.x.61.3-4).

The respective claims of the active and the contemplative life were the subject of much discussion during the Renaissance. It was generally agreed that action should precede contemplation. Landino even suggested that it might take precedence of it [62]. Spenser certainly assented to Landino's pronouncement "non datur igitur quies: nisi prius laboraveris", [63] but like the men of the Middle-Ages, he fully maintained the supremacy of contemplation [64]. On the whole, I do not find his attitude really typical of the Renaissance, not only on account of the mediaeval setting, but because, even while he gives the active life its full share in accordance with the Renaissance spirit and praises it from one standpoint, he does not hesitate to condemn it from another standpoint:

> Thence forth the suit of earthly conquest shonne,
> And wash thy hands from guilt of bloudy field:
> For blood can nought but sin, and wars but sorrowes yield.
> (I. x. 60. 7-9)

Landino sought to harmonize and relate the claims of action and contemplation. Spenser states them separately, and, while acknowledging both to be necessary, he considers the former to be inseparable from sin. This is certainly not a Renaissance attitude. It is not distinctly Calvinistic either [65]. But the duality is very largely mediaeval. The Middle Ages had seen no contradiction in extolling knightly deeds and yet proclaiming all earthly achievements to be contemptible, once the knight was turned into a hermit. It was not even the substitution of a divine for a purely earthly standpoint, for the deeds of arms were often praised as *gesta Dei.* It marked the substitution of the immediate quest of eternity for a divinely guided but temporal action, fulfilling the divine purpose in time only. From time to eternity, a leap had to be taken, and it meant renunciation of the world. With the leap, the standpoint changed utterly.

---

[62] *Disputationes,* f. LVI r°-v°. I translate: "... there are some ... who rank action before contemplation. Especially in our greener age, in which they would have the philosopher act, speak, administer the commonwealth, go to war and assume command".

[63] Quoted by Robb, *Neoplatonism,* p. 97.

[64] The men of the Renaissance, I must say, still maintained that "the end of the active or doing life ought to be the beholding, as of war, peace, and of paines, rest" (Castiglione, *Courtier,* p. 235). But in practice, they lay the emphasis on the former, and even in theory, their ideal was to harmonize them, to do away with the mediaeval duality.

[65] Spenser may have been influenced by the pessimism of Calvin, but Calvinistic influence is not directly traceable in the episode of the Mount of Contemplation. Siegel's attempt to present Spenser's reconciliation of the claims of action and contemplation as an "aspect common to Calvinism and neo-Platonism" is thoroughly unconvincing to my mind: see *SP* 41, pp. 220-21.

I believe the mediaeval duality affords the only possible psychological explanation for the otherwise incoherent pronouncements of the Hermit who urges St. George to fight for Una, and at the same time declares that blood can yield but sin. I further believe it accounts for the emphatic rejection of earthly love and earthly beauty by a poet who had earlier shown, in the *Amoretti* and the *Epithalamion,* that the love of man for woman, when chaste, answers God's own injunction. Again we find Spenser praising earthly love and beauty as "heavenly", just as he had praised the Queen of earthly Cleopolis, Gloriana, as "heavenly borne" (*F.Q.* I.x.59.9). And again we hear him proclaim that, once the sight of God is obtained, the beauty which formerly awoke love "Thenceforth seemes fowle, & full of sinfull blame" (*H.H.B.* 276). So had he invited the Red-Cross knight to turn form Cleopolis to Jerusalem: "For bloud can nought but sin, and wars but sorrowes yield" (*F.Q.* I.x.60.9).

Are these pronouncements instances of a change of mind? How could they be, when the different judgments are spoken nearly in one breath by the Hermit? In the Dedication to the *Fowre Hymnes,* Spenser again made it clear that he had no contempt for earthly love and beauty, since he praised his patrons for both.[66] Should we suspect conventionality in his denunciation of the world? The poet need not be impeached for insincerity, since he did not pretend he himself had reached the stage of contemplative life described in the fourth hymn. And he seems to be wholly sincere in his imaginative recreation of it. I believe he was fully convinced that the God who bade all creatures be fruitful and multiply had truly blessed human love; fully convinced, too, that the God who made all things fair in their time had never wished beauty to be the bait of sin. But I believe he no less truly felt that human love and the beauty of woman should "vanish into nought" in the light of divine beauty. The copy is fair, since the model is fair. But those who have been allowed to behold the model, thenceforth will needs spurn the copy, and be ashamed they ever loved it, if they loved it once for itself. And all human love will seem impure for the soul raised to divine love, even while remaining pure in the other souls. The one is at the threshhold of Jerusalem, the others are still in Cleopolis. It is characteristic of the Anglican poet who advocated celibacy for priests that he should have made chastity, in the stricter sense, a prerequisite of the contemplative life[67]. Once more his mediaeval inheritance, rather than the aesthetic asceticism of the Platonists, inspired a conception quite alien to Calvinism.

My purpose in this chapter has not been to deny either the poet's theological allegiance to Calvin nor his aesthetic allegiance to Plato, but to lay bare the mediaeval structure of his mind and sensibility. To all the suggestions of the Renaissance and the Reformation he more or less keenly responded. But he responded by inserting the newer notions in the ancient frame, and subtly attuning the never emotions to the traditions of mediaeval Christianity.

---

[66] "as to the most excellent and rare ornaments of all true love and beautie, both in the one and in the other."

[67] Implicitly in *H.H.B.*, explicitly in *F.Q.* V. vii. 9. 5-9.

CONCLUSION

The present study sprang from the conviction that a revaluation of Platonic influence over the poetry of Spenser was needed. The tracing of that influence had not only led to overstatement and misinterpretation of the poet's meaning: it had too often been confined to source-hunting. The ascertaining of sources, sometimes loosely or wrongly alleged, was a first requirement. But a mere array of parallels has little significance unless it helps the reader to gain an insight into the poet's mind. Moreover, since source-ascription must occasionally give way to the recording of affinities, a discrimination of actual influences required some insight into the influencing mind as well.

A chronological approach was felt to be useful since there had been no previous attempt to discover whether Spenser's interest in Platonism grew or declined with advancing years. But the date of Spenser's most distinctly Platonic poems, the first two *Hymnes,* was still a matter of debate. I had to show that in all likelihood they were written or re-written after the publication of *Colin Clout* in 1595. A late date of composition had already been assumed by some critics, but fresh evidence was offered. As the more Platonic sonnets in the *Amoretti* were probably composed in 1593-94, it looked as though Spenser's acquaintance with, or interest in, the niceties of the Neoplatonic philosophy of love and beauty had deepened in the later years of his life. Since increasing ease, precision and consistency in the handling of Platonic notions is a more likely evolution than increasing vagueness and looseness of language, a survey of the poetry written before the publication of the *Fowre Hymnes* was shown to support the chronological assumption. Accordingly the *Hymnes* were left for later consideration. But, whatever their date of composition might be, an analysis of the other poems disclosed a rejection of the metaphysical subtleties of Neoplatonism, a Christian transmutation of the Platonic philosophy of love, whether human or heavenly, and close links with mediaeval rather than Renaissance Platonism in the cosmology of the *Faerie Queene.*

Aesthetic or courtly Platonism, involving a theory of poetic inspiration and a philosophy of love and beauty, was first considered. But Platonic ideas were found to be deprived of their original implications in Spenser's statements. In the *Faerie Queene* Platonism was brought to earth and interpreted in terms of ethics. Platonic idealism merely invested with some of its own glamour a conception of love between man and woman that ran contrary to its very dictates. The divine origin of beauty had always been acknowledged by Christian tradition. Renaissance Neoplatonism was responsible for Spenser's insistence on a traditional theme, but the distinctive theories of the Neoplatonists, their metaphysical tenets and entities did not appear in the *Faerie Queene* nor in the *Teares of the Muses.* The distinction between beauty of body and beauty of mind was drawn on Petrarchan lines. The *Amoretti* offered the first instance of the poet's acquaintance with the Platonic ladder, yet the "steps" could not be traced in the sonnet sequence.

An analysis of Spenser's philosophy of love and beauty could not be confined to the poet's open statements since characters and episodes in the *Faerie Queene* had been construed into Platonic significance. A review of the least improbable interpretations showed that the contrast between the two Florimells was not meant to be a contrast between phenomenal and ideal beauty; that Belphoebe did not stand for the Heavenly Venus; that Gloriana, unlike the Heavenly Sapience, was described as a terrestrial ruler. Nor was Prince Arthur to be turned into a Platonic intermediary. The "continued allegory" was shown to be religious, ethical, historical or political, but hardly meant to illustrate Neoplatonic metaphysics.

Evidence for Platonic influence over the ethics of the *Faerie Queene* proved slender or inconclusive. What had been ascribed to Plato could often have been borrowed from Cicero or other sources. Besides, Spenser's conception of temperance and justice turned out to be closer to the spirit as well as the letter of Aristotelian ethics, contrary to current assumptions. The poet's notion of chastity, a subject of dispute, was elucidated in the light of his own poetry and popular Elizabethan ethics. The separate treatment of the moral virtues was further shown to be repugnant to the views of Plato.

Although Spenser must have been aware of the Neoplatonic significance attached to the classical myths, were it but through the Mythology of Natalis Comes, he had no use for the more esoteric and far-fetched interpretations. What Platonism could be found in the Mutabilitie Cantos was of mediaeval descent. A new interpretation of the Garden of Adonis steered clear of the pitfalls of sheer naturalism or pure Platonism and brought out both the largely mediaeval character of the philosophy and the Christian meaning of the allegory in accordance with the Augustinian and hexaemeral tradition. No Neoplatonic hierarchy of graded worlds was discovered in either myth. The mediaeval and astrological tradition on the one hand, and on the other hand classical literature, supplemented with information derived from popular Renaissance mythographers, fully accounted for the various descriptions and attributes of Venus in the *Faerie Queene*. The direct or indirect influence of the *Timaeus*, a mediaeval classic, over Spenserian cosmology was acknowledged. But the influence of the *Symposium* was first traced in Colin's account of cosmic love, a set speech probably inserted in *Colin Clout* as late as 1594-5.

Since unmistakable verbal borrowings could not be discovered and parallels could be offered from different sources, the poet's meaning, personal approach and frame of mind had to be defined before influences could be weighed and discriminated. In the survey of the Renaissance Neoplatonic treatises that Spenser may have known, source-ascription was not my main concern, though a fair number of reasons pointed to his acquaintance with Le Roy's *Sympose*, a hitherto neglected source. My object was to record affinities and discover trends, for real influence implies affinity and the discovery of affinity may point to influence when the trend is more distinctive than the material used. Le Roy's exposition of Platonic philosophy threw light on the continuity between the mediaeval and the Renaissance mind and justified the emphasis laid on the literary character of Spenser's Platonism as well as on its realistic and sensible avoidance of metaphysical subtleties and far-fetched allegories. Equicola's syncretistic *Libro di*

Natura d'Amore was also shown to be in harmony with the poet's conservative outlook and a likely source of information. On the contrary, the English poet was discharged of any real indebtedness to commonly alleged sources — Pico, Landino, Bruno and even Ficino — in the poetry published prior to the *Fowre Hymnes.*

The information obtained on Renaissance Neoplatonism and the knowledge gained as to Spenser's own philosophy and cast of mind could now be brought to bear upon his fullest exposition of the Platonic philosophy of love and beauty, the *Fowre Hymnes.* In the light of the preceding survey it was easy to distinguish in the first two hymns between non-Platonic materials, Platonic materials already used in earlier poetry and a more "technical" and systematic exposition of the Neoplatonic theory than Spenser had given as yet. The older elements could be disposed of readily. But their very presence afforded grounds for suspecting that the poet had digested the newer notions into his earlier consubstantial philosophy. And digestion implies transmutation of a kind. We were not surprised, therefore, to discover that Spenser's interest lay, not in the Neoplatonic steps, but in the identity of the lovers' souls. The discovery made it clear that he had followed a chapter of Ficino concerned with "enamoration" from the human standpoint only. The claims of Benivieni and even Castiglione in regard to source-ascription had therefore to be reduced and Ficino was fully reinstated in his rights.

The problem of interrelation between the "earthly" and the "heavenly" hymns was then considered and easily solved since my interpretation of the first pair of hymns made a complete break between the two inevitable. It gave further evidence of the conservative and Christian character of Spenser's philosophy of love, since its duality rests on traditional ethico-religious grounds and has little in common with the metaphysical duality of orthodox Neoplatonic doctrine. But the Renaissance Platonists themselves were by no means fully agreed in their conception of love, human and divine. Spenser was shown to discover kinship with Le Roy, Equicola, Bembo and Leone Ebreo, whose influence had never been considered, whereas he entirely rejected the orthodox Platonic ladder of Benivieni, Pico and Castiglione.

The controversy as to the dominantly Christian or Platonic character of the last two hymns called for attention. Spenser was defined as a Platonizing Christian, not a Christian Platonist, since internal evidence alone made it obvious that the poet intended the hymns to be Christian in tone, tenor and substance. Moreover, the poet's insistence on the "personality" of God in both hymns and his emphasis on divine love as a personal appeal of God to man in the third hymn were shown to be thoroughly un-Platonic. The fourth hymn was discovered to be in agreement with Christian tradition, both in the contemplation of God in his handiwork and in the final vision of the Scriptural Sapience, identified with the Second Person of the Christian Trinity. Yet, since Platonism defines love as a desire for beauty, whereas Christianity insists on self-surrender, I am prepared to own that the feeling expressed (not the dogmas illustrated) by the *Hymne of Heavenly Beautie* is more characteristic of Christian Platonism than suggestive of the more distinctly Christian approach to God. Spenser's heavens surpass each other in beauty:

> These thus in faire each other farre excelling,
> As to the Highest they approach more neare. (*H.H.B.* 99-100)

Dante's heavens surpassed each other in love. Beauty, to Spenser, was the cause of love; love, to Dante, was the cause of beauty [1]. Spenser's argument was: the higher beauty, the higher love. Dante's argument: the higher love, the higher beauty. Dante's experience of divine love was purely Christian. Spenser's conception of it in the fourth hymn is "theologically" and "historically" Christian since the object of love is the beauty of the Christian God. But "psychologically" the English poet, I admit, offers a compromise between Platonism and Christianity, directing love as a desire for beauty, not to the Intellectual Beauty of the Platonists but to the personal beauty of the Son-Sapience. Since he had fully illustrated the Christian conception of divine love in the third hymn, it is clear that both hymns are, on the whole, predominantly Christian from the psychological as well as from the historical point of view. But they remain an instance of the "muddled" feeling characteristic of the Renaissance, since no reconciliation is worked out between the two conceptions of love. To Spenser's discharge, and to the discharge of the Renaissance, it may be acknowledged that the contradiction had been more or less traceable in Christian thought whenever it came under Greek influence, whenever objective Beauty and the objective Good took precedence of subjective love and goodness [2].

Once Spenser's own position had been cleared, his affinities as a Christian Platonist with Le Roy, Equicola and Bembo were once more revealed. The identification of Sapience with the Second Person of the Trinity, already established on internal evidence, was confirmed by means of contemporary testimony. The influence of the Augustinian tradition, neglected so far, was duly stressed, and quotations from a sixteenth-century "manual" of devotion showed the popularity of the religious themes and the commonplaceness of the theological notions handled by the poet in the sacred *Hymnes*. Lastly, the peculiar blending of Scripture and Neoplatonism in the Sapience of Leone Ebreo's *Dialoghi* was found to offer the clearest illustration and the likeliest "source" for Spenser's portrait of Sapience.

Elucidation of the poet's meaning as a rule should take precedence of source-ascription. Yet when the discovery of a parallel affords an immediate clue to an interpreattion otherwise obtained by means of patient analysis and relentless illustration, its interest transcends mere historical curiosity. The main conclusions which followed upon an examination of the *Hymnes* could be anticipated, once the "seed" of the poet's inspiration was discovered in La Boderie's Epistle prefixed to his translation of the *Sopra l'Amore*. Both for the sake of emphasis and the sake of clarity, I therefore felt justified in placing that important parallel in the forefront of the chapters devoted to the *Fowre Hymnes*. Should the source-ascription be questioned, the parallel would retain its full value as an illustration, since the interpretation of the *Hymnes* it invites has been independently obtained.

---

[1] "... l'amor che mi fa bella" (*Paradiso* XII, 1.31). The nearer the souls are to God, the greater love they feel and the more beautiful they become.

[2] The latent contradiction I am stressing here is not unrelated to the contradiction between the notion of self-sufficiency and the principle of pleniture noted by A.O. Lovejoy in *The Great Chain of Being* (Harvard Univ. Press. 1936), pp. 42, 49, 72-81. The Good, like Beauty, is self-sufficient and only the object of love; love, craving an object, cannot be self-sufficient. The Christian poets and mystics never hesitated to contradict the notion of self-sufficiency.

Any discussion of Spenser's Neoplatonism implies an examination of his religious ideas. Besides, the poet's handling of Platonic notions had suggested the persistence of a mediaeval cast of mind. Confirmation could be sought in an analysis of his religious sensibility. Several layers were discovered. His conscious doctrinal allegiance to Calvinism was not denied but shown to be mainly intellectual and ethical; it hardly engaged his imagination and emotions. Platonism, on the contrary, was found to have had mainly an aesthetic attraction, but to have undergone a deep change in regard to doctrine and even to the "quality" of the feelings evoked, ethics — rather than metaphysics — ruling the poet's sensibility. Besides, both Platonic idealism and Christian mysticism appeared to be an imaginative rather than a heart-felt experience. Lastly, the traditional devotion to Christ expressed in the third hymn, however sincere, did not betray a high religious fervour. Spenser's deepest feelings certainly found expression in the cosmic passages of the *Faerie Queene.* Not pantheism, but the Christian naturalism of the Middle-Ages evoked the richest and fullest response of his religious sensibility.

The duality of action and contemplation, earthly and heavenly love, as disclosed in the poetry of Spenser, was further shown to reveal a frame of mind still mainly mediaeval and pre-eminently conservative. Such epithets may appear paradoxical when used to characterize the *Fowre Hymnes,* which at first sight seen to breathe the very spirit of the Renaissance. But critics now mostly agree that Spenser's thought in the *Faerie Queene* as in the *Complaints* was predominantly mediaeval. I have attempted to show that his mediaeval inheritance governed his response both to the Renaissance and to the Reformation. Never stifling his sensitiveness to the present appeal, it subtly influenced his reaction.

This interpretation is based on the survival of inherited notions in the poet's mind. Yet no interpretation can be valid unless it leaves room for the originating power of personal consciousness. I therefore consider that the traditions or conceptions Spenser accepted were coloured by his individual apprehension of them. But the present study was mainly concerned with the interplay of various influences and various traditions in the poet's mind. His own personality, but for the last chapter, was not directly studied. The Platonic themes ,indeed, afforded unsuitable ground, since they usually did not invite self-revelation. Yet my insistence on the poet's mediaeval inheritance, commanding his acceptance and understanding of newer notions, is not to be construed into an expression of social determinism. The cause of Spenser's traditionalism is not in the tradition, but in the mind of the poet who accepted a tradition he could have rejected. That is why the method of approach followed in the present study has a subjective as well as an objective significance. Spenser's conception of love, human and divine, was shown to be in harmony with an intellectual and emotional inheritance older than Renaissance Platonism: but that harmony expressed his *personal* choice. The Renaissance poet who went to Chaucer as to his master and long indulged in an archaic diction, the Renaissance courtier who kept contrasting "the image of the antique world" with the ruinous "state of present time" [3], the Renaissance allegorist who remembered the *Roman de la Rose* even while imitating Ariosto and Tasso, the Elizabethan churchman who urged celibacy

---

[3] *F.Q.* V. Proem I ff. Cf. Harvey, *Letter-Book* (ed. Scott, 1894), pp. 82-8: "You suppose the first age was the goulde age...".

for priests and revered hermits, in a word, the author of the *Faerie Queene* undoubtedly was among the most conservative spirits of his age.

"The publication of the *Shepheardes Calender*" Renwick observed, "meant the enrichment of English poetry not only through the naturalization of a new poetic form, but by the advent of a new poetic personality" [4]. Is it not illuminating that Spenser, for his "new" venture, should have chosen to speak the language of Chaucer and delighted in painting older customs, including the abhorred Popish ceremonies [5]? In his first published poem was revealed the bent of a mind that chose to think of the present in terms of the past. In his last published poems, the *Fowre Hymnes,* the newer language of Renaissance Platonism was used, partly at least, to convey an older meaning and older feelings: courtly, Petrarchan or Christian. From first to last the poet's cast of mind was discovered to be traditional and even retrospective.

---

[4] *Spenser,* p. 39.
[5] e.g. in *February,* ll. 207-10.

APPENDIX I

PARALLELS IN THE "FOWRE HYMNES" AND THE "FAERIE QUEENE"

Note: The distinction between parallels in diction and parallels in idea is sometimes a loose one. No undue strictness should be attached to the following classification.

I. *Hymne in Honour of Love.*

A — *Parallels in diction.*

H.L.	*F.Q.*
ll. 1-4.	*Ded. Sonnet* XVI, ll. 7. 9.
ll. 27-8.	I. i. 9. 6-7. Cf. VII. vii. 2.
ll. 25-6.	III. xi. 2. 3-4.
ll. 13-14.	III. xi. 44. 8-9.
l. 45.	III. xi. 49. 2.
ll. 11-13.	III. xi. 52. 3-5.
ll. 23-4.	IV. Pro. 5. 5-7.
ll. 11-14.	IV. vii. 1. 1-4.

B — *General Parallels in idea and diction.*

H.L.	*F.Q.*
ll. 22-9.	I. Pro. 3.
l. 196.	II. iii. 25. 6.
ll. 218 ff.	III. i. 49. 8-9. Cf. III. v. 1-2; IV. x. 26. 8-9.
ll. 22-8; 169-89.	III. iii. 1.
ll. 24. 27-8.	III. iii. 1. 1-2.
ll. 280-93.	III. vi. 29.
ll. 287-91.	III. vi. 41.
l. 287.	III. vi. 51.
ll. 122-3.	III. ix. 29. 1-5.
l. 262.	IV. x. 12, 13, 16.

C — *Important Parallels.*

H.L.	*F.Q.*
ll. 78-91 (cf. *H.H.B.* 197-201).	IV. x. 35.

II. *Hymne in Honour of Beautie.*

A — *Parallels in Diction.*

H.B.	*F.Q.*
ll. 65-7.	II. iii. 22. 4.
ll. 253-6.	II. iii. 25. 1-3.

B — *General Parallels.*

H.B.	*F.Q.*
ll. 161-88.	III. i. 49 and v. 53.
ll. 29-42.	III. vi. 12.
ll. 132-33.	IV. ix. 2. 6-8.

III. *Hymne of Heavenly Love.*

A — *Parallels in Diction.*

H.H.L.	*F.Q.*
l. 48.	II. x. 1. 1-2.
l. 1.	II. x. 1. 3.
l. 69.	II. xii. 39. 4.

B — *General Parallels.*

H.H.L.	*F.Q.*
ll. 8-21.	IV. Pro. 1.

IV. *Hymne of Heavenly Beautie.*

A — *Parallels in Diction.*

H.H.B.	*F.Q.*
l. 7.	I Pro. 2. 9.

B — *General Parallels.*

H.H.B.	*F.Q.*
ll. 267 ff.	I. x. 62.
l. 273.	I. x. 67. 9.

C — *Important Parallels.*

H.H.B.	*F.Q.*
ll. 36-42.	V. ii. 35.
ll. 197-201 (and *H.L.* 78-91).	IV. x. 35.

APPENDIX II

PROSODY

The style and prosody of the *Fowre Hymnes* have already been exhaustively studied by Dr. J. W. Bennett, according to Padelford's criteria, that is, the use of compounds, run-on lines, feminine endings and modifiers [1]. Both from her article and her later study of the *Faerie Queene,* it appears that the use of compounds, feminine endings and modifiers offers no safe indications as to the date of composition [2]. The lower or higher ratio of run-on lines is also liable to different interpretations, especially in late work, for Spenser seems to have tightened up his verse technique according to subject-matter or for other reasons after the first three books of the *Faerie Queene* [3]. Therefore, although the percentage of run-on lines in the *Hymnes,* much higher than in Book I, places them nearest to the *Cantos of Mutabilitie,* I would not rest on prosodic evidence alone my assumption that the *Hymnes* were written after the first six books of the *Fairie Queene.* But, within the *Hymnes,* a fairly uniform ratio of run-over lines would point to simultaneous composition, or, at least, revision. J. W. Bennett has already observed that "all four hymns show uniformity rather than difference". The first hymn is nearest to the last, "while the fewest run-over lines occur, not in either of the first two, but in the third hymn".

Though the figures given by J. W. Bennett fully support my conclusions in Chapter I, further investigation may not be unrewarding. Mathematical accuracy in the evaluation of run-over lines may not be so easily obtainable as prosodists usually assume. Punctuation (whether ancient or modern) and even syntax are not safe criteria. The absence of a comma is of no significance when the "turn" of the line dictates a pause. This is obvious in *H.B.* 6-7, among many other instances. Even when the lines are not single-moulded, the pause may be so strong as to make them actually end-stopped to the ear, as in *H.B.* 97-8:

> That golden wyre, those sparckling stars so bright /
> Shall turne to dust, and loose their goodly light.

---

[1] See *S P* 32, p. 155 ff. Cf. Padelford, *P M L A* 45, pp. 704-11.

[2] See *S P* 32, p. 156; *The Evolution of the Faerie Queene,* Appendix II, p. 268; Appendix III, p. 280.

Even the ejambment test affords no simple conclusion, as in the case of Shakespearian practice. "All considerations seem to point to a gradual increase in the use of enjambment from the inception of the poem until 1590 and to a conscious effort to decrease the enjambment in the second instalment" (*op. cit.* p. 272). This is of little help to date the first two *Hymnes,* since we do not know *a priori* whether they must be referred to the period of increase or decrease.

[3] See Bennett, *op. cit.,* p. 271 ff., and *note* 2 above.

Yet, in similar constructions, there may be overlapping both in sense and utterance. Some lines, indeed, may be differently spoken. The following should be classed among "doubtful" or "optional" instances of overruning. The lines definitely overlap if the pause after "forhead" is at least as strong as the pause after "behold". They hardly overlap if they are intoned according to the dominant pattern:

> Sometimes upon her forhead they behold
> A thousand Graces masking in delight, (*H.B.* 253-4)

But in the next lines the break in the second line definitely disrupts the pattern and the overrunning cannot be disguised in utterance:

> Sometimes within her eye-lids they unfold
> Ten thousand sweet belgards, which to their sight (*H.B.* 255-6)

When strong mid-line pauses after enjambment occur in succession, Spenser's stanzas may approach the flexibility of the blank verse paragraph. Instances are found in all the hymns:

> For sure of all, that in this mortall frame
> Contained is, nought more divine doth seeme,
> Or that resembleth more th'immortall flame
> Of heavenly light, then Beauties glorious beame.
> What wonder, then, if with such rage extreme
> Fraile men, whose eyes seek heavenly things to see,
> At sight thereof so much enravisht bee? (*H.L.* 113-19)

> Before this worlds great frame, in which al things
> Are now containd, found any being place,
> Ere flitting Time could wag his eyas wings
> About that mightie bound, which doth embrace
> The rolling Spheres, & part their houres by space,
> That high eternall powre, which now doth move
> In all these things, mov'd in it selfe by love. (*H.H.B.* 22-27)

Leaving out mere overrunning in sense and distinguishing between compulsory and optional overrunning in utterance, the following figures are obtained. To get the "average" figure one half of the optional instances have been added to the compulsory. These figures do not claim to be more than roughly accurate since the utterance will vary with different speakers in border-line cases.

Run-on lines

	Compulsory and Optional	Compulsory	Average
H.L.	1 to 6.02	1 to 8.29	*1 to 6.92*
H.B.	1 to 5.52	1 to 6.38	*1 to 5.92*
ll. 29-231	1 to 4.83	1 to 5.49	1 to 5.14
ll. 162-231	1 to 7	1 to 8.75	1 to 7.77
ll. 232-87	1 to 7	1 to 9.33	1 to 8
H.H.L.	1 to 7.175	1 to 8.69	*1 to 7.86*
ll. 1-154 and 260-87	1 to 5.87	1 to 7	1 to 6.38
ll. 155-259	1 to 11.66	1 to 15	1 to 13.12
H.H.B.	1 to 6.14	1 to 7	*1 to 6.55*

The above-listed results call for the following observations:

1° Since definite overlapping in utterance is required, the percentage of run-on lines is lower in all four hymns than it was according to the method of calculation followed by J. W. Bennett. Her figures were:

H.L. 1 to 4.95; *H.B.* 1 to 4.41; *H.H.L.* 1 to 5.53; *H.H.B.* 1 to 4.63.

2° Yet the general pattern is undisturbed. *H.B.* has the highest percentage. *H.H.B.* and *H.L.* come next with a slight difference. The percentage drops conspicuously in *H.H.L.*

3° Closer scrutiny of the rate of occurrence in the third hymn will afford an explanation for this surprisingly low percentage. If the fifteen devotional stanzas (ll. 155-259) devoted to a meditation on Christ crucified are left out, the ratio of run-on lines in the remaining stanzas will rise to 1 to 6.38, a figure not lower than the figures for the other hymns.

4° The percentage of run-on lines is so very low, indeed, in the devotional stanzas that the disparity suggests an incorporation of older material. For the amalgamation of poems belonging to fairly distant periods of composition is usually betrayed by a disparity in the enjambment ratio. I will give two examples in support of this assertion.

The Masque of Cupid in the third book of the *Faerie Queene* is commonly regarded as the rehandling of an early composition, and identified either with the *Court of Cupid,* or one of the *Pageants* which Spenser is said to have written in his youth [4]. The stiffness of the style and the mainly mediaeval character of the allegory contrasting with the flexibility and luxuriousness displayed in the Italianate House of Busirane support this assumption. Now, a study of the prosody reveals a much lower enjambment ratio in the Masque than either in the preceding description of the House of Busirane or in the remaining stanzas of Canto XII. Here are the figures according to my own method of computation:

	Compulsory and Optional	Compulsory	Average
The House of Busirane III. xi. 28-55	1 to 4.26	1 to 5.26	1 to 4.84
The Masque of Cupid III. xiii. 7-25	1 to 9.5	1 to 14.25	1 to 11.4
The rest of Canto xii	1 to 4.87	1 to 5.80	1 to 5.29

The difference is the more striking since there is the same enjambment ratio in Canto xi and in the stanzas of Canto xii that were written at the same time, the story of Britomart being continued in them, whereas the Masque stanzas were obviously embedded.

If we turn to *Colin Clouts Come Home again,* an interesting instance since it offers many parallels to the *Hymnes,* we notice two main variations in the enjambment ratio throughout the poem: one in the Lay of the Bregog and the Mulla, another in the second part of Colin's formal praise of love.

---

[4] Cf. Upton's, Buck's and Sandison's views recorded in *Variorum F.Q.* III, pp. 299-300.

	Compulsory and Optional	Compulsory	Average
a) Introduction: Raleigh's visit. ll. 1-103	1 to 10.30	1 to 25.75	1 to 14.71
b) The Lay of the Bregog and Mulla, ll. 104-55	1 to 5.77	1 to 10.4	1 to 7.43
c) Visit to England and Cynthia's Court, ll. 156-770	1 to 12.55	1 to 22.77	1 to 16.18
d) First part of Colin's praise of love, ll. 771-834	1 to 16	1 to 21.33	1 to 18.28
e) Second part of Colin's praise of love, ll. 835-94	1 to 5.45	1 to 8.59	1 to 7.06
f) Conclusion, ll. 895-955	1 to 12.2	1 to 20.33	1 to 15.25
g) Average enjambment ratio with b) and e) left out	1 to 12.39	1 to 22.78	1 to 16.06

While the enjambment ratio in the Lay and in the second part of Colin's speech compares with that of the *Fowre Hymnes,* it is remarkably low in the rest of the poem. It might be objected that the enjambment test should not be applied to short passages. But both Colin's speech and the shorter Lay clearly stand out as independent pieces of composition fitted into a narrative. There are no other passage, running to fifty lines at least, in which the enjambment ratio rises higher than 1 to 9.46, reckoning compulsory and optional run-over lines together (the strictures on Court life, ll. 648-70). It therefore seems reasonable to suppose that the disparity is due to some interruption in the even flow of composition.

The Lay of the Bregog and the Mulla, if Spenser sung it to Raleigh (*Colin,* l. 92) may have been originally a lyrical poem in stanzaic form, perhaps intended for insertion in the *Faerie Queene.* To insert it into *Colin Clout,* it would be necessary to re-write it, and the difficulty of moulding the same thought, and probably the same phrases, after a different verse and rhyme-pattern would result into overlapping.

As to Colin's praise of love, it may have been written as late as 1595 and embedded before publication. The different period of composition would account for the higher enjambment ratio. Or again, it may have been an adaptation of an earlier poem on love, and the remodelling may likewise have increased the percentage of run-on lines.

Accordingly it appears that, whenever an earlier or later poem is embedded in a different composition, the insertion is betrayed by a change in the enjambment ratio. The presence of a striking difference in the percentage of run-on lines within a given poem will then suggest an incorporation of older — or newer — material, especially when the assumption is supported by other characteristics of style. I therefore think it fairly probable that the devotional stanzas in the *Hymne of Heavenly Love* represent an earlier poem — or part of it. The very low enjambment ratio further implies that the original stanza pattern and rhyme scheme have been preserved, for otherwise the stanzas would have been entirely re-written and the percentage of run-on lines increased, as in Colin's "Lay".

5° J. W. Bennett has suggested that the more purely Petrarchan stanzas in the first two hymns represent what was left of the original hymns, after Spenser had given their final shape to all four hymns conceived as a unified exposition of the Neoplatonic theory of love [5]. We might therefore expect to find in the hymns of earthly love and beauty the same variations in the enjambment ratio as were noticed in the third hymn. But our expectation is frustrated, for, as the table shows, there is no striking difference between the Platonic and Petrarchan passages: uniformity prevails. In the second hymn, the patchwork should be more apparent since there is a solid group of Petrarchan stanzas at the close contrasting with another solid group of Platonic stanzas. Yet the enjambment ratio of the Petrarchan close is but slightly lower than the ratio for the whole hymn, and practically similar to the enjambment ratio in ll. 162-231, distinctly Platonic. And the utmost range of variation is from 8 to 5.14, whereas the range was from 13.12 to 6.38 in the third hymn.

It therefore seems probable that the first two hymns were written at a stretch. If any earlier material was incorporated, it must have been largely re-written. And it may be assumed that it originally belonged to a poem in a different stanza-form, for otherwise Spenser would have been tempted to embed the stanzas as they stood, and the insertion would have been betrayed by the enjambment ratio as in the third hymn.

Lastly, if it is assumed, as stylistic and prosodic evidence suggests, that the devotional stanzas in the *Hymne of Heavenly Love* are the earliest written material to be found in the hymns as they now stand, it leaves unsupported Long's contention that the metre used for the earlier hymns, e.g. rhyme royal, points to a period of composition contemporary with *Daphnaida* and the *Ruines of Time* [6]. For, if all four hymns were conceived and planned as a whole, the incorporation of the earlier devotional poem on Christ, decided from the first, may have commanded the choice of the metre. But it is not to be inferred either that the devotional stanzas were necessarily composed in the same period as the other poems written in rhyme royal. The selection of that metre must not be referred to chronology but to subject-matter. It was recognized in Spenser's time as the kind of verse best suited to grave subjects. Gascoigne ends his description of it with these words:

> "... this hath bene called Rithme royall, and surely it is a royall kinde of verse, serving best for grave discourses." [7]

It would be natural therefore to write a complaint on the Crucifixion in rhyme royal. But, had the first two hymns been written first, the choice of rhyme royal would have been largely accidental, if not unjustified, since the hymns of earthly love and earthly beauty are not particularly "grave" and certainly not mournful like *Daphnaida* and the *Ruines of Time* for which rhyme royal was surely chosen of set purpose.

---

[5] *SP* 28 (1931), pp. 55-6.
[6] *Eng. St.* 47 (1913), p. 200.
[7] *Certayne Notes of Instruction,* (1575), reproduced in *El. Crit. Essays,* I.54.

APPENDIX III

EDITIONS OF PLATO IN THE SIXTEENTH CENTURY

The Aldine edition of the Greek text was issued in Venice in 1513. There were later editions in Basel, one by S. Grynaeus in 1534, another by A. Arlenius in 1556.

Ficino's Latin translation had appeared in Florence as early as 1484. The Venice edition of 1491 is recorded in my Bibliography. Later editions in Venice, Basel, Paris and Lyons are briefly listed in Raymond Marcel's *Ficin* (p. 748). For a detailed account see *Joannis Alberti Fabricii Bibliotheca Graeca,* 4th ed., "curante Gottlieb Christophoro Harles" (Hamburg, 1793), vol. III, pp. 127-8. The handiest edition was published by De Tournes (Lyons, 1550, 16mo).

The *Opera* were also translated into Latin by the physician J. Cornarius (Basel, 1561) and by Serranus (Jean de Serres) with the advice of Henri Estienne (Geneva, 1575). The latter edition included the Greek text. Another Greek and Latin edition (Lyons, 1590) reproduced Ficino's translation corrected according to the new readings of Henri Estienne.

Many dialogues were separately printed in Greek and Latin versions or in translations into the vernacular. The more frequently issued are likely to have been the more popular and the more influential. A statistical study should review either all European editions or all editions in a single country to reach significant conclusions. A complete survey was hardly within the scope of the present work. Since a translation of the spurious *Axiochus* was the only dialogue published in England in the 16th century, a Continental nation must be selected. France will offer the best field of enquiry for French scholars edited or translated a great many dialogues and French works of scholarship were commonly used in England.

The following list is based on the articles of Lefranc (*Revue d'Histoire Littéraire,* t. 3, 1896, pp. 1-44, reprinted in *Grands Ecrivains Français de la Renaissance*) and Raymond Lebègue (*Association Guillaume Budé, Congrès de Tours et de Poitiers 1953,* pp. 331-51: "Le Platonisme en France au XVIe siècle"), and on the Ficinian bibliographies of Festugières and Raymond Marcel. Some items have been added, especially for the later period, from the *Bibliotheca Graeca* and from the catalogues of the British Museum and the following French libraries: Arsenal, Victor Cousin, Mazarine, Nationale, Sorbonne. The list may not be exhaustive, but it provides a sound basis for a comparative estimate. No distinction is drawn between genuine, supposititious or spurious Platonic dialogues. Works published in Strasbourg (Argentoratus), not yet a French town, are not included. Manuscript translations are not recorded. The list runs from the earliest editions down to 1596, since the publication of Spenser's *Fowre Hymnes* afforded a better landmark than the turn of the century for our present concern. Dialogues jointly published (e.g. *Axiochus* and *Hipparchus* in Dolet's *Second Enfer*) are recorded separately.

Dialogues	*Greek*	*Latin or Greek and Latin*	*French*
ALCIBIADES I	Lutetiae 1551		
AMATORES (i.e. ERASTAE)	Parisiis 1549	Parisiis 1551 Parisiis 1563 Parisiis 1573	
APOLOGIA SOCRATIS	Parisiis 1539 Parisiis 1541 Parisiis 1544		Lyon 1548 (tr. François Hotman)[1]
AXIOCHUS	Parisiis 1540 Parisiis 1547	Parisiis 1530 Parisiis 1548 Parisiis 1582	Paris 1510 (tr. Guil. Postel *teste* La Croix du Maine) Lyon 1544 (tr. Etienne Dolet, in *Le Second Enfer*)
CHARMIDES		Parisiis 1519 Parisiis(?) 1533	
CRATYLUS	Lutetiae 1527 Parisiis 1573		
CRITO	Lutetiae 1551 Lutetiae 1571		Paris 1542 (tr. Simon de Vallambert) Paris 1547 (tr. Philibert Du Val) Paris 1582 (tr. Jean Le Masle)
EPINOMIS	Parisiis 1573		
EPISTOLAE	Parisiis 1548 Parisiis 1551 Parisiis 1558	Parisiis 1544 Parisiis 1548 Parisiis 1549 Parisiis 1552	
EUTYPHRO		Parisiis 1560	
ERYXIAS		Lugduni 1543 Lugduni 1550	
GORGIAS			Paris 1553 (fragment in Le Roy's *Phaedo*)
HIPPARCHUS	Parisiis 1549	Parisiis 1560	Lyon 1544 (tr. E. Dolet in *Second Enfer*)
ION			Paris 1542? Paris 1546 } tr. Richard Le Blanc[2]
LEGES	Parisiis(?) 1547	Parisiis 1538	Paris 1562 — 1563 — 1566 — 1569 } fragment from Bk III, transl. by Le Roy
LYSIS			Lyon 1544 (in *Oeuvres de Bon. Des Periers)* Paris 1579 (tr. Blaise de Vigenère in *Trois Dialogues de l'amitié*)
MENO		Lugduni 1543 Lugduni 1550	
MINOS		Parisiis 1558	

[1] *Fabricii Bibliotheca Graeca* records an earlier translation by Antonius Verderius (Paris, 1542?).

[2] Le Blanc's translation is dated 1542 by Lanson, 1546 by R. Marcel.

PHAEDO		Parisiis 1536	Paris 1553 — tr. Loys Le Roy
		Parisiis 1553	— 1581 — tr. Loys Le Roy
		Parisiis 1554	
PHAEDRUS	Lutetiae 1581		Paris 1553 (fragment in Le Roy's *Phaedo*)
POLITICUS	Parisiis 1548		Paris 1567
REPUBLICA (DE)	Parisiis 1551	Parisiis 1544	Paris 1553 (Bk X in Le Roy's *Phaedo*)
	Lutetiae 1587	(Bks I-II)	Paris 1555 (Bks I-II, tr. Le Roy)
		Parisiis 1556	Paris 1559 (Bk II, tr. Le Roy,) [3]
SYMPOSIUM	Parisiis 1543		Paris 1556 (tr. Math. Héret)
	Parisiis 1551		Paris 1558 (tr. Le Roy) [4]
			— 1559 id.
			— 1581 id.
THEAGES	Parisiis 1549		
	Parisiis 1551	Parisiis 1558	Lyon 1563-4 (tr. P. Trédéhan, in verse)
TIMAEUS	Parisiis 1532	Parisiis 1520	Paris 1551 — tr. Le Roy
	Parisiis 1536	Parisiis 1536	— 1581 — tr. Le Roy
	Parisiis 1540	Parisiis 1540	
	Parisiis 1542	Parisiis 1544	
	Parisiis 1580(?)	Parisiis 1550	
		Parisiis 1561	
		Parisiis 1563	
		Parisiis 1569	
		Parisiis 1578	
		Parisiis 1579	

From the list an order of precedence emerges and the discovery of other editions would not fundamentally alter it. The dialogues most frequently issued were:

1. TIMAEUS (17)
2. AXIOCHUS (not by Plato), EPISTOLAE, SYMPOSIUM (7 to 6)
3. CRITO, PHAEDO (5).

LEGES and DE REPUBLICA may be included in Group 2 if partial translations are reckoned. APOLOGIA SOCRATIS may belong to Group 3. THEAGES and HIPPARCHUS rank next. The PHAEDRUS lags far behind.

Greek editions were meant for scholars. Since we are chiefly concerned with the influence of the dialogues over poets and courtly readers, French and Latin (or Greek-Latin) editions might be considered alone. But little change would result:

1. TIMAEUS (12)
2. AXIOCHUS, PHAEDO and fragments of LEGES and DE REPUBLICA (5)
3. EPISTOLAE, SYMPOSIUM, AMATORES, CRITO (4 to 3).

But translations into the vernacular are the safest criterion of popularity. Should these alone be listed, the order would be perceptibly altered:

---

[3] A complete translation by Le Roy appeared in 1600.

[4] The 1559 edition alone is usually listed, but see Catalogue Bibl. Nat. "Platon", Nos 616-17.

1. SYMPOSIUM and fragments of LEGES (4)
2. CRITO and fragments of DE REPUBLICA (3)
3. AXIOCHUS, LYSIS, PHAEDO, TIMAEUS and perhaps APOLOGIA SOCRATIS and ION (2)
4. HIPPARCHUS, POLITICUS, THEAGES and fragments of GORGIAS and PHAEDRUS.

This statistical study calls for the following observations:

1. The impressive number of Greek and Latin editions shows that the *Timaeus* still held the first rank in the favour of scholars and the two translations into French further imply that its influence was by no means confined to the more scholarly readers.

2. To the translations of the *Symposium* should be added a paraphrase of the speech ascribed to Aristophanes by Antoine Héroet (*L'Androgyne,* Lyon 1543, 1547; Paris, 1568) and the three French editions of Ficino's *In Convivium* (see Bibl.). The *Symposium* is thus placed far ahead of any other dialogue in the favour of the widest audience, independently from its diffused influence through the trattati d'amore.

3. The popularity of the political dialogues (*Leges, De Republica*) is noteworthy. Besides the editions listed, *Excerpta de Republica et Legum* were published in Paris in 1506, 1526 and 1543.

4. The *Phaedo* holds an honourable rank, but cannot compete in popularity with the *Timaeus* or the *Symposium.* The influence of the *Ion* must have been indirectly enhanced by the *trattati* and Minturno's *De Poeta.*

5. The *Phaedrus* did not attract attention. There was only one Greek edition designed for scholars and a mere fragment was included in Le Roy's translation of the *Phaedo.* This is unexpected since the myth of the chariot with the winged horses and the figure of the winged soul are frequent enough in French Renaissance Poetry. But the poets may have known of them through various commentaries and *trattati* (e.g. Ficino's *In Convivium,* IV.iv) or through the poetic paraphrases of the scholarly Héroet: *Parfaicte Amie,* ll. 875-913.

These conclusions, based on the number of separate editions, are largely in agreement with the conclusions reached by French scholars in tracing influences: "Les dialogues de Platon qui ont eu en France, au XVe siècle, le plus de diffusion et d'influence, sont le *Banquet,* la *République,* le *Timée,* le *Phédon* et l'*Ion*" (R. Lebègue, *op. cit.,* p. 343). Now, such findings may have some bearing on the controversy concerning Spenser's knowledge of Plato. It has been shown that the influence of the *Timaeus* and the *Symposium* is traceable in his poetry, whereas he badly blundered in his allusions to the *Phaedrus* and the *Phaedo* (see p. 96). This is at first sight surprising, but the wonder is removed by the order of precedence just established. Since the *Phaedrus* was not a Renaissance favourite and since the *Phaedo* was outshone by the *Timaeus* and the *Symposium,* one need not infer from the poet's blunders that he is unlikely to have known "any Platonic work at first hand", as A.E. Taylor suggested (*MLR* 19, p. 210). Conversely, his acquaintance with the two best known dialogues is no proof that he was widely and deeply read in Plato.

ABBREVIATIONS

I. SPENSER'S WORKS.

Colin	*Colin Clouts Come Home Againe*
F.Q.	*Faerie Queene*
Hubberd or M.H'sT.	*Mother Hubberds Tale*
H.L.	*Hymne in Honour of Love*
H.B.	*Hymne in Honour of Beautie*
H.H.L.	*Hymne of Heavenly Love*
H.H.B.	*Hymne of Heavenly Beautie*
R.T.	*Ruines of Time*
S.C.	*Shepheardes Calender*
T.M.	*Teares of the Muses*
View	*View of the Present State of Ireland*

Other titles are given in full.

II. EDITIONS OF SPENSER.

Calendar. *The Shepherd's Calendar*. Edited by W.L. Renwick.

Complaints. *Complaints*. Edited by W.L. Renwick.

Daphnaida. *Daphnaida and other poems...* Edited by W.L. Renwick.

Variorum, F.Q. I to VII. *The Works of Edmund Spenser. A Variorum Edition. The Faerie Queene*. Books I to VII. (Bks VI and VII are included in vol. VI.)

Variorum, M.P. I, II. *The Works of Edmund Spenser. A Variorum Edition. The Minor Poems*. Volumes One and Two.

Winstanley. *Fowre Hymnes*. Edited by L. Winstanley.

III. SPENSER'S SOURCES.

Abbreviated titles are used in the Notes and the titles of articles usually omitted. The Bibliography is so arranged as to make identification easy by looking up the author's name.

For the various translations of Ficino's *Commentarium in Convivium*, the following abbreviations have been used:

Commentaire for the translation by Jean de la Haye (1546).

Discours for the second edition of the *Discours de l'honneste amour*, translated by Le Fèvre de la Boderie (1588).

— A translation of Pico's *Commento* is included in the 1588 edition of the *Discours*.

Jayne for S.R. Jayne's English translation of Ficino's *In Convivium* (1944).
Marcel for Raymond Marcel's French translation (1956).

IV. PERIODICALS.

The standard abbreviations have been used.

Note on the Quotations.

In ancient texts, all contractions have been expanded, u's and v's, i's and j's distinguished. The spelling has otherwise been respected and misprints have not been corrected.

I intended to quote only from editions that Spenser could have used. This has not always proved possible in the last stage of composition. But in all quotations from later editions of Cicero, Augustine, etc., the text is substantially that which the poet must have read.

BIBLIOGRAPHY

General Plan.

A. Editions of Spenser.
B. Sources and Analogues.
C. Studies on Platonism.
D. Spenserian Criticism.

A. EDITIONS OF SPENSER.

For early editions the reader is referred to:

JOHNSON, R.R. *A critical Bibliography of the Works of Edmund Spenser printed before 1700.* Baltimore: The John Hopkins Press, 1933. In-4°; XIII-61 p.

The standard critical edition is:

The Works of Edmund Spenser. A Variorum Edition. Edited by Edwin Greenlaw, Charles Grosvenor Osgood, Frederick Morgan Padelford, Ray Heffner. Baltimore: The John Hopkins Press, 1932-49.

The ten volumes include:

The Faerie Queene. Books I to VII, in six volumes. 1932-38.

The Minor Poems. Volume One. 1943.
Volume Two. C.G. Osgood, H.G. Lotspeich, Special Editors, Assisted by D.E. Mason. 1947.

The Prose Works. Special Editor Rudolf B. Gottfried. 1949.

The Life of Edmund Spenser. By Alexander C. Judson. 1945.

Other editions mentioned in the present study are:

Fowre Hymnes. Edited by L. Winstanley. Cambridge University Press, 1907.

Complaints. Edited by W.L. Renwick. London: The Scholartis Press, 1928.

Daphnaida, and other Poems. Edited by W.L. Renwick. London: The Scholartis Press, 1929.

The Shepherd's Calendar. Edited by W.L. Renwick. London: The Scholartis Press, 1930.

The Axiochus of Plato. Translated by Edmund Spenser. Edited by F.M. Padelford. Baltimore: The John Hopkins Press, 1934. (The ascription of the translation to Spenser is controverted.)

Spenser. La Reine des Fées. (*The Faerie Queene*). Extraits. Introduction, traduction et notes par Michel Poirier. Paris: Aubier, 1950.

B. SOURCES AND ANALOGUES.

ALBERTUS MAGNUS. *Opera.* Lugduni, Sumptibus Claudii Prost., etc., 1651. 21 vols. in-fol.

ALIGHIERI, Dante. *Opere Minori*. Ed. G.L. Passerini. Firenze: G.C. Sansoni, 1910-18. 3 vol.

ARIOSTO, Lodovico. *Orlando Furioso*. Firenze: Successori Le Monnier, 1911. 2 vol. in-8°.

AUGUSTINE (Saint). *Opera. Tomis Decem Comprehensa*. Parisiis, Cum Privilegio, 1586. 10 tomes in 6 vol. in-fol.

— *Opera omnia ... accurante J.P. Migne*. Parisiis, 1841-2. In-4°. (*Patrologia Latina*, vol. 32-46.)

— *Certaine Select Prayers, gathered out of S. Augustines Meditations*. London, Richard Daye, 1565. In-8°.

BARTHOLOMAEUS ANGLICUS. *Liber de proprietatibus rerum*. Argentinae, 1505. In-fol.

— *Batman uppon Bartholome his booke De Proprietatibus rerum, enlarged and amended*. London: T. East, 1582. In-fol.

BASILIUS (Saint). *L'Hexaéméron de Saint Basile*. Ed. Stanislas Giet. Paris: Editions du Cerf, 1950, 539 p.

BEMBO, Pietro. *Gli Asolani*. Vinegia, G. Giolito, 1558. In-12, 238 p.

— *Gli Asolani. Translated by Rudolf B. Gottfried*. Bloomington: Indiana Univ. Press, 1954. XX-200 p.

BENIVIENI, Girolamo. *Opere ... con una canzona dello amor celeste et divine, col commento dello ill. S. conte Giovanni Pico Mirandolano*. Venegia: G. di Gregori. 1524. In-8°; 208 p.

BERNARDUS SILVESTRIS. *De Mundi Universitate libri duo...* Herausgegeben von C.S. Barach und J. Wrobel. Innsbruck, Verlag der Wagnerischen Universitaets Buchhandlung, 1876. XXI-71 p.

BOCCACCIO Giovanni. *La Genealogia degli Dei de Gentili*. Venetia: G.A. Bertano, 1584. In-4°; VIII-263 f.

BOETHIUS, Anicius. *Philosophiae Consolationis Libri Quinque*. Lipsiae, in aed. B.G. Teubneri, 1871.

— *Boethius De Consolatione Philosophie*. Chaucer's translation: see CHAUCER.

BOSTOCKE, Richard. *The difference betweene the auncient Phisicke, first taught by the godly forefathers, consisting in unitie peace and concord: and the latter Phisicke, proceeding from Idolaters, Ethnickes, and Heathen: as Gallen, and such other, consisting in dualitie, discorde, and contrarietie. By R.B. Esquire*. London, for R. Walley, 1585. In-8°; 186 p.

BRUNO, Giordano. *De gl'Heroici Furori*. Parigi, A. Baio, 1585. In-8°; sig. A-Q.

— *Des Fureurs Héroïques. De gl'Heroici Furori*. Ed. and Transl. by Paul-Henri Michel. Paris: Belles Lettres, 1954.

CALVIN, Jean. *Institution de la Religion Chrestienne*. Genève: F. Perrin, 1566. In-fol.; XXVI-1034 p.

CASTIGLIONE, Baldassaro. *The Book of the Courtier*. Everyman's Library. London: Dent, 1928. (Hoby's translation, first printed in 1561.)

CHAUCER, Geoffrey. *The Complete Works*. Ed. by W.W. Skeat. Oxford: University Press, 1927.

CICERO, Marcus Tullius. *Opera*. Basileae, ex off. Hervagiana, 1540. 5 tomes in 2 vol. in-fol.

— *Somnium Scipionis*. Introd. et Notes par V. Cucheval. Paris: Hachette, 1882.

CONTI, Natale. (COMES, Natalis). *Mythologiae ... libri decem*. Parisiis; apud Arnoldum Sittart, 1583. In-8°, 1112 p.

DESPORTES, Philippe. *Œuvres.* Ed. Alfred Michiels. Paris: Delahays, 1858.

DIONYSIUS (Pseudo). *S. Dionysii Areopagitae ... opera.* Coloniae, ex off. haeredum J. Quentel, 1556. In-fol., 44-951 p.

DU BARTAS (Guillaume de Saluste, sieur). *Commentaires sur la Sepmaine de la création du monde* (with the text). Rouen, T. Mallard, 1589. In-12, 328f.

EQUICOLA, Mario. *D'Alveto di Natura d'Amore.* Vinegia, appresso Gabriel Giolito de'Ferrari, 1563. In-8°; 408 p.

FICINO, Marsilio. *Opera.* Basileae, ex off. Henricpetrina, 1576. 3 parts in 2 vol. in-fol. Also Parisiis, apud Guilhelmum Pele, 1641, 2 volumes.

— *Sopra l'Amore, overo Convito di Platone.* Firenze, per F. Giunti, 1594. In-8°, 251 p.

— *Le Commentaire de Marsile Ficin, Florentin: sur le banquet d'Amour de Platon: faict François par Symon Sylvius, dit I. De la Haye, Valet de Chambre ... Marguerite de France, Royne de Navarre.* Poictiers, à l'enseigne du Pélican, 1546. In-8°, III-CXVII f.

— *Discours de l'honneste amour sur le Banquet de Platon, par Marsile Ficin... Traduit de toscan en françois par Guy Le Fèvre de la Boderie.* Paris: J. Macé, 1578. In-8°, 391 p.

— *Discours de l'honneste amour sur le Banquet de Platon, par Marsile Ficin ... traduit de Toscan en françois par Guy Le Fèvre de la Boderie ... avec un Traicté de I. Picus Mirandulanus sur le même subject.* Paris, A. L'Angelier, 1588. In-8°; 260 f.

— *Marsilio Ficino's Commentary on Plato's Symposium.* The text and a translation, with an Introduction by Sears Reynolds Jayne. University of Missouri, Columbia, 1944.

— *Marsile Ficin. Commentaire sur le Banquet de Platon.* Texte du manuscrit autographe présenté et traduit par Raymond Marcel. Paris: Belles Lettres, 1956.

— *De la Religion chrestienne, par Marsile Ficin, ... avec la harangue de la dignité de l'homme, par Jean Picus comte de Concorde et de la Mirandole. Le tout traduit de latin en françois par Guy Lefevre de La Boderie.* Paris: G. Beïs, 1578. In-8°; XIV-440 pp.

JULIAN of Norwich. *Revelation of Divine Love.* A version from the MS... edited by Grace Warrack. London: Methuen, 1912.

LANDINO, Cristoforo. *Christophori Landini ... Camaldulensium disputationum, opus doctrinae et elegantiae plenissimum...* Parisiis, pro Joanne Parvo, 1511. In-4°; VII-86 f.

LA PRIMAUDAYE, Pierre de. *Académie Françoise.* Paris, Guillaume Chaudière, 1581. 2 tomes in-fol. (first ed. 1577; Second Part, 1580).

LEONE EBREO or LEO HEBRAEUS, i.e. Jehudah ABRAVANEL or ABRABANEL. *Dialoghi di amore ... di nuovo con diligenza correti* (da M. Lenzi). Venetia; appresso D. Giglio, 1558. In-8°; 246 f.

— *Leone Ebreo. Dialoghi d'Amore. Hebraeische Gedichte.* Ed. Carl Gebhardt. Curis Societatis Spinozanae. Heidelberg: Carl Winter, 1929.

— *The Philosophy of Love.* Transl. by F. Friedeberg Seeley and J.H. Barnes. London: Soncino Press, 1937.

LE ROY (Loys or Louis). *Le Sympose de Platon, de l'Amour et de Beauté, Traduit du Grec en François, avec trois livres de Commentaires, extraitz de toute Philosophie ... par Loys le Roy; dit Regius ... Plusieurs passages des meilleurs Poëtes Grecs et Latins, citez aux Commentaires, mis en vers par J. du Bellay Angevin.* Paris, pour Jehan Longis & Robert le Mangnyer, 1558. In-4°; IV-200 f.

— *Le Timée de Platon ... translaté du grec en françois par Loys le Roy...* Paris, A. L'Angelier, 1581. In-4°; 158 f.

LING, Nicholas. *Politeuphuia. Wits Common-Wealth.* London, I.R. for Nicholas Ling, 1597. In-12, 260 fol.

LORRIS (Guillaume de) and JEAN DE MEUNG. *Le Roman de la Rose.* Publié par Ernest Langlois. Paris: Firmin-Didot, 1914. 5 vol.

MACROBIUS, Aurelius. *Aurelii Macrobii ... In Somnium Scipionis Libri II. Ejusdem Conviviorum Saturnaliorum Libri VII.* Parisiis, (H. Stephani), 1585. In-8°; 578 p.

MARGUERITE DE NAVARRE. *Les Marguerites de la Marguerite des Princesses.* Paris, Cabinet des Bibliophiles, 1873. 4 vol.

OVID (Publius Ovidius Naso). *The XV Bookes of P. Ovidius Naso, entytuled Metamorphosis, translated oute of Latin into English meeter, by Arthur Golding.* London, Willyam Seres, 1567. In-fol. (Reprinted as *Shakespeare's Ovid* by W.H.D. Rouse for the King's Library, London, The De La Mare Press, 1904.)

PALINGENIUS, Marcellus (MANZOLLI, Pietro Angelo). *Zodiacus Vitae.* Lugduni, apud J. Tornaesium, 1581. In-16, 336 p.

— *The Zodiake of Life. Translated by Barnabie Googe.* London, Robert Robinson, 1588 (first complete edition in 1565).

— *The Zodiake of Life.* Ed. by Rosemond Tuve. Scholars' Facsimiles & Reprints, New York, 1947.

— *The Zodiacus Vitae ... An old schoolbook.* Ed. by F. Watson. London: P. Wellby, 1908.

PETRARCH, Francesco. *Opera.* Basileae, per S. Henricpetri, n. d. 4 tomes in 1 vol. in-fol. 1131-305 p.

— *Le Rime.* Restituite nell'ordine e nella lezione del testo originario ... da Giovanni Mestica. Firenze: G. Barbèra, 1896.

PICO DELLA MIRANDOLA, Giovanni (the elder). *Commento* on Benivieni's *Canzone* in BENIVIENI's *Opere.*

— *Le Commentaire du tres-illustre seigneur Comte Jean Picus Mirandulanus, sur une Chanson d'Amour; composé par Hierosme Benivieni ... selon l'opinion des Platoniciens. Mis en françois par C.G.T.* Included in the 1588 edition of the *Discours de l'honneste amour.* See FICINO.

PICO DELLA MIRANDOLA, Giovanni (the nephew). *De Amore Divino, libri quattuor.* Romae, per Jacobum Mazochium, M.D.XVI. In-4°; sig. A-O.

— *Hymni heroici tres, Ad sanctissimam Trinitatem, Ad Christum et Ad Virginem Mariam..* Impressum Vienne Austriae, per Hieronymum Vietorem, a.d. 1517. In-4°; sig. A-H.

PLATO. *Platonis Opera, latine interprete Marsilio Ficino, cum Vita Platonis ab eodem Ficino.* Venetiis, per B. de Choris et S. de Luero, impensis A. Toresam de Asula, 1491. In-fol.; 444 f.

— *Platonis Timaeus interprete Chalcidio cum ejusdem commentario.* Ed. J. Wrobel. Lipsiae: Teubner, 1876.

— *Timée. Critias.* Trad. Albert Rivaud. Paris: Belles Lettres, 1949.

PLUTARCH. *Plutarchi Chaeronensis Quae Extant Omnia. Cum Latina Interpretatione Hermanni Cruserii..* Francofurti, Apud Andreae Wecheli heredes, 1599. 2 vol. in-fol.

— *Isis et Osiris.* Tr. Mario Meunier. Paris: L'artisan du Livre, 1934. In-8°; 236 p.

PLOTINUS. *Les Ennéades.* Ed. Emile Bréhier. Paris, Les Belles Lettres, 1934-1938. 7 volumes in-8°.

PONTANO, Giovanni, Giovanno. *Opera.* Basileae, ex officina Henricpetrina, 1556. 4 volumes in-8°.

SPERONI, Sperone. *Dialogi di M.S. Speroni...* In Vinegia, in casa de figliuoli di Aldo, 1543. In-8°; 171 f.

TASSO, Torquato. *Gierusalemme Liberata.* In Ferrara, D. Mammorelli, e G.C. Cagnacmi, 1582. In-12°; 576 p.

— *Opere.* Vol. VI: *Rime Amorose, Eroiche, Sacre, E Morali.* Venezia, Appresso Steffano Monti, 1736.

THOMAS AQUINAS (Saint). *Summa Totius Theologiae.* Antverpiae, Ex off. Christophori Plantini, 1585. In-fol.

VARCHI, Benedetto. *L'Ercolano e Lezioni Quattro sopra Alcune Quistioni d'Amore.* Milano: Edoardo Sonzogno, 1880. 356 p.

C. STUDIES IN MEDIAEVAL AND RENAISSANCE PLATONISM.

Only works cited in the present study are listed. For fuller information see the bibliographies of Festugières, Kristeller and Robb (in works listed below) and the bibliographies of Jayne and Marcel in their editions of Ficino's *In Convivium.*

For the sake of convenience other works concerning the history of ideas are included in this section.

CASPARI, Fritz. *Humanism and the Social Order in Tudor England.* University of Chicago Press, 1954. IX-292 p.

CASSIRER, Ernest. *Die Platonische Renaissance in England und die Schule von Cambridge.* Berlin-Leipzig: Teubner, 1932. VIII-143 p.

ELTON, Oliver. "Giordano Bruno in England", in *Modern Studies.* London: E. Arnold, 1907.

FESTUGIÈRES, Jean. *La Philosophie de l'Amour de Marsile Ficin, et son influence sur la littérature française au XVIe siècle.* Paris: Vrin, 1941. VIII-168 p.

GILSON, Etienne. "La Cosmogonie de Bernardus Silvestris", in *Archives d'Histoire Doctrinale et Littéraire du Moyen-Age,* t. III (1928), pp. 5-24.

— *Introduction à l'Etude de Saint-Augustin.* Paris: Vrin, 1929.

— *L'esprit de la philosophie médiévale.* Paris: Vrin, 1944.

— *La Philosophie au Moyen-Age.* Paris, Payot, 1944 (2nd ed.).

— *Le Thomisme.* Paris: Vrin, 1945.

IVANOFF, N. "La Beauté dans la philosophie de Marsile Ficin et de Léon Hébreux", in *Humanisme et Renaissance,* t. III, 1936.

JACQUOT, Jean. *Georges Chapman.* Sa vie, sa poésie, son théâtre, sa pensée. Paris: Belles-Lettres, 1951. IV-308 p.

— "L'élément platonicien dans l'*Histoire du Monde* de Sir Walter Ralegh", in *Mélanges Henri Chamard.* Paris, Nizet, 1951 (pp. 347-53).

JAYNE, Sears. «Ficino and the Platonism of the English Renaissance». *Comparative Literature* 4 (1952), 214-38.

JOHNSON, F.R. *Astronomical Thought in Renaissance England.* Baltimore: The John Hopkins Press, 1937. XI-357 p.

KLIBANSKY, Raymond. *The Continuity of the Platonic Tradition during the Middle-Ages.* London, The Warburg Institute, 1939. In-8°; 58 p.

KRISTELLER, Paul Oskar. *The Philosophy of Marsilio Ficino,* Translated by Virginia Conant. New-York, Columbia University Press, 1943. XIV-441 p.

— "Francesco da Diacceto and Florentine Platonism in the Sixteenth Century", in *Miscellanea Giovanni Mercati,* vol. IV, pp. 260-304. Bibliotheca Apostolica Vaticana, 1946.

LEFRANC, Abel. "Le Platonisme et la Littérature en France à l'époque de la Renaissance", in *Grands Ecrivains Français de la Renaissance*, Paris, Champion, 1914. In-8° (pp. 63-137).

MAC COLLEY, Grant. "Nicholas Copernicus and an Infinite Universe". *Popular Astronomy* 44 (1936), 525-33.

MARCEL, Raymond. *Marsile Ficin*. Paris: Les Belles Lettres, 1958. 784 p.

MOENCH, Walter. *Die Italienische Platonrenaissance und ihre Bedeutung für Franckreichs Literatur und Geistesgeschichte*. Berlin, E. Ebering, 1936. XXIV-399 p.

RAYNAUD DE LAGE, G. *Alain de Lille, Poète du XIIe siècle*. Paris: Vrin, 1951. 187 p.

RIVAUD, A. *Le problème du Devenir et la notion de la matière dans la philosophie grecque*. Paris: Alcan, 1905.

ROBIN, Léon. *Aristote*. Paris: Presses Universitaires de France, 1944. 322 p.

ROBB, Nesca A. *Neoplatonism of the Italian Renaissance*. London: G. Allen and Unwin, 1935. 315 p.

SAVINO, L. *Di alcuni Trattati e trattatisti d'amore italiani della prima meta del secolo XVI*. T. IX (pp. 222-435) and X (342 p.) in *Studi di letteratura italiana*. Napoli: N. Jovene, 1909-14. In-8°.

SAITTA, Guiseppe. *La philosophia di Marsilio Ficino*. G. Principato; Messina, 1923. 285 p.

SCHIRMER, Walter. *Antike, Renaissance und Puritanismus*. München: M. Hueber, 233 p.

SCHROEDER, Kurt. *Platonismus in der Englischen Renaissance vor und bei Thomas Elyot*. Berlin: Mayer & Muller, 1920. IX-158 p. (Palaestra LXXXIII.)

SCHOELL, Frank L. *Etudes sur l'humanisme continental en Angleterre à la fin de la Renaissance*. Paris: Champion, 1926. VII-270 p.

SHOREY, Paul. *Platonism Ancient and Modern*. Univ. of California Press: Berkeley, 1938. In-8°; 259 p.

TAYLOR, A.E. *Platonism and its influence*. London: G.G. Harrap, n. d. In-8°; 153 p.

TONELLI, Luigi. *L'amore nella poesia e nel pensiero del Rinascimento*. Firenze: G.C. Sansoni, 1933, 323 p.

WEISS, R. *Humanism in England during the Fifteenth Century*. Oxford: Blackwell, 1957. XXIII-202 p. (Ist ed. 1941).

D. SPENSERIAN CRITICISM.

Only works cited in the present study are listed.

1. *Books.*

BENNETT, Josephine Waters. *The Evolution of the Faerie Queene*. Chicago: The Univ. of Chicago Press, 1942. VIII-299 p.

BHATTACHERJE, Moninomohan. *Studies in Spenser*. Univ. of Calcutta, 1929, 93 p.

— *Platonic Ideas in Spenser*. Bombay, Calcutta, Madras: Longmans, Green, 1935. XII-200 p.

BRADNER, Leicester. *Edmund Spenser and The Faerie Queene*. Univ. of Chicago Press and Cambridge Univ. Press, 1948. IX-190 p.

COLLINS, Joseph B. *Christian Mysticism in the Elizabethan Age with its Background in Mystical Methodology*. Baltimore: The Johns Hopkins Press, 1940. In-8°; XIV-251 p.

DAVIS, B.E.D. *Edmund Spenser, a critical study*. Cambridge Univ. Press, 1933. IX-267 p.

GRIERSON, Sir Herbert. *Cross-currents in English Literature of the XVIIth Century*. London: Chatto & Windus, 1929, XIV-344 p.

HARRISON, John Smith. *Platonism in English Poetry of the Sixteenth and Seventeenth Century*. New-York: Macmillan, 1903, 234 p.

HIGGINSON, J.J.: *Spenser's Shepherd's Calender in Relation to Contemporary Affairs*. New-York, 1912.

HUGHES, Merritt Y. *Virgil and Spenser*. Univ. of California Publications in English. vol. II, n° 3. Berkeley: Univ. of California Press, 1929 (pp. 263-418).

JONES, H.S.V. *A Spenser Handbook*. New-York: F.S. Crofts, 1930. VIII-419 p.

LEGOUIS, Emile. *Edmund Spenser*. Paris, Bloud et Gay, 1923. XVI-359 p. *Anr. ed.*: Paris: Didier, 1956. XIII-333 p.

LEWIS, C.S. *The Allegory of Love. A study in medieval tradition*. London: H. Milford; Oxford University Press, 1936. IX-379 p.

LOTSPEICH, H.G. *Classical Mythology in the Poetry of Edmund Spenser*. Princeton University Press, 1932. X-126 p.

MUELLER W.R. and D.C. ALLEN, editors. *That Soveraine Light. Essays in Honor of Edmund Spenser*. Baltimore: The Johns Hopkins Press, 1942, 133 p.

RATHBORNE, I.E. *The Meaning of Spenser's Fairyland*. Columbia Univ. Studies in English and Comparative Literature, n° 131. New-York, 1937.

RENWICK, W.L. *Edmund Spenser, An Essay on Renaissance Poetry*. London: E. Arnold & C°, 1925. In-8°.

SCOTT, Janet G. *Les Sonnets Elisabéthains. Les sources et l'apport personnel*. Paris: Champion, 1929. 343 p.

SPENS, Janet. *Spenser's Faerie Queene: An Interpretation*. London: E. Arnold & C°, 1934, 144 p.

WHITAKER, Virgil K. *The Religious Basis of Spenser's Thought*. Stanford (Calif.): Stanford Univ. Press, 1950. 70 p.

2. *Studies in Periodicals.*

The following list includes:

a) Articles in which Platonic or Neoplatonic influences are discussed; they are marked out by an asterisk placed before the title.

b) Articles cited in the discussion on Spenser's thought and on the chronology and interpretation of his poetry.

ALLBRIGHT, Evelyn M. "Spenser's Reasons for rejecting the Cantos of Mutability." *SP* 25 (1928), 93-127.

* "Spenser's Cosmic Philosophy and his Religion." *PMLA* 44 (1929), 715-59.

ALLEN, D.C. "Arthur's Diamond Shield in *The Faerie Queene*", *JEGP* 36 (1937), 234-43.

BENNETT, Josephine W. * "The Theme of Spenser's *Fowre Hymnes*." *SP* 28 (1931), 18-57.

* Spenser's *Fowre Hymnes:* Addenda. *SP* 32 (1931), 138-57.
* "Spenser's Garden of Adonis." *PMLA* 47 (1937), 46-78.
* "Spenser's Venus and The Goddess Nature of the Cantos of Mutability." *SP* 30 (1933), 160-192.
* "Spenser's Garden of Adonis Revisted." *JEGP* 41 (1942), 54-78.

BROOKE, N.S. "C.S. Lewis and Spenser: Nature, Art and the Bower of Bliss." *Cambridge Journal*, 2 (1949), 420-34.

BUYSSENS, E. "Calvinism in the *Faerie Queene* of Spenser" *Rev. Belge de Philologie et d'Histoire*, 5 (1926), 37-70, 381-400.

CASADY, Edwin. * "The Neo-Platonic Ladder in Spenser's *Amoretti*." *PQ* 20 (1941), 284-95.

— Reprinted in *Renaissance Studies in Honor of Hardin Craig*, pp. 92-103.

CUMMING, W.P. "The Influence of Ovid's Metamorphoses on Spenser's Mutabilitie Cantos." *SP* 28 (1931), 241-56.

FLETCHER, Jefferson A. "The Puritan argument in Spenser." *PMLA* 58 (1943), 534-48.

FLETCHER, J.B. "Mr Sidney Lee and Spenser's *Amoretti*." *MLN* 18 (1903), 111-13.

— "Spenser the Cosmopolitan Poet." *English Graduate Record.* Columbia University, 1905. Pp. 65-80.

— * "Benivieni's Ode of Love and Spenser's *Fowre Hmnes*." *M.P.* 8 (1911), 545-60.

— * "A Study in Renaissance Mysticism: Spenser's *Fowre Hymnes*." *PMLA* 26 (1911), 452-75.

GREENLAW, Edwin. "Spenser and Lucretius." *SP* 17 (1920), 439-64.

— * "Some Old Religious Cults in Spenser." *SP* 20 (1923), 216-43. See also pp. 241-42.

— "Spenser's Mutabilitie." *PMLA* 45 (1930), 684-703.

HARRISON, T.P. Jr. * "Divinity in Spenser's Garden of Adonis." *Univ. of Texas Studies in English* (*1939*), 48-73.

HANKINS, J.F. "Spenser and the Revelation of St-John." *PMLA* 60 (1945), 364-81.

HOOPES, Robert. "'God Guide Thee, *Guyon*': Nature and Grace Reconciled in *The Faerie Queene*, Bk II." *RES* 5 (1954), 14-24.

HUGUES, Merritt Y. * "Virgilian Allegory and the *Faerie Queene*." *PMLA* 44 (1929), 696-705.

— "The Arthurs of *The Faerie Queene*." *Etudes Anglaises* 6 (1953), 193-213.

JONES, H.S.V. "*The Faerie Queene* and the Mediaeval Aristotelian Tradition." *JEGP* 25 (1926), 282-98.

— "Magnanimity in Spenser's Legend of Holiness." *SP* 39 (1932), 200-206.

KAHIN, Helen A. * "Spenser and the School of Alanus." *ELH* 8 (1941), 257-72.

KNOWLTON, E.C. * "Spenser and Nature." *JEGP* 34 (1935), 366-76.

LANDRUM, Grace W. "Spenser's Use of the Bible and his alleged Puritanism." *PMLA* 41 (1926), 517-44.

LEE, R.W. * "Castiglione's Influence on Spenser's Early Hymnes." *PQ* 7 (1928), 65-77.

LEVINSON, R.B. * "Spenser and Bruno." *PMLA* 43 (1928), 675-81.

LONG, Percy W "Spenser and Lady Carey." *MLR* 3 (1908), 257-67.

— "Spenser's Sonnets 'as published'." *MLR* 6 (1911), 390-97.

— "The Date of Spenser's Earlier Hymnes." *Eng. St.* 47 (1913), 197-208.

MAC LANE, P.E. "Spenser's Political and Religious Position in the *Shepheardes Calender*." *JEGP* 49 (1950), 324-32.

MILLER, Milton. "Nature in the Faerie Queene." *ELH* 18 (1951), 191-200.

MOLONEY, M.F. "St Thomas and Spenser's Virtue of Magnificence." *JEGP* 52 (1953), 58-62.

OSGOOD, C.G. * "Spenser's Sapience." *SP* 14 (1917), 167-77.

— * "Comments on the Moral Allegory of the *F.Q.*" *MLN* 46 (1931), p. 506.

PADELFORD, F.M. "Spenser and the Puritan Propaganda." *MP* 11 (1913), 85-106.

— "Spenser and the Theology of Calvin." *MP* 12 (1914), 1-18.

— * "Spenser's Fowre Hymnes." *JEGP* 13 (1914), 418-33.

— * "Spenser's Fowre Hymnes. A Resurvey." *SP* 29 (1932), 207-32.

— "Spenser and The Pilgrimage of the Life of Man." *SP* 28 (1931), 211-18.

— "Spenser or Anthony Munday. A Note on the Axiochus." *PMLA* 50 (1935), 903-13.

RICKS, Beatrice. "Catholic Sacramentals and Symbolism in Spenser's *Faerie Queene*." *JEGP* 52 (1953), 322-31.

SAURAT, Denis. * "Les Idées philosophiques de Spenser." *Yearbook Lund Society of Letters,* I, 1924.

— "La 'Sapience' de Spenser et la 'Schekina' de la Cabale." *Rev. de Litt. Comparée* (1926), 5-15.

SCOTT, Janet G. * "Sources of Spenser's *Amoretti*." *MLR* 22 (1927), 189-95.

SHANLEY, J.L. "Spenser's Temperance and Aristotle." *MP* 43 (1946), 170-74.

SIEGEL, Paul N. "Spenser and the Calvinist View of Life." *SP* 41 (1944), 201-22.

SIRLUCK, E. * "The *Faerie Queene,* Bk II, and the *Nichomachean Ethics*." *MP* 49 (1951-2), 73-100.

SMITH, C.G. * "The ethical allegory of the two Florimels " *SP* 31 (1934).

— * "Spenser's Theory of Friendship: An Elizabethan Commonplace." *SP* 32 (1935), 157-69.

— * "Sententious Theory in Spenser's Legend of Friendship." *ELH* 2 (1935), 165-91.

STAMPFER, Judah L. "The Cantos of Mutability: Spenser's Last Testament of Faith." *Univ. of Toronto Quarterly* 21 (1951-2), 140-56.

STIRLING, Brents. * "The Concluding Stanzas of Mutabilitie." *SP* 30 (1933), 193-204.

— * "The Philosophy of Spenser's Garden of Adonis." *PMLA* 49 (1934), 501-38.

— * "Two Notes on the Philosophie of Mutabilitie." *MLN* 50 (1935), 154-5.

TAYLOR, A.E. * "Spenser's Knowledge of Plato." *MLR* 29 (1924), 208-10.

TUVE, Rosemond. * "A Mediaeval Comonplace in Spenser's Cosmology." *SP* 30 (1933), 133-47.

— * "Spenser and the Zodiacke of Life." *JEGP* 34 (1935), 1-19.

WOODHOUSE, George. "Nature and Grace in *The Faerie Queene*." *ELH* 16 (1949), 194-228.

— "Nature and Grace in Spenser: A Rejoinder." *RES* 56 (1955), 284-87.

INDEX

I. INDEX OF SOURCES AND ANALOGUES

The reference is to page number. The figure is followed by "n" when the reader is specially referred to a note on the page mentioned. The more important references are given in italics.

A. GREEK, LATIN AND FOREIGN AUTHORS

B. ENGLISH AUTHORS MENTIONED

II. INDEX OF SPENSER'S WORKS

III. SUBJECT INDEX

TABLE OF CONTENTS

TABLE OF CONTENTS